The Ann Oakley reader

Gender, women and social science

Written and edited by Ann Oakley

Foreword by Germaine Greer

First published in Great Britain in June 2005 by

The Policy Press
University of Bristol
Fourth Floor, Beacon House
Queen's Road
Bristol BS8 1QU
UK

Tel +44 (0)117 331 4054
Fax +44 (0)117 331 4093
e-mail tpp-info@bristol.ac.uk
www.policypress.co.uk

North American office:
The Policy Press
c/o International Specialized Books Services (ISBS)
920 NE 58th Avenue, Suite 300
Portland, OR 97213-3786, USA
Tel +1 503 287 3093
Fax +1 503 280 8832
e-mail info@isbs.com

© Ann Oakley 2005
Illustrations contained herein © as specified, where known

Transferred to Digital Print 2011

The author would like to thank the following for kind permission to publish their cartoons: Jackie Fleming
("Strange black ring") and Leeds Postcards ("Oh, that explains the difference in our pay").

British Library Cataloguing in Publication Data
A catalogue record for this book is available from the British Library

Library of Congress Cataloging-in-Publication Data
A catalog record for this book has been requested

ISBN 978 1 86134 691 9 paperback

A hardback version of this book is also available.

Cover design by Qube Design Associates, Bristol.
Cover photograph taken on Eel Pie Island, 2001, kindly supplied by Philip Marlow/Magnum Photos.
Printed and bound in Great Britain by Marston Book Services, Oxford.

Contents

Sources of extracts

Part 4: Doing social science

Foreword by Germaine Greer

Twenty-first-century feminisms come in many versions, most of them, according to the common perception, remote from the reality of women's lives. The shelves of university libraries are freighted with books dealing with all aspects of the ramifying cultural manifestations of gender, none of which could ever resolve the conundrums that Ann Oakley has been wrestling with all her life. Women are still at work for most or even all of their waking hours, and most of that work is still done without hope of reward.

The relatively small proportion of women's work that is paid is undervalued by comparison with the work done by men. Yet even ancient ladies whose time is their own will say proudly, 'I keep busy', polishing their dwellings until they shine and knitting garments that nobody wants to wear. The feminist most likely to explain to us women's irrational attachment to unappreciated work is Ann Oakley.

Though the media tell us every day that feminism is over, and even that feminism has gone too far, for the vast majority of the world's women liberation is not even a gleam on the horizon. Globalisation has transported the feminine stereotype into every hovel on the planet. Along the noisome alleys of the slum towns that have grown up wherever big business has driven peasants off the land, amid rivulets of raw sewage, women whose mothers were farmers teeter on spike heels as they wait for clients. Prostitution expands globally; pornography balloons into cyberspace. The consumer in both cases is male. The evidence is that in the cut-throat competition for the client dollar, commercial pornography becomes ever more sadistic and more misogynistic. When Ann Oakley was writing *Sex gender and society*, published in 1972, videos of depilated teenage women enduring 'double anal' penetration were not on sale in every shopping mall; they are now. Sex workers were not at risk from HIV; they are now, and there is little or nothing they can do to protect themselves if the client refuses to use a condom.

Ann Oakley's writing was the 'coming to consciousness' for many women in the seventies - the first analysis of the circumstances in which they found themselves. Her cool, clear and amazingly concise descriptions were immediately recognisable as the complex of contradictory expectations which so tormented them. Understanding then as now was the key to developing strategies for survival. Oakley has edited her earlier accounts, including more and more precise references; what is surprising and depressing is how relevant her analysis of the basic mechanisms of women's oppression still is. In the updated version, even more information and debate has been compressed and organised into cool and cogent discussion.

Women are sometimes accused of being practical rather than creative, useful rather than brilliant. One of the great pleasures of rereading Oakley on any subject is her stubborn resistance to the lure of footling brilliance. Though she is aware that she is likely to be reviled as a logical positivist, she remains stolidly committed to reality as the ultimate test of theory. She can see and applaud the elegance of many of the postmodernists' arguments, but she herself returns again and again to the mundane. Sure, gender is a cultural construct, and yes, she can see that even sex could be construed as a social construct and must therefore be mutable rather than necessary, but, men don't menstruate and that, ladies and gentlemen, remains a fact. While the suffering of women remains real and apparently intractable, it has to be practically dealt with, not argued out of existence. Oakley's training as a social scientist (about which she feels more than slightly ambivalent) is what distinguishes her from the more spectacular feminist polemicists, most of whom were trained in literature and were never required to acquire or exert methodological rigour.

Oakley is as radical as any feminist alive today but what she displays for us is not her personal convictions but her evidence. Her conclusion about housework may seem verbally mild: "Housework remains an incredibly important limit on what women are able to do and become" (p 116). The word 'incredibly' could offer nothing but emphasis, but press it just a little and it refers to the puzzlingness of women's continuing involvement in pointless, repetitive labour which they resent. Go to any student digs and you will see women who are not governed by the needs and desires of husband or children doing all the housework, while the boys do none. The girls buy the coffee and the toilet paper, and wash the coffee pot and cups and clean the toilet. The boys don't care if these jobs are not done; the girls do. We still don't know why.

Oakley is one of the many feminists who have drawn attention to the negative experiences of birthing mothers. With characteristic modesty she allows the mothers to speak for themselves, but once again her conclusion is potentially chilling: "… the capacity for loving children is what ensures women's continuing oppression, because the cycle of mothering is constantly reproduced, and with it the gender-divisive consequences of maternal love" (p 181) – women are oppressed because they love children; or (alternatively put), if they didn't have children, women no longer would be oppressed. The point is the same as that made long ago by radical feminist Shulamith Firestone in *The dialectic of sex* (1970): as long as women undergo pregnancy and birth, they will not be free. Faced with the steadily declining birth rate, and ever-increasing recourse to techniques of assisted reproduction, we should perhaps be asking if freedom from child-bearing might not be the answer to the men's perennial question, 'What do women want?'. Is some such loss of embodiment essential to our liberation, or will women, like Vietnamese villages, be liberated only by being destroyed?

The fourth and last part of *The Ann Oakley reader*, 'Doing social science', deals with her struggles within the sociological intellectual establishment to arrive at a methodology that would be of material use in designing strategies for emancipating the mass of the population and, in particular, women. It is the more difficult for Oakley because of her deep distrust of social scientists' obsession with methodologies of analysis and their concomitant reluctance to address existing, pervasive and obvious social problems. In defending herself from allegations of abandonment of qualitative analysis for the more orthodox quantitative approach, she demonstrates once more her way of anchoring her interpretation by a million

Lilliputian threads to what she can see and hear happening all around her all the time.

Throughout her career Oakley has found her work sidelined and discounted because she is a declared feminist, as if a social scientist is one who is prevented by intellectual protocol from having any moral or political views whatever. To qualify as a sociologist, one is required to see the world through male spectacles; Oakley's great achievement is to succeed in laying by the distorting glasses and fighting her way through to a vantage point from which her woman's eyes can see what is really there.

Preface

Republishing some of one's own work may seem (and it certainly feels) like a form of self-indulgence, but *The Ann Oakley reader* is a response to many complaints I have had about work being out of print. Most of my early books can only be found in libraries, and it seems (from the many enquiries that reach my email inbox) that what students, in particular, want is some easily accessible compendium of my writings, beginning several decades ago, about gender, women, motherhood, social science and other such tricky subjects.

The Ann Oakley reader contains extracts from *Sex, gender and society* (1972), *The sociology of housework* (1974; revised, 1985), *Becoming a mother* (1979, later reprinted as *From here to maternity*, 1981), *Women confined: Towards a sociology of childbirth* (1980) and *Subject women* (1981). It thus encompasses the three early projects on which I worked: the social representation of sex differences, housework and the transition to motherhood. This is the 'historical' Ann Oakley – the work most often quoted and used on social science, women's studies and other school and higher education courses. However, the anonymous reviewers who read the book proposal for The Policy Press (to whom many thanks for their valuable comments) suggested it would be helpful to include some of my more recent work, especially parts of it that relate to the interminable debate about the appropriateness of 'quantitative' and 'qualitative' methods. There are thus several papers on that theme, including a fairly recent statement about my own personal position on paradigm warfare. The first section of the book also concludes with an edited version of a paper I published in 1998, arguing that the project of an emancipatory social science requires both continued use of the term 'gender' and rehabilitation of the 'science' element; such a response is urgent in view of threats such as postmodernism.

Large chunks of my work are not represented in this volume; these include a historical study of the evolution of medical care for pregnant women (*The captured womb*, 1974b); the substantial findings from a large intervention project concerned with providing support for mothers of young children (*Social support and motherhood*, 1992), and my more recent, collaborative work exploring experimental methods and applying the technique of systematic reviewing to the evidence base for social policy. This more recent work – much of it undertaken with my colleagues at the Social Science Research Unit, the Institute of Education, University of London – expands on my earlier reputation as a feminist social scientist, but exemplifies exactly the same concern with developing an informed understanding of how best to promote human welfare and wellbeing. References to these other works can be found in the 'Ann Oakley: further reading' section of this book.

The central themes of *The Ann Oakley reader* are developed much more fully in my two most recent books: *Experiments in knowing: Gender and method in social science* (2000), and *Gender on planet earth* (2002). At the time of writing, these are both in print (see my website www.annoakley.co.uk for up-to-date information and a full list of publications).

Rereading and editing one's own work is an informative experience. The extracts reproduced here *are* heavily edited – in the interests both of space and of intelligibility. I was a more long-winded writer 40 years ago than I am now. I was also somewhat less punctilious about the way I referenced sources, so there are some gaps in the Bibliography that I have not been able to fill.

In terms of intellectual content, there is not much I would disagree with, although the language and approach has changed. We do not, for example, talk about 'housewives' or 'sex roles' in the same way now as we did in the 1970s. There have also been shifts in research traditions. My early work drew heavily on many small empirical studies, for example, of the furnishing of boys' and girls' rooms, or of the representations of women in drug advertising; such studies seem much thinner on the ground today (perhaps partly because people believe there is no longer anything worth studying there?). Yet other themes discussed in some of the extracts which were unusual then – for example, sex differences in brain function, or the domestic oppression of creative women such as Sylvia Plath – have since entered everyday discourse on gender. So the new becomes old, and maybe also, there is space for the old to become new again.

In putting this reader together, I have been supported by the encouragement of Dawn Rushen at The Policy Press and the invaluable editorial help of Matthew Hough. My colleagues in the Social Science Research Unit have provided inspiration and forbearance far beyond the call of duty. My grandchildren have seen rather less of me because of this book, but I hope they will understand.

Part 1: Sex and gender

SEX: "... the two divisions of ... human beings respectively designated as male or female"

GENDER: "... any of two or more subclasses ... that are partly arbitrary, but also partly based on distinguishable characteristics such as ... sex (as masculine, feminine...)"

SOCIETY: "... an enduring and cooperating social group whose members have developed organised patterns of relationship through interaction with one another ... a broad grouping of people having common traditions ... collective activities and interests"

from Webster's *Third New International Dictionary*

Introduction

Anyone trying to understand the social positions of men and women must sooner or later confront the question of causality. The impressive repertoire of differences seemingly inscribed on the 'fault' line of femininity/masculinity suggests an underlying conspiracy on the part of Mother Nature to make women unequal, but the stuff of social science is complex social systems, and there is nothing simple about gender.

The main extracts in this section come from my first book, *Sex, gender and society* (1972), and from an update of this material published as a women's studies textbook, *Subject women* (1981). These arose from my own naive inquiries during the course of a PhD on housework (see Part 2) as to why women appeared to do the bulk of the world's work, unpaid, unrewarded and largely unrecognised. The need for some conceptual distinction between bodily constraints and social oppression was also directly prompted by second wave feminism in Europe and North America; the politics of a new awareness relating to sex inequality demanded a new academic consciousness and analytic technology. The paired terms 'sex' and 'gender' seemed to offer just that: while one signalled bodily prescription and proscription, the other counterposed the heavy weight of culture, economics and tradition in allowing only certain kinds of possibilities.

Sex, gender and society is credited in *The Oxford English Dictionary* with initiating into the language a new use of the term 'gender', and specifically with introducing this use into lexicons of social science (see, for example, Segal, 1987; Delphy, 1993; Oudshoorn, 1994; Hood-Williams, 1996; David, 2003). This book came to be regarded as something of "a feminist primer" (Franklin, 1996, p xiii), promoting a circulation throughout the social sciences of the 'sex/gender binary'. This permitted what was much needed at the time: a conceptual framework for "a material account of women's oppression" (Hird, 2000, p 348).

The research on which *Sex, gender and society* was based drew particular inspiration from two sources: the work of American psychiatrists treating people with various disruptions of the (statistically) normal sex/gender model; and anthropological work on the positions of men and women in non-Western cultures. Both these areas of work suggested a new way of seeing what sociologists had until then, rather restrictively, termed 'sex roles'. Making a distinction between 'sex' and 'gender' had the clear advantage of permitting connections to be made between inequitable social structures, on the one hand, and the development of individual personalities and behaviours, on the other. At the same time, it yielded a theory to accommodate the cross-cultural data. Gender also connected nicely with (i) evolving theories of patriarchy, which added in the all-important notion of a gender *hierarchy* (Johnson, 1997), and with (ii) the notion of a 'system' of gender oppression, within which different structures and sites have both linked and autonomous effects in shaping patterns of inequality (Walby, 1990).

Since 1972, sex and gender have enjoyed an eventful history. The blossoming of women's studies meant that a great deal of the basic descriptive and theoretical work was accomplished in the areas touched on in these extracts: for example, gender and both physical and mental health (Stacey, 1988), menstruation (Weideger, 1978), gender identity development (Chodorow, 1978), interactional analysis (Spender, 1980) and global economic divisions of labour between men and women (Waring, 1988). Interestingly, nothing really competes with the encyclopaedic volumes on sex differences by Eleanor Maccoby and Carol Jacklin (1974) (see Hyde, 1996), on which my work drew heavily (though also see Renzetti and Curran, 1992). As a result of these activities, 'gender' came into common usage in the social sciences, arts and humanities, and by 2001 even in the natural sciences there was more than one use of gender for every two of sex (Haig, 2004). 'Gender' also increasingly substituted for sex as a politer and more fashionable term (Pryzgoda and Chrisler, 2004).

Since the early rush of energy documenting and attempting to explain gender differences, a number of developments have arrived on the scene to threaten the validity of the distinction between sex and gender – or at least to ask awkward and important questions about it.

The first such development was the persuasive argument that sex, as well as gender, is socially constructed. The classic work here is Thomas Laqueur's elegant exposé of how historical thinking about sex and gender elides the two: "almost everything one wants to say about sex ... already has a claim in it about gender" (Laqueur, 1990, p 11). Sex can only be understood in terms of the interaction between gender and power. Gender may even be regarded as the primary classification; it is the social division of labour between men and women which leads to the use of biological sex to determine the distribution of people into dominant and subordinate classes (Delphy, 1993).

There is a situational diversity about sex as well as gender, and both are victims of a patriarchal, phallocentric ideology. The second development, which has embellished the original binarism of sex and gender, is the insistence, deriving from intersex and queer politics, that gender is something to be acted out, played at, and even intentionally parodied, on the assumption that all such boundaries are oppressive, and that transgressing boundaries is one way to demolish them entirely (Lewins, 1995; Rothblatt, 1995; Ekins and King, 1996; Feinberg, 1996; Phelan, 1997; More and Whittle, 1999). There have been linked calls to recognise more than two sexes – three (Herdt, 1996) or possibly five (Fausto-Sterling, 1993). Transsexual and 'transgender' narratives have highlighted the sex-, gender-, heterosex- and literal phallocentr-ism of the common medical practice whereby most ambiguous bodies are surgically reassigned as female because what makes a man is a penis big enough – at least 2.5 cm long (Kessler, 1998, p 43) – to insert into a woman (Hird, 2000; Diamond, 2002). Sexual surgery of this kind joins routine female and male circumcision and the practice of episiotomy in childbirth (see Part 3) as a form of genital mutilation (Chase, 1998).

Both *Sex, gender and society* and *Subject women* bear the hallmarks of an emerging feminist social science that felt it had to do battle with such repositories of myth as Freudian psychology and simplistic forms of biologism that reduced women to weepy uteruses on legs, ill-fitted for most forms of public life. Time has moved on, and some of this, fortunately, reads as outdated now. New forms of resistance, however, have taken the place of old myths. Today's pronounced backlash against feminism reinstates a revamped sociobiology and an obsessional chase for genes that explain everything as a major strategy for closing the door on sociological understandings of difference (Oakley, 1997; Lewontin, 2000). This is the third development which challenges the sex/gender distinction. Not only bodies but brains have sex, and this is effectively their gender (Moir and Jessel, 1989). The attractively radical idea that socialisation can override biology has been subject to some of the same kinds of conservative qualifications as certain brands and exponents of feminism (Money, 1994; see Stacey, 1986).

One major plank of backlash ideology is postmodernism, which provides a fourth critique of sex and gender and, indeed, of many of the concepts which have been central to feminist social science over the last 30 years. Postmodernist theory disputes stable reality and categories of meaning, historical time and objective facts, and turns its back on the Enlightenment belief that science can help us to understand both natural and social worlds (Lyotard, 1984). It is aligned with post-structuralism as a theory of knowledge and language which disputes the notion of a unified, essential self (Culler, 1983). These perspectives would seem to put decisive nails in the coffin of gender. Described as a form of 'masturbation' engaged in mainly by White, middle class intellectual men (Brodribb, 1992, p 8), postmodernist theory and poststructuralism exhibit a severe disconnection from the material experiential base of people's lives. In this sense, they are antagonistic to the emancipatory objectives that have been an important traditional engine for social science (Taylor-Gooby, 1994). The arguments of postmodern feminists have especially weakened the political uses of gender, since such arguments suspend the categories 'women' and 'men', and refute 'the grand narrative of gender difference' (Butler, 1990; Nicholson, 1990; Wittig, 1992). Both sex and gender are reduced to 'performative' aspects of life, a reductionism which is fatal for gender, in particular, rendering it a 'postmodern category of paralysis' (Hoff, 1994).

The battle today is between those who consider that we still need gender, and those who regard it as an outdated misnomer. But, at the same time, in some circles, there are some people who are still trying to get the original distinction straight, helped by the aphorism that 'sex is what you want; gender is what you have to do to get it' (Ebrahim, 2003). Such efforts are motivated by mounting evidence that, in areas such as health research, gender relations and sex-linked biology are best treated as independent and sometimes synergistic variables (Krieger, 2003). While the range of human social arrangements may theoretically be infinite, the signifiers 'man' and 'woman' and the linked structures of gender relations, heterosexism and masculine power exhibit common, sufficiently stable features to constitute a focus for research and theory in the social sciences and elsewhere (Walby, 1992; Assiter, 1996; Oakley, 2002).

The final extract in Part 1 is an edited version of a paper which was originally published in the journal *Women's Studies International Forum* in 1998. The paper addresses the challenge of postmodernism to gender directly, but at the same time asks questions about science. Science and gender have been the main victims of postmodernism, but they have occupied very different positions in feminism's methodological toolkit. In 'Science, gender and women's liberation: an argument against postmodernism', I argue that understanding the epidemiology of women's position requires both the concept of gender and the approach of science: what is needed, above all, is a grounding of theory and political claims in the evidence of real women's lives. This extract could equally well have come at the end of Part 4 of this book, 'Doing social science', since it synthesises much of what my research and thinking have been about since the first naïve enquiries into sex and gender. I include it here because it is an important statement of my own position about gender, and because I enjoy the sense of order which comes from ending up in a new version of the place where I began.

The difference between sex and gender

Everybody knows that men and women are different. But behind this knowledge lies a certain uneasiness: *how* different are they? What is the extent of the difference? What significance does it have for the way male and female behave and are treated in society?

While the first questions are factual ones, the last is a question of value. In practice, of course, fact and value are not always separated, and the confusion between them has been crucial in the debate about sex differences.

This debate has been carried on much more keenly during some historical periods than others. It seems to be revived at times when the existing roles and statuses of male and female are changing, and three periods in particular stand out: the century from about 1540 to 1640, the Victorian era, and the present time [the early 1970s]. In the last two periods, distinct 'women's movements' have arisen, and their existence suggests that, since the 17th century and the growth of industrialisation, basic issues to do with the role of women have never been solved.

The enduring questions are these: Does the source of the many differences between the sexes lie in biology or culture? If biology determines male and female roles, how does it determine them? How much influence does culture have?

The starting point for the study of sex differences is biology. But biology also demonstrates the *identity* of male and female – their basic similarities, the continuity in their development. Far from falling into two discrete groups, male and female have the same body ground-plan, and even the anatomical difference is more apparent than real. Neither the phallus nor the womb are organs of one sex only: the female phallus (the clitoris) is the biological equivalent of the male organ, and men possess a vestigial womb, whose existence they may well ignore until it causes enlargement of the prostrate gland in old age.

What is 'sex'? How do the differences and similarities of the sexes arise? In ordinary usage, the word 'sex' has two meanings: it refers to the differences between individuals that make them male and female, and also to a type of behaviour – the 'mating' behaviour that begins sexual reproduction. Not all organisms, of course, do reproduce in this way; some reproduce asexually by releasing a cell or group of cells from one organism alone. In humans, reproduction is sexual because there is an exchange of nuclear cell material between different mating types – male and female. This process of exchanging and mixing genetic material is what biologists mean by 'sex'. In evolutionary terms, the division of a species into male and female has adaptive advantages: greater variation between individuals is possible and genetic weaknesses can be bred out.

'Sex' is a biological term; 'gender' is a psychological and cultural one. Common sense suggests that they are merely two ways of looking at the same division and that someone who belongs to, say, the female sex will automatically belong to the corresponding (feminine) gender. In reality, this is not so. To be a man or a woman, a boy or a girl, is as much a function of dress, gesture, occupation, social network and personality, as it is of possessing a particular set of genitals.

This rather surprising contention is supported by a number of facts. For example, anthropologists have reported wide variation in the way different cultures define gender (Mead, 1935, 1950; Leith-Ross, 1939; du Bois, 1944; Ford and Beach, 1952; Kaberry, 1952; Henry, 1964; Turnbull, 1965). It is true that every society uses biological sex as a criterion for the ascription of gender but, beyond that simple starting point, no two cultures would agree completely on what distinguishes one gender from the other. Needless to say, every society believes that its own definitions of gender correspond to the biological duality of sex.

Culturally, therefore, one finds the same biological distinctions between male and female coexisting with great variations in gender roles. However, one also finds individual people whose culturally defined genders coexist with indeterminate sex. These people are the intersexed, and recent studies of them in Britain and the United States have shown that someone who is neither male nor female can be masculine or feminine – just as masculine or just as feminine as those who are biologically normal (Money, 1965; Stoller, 1968).

Dr Robert Stoller, in his book *Sex and gender*, defines the relationship between the two as follows:

> … with few exceptions, there are two sexes, male and female. To determine sex one must assay the following physical conditions: chromosomes, external genitalia, internal genitalia (eg uterus, prostate), gonads, hormonal states, and secondary sex characteristics.… One's sex, then, is determined by an algebraic sum of all these qualities and, as is obvious, most people fall under one of two separate bell curves, the one of which is called 'male', the other 'female'.…

> Gender is a term that has psychological and cultural rather than biological connotations; if the proper terms for sex are 'male' and 'female', the corresponding terms for gender are 'masculine' and 'feminine'; these latter may be quite independent of (biological) sex. Gender is the amount of masculinity or femininity found in a person, and, obviously, while there are mixtures of both in many humans, the normal male has a preponderance of masculinity and the normal female a preponderance of femininity. (Stoller, 1968, pp 9-10)

Much of the confusion in the debate about sex roles comes from the fact that we tend to speak of 'sex differences' when we are really talking about differences of gender. Because of this, the rationale of a society organised around sex differences is never made clear, and the idea of a society based on liberation from conventional gender roles is written off as an impossibility.

The aura of naturalness and inevitability that surrounds gender-differentiation in modern society comes, not from biological necessity, but from the beliefs people hold about it. In particular, most people believe that there are inborn differences between the sexes; that differentiation increases social efficiency; and that differentiation is a natural law. The most influential of these three beliefs is the first – that gender differences mirror innate differences between the sexes. Throughout the centuries, this belief has accounted for much of the passion in the debate about sex differences.

It is no coincidence that, each time the debate is renewed, more or less the same sentiments are voiced as reasons for strengthening the system of gender-differentiation in places where it is being eroded by feminism. Various techniques are used to do this, the basic being the 'gynaecological' one. One example is found in an article on 'The potential of women' by a gynaecologist, Edmund Overstreet, who puts forward the historically recurring view of woman as a string of endocrine glands, controlling two ovaries in charge of a uterus. Overstreet (1963) recounts the differences in hormonal secretion between the sexes, and the physiological basis of menstruation and reproduction, arguing that "these structural and functional differences, by their very nature, produce mentational and emotional behaviour in the woman which is different from that of the man" (p 13). He ends: "When you come right down to it, perhaps women just live too long. Maybe when they get through having babies they have outlived their usefulness – especially now that they outlive men by so many years" (p 22). Mary Wollstonecraft, in her introduction to the *Vindication of the rights of women* (1792), quotes a comment which is the exact predecessor of Overstreet's: one writer, she says, "asks what business women turned of forty have to do in the world".

In reality, of course, as opposed to popular myth, the biological differences between the sexes are often no more significant than those between individuals. Biological variability between individuals increases the further up the evolutionary scale one goes, so that a very wide range of size and function is found in most human organs, tissues and secretions (Williams, 1956).

The female clitoris and male penis vary enormously in size, and so do the stomach, the oesophagus, the duodenum, the colon, the liver, the bladder, the heart and the heart rate, the distribution of muscle and fat, the chemical make-up of blood and saliva, the weight and shape of the

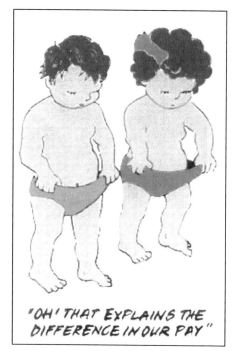

"OH! THAT EXPLAINS THE DIFFERENCE IN OUR PAY"

Low pay–sexist difference © Leeds Postcards

thyroid gland, and so on. Sometimes the range of difference is not just 50% or 100% but 10 or 50 fold. For example, the size of normal ovaries varies from 2 grams to 10 grams; normal heart rates of normal males range from 45 to 105 beats per minute, and the heart's pumping capacity may be normally 3.16 litres of blood per minute or 10.81. On all these measures, females vary as much as males, so a significant proportion of males and females are in the same group with respect to size, height, heart rate and hormone levels, to name a few of the parameters. Even in the form of the external genitals, there is a range extending from very female to very male, and it is along this range that all individuals – male and female, normal and abnormal – fall. Some experts on intersexuality have said that it is impossible to define male and female genital morphologies as distinct: they exist as a continuum of possible developments and are thus a constant reminder, not of the biological polarity of male and female, but of their biological identity. The same is true of the evidence that there may be differences in the hormonal sensitivity of the central nervous system in men and women. This would not create two distinct types – male and female – but a whole range from very male to very female over which individuals would be distributed as they are for other variables.

The argument for the 'social efficiency' of our present gender roles centres around woman's place as housewife and mother. There is also the more vaguely conceived belief that any tampering with these roles would diminish happiness. 'Happiness' can be a cover-term for conservatism, and countless evils can be sanctioned in the name of some supposed short-term psychic gain. The most famous historical example is the subjection of Black people to slavery.

The assumption that a woman's place is in the home implies that it is not in a career. When women do take jobs outside the home, they find themselves almost always doing traditional 'feminine work', conforming to conventional ideas of gender roles (Klein, 1965; Sullerot, 1971). This extension of 'feminine' activities is based on the way we live, in families. The asymmetrical structure of the family allows a connection to be made between such diverse activities as the feeding of tiny babies, the cleaning of houses and the washing of dirty socks. In reality, while childbearing is a biological function, and therefore female, domestic work is a social/economic one, and therefore sexually neuter; but, where both are in practice feminine, the biological role of motherhood takes on a whole aura of domesticity and cultural femininity. The lines are tied between the act of giving birth and the act of cleaning the house, and the status of women as a group is coloured by these secondary cultural consequences of the primary biological specialisation. From that point on, it is not biology that determines the role of women, but domesticity.

Gender-differentiation persists in industrial society, basically because of the importance people continue to attach to masculinity and femininity. They see a whole mass of distinctions between male and female as necessary to social life (UNESCO, 1962; Holter, 1970). But is our form of gender-differentiation actually related to any goal of social or economic efficiency? Moreover, do men and women like being 'masculine' and 'feminine': are they happy in their gender identities? What difference does sex make? What difference should it make?

Looking at the ways in which our practice of gender differentiation contradicts our ideology, it is noticeable that, while small-scale societies often have less gender-differentiation in practice than they do in theory, we seem to have reversed the order. This is odd. Societies lacking in technology are more bound in every way by the reproductive specialisation of male and female. If our own society is largely independent of these constraints, its organisation of gender roles around the division of work and home does have a certain function: it guarantees the servicing of the (predominantly male) industrial work force by the (predominantly female) domestic work force. Further, it provides society with an army of consumers – housewives – whose economically unproductive role has been essential to the success of Western capitalism.

But, in the end, it is not the argument from social efficiency that keeps gender roles in being; it is the simple belief that a society without gender differentiation is somehow wrong in itself. This mechanism of belief sustains gender-differentiation, just as a similar mechanism sustains differences of caste. Gender, like caste, is a matter of social ascription which bears no necessary relation to the individual's own attributes and inherent abilities. In this sense, gender and 'caste' are sociologically identical and the capacity of caste to survive change is shared by gender.

Most of the debate about sex differences is angled at proving that women are, or are not, different from men, rather than proving that men are, or are not, different from women. If this fact needs explaining, it is enough to point out that the bias of our culture is still patriarchal; it is women who are claiming the rights of men and who need to be defended against charges of inferiority. Perhaps there is only one area in which attempts are made to prove the reverse – that men are not inferior to women – and that is the home. But even the most participatory father is not shamed by either real or imputed failure, since he retains the prestige of masculinity, and indeed it is in terms of this masculinity that his inability to care sensitively and tirelessly for small children is explained.

Although the emphasis is on the condition of womanhood, the roles of both sexes are under scrutiny, and, if women suffer from their status as second-class citizens, men certainly suffer from the exercise of privilege. The strains of playing the masculine role in modern civilisation show signs of mounting to breaking point. Social stress diseases are killing proportionately far more males now than they were at the beginning of the 20th century.

Perhaps it is a condition of civilisation that men should be excluded from the care of the next generation and from all the qualities and habits associated with maternity; but what kind of civilisation is this? If it is a civilisation that encourages three-year-old boys to fight back, that disciplines them with the hand rather than with the word, precisely in order that they should become strong, punitive, aggressive men in their turn, then the political machinations which lead to war have their beginning in the nursery, and neither men nor women can expect men to stop fighting wars until the experience of the small boy teaches him to value love and tenderness, non-violence and the urge to protect, instead of the will to destroy, and to see these as human, rather than feminine, qualities. If it is a civilisation that gives dolls to female children so they can have practice at mothering, it is a civilisation that teaches girls to expect their greatest achievements to be maternal ones, to repress and inhibit the development of all their other capacities, so that their maternal destinies can be fulfilled in a world which is already over-populated and able to offer them, at best, less than a decade of active maternity.

While our society is organised around the differences rather than the similarities between the sexes, these two extremes of masculinity and femininity will recur, so apparently confirming the belief that they come from a biological cause. Whatever biological cause there is in reality, however influential or insubstantial it may be, thus tends to become increasingly irrelevant and the distorted view of its importance becomes increasingly a rationalisation of what is, in fact, only prejudice. In this matter, human beings are probably more conditioned by their own gender-differentiated upbringing than they are able, or would care, to admit.

Genes and gender

Whatever nature does or does not determine in the psycho-sexual differentiation of females and males, many people today believe that innate genetic qualities of individuals are extremely important in shaping gender-differentiated behaviour. This draws attention to the central conceptual distinction between 'sex' and 'gender'. 'Sex' refers to the biological division into female and male; 'gender' to the parallel and socially unequal division into femininity and masculinity.

What makes a male?

Most remarkably, the first question is not 'What makes a female?' but 'What makes a male?'. In most other fields, the issue is framed as one of women's differences from men: women are seen as a 'problem', a special group, a disadvantaged minority, and so forth. In the biological field, our vision has to shift. In the first place, of the 46 chromosomes coding the genetic inheritance a child receives from its parents, only two relate directly to its sex. Secondly, men have only themselves to blame for creating a second sex. All female ova contain one of the sex chromosomes, the X chromosome, and the original battle of the sexes takes place in the discharge of paternal sperm, which are divided into those bearing the X (female-determining) and those bearing the Y (male-determining) chromosome. The Y chromosome has been described as an incomplete X, one fifth of its size: "the shape of a comma, the merest remnant, a sad-looking affair" (Montagu, 1968, p 73).

The development of the fertilised ovum is basically female. Until about seven weeks of pre-natal life, the internal and external genitalia look the same in both 'sexes'. The basic human form is female and maleness represents an addition to this structure. This has been dubbed 'the natural superiority of women' (Montagu, 1968). Many of the male's troubles are due to the fragility of his biological status as an addition to the basic female groundplan. Physically, maleness is brought about when the embryonic gonads (the glands that become either ovaries or testes) start to produce the male hormone testosterone at around seven weeks of intrauterine life. This causes the genitals to assume the male form and is later responsible for the secondary sexual characteristics of puberty. The lack of the second X chromosome, and its replacement by the Y chromosome, puts men at a biological disadvantage. In the first place, this is the mechanism by which men express sex-linked diseases in greater numbers than women do. Some of these can only be passed by fathers to sons via the Y chromosome. Yet other diseases and disabilities are more likely to occur in males simply because, if they are carried by one X chromosome, there is no second X chromosome to counteract this effect. Haemophilia and red-green colour blindness fall into this category, and are among the 100 or so known disorders that are sex-linked and found mostly in males.

Being male is associated with higher mortality during gestation and afterwards, throughout childhood and adult life. "Take 20,000 newborn babies, equal numbers of boys and girls, and apply current mortality rates: after 70 years there would be 5743 men and 7461 women still alive" (*British Medical Journal,* 18 June 1977). In 1971-73 British men and women aged 60 could expect to live to 75 and 80 respectively; this difference in life expectancy is typical of many countries. [In 2002, the life expectancy of men and women aged 65 was 81 and 84 respectively (www.statistics.gov.uk, accessed 17 November 2004).] At the other end of the life cycle, more males are miscarried after early pregnancy and stillborn than females. More males than females are usually born (about 106:100), although this sex ratio varies between different societies, probably reflecting environmental influences on pregnancy loss and perinatal mortality.

Many diseases of childhood and adult life are more common in males than females. During the first year of life, one third more males than females die, primarily from infectious diseases (Barfield, 1976, p 67). [This has now fallen to around a quarter more (www.statistics.gov.uk, accessed 17 November 2004).] Boys are more often the victims of childhood accidents – both in and outside the home – and 'violent deaths' in adulthood are a male speciality (Brown and Davidson, 1978; Office of Health Economics, 1978). In middle age, men are 1.95 times more likely than women to die of heart disease, cancer, chest illnesses, kidney diseases and digestive disorders (*New England Journal of Medicine*, 20 October 1977, p 863).

The reasons for men's pronounced physical vulnerability are, in part, biological. Resistance to infectious diseases has a genetic component, and it has been suggested that the synthesis of immunoglobulin is affected by genetic loci on the X chromosome, so that the female with two X chromosomes is better off than the male with one (*The Lancet*, 18 October 1969, p 826). Other physical differences between males and females, such as the male's greater size and weight, may be implicated in the disease-and-mortality-differential – for example, in the greater male susceptibility to birth trauma.

It has been suggested that one reason why adult men die more often than women is because they seek medical help less readily; help-seeking is not concordant with the ideology of the masculine role (*New England Journal of Medicine,* 20 October 1977, p 863). Some male mortality and disease is occupationally related: heart disease to dietary and activity patterns that may be more pronounced in masculine occupations; certain types of cancer to contact with industrial chemicals or radiation. In a study of men and women living in religious cloisters with similar diets, housing, occupation, etc, life expectancies were raised in both sexes, but women still fared better, especially in relation to degenerative diseases (such as heart disease) (Madigan, 1957).

If men's and women's lives are more alike now than they used to be, is the gap between their physical vulnerabilities narrowing?

There is certainly an increase among women of certain types of 'masculine' behaviour known to be related to the mortality differential: they drink more, smoke more and go out to work more. It is arguable whether increases among women in alcoholism and smoking-related illnesses are unintended consequences of women's 'liberation' or signals of stress pointing to the *failures* of our society in this direction. But what they do demonstrate is an interaction between the protective effect of biological femaleness and the corrosive impact of participation in a socially stressful world.

Changing social mores influence biological indicators of gender differences. These biological indicators themselves are associated with another complex group of factors. Many attributions of biological cause and social effect in everyday life appeal to hormones as a Pandora's box of explanations.

Of mice and men

'Hormones' are secretions of the endocrine glands (the pituitary, adrenal glands, thyroid, pancreas, ovary and testis). The number and range of hormones circulating in the bodies of males and females is virtually the same, but women produce a preponderance of what are somewhat incorrectly dubbed the 'female' sex hormones, oestrogen and progesterone, and males a preponderance of testosterone and the general group of hormone, known as 'androgens' or 'male' sex hormones. Individual variations mean that it is not uncommon to find women with higher androgen levels than those of the 'average' man, and men with higher oestrogen levels than those of the 'average' women. Androgen and oestrogen are also interconvertible in normal body processes. In both men and women, the sex hormones are manufactured not only by ovaries and testes, but by the adrenal glands as well. Their function is primarily to ensure the differentiation of reproductive anatomy and physiology. However, other effects are possible, and three of these have been singled out in sex differences research: the impact of hormones on the central nervous system, on aggression and on the periodicity of women's state and behaviour.

It's all in the mind

During embryonic and fetal life, when different hormone profiles distinguish between male and female sexual development, there is also an effect on the brain. The hypothalamus (the brain's control centre for several basic bodily systems) is converted either to a cyclical female or acyclical male rhythm. Like much evidence in this field, this demonstration of an effect on the central nervous system is derived from animal experiments (Money and Ehrhardt, 1972). The fact that in animals some areas of the brain are clearly sensitive to hormones pre-natally raises the question whether there is some more general effect. One such area intensively investigated is that of intellectual functioning. Sex differences here, it is now generally (although not incontrovertibly) agreed, relate not to general intelligence but to specific skills. From puberty onwards, females exceed males in verbal ability, and males are slightly better than females at visual–spatial tasks (Maccoby and Jacklin, 1974).

The hypothesis about the relevance of pre-natal brain differentiation to these

sex differences goes as follows: the left side of the brain controls language function and the right side is responsible for spatial and non-verbal functions. The left side is usually dominant in both sexes after about the age of two. But this dominance is more complete and develops at an earlier age in females, accounting for their verbal superiority and for the superiority of visual–spatial ability in males. Evidence relevant to this hypothesis comes from various kinds of studies and is contradictory (Gray and Buffery, 1971; Levy, 1972; Sperry, 1974; Witelson, 1976). Yet another problem is that the 'package' of skills localised in each hemisphere does not correspond to the 'known' sex difference in abilities (Star, 1979).

Whatever the biological basis of observed gender differences, adult gender identity and role vary between cultures and within the same culture, according to ethnic and socio-economic group. Margaret Mead's famous study, *Sex and temperament in three primitive societies* (1935), is not the only anthropological research to document this, although it is by far the best known. She found three societies exhibiting three different gender patterns: the Arapesh, where both sexes were gentle and 'maternal'; the Mundugumor, where hostile, vigorous and unmaternal personalities were the norm for both sexes; and the Tchambuli, where the traditional western model was reversed, and assertive, business-minded women with shaved heads were complemented by 'skittish', gossipy, adorned male-housewives (Mead, 1962, p 107). Reviewing the literature on the anthropological perspective more recently, Strathern (1976) observed that "… while attention to gender is universal, in many societies a major preoccupation, there are a handful of cultures which do not seem to utilize it to any great extent. This should alert us to the question of what its uses might be" (pp 51-2).

A male problem

Greater physical activity, strength and aggression in males have represented a stereotype of enormous importance in the evolution of sex differences research. In social terms, aggression (however defined, and often it is not) is a male problem: men beat and rape women rather than vice versa; most crimes of violence are committed by males; men are more likely to engage in dangerous and violent sports than women; and so on. Jessie Bernard (1975) has put the position (from women's point of view) in a nutshell: "I think I have no hang-ups about sex differences. I am quite willing to concede male superiority in offensive aggressiveness" (p 23).

In Maccoby and Jacklin's review (1974) of sex differences research, aggression emerges as one of three sex-differentiated traits (the others are visual–spatial and verbal ability) for which there is reasonably sound evidence. Before the age of about two years, most studies show no sex difference. There is clear evidence that aggression is a learned capacity (Patterson et al, 1967; Bandura, 1973; see also Scherer et al, 1975). There is also evidence that hormones play a role. Genetic females hormonally masculinised in the womb have elevated levels of threat behaviour and rough-and-tumble play, an effect that has been demonstrated in humans, monkeys and rats. But for both humans and animals, it is too simplistic to say that individual differences in aggressive behaviour correlate with different levels of male hormones. In monkeys, dominant males have higher testosterone levels than non-dominant males, but this is affected by social context, and low-dominance males caged with females show markedly raised testosterone levels (Rose et al, 1972).

Summarising their review of the evidence on the biological predisposition to aggression in males, Maccoby and Jacklin (1974) comment that:

> We have been emphasizing male aggression to the point of allowing females to be thought of, by implication, as either angelic or weak. Women share with men the human capacity to heap all sorts of injury upon their fellows. And in almost every group that has been observed, there are some women who are fully as aggressive as the men. Furthermore, an individual's aggressive behaviour is strengthened, weakened, redirected, or altered in form by his or her unique pattern of experiences. (p 247)

Accordingly, as these experiences change, so ought the social record of gender patterns in aggression. Beginning in the 1960s, there were suggestions that women were becoming more involved in 'criminal' types of activity. For example, there was a 225% rise in violent offences committed by women over the period from 1965 to 1967 (100% for men) (Smart, 1979).

Whatever the 'real' change in women's behaviour, the altered disposition of law-enforcing agencies to find more women guilty of criminal behaviour is important. For women criminals, a different and more gender-appropriate version of the biological model has operated: the view that women's behaviour is controlled by the hormones of their menstrual cycle.

The curse of women

Menstruation has been a murky field throughout women's history. In the 19th century, it was the reason doctors gave why women could not expect (or hope) to live the same sort of life as men. In the 20th century, less overt biological determinism has predominated among 'experts', but there is still a widespread suspicion that the periodicity of women's hormone levels makes them unequal citizens.

Women are held to be victims of the recurrent 'normal crises' of menstruation, exemplifying in their moods and behaviour the ebb and flow of their hormones. This is the reproductive machine model of women, according to which the body–mind connection is so close that women's behaviour can only be explained in terms of their possession of a uterine physiology (Oakley, 1980). Menopausal and post-menopausal women do not escape from this distorted view, but are special victims, since the menopause is seen both as something really terrible and as an invented feminine neurosis: moreover, it provides a convenient excuse for the behaviour of all middle-aged women (Weideger, 1978).

The menstrual hypothesis of gender differences boils down to the description and consequences of something called 'the pre-menstrual syndrome'. This was introduced by Frank in 1931 as a feeling preceding menstruation of "indescribable tension", irritability and "a desire to find relief by foolish and ill-considered actions" (Frank, 1931, p 1054). The pre-menstrual syndrome has since been associated in a proliferation of studies with such varying types of behaviour as violent crimes (Cooke, 1945; Morton et al, 1953; Dalton, 1961; Ribeiro, 1962), death from accidents or suicide (MacKinnon and MacKinnon, 1956; Mandell and Mandell, 1967), accidents (Dalton, 1960), admission to hospital with acute psychiatric illness (Dalton, 1959; Janowsky et al, 1969), taking a child to a medical clinic (Dalton, 1966) and loss of control of aircraft (Whitehead, 1934).

This seems an impressive record. Five main problems are identified by Mary Brown Parlee (1976) in her critical review of these studies:

1) Many are correlation studies, which do not establish causal relationships. Many are vague or weak on the issue of establishing the timing of menstruation.
2) Where actual data on pre-menstrual symptoms are collected, the manner of collection usually leaves a great deal to be desired. For example, how do symptoms experienced by individual women prior to menstruation compare with those experienced at other times in the cycle? What *are* the symptoms of the pre-menstrual syndrome? Over 150 are mentioned in the literature; this seems rather a lot.
3) In a study by Paige (1971) of pill-users and non-pill users, severity of bleeding turned out to be a better predictor of pre-menstrual anxiety in all the women, suggesting the common-sense conclusion that some pre-menstrual anticipation is due to the inconvenience and discomfort of the physical event of menstruation itself.
4) Most of the studies of the pre-menstrual syndrome are consistent with an interpretation of a mid-cycle peak having positive traits, as well as of a pre-menstrual syndrome of negative symptoms. So why is there such an exclusive emphasis on *negative* symptoms?
5) Men have moods too. Monthly cycles in men have been reported for body temperature (Kuhl et al, 1974), weight (Luce, 1970), beard growth (Harkness, 1974) and pain threshold (Smolensky et al, 1974). Male cycles have also been documented in schizophrenia, manic-depression and epilepsy (Richter, 1968). In Denmark, researchers charting urine levels of male hormones in a sixteen-year study found a pronounced 30-day rhythm (Luce, 1970, p 111).

The politics of 'sex differences' research

A curious relationship between the size of people's feet, their sex, and whether they are left- or right-handed has been discovered by American researchers. After measuring the foot sizes of 150 individuals, they were able to show that there was a strong association between right-handedness and a right foot bigger than the left – and vice versa – in men. In women, the reverse is true: right-handed women tend to have bigger left feet, and vice versa. (*The Sunday Times,* 25 June 1978)

Unless this research was prompted by some charitable intention on the part of shoe-manufacturers and retailers to sell different-sized shoes to accommodate people's different-sized left and right feet, it is difficult to see what relevance it could have to any aspect of social or personal life. Like most of the 'scientific' research on sex and gender differences, it is based on the assumption that sex differences matter – and that they matter more than sex similarities. In this way, scientific work starts from, and reinforces, the status quo of everyday beliefs about the roles of men and women.

In one longitudinal study in which 35 categories of behaviour were rated yearly for 57 females and 58 males, 7 per cent of 442 female–male differences achieved the 5 per cent level of significance. This is hardly greater than the number of 'findings' that would have been expected to occur by chance (Tresemer, 1975). A second important point is that socialisation processes are quite sufficient to account for most of the observed and 'documented' sex differences. The socialisation effect cannot be dismissed even from research on neonates, one of the two fields to which sex differences researchers have most hopefully looked for 'pure' data (the other field is the cross-cultural one). A striking omission is that much of this research does not control for the impact of circumcision, which is an injury inflicted on 80-90 per cent of North American male babies with relevant identifiable behavioural consequences in the direction of altered arousal levels, more wakefulness and more irritability (Richards et al, 1976).

A third point to note is that much sex differences research is conducted on the assumption that conclusions about human behaviour may be drawn from studies of animal behaviour. Such extrapolations ignore (a) the importance of learning in humans, (b) the much greater complexity of humans' verbal communication, and (c) the tremendous extent to which humans are able to manipulate their environment.

Fourthly, biology is not a 'given', a cultural constant. The biological body and its 'natural' divisions are not perceived in the same way in all cultures, or by different social groups within the same culture (Ardener, 1978; see also Ardener, 1971, 1977; Williams, 1975). One reason why the nature versus nurture debate is outmoded, in other words, is because nurture affects nature.

The Isle of Wight 1970 © Paul Popper

Last, but by no means least, the status quo that much scientific research on sex differences claims to discover is one that legitimises the social inferiority of women.

Among the stimuli within the scientific community that led the debate about sex differences to assume the form it did in the late 1970s were (1) the counting of chromosomes first made possible by the work of Tjio and Levan in 1956; (2) the development of the radio–immunoassay method of measuring body hormones in the late 1960s; and (3) the demonstration of cellular uptake of radioactively labelled oestrogen in individual brain cells in the early 1960s (Michael and Glascock, 1963). All of these paved the way for speculations about the hormonal basis of adult gender differences. They can hardly be considered to be completely accidental discoveries, occurring as they did in the political context of a sexist medical/scientific community with a shared ambience and shared standards of rewarded achievement (Kuhn, 1962), and publicised in a society in which the position of women had come, once more, to be regarded as something of a riddle. As Crook (1970) has pointed out, in situations of social change, biological explanations may assume the role of an ethical code akin in their moral persuasiveness to religion. They provide powerful, easily understood arguments about the undesirability of change by fuelling a retreatist emphasis on the immutability of the natural world.

A kind of person

Homo sapiens

The name of the race is Man. *Homo erectus* became *homo sapiens*, the noun 'embracing' woman but relegating her to a sub-group, its adjectival qualification suggesting that the wisdom marking Man's descendancy from animals is a male trait. The labelling habits of the 19th-century evolutionists were contiguous with the conventions of their culture: men represented the norm with which women were (usually invidiously) compared (Morgan, 1972). They still do. Femininity is defined in relation to masculinity, not the other way round: the media offer special programmes or features for women, but not for men, since men are the general audience at whom the bulk of media provision is aimed; in textbooks on sex roles, aggression appears first and is discussed as a positive trait, while feminine passivity comes second and is negatively valued (see, for example, Weitz, 1977); questions about inequality in patterns of female and male employment are phrased as questions about the 'failure' of women to make use of their opportunities, in terms of the 'under-achievement' of women (what about the under-achievement of men in the home?).

In a very important sense, it is normal to be a man and abnormal to be a woman. Rosenkrantz and his colleagues (1968) asked 154 people to rate 122 bipolar personal qualities (for example, 'not at all aggressive' versus 'very aggressive') in terms of their relevance to the 'average female' and the 'average male'. A third of the qualities were differentiated by gender in the sample's ratings and 71 per cent of these 'stereotypic' items had the masculine pole designated as more socially desirable. In a second study, the Rosenkrantz questionnaire was given to 79 mental health clinicians (Broverman et al, 1970). The hypothesis was that personality traits regarded as socially desirable are positively related to ratings of normality, mental health and adjustment. The clinicians were divided into three groups: the first group was asked to fill in the questionnaire with normal adult men in mind; the second group for normal adult women; and the third group was asked to describe a 'healthy, mature, socially competent person'. Socially desirable masculine characteristics were seen as healthier for men than for women. Healthy women were more submissive, less aggressive, less competitive, more excitable, more easily hurt, more emotional, more conceited about their appearance and less objective than healthy men. This points to a double standard of mental health: for a woman to be considered mature and healthy, she must behave in ways that are socially undesirable and immature for a competent adult.

This conflict, between being a woman and being a person, is central to women's psychological development. The 17-year-old Sylvia Plath wrote:

> I want to be free – free to know people and their backgrounds – free to move to different parts of the world so I may learn that there are other minds and standards besides my own. I want, I think, to be omniscient....

In the same piece, 'Reflections of a seventeen year old', she also said,

> I have a terrible egotism ... I am 'too tall' and have a fat nose, and yet I poke and prink before the mirror ... I have erected in my mind an image of myself – idealistic and beautiful. Is not that image, free from blemish, the true self.... (Plath, 1977, pp 37-8)

In terms of outward appearance, Sylvia was a very feminine person. But she was also a very determined person, with a strong commitment to a writing career. Between the ages of 17 and 24, she had many minor publishing successes and added a long list of scholastic achievements to an already impressive record. A suicide attempt at 21 followed some minor setbacks; she convinced herself she would never succeed as a writer. Readjusted with psychiatric help, which she later satirised in her autobiographical novel, *The bell jar* ("'Suppose you try and tell me what you think is wrong?', said the psychiatrist. 'What did I *think* was wrong? That made it sound as if nothing was *really* wrong, I only *thought* it was wrong", Plath, 1963, p 137), Sylvia continued her search for freedom, omniscience and femininity. In Cambridge she met and later married a fellow poet, Ted Hughes. Sylvia housekept in a three-room rented flat ("I'll make it like an ad out of *House and Garden*", Plath, 1977, p 324), and finally in a rambling Devon farmhouse. When Ted's first book of poems was accepted for publication, she said:

> I am more happy than if it was my book published! I have worked so closely on these poems of Ted's and typed them so many countless times through revision after revision that I feel ecstatic about it all.

> I am so happy *his* book is accepted *first*. It will make it so much easier for me when mine is accepted ... I can rejoice then, much more, knowing Ted is ahead of me. (Plath, 1977, p 340)

At the beginning of 1960, her first child was born. Sylvia did all the housework, trying to fit it into a schedule so that it did not intrude into her writing time. Ted Hughes started a relationship with another woman and four months later he left Sylvia. The separation was a relief for her in some ways, but managing without Ted proved difficult: housing and money problems, the bitterly cold strike-ridden winter of 1962-63 and her own and the children's ill-health wore her down. Some weeks before her death from suicide, she said:

> I just haven't felt to have any *identity* under the steamroller of decisions and responsibilities of this last half year, with the babies a constant demand.... How I would *like* to be self-supporting on my writing! But I need *time*.

I guess I just need somebody to cheer me up by saying I've done all right so far. (Plath, 1977, pp 570, 583-4)

Although she lived in the shadow of Ted Hughes, death made Sylvia Plath famous. The women's movement adopted her as a martyr, a symbol of man's oppression of woman. Her life illustrates the opposed pull of the two motivations in women's personalities: to become and be a person, making a contribution to society based on individual worth, and to become and be a woman, matching conventions of femininity.

Of course, Sylvia Plath's life also illustrates a great many other relevant aspects of women's lives: the frustration of creativity by domestic responsibility; the function of mental illness as an acceptably feminine escape route; the economic vulnerability of women and children as dependents of men. But these are also related to the structural *ambivalence* surrounding the character and position of women in industrial society (Oakley, 1974a, pp 80-90). Two central qualities of femininity are passivity and instability.

Standing (or lying) still: feminine passivity

In *Ways of seeing,* John Berger (1972) describes the representation of women in art, the passive female contrasting with the active male:

A man's presence is dependent upon the promise of power which he embodies.... A man's presence suggests what he is capable of doing to you or for you....

By contrast, a woman's presence expresses her own attitude to herself.... Her presence is manifest in her gestures, voice, opinions, expressions, clothes, chosen surroundings, taste....

One might simplify this by saying: *men act* and *women appear.* Men look at women. Women watch themselves being looked at.

The idea that women are naturally passive has a long history:

Men have been generals, kings, writers, composers, thinkers and doers; women have been wives, mistresses, companions, friends, and helpmates. The very word woman, in fact, emphasizes this passive anonymous position. It derives from the Anglo Saxon *wifman*, literally 'wife-man'.... (Bullough, 1974, p 3)

However, as Bullough points out, we do not really know whether or how women experienced this passivity, since most historical records are written by men. In such records, it is often sexually scandalous behaviour on the part of women that ensures their notoriety: Cleopatra, Lucrezia Borgia, Eleanor of Aquitaine, Catherine the Great of Russia – these 'leaders' of 'men' have their places in history defined by their active and unusual sexuality. Elizabeth I of England, who was not sexually scandalous in this way, puzzled historians with her unconsummated love affairs and refusal to marry; some, therefore, concluded she was really a male in drag (Bullough, 1974, p 4).

Two processes have exacerbated this tendency to cast women in a mould of necessary inactivity. The first is the assurance with which many religious ideologies have defined women's place. The second is the massive upheaval in gender roles and perceptions that has accompanied the industrialisation of work.

Capitalism and Protestantism are connected 'revolutions'. The Protestant idealisation of the home and the family (and women) was "an inheritance given substance by the capitalistic division of the world into work and home" (Hamilton, 1978, p 22) and, reciprocally, Protestant ideology gave capitalists the tool with which to mythologise the activity of women. What was most important about this mythology was its fabrication of a natural feminine passivity, a tradition that Freud, who has done more than anyone else to equate female biology with feminine passivity, himself inherited. The families into which he was born and which he founded were models of conventionality: wife-mother kept house, reared the children and was submissive to the male head of the household (Puner, 1947). Freud was bitterly attacked by the Church for his irreligious 'science' of psychology, and yet his theory really represents the secularisation and apotheosis of Protestant ideology on the subject of the human, and especially the feminine, character.

Freud observed (incorrectly): "The male sex-cell is actively mobile and searches out the female one, and the latter, the ovum, is immobile and waits passively. The behaviour of the elementary sexual organism is indeed a model..." (Freud, 1964, p 114). Noting three meanings of 'masculinity' and 'femininity' in everyday language – the equation with activity-passivity, the biological and the 'sociological' – he was in no doubt as to their relative importance: "The first of these three meanings is the essential one" (Freud, 1962, p 85). The distinction between masculine activity and feminine passivity was absolutely central to his work. It enabled him, for example, to characterise women as constitutionally passive, to say that auto-eroticism in women was phallic in nature, and to construct the libido (sexual drive and life-force in general) as "regularly and lawfully of a masculine nature whether in the man or the woman" (Freud, 1964, pp 612-13).

As pure description, the Freudian paradigm has a certain merit. The prescription to be passive is to some extent internalised in the social system of which Freud writes and women tend to experience themselves as passive, as objects of other people's experiences rather than subjects of their own. The passive victim lacks a voice of her own: inarticulateness is the mark of an oppressed group. Patterns of verbal communication are thus one way in which the stereotype of the feminine character is expressed in the reality of female behaviour.

For example, women specialise in what Lakoff has termed 'tag questions' ('I did lock the door, *didn't I*?'). These are used "when the speaker is stating a claim, but lacks full confidence in the truth of that claim" (Lakoff, 1975, p 15). A related device is the feminine intonational pattern of a rising inflection at the end of an answer to a question, for example,

'When will dinner be ready?'

'About six o'clock?'

"The effect is", says Lakoff, "as though one was seeking confirmation, though at the same time the speaker may be the only one who has the requisite information" (Lakoff, 1975, p 17).

Women's reticence is balanced by men's assertiveness. Barbara and Gene Eakins (1978) taped a year's worth of university faculty meetings, counting 'speaker turns'. The males surpassed the females in number of turns taken and they spoke for much longer (average *longest* female turn, 10 seconds; average *shortest* male turn, 10.66 seconds). Moreover the number of turns followed a hierarchy of power or status, according to rank, importance or length of time in the department. A study by Zimmerman and West (1975) looked at 'overlaps', interruptions and silences in same-sex and dual-sex conversations recorded in coffee shops, drug stores and other public places in a university community. In same-sex conversations, interruptions and overlaps (an intrusion at the end, rather than in the middle, of a statement) were equally distributed between both speakers. But in female–male conversations, 96 per cent of the interruptions and 100 per cent of the overlaps came from males.

Such feminine–masculine polarities are at a premium in intimate relationships; the more intimate the setting, the bigger the difference. Pamela Fishman set up a tape recorder in the apartments of three couples and analysed 52 hours of tape-recorded conversation. Some of her findings were as follows:

1) The men were consistently successful in initiating interactions, while the women's attempts often failed because the men did not do any 'interactional work'.
2) The women asked two and a half times more questions than the men.
3) The women used attention-getting devices (such as 'Do you know what?') and the men did not.
4) The men more often used monosyllabic responses (such as 'yeah'). When women used them, they did so to punctuate a masculine stream of talk: 'support work'.

Fishman called her article 'Interactional shitwork', and concluded that interactional work is tied up with feminine identity: "It is not seen as something we do, but is part of what we are" (Fishman, 1977, p 101).

Similarly with humour. It is, of course, important that, as Lakoff (1975, pp 81-2) notes, our culture contains:

a whole genre of antiwomen jokes, based on sexual stereotypes as antiethnic jokes were (and are) based on ethnic stereotypes: women as a group and any woman because of belonging to that group are vain, fuzzy-minded, extravagant, imprecise, long-winded … and numerous variants on those themes, concerning jealousy of other women, hat buying, driving, and so on. There are to my knowledge no parallel joke types based on stereotypes of men in general.

Responding well: feminine instability

Stephen Spender once compared Sylvia Plath's poetry with that of Wilfred Owen, the British war poet:

> … being a woman, her warning is more shrill, penetrating, visionary than Owen's. Owen's came out of the particular circumstances of the trenches, and there is nothing to make us think that if he had not been on the Western Front – the mud and blood into which his nose was rubbed – he would not have warned anyone about anything at all. He would have been a nice chap and a quiet poet. With Sylvia Plath, her femininity is that her hysteria comes completely out of herself, and yet seems about all of us. And she has turned our horrors and our achievements into the same witches' brew. (Spender, 1966, p 26; cited in Ellmann, 1968, pp 84-5)

Despite the demise of the ancient Greeks, hysteria remains a prominent theme in the feminine stereotype. In very many aspects of life, the view prevails that women cannot be trusted because they have poor control of their emotions. Feminine instability is seen as a core female trait (Holter, 1970, p 124) and is one of the common sense understandings about women in industrial societies.

In an interesting analysis of reviews of Emily Brontë's *Wuthering heights*, Carol Ohmann has explored the different characterisations associated with male and female authorship. *Wuthering heights* was first published under a male pseudonym (Ellis Bell), as were all the Brontë sisters' works. Charlotte later noted the reason, still appropriate today:

> We did not like to declare ourselves women, because – without at that time suspecting that our mode of writing and thinking was not what is called 'feminine' – we had a vague impression that authoresses are liable to be looked on with prejudice; we had noticed how critics sometimes use for their chastisement the weapon of personality, and for their reward, a flattery, which is not true praise. (cited in Ohmann, 1971, p 906)

Ohmann shows how differently *Wuthering heights* was interpreted when written by Ellis Bell as opposed to Emily Brontë. With the former author, the novel was taken to be a representation of brutality and violence, a celebration of masculine sexual power. One reviewer described the author as "a rough sailor [with] a powerful imagination" (George Washington Peck, cited in Ohmann, 1971, p 908). He said that the author pretended to understand women but only really understood his (male) view of them. In the reviews of the second edition, when Emily Brontë was its author, the word 'original' – prominent the first time around – is missing; it became a work of 'female genius', a tale typical of women's imagination and peopled by male monsters whose creation was due to the fact that their female author did not understand men. It became principally a love story concerned with the portrayal of emotion, a task for which female writers were, of course, specially equipped.

Another mark of women's instability is the tendency of women to specialise in mental illness. In most industrialised societies, many more women than men are classified as having 'neurotic' disorders, and females predominate in all psychosomatic disorders (Silverman, 1968). The female preponderance in depression is commonly 2:1.

If 'depressive psychoses' and 'psychoneuroses' are categories in which women cluster, the social situation of those thus afflicted contains some clues. Gove (1972) and Gove and Tudor (1973) have shown how statistics concerning mental illness reveal a pattern of higher male rates in never-married, divorced and widowed categories and higher female rates in the married population. Using 12-month records from a sample of London GPs, Shepherd and his colleagues found that 18% of women in the practices had visited their doctors and had been given some kind of psychiatric 'diagnosis', compared with 10% of the men. More of the women than the men who were given a psychiatric diagnosis were classed as neurotic. Mood-altering ('psychotropic') drugs are more often given to women than to men by GPs (Skegg et al, 1977). [Nowadays, women use twice as many such drugs as men (Van der Waals et al, 1993).]

There is little evidence that such drug treatment of depressed women is effective in curing depression. If medical treatment does not cure depression, then it is a way of exercising control over the social functions of women. Michèle Barrett and Helen Roberts (1978) studied the consulting patterns of middle-aged women and found that GPs often attributed women's anxiety and 'depression' to their inadequate adjustment to domesticity, and that 'readjustment' to domesticity was the dominant aim of treatment. Accordingly, the commercial promotion of psychotropic drugs relies on a heavily reactionary mythology of women. One advertisement in an Australian medical journal shows a typical 'before' and 'after' situation in which a lethargic, sedentary housewife nursing an inactive vacuum cleaner is transformed into a bright, cheerful, hoover-pushing housewife via the medical administration of a magic potion (Chapman, 1979). [Advertising of psychotropic drugs today continues to be aimed at women (Lövdahl et al, 1999).]

Women's energies in our kind of society appear to be devoted to 'doing good and feeling bad'. Masculine culture delegates to them the care of not only humanity's lowest needs (the 'lavatorial' function of housework, the cleaning of small children, etc) but its 'highest necessities' – "the intense, emotionally connected co-operation and creativity necessary for human life and growth" (Miller, 1976, pp 25-6). Sociologists have called this the 'expressive' role, and seen its performance by women as essential to the stability of the family and society. Yet it is the very *sensitivity* of women to other people's needs that is likely to produce the appearance and the consequence of mental instability: women's instability stabilises the world.

Dominant standards

Most research on ideas of feminine personality has used white, middle-class and university-educated populations. Yet there are likely to be significant social class and ethnic differences. For example, Turner and Turner (1974) found in a study of black and white students that white men differed from black men, white women and black women in rating 'most women' especially low on the effectiveness/efficiency dimension. They suggest that this is because of cultural differences in the role of women, which in black culture has traditionally been a great deal more 'instrumental' than in white culture.

Predictably too, investigations of ethnic differences have rarely moved beyond the confines of the industrialised West. One study that did this was that by Huang (1971). She asked some Chinese students (again, the student bias) from Taiwan and some American students to complete Rosenkrantz's questionnaire (Rosenkrantz et al, 1968; see p 21). There were many similarities in the ratings made by both sexes of feminine and masculine characteristics in the two samples, but some differences. By comparison with the American women, the Chinese women saw women as "having a poorer sense of humour and a weaker personality; less conscientious and less resourceful; more selfish; giving up more easily; less dominant; less adventurous, less inclined to act as leader; and more timid, more afraid to be different, and less creative" (Fransella and Frost, 1977, p 46). Chinese men were even more negative about women, and the gulf between the sexes was much bigger than in the American sample.

Women's personalities, self-perceptions and feminine ideals are formed as part of a male-dominated culture. Women have historically been subject to many of the same sorts of social, economic and psychological discrimination as have black people. This means that their psychology and the idealised construction of feminine personality can very largely be seen as an embodiment of subordinate group status.

Jean Baker Miller (1976) puts this interpretation in *Toward a new psychology of women*. Examining the relations between men and women under the more general titles of 'dominants' and 'subordinates', she shows how both the designated roles of women and their personality types flow from the dominant–subordinate relation. Personality characteristics of subordinate groups form a familiar cluster:

> submissiveness, passivity, docility, dependency, lack of initiative, inability to act, to decide, to think and the like. In general this cluster includes qualities more characteristic of children than adults – immaturity, weakness and helplessness. If subordinates adopt these characteristics they are considered well-adjusted. (Miller, 1976, p 7)

A further implication is that the dominant group's model of itself becomes the paradigm of 'normal' human personality and relationships.

The dominant–subordinate split makes for the over-valuation of some aspects of the human potential and the under-valuation of others. Perhaps the most important point is, as Miller puts it, that women as subordinates have become "the 'carriers' for society of certain aspects of the total human experience – those aspects that remain unsolved" (1976, p 23). These have to do with emotional connections between individuals, which are an essential part of human social life and individual psychic health. Connectedness is not possible without the qualities of vulnerability, weakness, helplessness and dependency. It is immediately obvious that the central paradox is that these qualities are negatively described as constitutionally feminine and thus necessarily undesirable (from the dominant group's point of view). Women's involvement in this kind of emotional work has been at great cost to themselves; they have been led to believe that effective thought and action will jeopardise their chances for satisfying emotional experience. The capacity and need for emotional connection becomes a liability, not an asset: women experience powerlessness and low self-esteem and are unable to regard their traditional activities as enhancing self-development and self-fulfilment. 'Real work' in the dominant group's paradigm is what men do for themselves and for financial gain.

Childhood lessons

Doctor: "Come on junior. Only a lady could cause so much trouble. Come on, little one [baby is delivered]."

Mother: "A girl."

Doctor: "Well, it's got the right plumbing."

Mother: "Oh, I'm sorry, darling."

Father: [laughs]

Doctor: "What are you sorry about?"

Mother: "He wanted a boy." (Macfarlane, 1977, p 631)

Conversations of this kind set the scene for a lifetime's lessons.

It's a baby

Moss (1967) looked at the way mothers and their first-born infants behaved in the first three months of motherhood. Dimensions of behaviour examined included crying, fussing and sleeping in the infant, and holding, feeding, rocking, talking to and stimulating in the mother. He found that male babies 'fussed' more and that the mothers of sons held, attended to, stimulated and looked at their babies more than the mothers of daughters, who characteristically imitated their daughters' vocalisations more than did the mothers of sons. Mothers also hovered over male babies more, trying to anticipate a restlessness that might need maternal intervention.

Infants are not *tabula rasa* on whom parents inscribe easily decipherable gender messages. Males inherit a certain biological disadvantage along with their chromosomal constitution. But what parents do and how babies behave reflect a two-way influence of biological potential and cultural determinism in which biological and cultural inputs are not likely ever to be clearly identified.

Few parents are indifferent to the sex of their child. In my own study of London women having their first babies in 1975-76, three quarters said in pregnancy they had a definite sex preference and many of those who said they 'didn't mind' added, after the child was born, that they had minded, but hadn't wanted to voice a preference for fear of being disappointed, or because to do so is regarded superstitiously as bringing bad luck. Table 1 shows how many women wanted boys and girls, and what their reactions were: 93% of those who had boys were

Table 1: Sex preferences and reactions (%)

Wanted girl	22
Wanted boy	54
Didn't mind	25
Had girl: pleased	56
Had boy: pleased	93
Had girl: disappointed	44
Had boy: disappointed	7

Source: Oakley (1979, p 118)

pleased; and 44% who had daughters were not (as in the delivery room scene above). The question arises whether adult women's stated preferences are theirs or those of their male partners. Do they really want boys, or do they want boys because men do and they want to please men?

Sex preferences are conscious; gender-differentiated treatment of children often is not. Lake (1975) gave five young mothers Beth, a six-month-old in a pink frilly dress for a period of observed interaction; five others were given Adam, a six-month-old in blue overalls. Compared with Adam, Beth was smiled at more, offered a doll to play with more often and described as 'sweet' with a 'soft cry'. Adam and Beth were the same child.

Conceiving gender

Money and Ehrhardt (1972) have suggested that a relevant analogy for the development of gender identity is that of bilingualism. A child growing up in a bilingual environment is presented with two languages that require two different sets of behavioural responses. So with gender: there are two sets of stimuli to be programmed by the brain into two different complexes of behaviour. The child's task is to identify with one and reject the other; the parents' conscious or unconscious duty is to provide the means whereby little girls identify with the feminine model and little boys with the masculine one.

'Identification' is the key concept. Most theories of gender-identity development reserve an important place for it. Because it implies the idea of a 'model' with whom identification can take place, most theories also stress the importance of parents as the primary teachers of gender. The three main theories are the cognitive–developmental, the social learning and the psychoanalytic.

The first of these builds on the work of Piaget (1952) and says that gender is based on genital sex and so is a physical property of people that has to be learnt in the same way as other unchanging physical properties. The thinking is: I am a girl; therefore I like girl things; therefore doing girl things is rewarding (Kohlberg, 1967; Kohlberg and Ullian, 1974).

The second theory, that of social learning, contends that the development of gender identity involves a learning process that is essentially the same as other learning processes. A little girl observes her parents performing feminine and masculine roles, but, when she imitates the various behaviours she sees, she is only rewarded for those considered appropriate to her gender. Through such differential reinforcement, feminine behaviours come to be positively evaluated and masculine ones rejected: I want rewards; I am rewarded for doing girl things; therefore I want to be (am) a girl. The result is a generalised tendency to imitate all same-gendered 'models' (Mischel, 1967, 1970).

Thirdly, we have the psychoanalytic view of gender–identity development. In this, awareness of genital difference comes first and paves the way for an identification with the parent who has a similar set of genitals. The formula runs: I do not have a penis; therefore I am a girl. Freud did not concern himself with the notion of 'gender identity' since he regarded genital–sexual identity as synonymous with the cultural meaning of femininity and masculinity. The way in which the anatomical sex difference is reflected in the different psychic constitutions of men and women is determined in Freud's theory by the structure of the family. Because women rear children, the love of both girls and boys is originally centred on the mother. This, combined with an early unawareness in small children of the genital difference, means that at first the psychological development of females and males is the same. But, when the girl discovers that she has no penis, she also recognises that her mother shares the same fate and blames her for her disadvantaged condition. This leads to a rejection of the mother as a love object; the girl turns to her father instead, a move that lays the foundation for her adult sexual attraction to males and her desire to bear male children.

All three theories – the cognitive–developmental, the social–learning and the psychoanalytic – take the actual processes that are involved in the emergence of adult femininity and masculinity as in need of explanation. All assume that some identification with the same-sexed parent has to take place and is the main precursor of the desire to be seen as feminine or masculine. This 'motivational consequence' is not only a necessary element in the continuing gender socialisation of children ('self-socialisation'), but is, of course, an absolutely central means for the cultural transmission of gender concepts from one generation to another. Lessons learnt in childhood become the lessons that parents want their own children to learn.

The following points summarise some of what has been written on the available empirical evidence for the different theories, particularly Eleanor Maccoby and Carol Jacklin's (1974) careful and comprehensive review of the literature on gender differences.

1) Children know their own gender – they describe themselves accurately as boys or girls and choose gender-appropriate toys and activities – before they are able to relate this to genital sex differences.
2) Understanding of gender invariance follows rather than precedes the establishment of 'correct' gender preferences in toys and activities.
3) Gender identity is fundamentally formed in the first two years of life.
4) Parents' distinctions between boys and girls are not wholly sufficient to explain the gap between the feminine and masculine self-concepts that are developed.
5) Children do not tend to identify with same-gendered models, even after the age at which quite rigidly differentiated gender identities are formed.

6) Parent–child similarities on a range of attributes are not strong and, in particular, there are no stronger correlations between children and same-gendered parents than between children and parents of the other gender.
7) The activities preferred by children, though gender-differentiated from nursery school age on, often do not follow any pattern that they have been exposed to in their own families. For example, the daughter of a doctor ardently declares only men can be doctors when her own mother is one (Maccoby and Jacklin, 1974, p 364).

The cognitive–developmental view is supported by points 1, 4, 5, 6 and 7, and is not supported by points 2 and 3. In other words, this theory is quite compatible with the fact that modelling specifically on *parental* behaviour may not be the core phenomenon; the problem is that gender identity in many senses happens before the idea takes root that gender is a fixed attribute. The social learning view is contradicted by points 4, 5, 6 and 7 but supported by points 1 to 3. In this approach, the importance of parents as models and as differential reinforcers of gender-appropriate and gender-inappropriate behaviours is critical.

The psychoanalytic interpretation is really not supported by any of these findings. Physical sex differences are not the most salient determinant of gender identity for children. Identification with a parental model is not, apparently, the most powerful force establishing adult gender differences.

Penis and other envies

Feminist descriptions of the imprisonment of women in a feminine mould blame 'society' in general for their captivity. It is the 'over determination' of gender that is implicated. In Simone de Beauvoir's famous words,

> One is not born, but rather becomes, a woman. No biological, psychological, or economic fate determines the figure that the human female presents in society; it is *civilisation as a whole* that produces this creature, intermediate between male and eunuch, which is described as feminine. (De Beauvoir, 1960, p 8; emphasis added)

'Civilisation' is not feminine; it is 'a man's world'. Of all the lessons girls learn, this is the most important one. Freud, from his enviable position of masculine hegemony, called it 'penis envy', but it is not the penis that women want. Clara Thompson, one of the small band of female analysts who challenged Freud's thinking, wrote

> ... one can say the term penis envy is a symbolic representation of the attitude of women in this culture ... the penis is the sign of the person in power in one particular competitive set-up in this culture, that between man and woman. The attitude of the woman in this situation is not

qualitatively different from that found in any minority group in a competitive culture. So, the attitude called penis envy is similar to the attitude of any underprivileged group toward those in power.... (Thompson, 1974, pp 53-4)

Women envy men their power. Small children learn effortlessly about masculine power within the asymmetrical nuclear family. But in fact, and paradoxically, dominance and nurturance are the two adult qualities that most attract children to identify with parents (Bandura and Huston, 1961; Hetherington, 1965; Hetherington and Frankie, 1967). This contradiction illuminates many of the difficulties men and women have in adjusting their identities to fit the standard gender formulae.

Florence Nightingale was the second daughter, intended to be a son, of ill-matched parents. Fanny Nightingale was six years older than her husband, a dedicated hostess married to an indolent and charming dilettante. Florence's biographer, Cecil Woodham-Smith (1952), comments that her main attachment in childhood was to her father. He educated both Florence and her elder sister Parthenope (Parthe) himself, teaching them Greek, Latin, German, French, Italian, history and philosophy. Parthe rebelled and joined her mother in domestic activities.

Florence found the life of a Victorian lady boring, debilitating and depressing. "All I do is done to win admiration" she complained in a private note. When she was 16, Florence received her first call from God. The voice reappeared three more times: in 1853, just before she took up her first post at the Hospital for Poor Gentlewomen in Harley Street; before the Crimean War in 1854; and after the death of her friend and 'Master', Lord Sidney Herbert in 1861. Seven years after the first call, and after an intense inner struggle, Florence became certain that her vocation was to nurse the sick. It took nine more years to convince her family that this was what she should be allowed to do. Her mother was 'terrified' and 'angry', her sister 'hysterical'. Her father was disappointed that his education of Florence had led to this unsuitable wilfulness, but he did eventually grant her an allowance of £500 a year and later bought her a house. In his last years, they were reconciled and had 'long talks on metaphysics' together.

The role played by fathers as powerful and affectionate representatives of non-domestic culture can, of course, be taken by mothers as well. Daughters of 'working' mothers have less rigid conceptions of gender roles than daughters of 'non-working' mothers (Hansson et al, 1977; Morantz and Mansfield, 1977). They tend to have less 'feminine' identities, stressing such masculine qualities as independence and self-reliance (Hoffman and Nye, 1974).

In a very different society, that of the !Kung bush people of the Kalahari desert, the same general importance of women's socially valued productivity is seen. Among the !Kung, women's agricultural work is crucial to everyone's physical survival. Women have a great deal of autonomy and influence over the economic resources of the community as well as its ceremonial and power relations:

A common sight in the late afternoon is clusters of children standing on the edge of camp, scanning the bush with shaded eyes to see if the returning women are visible. When the slow-moving file of women is finally discerned in the distance, the children leap and exclaim. As the women draw closer, the children speculate as to which figure is whose mother and what the women are carrying in their karosses. (Draper, 1975, p 82)

Women's work is part of their childhood games, of female socialisation:

We ... played at being hunters and we went out tracking animals and when we saw one we struck it with our make-believe arrows. We took some leaves and hung them over a stick and pretended it was meat. Then we carried it back to our village. When we got back, we stayed there and ate the meat and then the meat was gone. We went out again, found another animal and killed it. We again threw leaves over the stick, put other leaves in our karosses, and brought it back. We played at living in the bush like that. (Interview with !Kung woman, *Spare Rib*, October, 1975, pp 15-16)

In a society where small children of both sexes are brought up by women but expected to learn to be different genders, girls have an obvious advantage. There is no room for doubt as to who they are expected to be like. Two linked findings are consistent products of the research on childhood gender differences: first, girls *are* more androgynous than boys until puberty; and, second, the male 'cissy' is more uniformly feared and denigrated than the female 'tomboy'.

Artefacts of gender

Parental work in the area of teaching gender also takes place within the broad context of cultural artefacts that separate the world of girls from the world of boys.

Gender-appropriate toys are both the cause and the proof of correct gender identification. In the case of a boy whose penis was accidentally removed and who was reassigned as a girl at the age of 17 months:

The mother reported: 'I started dressing her not in dresses but, you know, in little pink slacks and frilly blouses ... and letting her hair grow'. A year and six months later, the mother wrote that she had made a special effort at keeping her girl in dresses, almost exclusively, changing any item of clothes into something that was clearly feminine. 'I even made all her nightwear into granny gowns and she wears bracelets and hair ribbons'. The effects of emphasizing feminine clothing became clearly noticeable in the girl's attitude towards clothes and hairdo another year later, when she was observed to have a clear preference for dresses over slacks.... (Money and Erhardt, 1972, p 119)

The girl asked for dolls, a dolls' house and a dolls' pram for Christmas: her brother, a toy garage with cars.

Walum's analysis of the 1972 edition of the Sears Roebuck Christmas toy catalogue found that 84% of the toys portrayed as suitable for girls fell under the heading of 'preparatory for spousehood and parenthood', whereas none of those portrayed for males did so; 75% of male toys were 'manipulatory' in character and 25% related to male occupational roles (Walum, 1977). As Alice Rossi once remarked, a girl may spend more time playing

Boy with a toy crane © Fotolink

with her dolls than a mother will ever spend with her children (Rossi, 1964, p 105). Toys such as Palitoy's 'Girl's World' take over from the dolls stage:

> It is a near life-size orange-pink plastic bust with a thick brown wig. The face is a pert young teenage Miss, and under the base of the shoulders are large plastic suckers so you can stick it to the table while you brush its hair. Its jaunty face, with a retroussé nose, and full curvy lips, looks not entirely unlike the sort of thing you might find in a porn shop, only it hasn't got a body. (*The Guardian*, 17 December 1979)

The child's own space within the home is full of gender signals. In a middle-class area of a university community, "a locale that would presumably be on the less differentiated end of the sex role socialization spectrum" (Weitz, 1977, p 61), the bedrooms of boys and girls were instantly identifiable. Boys' rooms "contained more animal furnishings, more educational art materials, more spatial–temporal toys, more sports equipment and more toy animals. The rooms of girls contained more dolls, more floral furnishings and more 'ruffles'" (Rheingold and Cook, 1975, p 461). The 48 girls' rooms boasted 17 toy vehicles; the 48 boys', 375; 26 of the girls' rooms had dolls, compared with three of the boys'.

Another potent source of gender messages is children's literature. In a survey by Weitzman and colleagues (1976) of prizewinning books, the male: female sex ratio in pictures of people was 11:1 (for animals it was 95:1). Most of the plots centred on some form of male adventure and females figured chiefly in their traditional service function or in the more imaginative, but ultimately no less restrictive, roles of fairy, fairy godmother and underwater maiden.

Examining the material over time, Czaplinski (1976) has shown that sexist bias (as judged by the relative representation of female and male characters) decreased during the 1940s and 1950s, and increased markedly in the 1960s. During the war and immediately after, women's participation in public life was raised, but the 1950s and 1960s were the era of the 'happy housewife heroine'.

Many heroines of children's fiction follow in the respectable fairytale tradition. As Belotti (1975) observes in her retelling of some traditional fables, the pervasive stupidity of women is a common theme:

> 'Little Red Riding Hood' is the story of a girl, bordering on mental deficiency, who is sent out by an irresponsible mother through dark wolf-infested woods to take a little basket full to the brim with cakes, to her sick grandmother. Given these circumstances her end is hardly surprising. But such foolishness, which would never have been attributed to a male, depends on the assurance that one will always find at the right moment and in the right place a brave huntsman ready to save grandmother and granddaughter from the wolf. (Belotti, 1975, p 102)

Out of place

All cultures have a division of labour by gender, but some are more divided than others. The need to differentiate children's roles and identities by sex is therefore immensely variable. Such variation must be borne in mind when viewing our own arrangements, which are not the only way of grouping children in readiness for their adult life.

The Tanulong and Fedilizan peoples of Southeast Asia teach their female and male children the lesson that gender is not an important discriminator of personal identity or occupational role. They are a mountain-dwelling people with a staple diet of rice and sweet potatoes, supplemented with other vegetables, coffee and the keeping of a few animals, such as chickens and pigs. Kinship is bilateral (descent through both mother and father is important) and it is assumed that both man and woman will bring property (such as rice fields) to marriage. The adult division of labour shows a high degree of interchangeability: an activity that is said to be usually women's is often done by men, and vice versa; there are also many jobs men and women habitually do together. Albert Bacdayan (1977), who studied these people, writes:

> The ethnographer there cannot miss the predominantly bisexual nature of most work and activity groups in the fields and the village. In subsistence production, for instance, one is likely to see men, women and children of both sexes engaged in the same tasks, harvesting, preparing the soil for planting, bundling seedlings, and planting. In cases where they are seen performing different tasks they are still working together: if men are repairing broken terraces, using a carabao to plow, or hauling the harvested rice home to the village, the women are likely to be close

by smoothing the soil, cutting the grass around the field, or harvesting the rice to be hauled away.

This pattern of working together is observable in the domestic scene too. During the harvest season, one is likely to find the entire family bent over a huge basket outside their home removing the beans from their pods, spreading bundles of rice to dry, or carrying the rice inside to store in the granaries. At other times they may be pounding rice or cooking together. Even childbirth is a bisexual affair. The husband is likely to deliver his wife, attended or helped by older children and maybe an older female relative such as his own mother or the wife's mother. Many of the relatives of both sexes gather around for the birth process. (p 286)

Economic decisions and 'public display of economic power' are shared, as is participation in village politics. So far as children's preparation for this society is concerned, the birth of boys and girls is welcomed, with a slight edge in favour of girls, who are thought to be more likely to stay in the village as adults. The people have a saying 'a girl is also a boy and a boy is also a girl', which reflects their perception of the equivalent position of the two genders in the occupational division of labour. In the inheritance of property, the significant variable is age, not sex: the first born, whether boy or girl, is given the family's best rice fields. Their socialisation is even, with neither sex awarded particular privileges; when meat, a rare commodity, is available at meals, each child is given a piece of fat and a piece of lean meat, but older people receive larger portions than the young. Both parents participate in the rearing of children, who are initiated at an early age into the chores of agricultural and domestic labour.

A Kikuyu woman carries her load of wood while her daughter trudges behind with a lighter load on her head © Paul Popper

The Tanulong and Fedilizan are not unique among pre-literate cultures described by anthropologists; see, for example, the Mbuti pygmies studied by Turnbull (1965) and the !Kung bushmen of the Kalahari desert, studied by Draper (1975). In general, the socialisation of boys and girls is in step both with the requirements of the economic system and the personality values of a culture (Barry et al, 1959; Whiting, 1963). The bipolar sex and gender categories – *either* female or male, *either* feminine or masculine – of Western industrial civilisation would puzzle many pre-industrial peoples, whose thought and attitudes allow not only for the irrelevance of biological sex to cultural gender attribution but also for the possibility of physical sex states that are neither female nor male (Martin and Voorhies, 1975).

Science, gender and women's liberation

Both 'science' and 'gender' are concepts that many current positions within feminism contest as having no appropriate or useful place in feminist discourse. Science has been discredited as a useful feminist concept for a considerably longer time than gender. Within contemporary feminist debates, the 'old' notions of science and gender are reframed in different ways: for example, as issues concerning sexual difference (Irigaray, 1985) or epistemology (Code, 1991). This chapter argues that rehabilitating both science and gender offers an important step forward for feminism and for women. The reasons the two concepts are valuable overlap in two aspects: (a) the desirability of revitalising the original agenda of second-wave feminism as committed to the practical liberation of women, and (b) in understanding the relationship between gender as an ideological structure, on the one hand, and knowledge and ways of knowing as socially constituted, on the other. The chapter discusses the context and background of contemporary feminist arguments against science and gender. It then examines the case study of women's health to illustrate how these concepts remain useful in addressing continuing oppressive features in women's situation.

Science

Second-wave feminism inherited, and reacted against, a science not often sympathetic to the interests of women as a social group (Rose, 1994). Moreover, this science came wrapped in the trappings of logical positivism and with a stress on 'quantification', 'objectivity', and 'control' that seemed at odds with the political values of feminism, and particularly with the formation of a feminist 'social' science that tried to be *for* women rather than *about* them.

The hostility between feminism and science goes back a long way. It involves the dialectical relationship between natural and social science, and the long-standing debate about the status of knowledge and different methodological traditions. What we call 'science' is the product of an ancient tradition of rational enquiry that at first used reason, experience, theory and argument in an attempt to know the human world, the cosmos and God. In the 18th century, philosophy and science divorced one another under the influence of Humean and Kantian propositions to the effect that whatever lies beyond experience is not science (Manicas, 1987). Thereafter, science became increasingly restricted to the empirically and systematically knowable, although the specific association of science with images of men in white coats carrying out experiments in laboratories dates only from the 1900s (Schiebinger, 1989).

Social science was born in the space between images of science and the scientific method, on the one hand, and the actual practices of scientists, on the other (Lepenies, 1988). Like all human knowers, scientists work and know within specific social and material contexts (Kuhn, 1962; Gould, 1981). But, while social science struggled to settle on an identity between science and fiction, scientific ways of knowing possessed a unitary character as *systematic, empirically based* enquiry. What distinguished science was not its subject matter, but its method (Pearson, 1892; see also Cohen, 1994). Social science was the natural science of society. Many social scientists were also natural scientists, and vice versa (McDonald, 1993).

Despite this epistemological interplay between social and natural sciences' ways of knowing, the history of the way natural science was sometimes done, particularly its ethically dubious use of animal and human experiments, suggested an opposition between it and the interests of women as a group. By the late 19th century, science, in the sense of what men do in laboratories and with experimental and quantitative ways of knowing about the human and material world, had emerged distinctively as an enemy of women. Indeed, women and nature had successively been merged as objects of the masculine scientific gaze (Jordanova, 1989). Science thus acquired its modern character as a major cultural agent in transmitting "oppressive fictions" about women's bodies and minds.

The relationship between feminism and science increased in complexity as the scholarship of second-wave feminism developed, and as women like Sandra Harding (1986), Nancy Hartsock (1987) and Hilary Rose (1986) argued the existence of a feminist standpoint position, and the need for a science that respects both this and the foundations of women's knowledge of the world in their work and love of caring for, and about, others. Such critiques of science joined a range of other positions against positivism as the epistemological basis of social science. Since the late 1960s, these alternative positions have gathered weight. The result is two contesting methodological paradigms that argue, rather than converse, with one another (Guba, 1990). According to the 'qualitative' paradigm, an authentic social science engages only in relative, reflexive ways of knowing, capable of respecting multiple subjectivities; whereas the 'quantitative' paradigm speaks to 'pre-postmodern' ideas of validity, reliability, objectivity and truth (Bryman, 1988). Feminist debates about methodology have privileged qualitative methods, which have consequently acquired a hegemonic correctness for feminist social science researchers (Reinharz, 1992; Stanley and Wise, 1993). Postmodernism and feminism both reject foundationalism; that is, the singularity and the universality of the scientific method (Curthoys, 1997). Indeed, knowledge itself is a problem within postmodernist and feminist critiques. Most contemporary feminist epistemology argues that knowledge is always "provisional, open-ended and relational" (Luke and Gore, 1992, p 7).

Behind the clash of methodological paradigms lies a long and complex history according to which *methodology is itself gendered*; that is, the dualism of the qualitative and quantitative/experimental paradigms and their respective associations with women/feminism and men/patriarchy is the problem to be explained. This gendering of knowledge and ways of knowing is what produced the case for feminism to attack: the identification of science, quantification and experimentation as the main enemies.

In other words, it is important to understand the history of science, social science and methodology as part of that same nexus of cultural and material processes that produces patriarchy itself. It is within this framework that femininities and masculinities are created and sustained as ideational representations linked in systematic ways to institutionalised forms of power. This is one of a number of ways in which the concept of gender is a useful analytic tool within women's studies.

Who needs gender?

Every revolutionary movement generates its own political language, and gender provided a key political concept for second-wave feminism (Franklin, 1996; Oakley, 1997). The concept of gender originated in grammar, and in the work of American psychiatrists in the late 1960s, who needed a technical language with which to talk about the lives and experiences of people for whom biological and social sex diverged (Stoller, 1968; see Oakley, 1972). At about the same time, a very similar problem and need for a new conceptual language emerged among feminists. The invention of gender and its separation from sex allowed Betty Friedan's 'problem with no name' to be understood as nothing more nor less than the social construction of an oppressive, antidemocratic femininity (Friedan, 1963). Within social science, 'gender differences' came to be substituted for 'sex roles' and 'socialisation' – terms that resonated with a latent functionalism and biologism. From the early 1970s onward, feminist social scientists created a substantial literature that deconstructs sociobiological arguments about women. This literature used the wedge of sex and gender as an oppositional nature/culture dualism to identify an agenda of preventable differences between the sexes, and thus effectively to force open the door of oppression and discrimination. As Hausman observes "... the hegemony of 'gender' as feminism's category of analysis cannot be denied, as its use has allowed feminists to claim the social construction of women's inequality (and therefore the possibility of its rectification)" (Hausman, 1995, p 8).

Since the 1970s a number of social and intellectual developments have complicated these original relationships between sex, gender and feminism. A somewhat insidious synonmity between 'women' and 'gender' developed; men remained the sex, while women became the gender. This is also the sense in which women's studies came to be reconstituted as gender studies and 'gender' was substituted for 'women' in research grant applications because it was more profitable to suggest the goal of understanding men's ways of being (McLean et al, 1996) than to study women, using women's ways of knowing (Belensky et al, 1986). More fundamentally, the development of postmodernist thinking encourages us to consider late capitalist culture as paradoxical, ambiguous and uncertain, with ourselves as irremediably fragmented subjects; language, things, people and ways of knowing have all been reconstituted as fragile, conditional and problematic (Latour, 1993; Fraser, 1995). Because the specific artefacts of science and technology are rooted in Western metaphysics, they are only partially relevant to the conditions of globalisation (Smart, 1993).

Postmodernism introspects and deconstructs; everything becomes much more complex than it seems. This includes feminist discourse, which has been substantially reshaped by drawing on the theories of the 'grand masters' – Foucault, Derrida, Lacan, Habermas, Bakhtin and Bourdieu. Gender has thus fallen into disrepute for its failure to signify the fluid and contextual nature of 'knowledge' categories. Its disappearance is also a feature of theoretical developments within social science contending that 'fixed' categories are not useful, and that neither old-style positivism nor a more modern empiricism can be taken as valid models for the social sciences (Manicas, 1987; see Phillips, 1992).

The backlash, gender, and feminism

The theorisation of postmodernity and contemporary social science passes by many of those with a personal and/or professional interest in the politics of sex and gender. But, in the late 1990s, ideological representations in North America and many European countries construe feminism and femininity as implacably imposed, just as they used to in earlier eras of reactions against feminism (Oakley and Mitchell, 1997). In this backlash against feminism, a nostalgia is articulated for a golden past of sexual difference. Since feminism created a need for the vocabulary of gender, antifeminism means getting rid of it. The device of redefining gender as sex is one of two central ideological manoeuvres in the backlash; the other is returning women to the family. The two strategies are linked in important ways, because denying the social construction of femininity as an illiberal condition is a necessary part of the argument as to why women really do belong in the family after all. The linkage between the two arguments can be seen in texts such as *The war over the family* (Berger and Berger, 1983). The Bergers assert that "the family is a problem", and note that the concept of 'gender roles' is merely "femspeak" – a technique for arguing that the assignment of roles within the family is arbitrary and that it can/should be changed, so as to advance women's welfare (p 64). The denial of natural differences, say the Bergers, unhelpfully undermines the democratic and nurturant functions of the family.

Reifying 'the' family is hard-core antifeminism, and assigning democracy to 'the family' rather than to individuals within it is one of the most effective ways of disenfranchising women. Other antifeminist arguments are equally simple. These days, gender differences are found in genes, brain cells and in all sorts of other bodily sites (see Oakley, 1997). Like housework, contemporary sociobiology expands to fill any number of apparent spaces, and an ever-expanding cascade of 'scientific' discoveries about sex/gender differences reaches us every day via the media, and 'popular' as well as scientific literature (see, for example, Pool, 1993). Both issues of gender (Davidson, 1988) and sex (Paglia, 1992) are said to be "too important" to leave to feminists; Paglia's analogy is that "leaving sex to the feminists is like letting your dog vacation at the taxidermists" (Paglia, 1992, p 50). According to her, academic feminism has lost itself in a fog of social constructionism.

But, significantly, the disappearance of gender is advocated by both antifeminists and by feminists. One major criticism of gender put by some feminists derives from the argument that the political goal of gender equality may produce different social consequences from the goal of liberating women. Gender can act to hide power, because it suggests parallel sets of ideological representations of femininity and masculinity. Although these are *hierarchically ordered* – gender *is* about power – the power dimension is not immediately apparent in the same way it is when one speaks about class. Like the family, gender suggests democracy, but in both cases – that of the family and of gender – the relations of men and women follow a patriarchal logic. The difficulty with gender and power has led some theorists, for example Catherine MacKinnon, to reject gender as merely the sexualisation of inequality between men and women. MacKinnon (1990) argues that, because the idea of difference is a conceptual tool of gender and inequality, "it cannot deconstruct the master's house because it has built it" (p 214). Analysis of the social positions of men and women in terms solely of gender will lack the materialist base of a Marxist analysis. In this sense, MacKinnon's quarrel with gender would be partially supported by the arguments of dual systems theorists, such as Hartmann (1979) and Eisenstein (1981), and, somewhat differently, by the reformulation of gender as 'gender class' offered by materialist feminists, such as Delphy and Leonard (1992). One key point is, of course, that power, like class, is itself a gendered concept (Gatens, 1992).

Much recent feminist literature in sociology and cultural studies uses gender as a synonym for sex. Another device used to conflate or dissolve the dualism is their linking – as in "sex-gender identity" or "the sex/gender system" (Rubin, 1975). Under the influence of post-structuralism and psychoanalysis, yet other brands of feminist thinking prefer to deliver both sex and gender back to sexuality by creating a pandora's box of 'sexual difference' (see, for example, Adams and Cowie, 1990). Following Foucault, Judith Butler (1992) and others argue that both sex and gender are "discursive terms" and "technologies" that unify schemes of anatomy and social classification as ontological facts. As sex is an 'essentialist' distinction, gender is to be preferred. Once one understands what people such as Derrida, Lacan and Foucault have to say about how the social body is constituted, any distinction between biology and society becomes difficult to maintain (Hood-Williams, 1996). Rather than sex being the primary condition and gender a secondary accretion, the idea of sex is *itself* mediated by the conceptualisation of gender, and gender in the sense of 'engender' is what produces (rather than describes) observable differences between men and women. Such critics point to recent work on historical conceptions of the body and the archaeology of sex hormones that shows sex to be subject to some of the same processes of social construction as gender, and also to the medical industry of 'sex change,' which exemplifies gender as yet another story about the complicitness of technology and science in creating normative bodies (Hausman, 1995). For these reasons, and in these ways, it is argued that there is no "unmediated natural truth of the body" (Oudshoorn, 1994, p 3).

The discrediting of gender and the rejection of science are linked because modern biological science is a target that is responsible for the myth of sex as a biologically given dualism (Fausto-Sterling, 1993). A second link is, of course, the whole disputation of positivism. Here, the notions of woman as a category and of power in relationships as something it is relatively easy to recognise have also been discredited as hiding the multiple meanings characterising subjectivity in different cultural contexts (see, for example, Hooks, 1981; Kristeva, 1981; Haraway, 1991). In its most extreme form, this argument results in the gender of woman being abandoned on the grounds that it is nothing more nor less than an "oppressive fiction" (Di Stefano, 1990, p 65). It is suggested that women have no sex at all (Wittig, 1981) or that they constitute 'a sex which is not one' (Irigaray, 1985).

There is something very attractive to a feminism that has become feminism*s* in defending a multitude of theoretical, epistemological and methodological positions. Complexity and difference intuitively appeal as anti-authoritarian. Moreover, the simple Enlightenment view of woman, gender and power as unitary categories undoubtedly denied class and ethnicity as factors shaping women's experiences (see, for example, Jarrett-Macauley, 1996).

Women's health

The case for rehabilitating science and gender could be argued from many premises. A useful example is the area of women and health. This demonstrates the existence of *practical* problems faced by millions of women every day with the cultural construction of womanhood through the discourses of medical 'science'. Such problems demand a matching practical feminism that will engage productively with debates about women's bodies, minds and lives, and what is considered 'scientific' knowledge.

The cultural representation and material position of women is interrelated with their health in significant ways. There are direct health effects of discrimination (WHO, 1994) and of material social position (Graham, 1984; Oakley, 1994). The healthcare system is a source of discrimination against women. For example, women are less likely than men to receive a kidney transplant (Kutner and Brogan, 1990), and women smokers are less likely to have tests for lung cancer than men smokers (Wells and Feinstein, 1988). Presenting with symptoms of heart disease, women are more likely than men to have their symptoms judged as less serious, they are less often referred for tests, have to wait longer, are less often admitted to an intensive care unit, and are less often candidates for coronary bypass surgery (Tobin et al, 1987; Gijsbers van Wijk et al, 1996). Some of these differences proceed from the well-known processes of misogynist treatment by doctors (see, for example, Birdwell et al, 1993). But medicine is also more fundamentally involved in the phenomenon of gender, as Nellie Oudshoorn (1994) shows in her history of research on sex hormones. The hormone industry settled on women and female hormones on account of women's greater accessibility as patients; there was no parallel institutional structure for men.

In developed societies, a significant aspect of women's health is its overdetermination by medical ideologies and technologies. During the 20th century, science, medicine and technology have vastly expanded the domain of who is considered to be at risk of what. In this respect, women's bodies form a major site of contemporary discourses about risk. A study of the occurrence of the term 'risk' in the titles and abstracts of medical journals over the period from 1967 to 1991 showed that the term occurred 50 times more often in 1991 than in 1967; this increase was most marked for obstetric and gynaecology journals, that is for those health discourses exclusively concerned with women (Skolbekken, 1995). As participants in mass screening programmes, women are major targets of medical surveillance and, in the area of the prevention and promotion of childbirth, they are subject to multiple medical and surgical interventions. The 'burden' of women's poorer mental health leads to a greater use of psychotropic (mood altering) drugs (van der Waals et al, 1993).

'Medicalisation' has become a salient and taken-for-granted feature of women's lives; most women, including feminists, tend to accept as relatively uncontentious and necessary much of what doctors do and say they ought to do. But most of the medicalisation of women's health cannot be justified in terms of scientific evidence about effectiveness and safety.

Two examples are cervical cancer screening and hormone replacement therapy (HRT).

Cervical cancer screening

Women in many developed societies are encouraged to present for cervical cancer screening on a regular basis. The current policy in England is for women to attend every three to five years between the ages of 25 and 64.

Cervical cancer screening is one example of a preventive health programme. Routine cervical cancer screening depends on two contentions: that screening is an effective method of prevention and that cervical cancer is a significant cause of death. However, neither statement is true. The biggest killer of women under 35 is motor-vehicle accidents, which cause four times as many deaths as cervical cancer, and suicide, which is responsible for three times as many. Among women as a group, lung cancer kills nearly eight times as many women as cervical cancer (Raffle, 1996); rates of female death from lung cancer are increasing, while male death rates are falling (DH, 1995).

In terms of effective prevention, we lack reliable evidence to prove that decreased deaths from cervical cancer result from the introduction of mass screening programmes; indeed, the biggest drops in death rates have been among older women who have never been screened (Raffle, 1996). Cervical cancer screening has the status of a 30-year uncontrolled experiment. The balance between risks and benefits is uncertain. The risks of screening include over-diagnosis, with thousands of women being investigated for a disease they do not have (Raffle et al, 1995); cross-infection due to inadequate sterilisation of specula; and anxiety caused by the test and the stigma of positive smears. The antipathy many women feel to the invasive nature of the test (McKie, 1995) echoes a concern voiced by others that scraping the surface of the cervix 13 or more times over a woman's lifetime may itself cause problems.

The doctor who was largely responsible for setting up the British screening programme observed that "it is absurd to conduct a screening test in such a way that nearly forty women are referred for an expensive and possibly hazardous procedure for every woman who is at risk of developing serious disease" (Smith, 1988, p 1670).

Hormone replacement therapy (HRT)

The hormones oestrogen and progesterone were first synthesised in the laboratory in the early 1900s, and their early use was for the treatment of menstrual disorders. In the late 1930s, pharmaceutical companies manufacturing hormones decided that the most profitable route was to make women concerned about menopause the principal target of their advertising campaign for these drugs (Oudshoorn, 1994). The hormones used in HRT are now the most widely used drugs in the world, and indeed in the entire history of medicine (Oudshoorn, 1994).

Women are encouraged to take HRT for a variety of reasons, including the relief of menopausal systems, and the prevention of osteoporosis and heart disease. HRT is taken by significant numbers of women in many countries: about one in three women in the UK and probably a similar proportion in the US, Australia and Finland (Topo, 1997). In order to support prescription rates at this level, a wide range of health problems are attributed to the menopause, including hot flushes, sweating, tiredness, joint and muscle pains, insomnia, nervousness, weight gain, headaches, back pain, irritability, mood swings, frequent and/or involuntary urination, depression, forgetfulness, low esteem, palpitations, dizziness, shortness of breath, loss of feeling in hands and feet, lack of energy, and restless legs (Kaufert et al, 1988; Holte, 1991; Oldenhave et al, 1993). Yet all these symptoms, except hot flushes and excessive sweating, are as common in middle-aged men as in middle-aged women (Hunter, 1990; Holte, 1991).

HRT is effective in relieving hot flushes and the problem of excessive sweating (Topo et al, 1993). But the health-promoting benefits of HRT are unproven at the population level and the jury is still out on the long-term effects (Hemminki, 1995; Topo, 1997). [Recent evidence shows enhanced risks of breast cancer and coronary heart disease (McPherson, 2004).] Assessments of the evidence suggest that HRT does promote bone density, but only for so long as it is used, so if preventing osteoporosis is the aim, then women must take HRT for the rest of their lives (WHO, 1994; Office of Technology Assessment, 1995). But, while research shows an effect on bone density, there is no evidence that the use of HRT actually prevents fractures (School of Public Health et al, 1992).

There is evidence that taking oestrogen leads to dependence, with higher and higher doses required over time to give a uniform effect (Bewley and Bewley, 1992). Rates of breast cancer are raised by as much as 50% in HRT users (McPherson, 1995), and the risk of deep vein thrombosis and pulmonary embolism is between two and four times as high as in non-users (Wise, 1996). Recent analysis of the evidence from 22 studies in six countries does not support the theory that HRT prevents heart disease (Hemminki and McPherson, 1997).

Research needs and women's health

Neither in the case of cervical cancer screening nor in the case of HRT, nor in the case of many other examples of interventions in women's health, are current medical recommendations based on sound evidence of effectiveness and safety. There are clearly enormous gaps in women's health research. Research on women and health has a 'ghetto' tendency, whereby women are excluded from major studies of "important" health topics, such as cancer and heart disease. Thus, the large studies that have influenced the treatment and prevention of heart disease have all only included men (Mastroianni et al, 1994). It is on the basis of such research that cholesterol-lowering diets have been widely recommended, but these may increase rather than decrease the risk of heart disease in women (Crouse, 1989).

There has been very little attempt to design research studies that explore topics and approaches that women themselves consider important. For examples, studies of different treatments for excessive menstrual bleeding commonly ignore women's concerns about pain, energy, sex life, emotions and the effect of bleeding on work (Coulter, 1993). So long as artificial hormones are the treatment for the 'disease' of being an older woman, alternative approaches to promoting women's health are likely to remain untested – for example, exercise or dietary changes. One rather well-kept secret is that alcohol increases bone mineral density (Felson et al, 1995). There is certainly evidence that exercise is an effective means of preventing fractures in older people (Oakley et al, 1996). But walking, running, and taking calcium and other dietary supplements are treatments that cost either nothing or very little, so it is not in the interest of the pharmaceutical industry to promote them. One of the largest gaps in women's health research is the lack of well-designed prospective studies of different approaches to prevention and treatment. Such studies, otherwise known as 'randomised controlled trials', have in the past not met the kinds of criteria for feminist research that have been established within women's studies over the last 20 years. But there is absolutely no reason why they cannot do so and there is every reason why this should be one of the challenges of feminist research in the future.

Postmodernism and women's liberation

These examples from the field of women and health indicate some of the ways in which in the real world women remain oppressed through being constructed as a gendered 'Other'. Contesting this requires forms of knowledge that are *relevant* and *useful* in terms of advancing women's freedom and welfare. It is for this reason that this chapter argues against the postmodern rejection of science and gender.

Whose science?

As Lynn McDonald shows in her *The early origins of the social sciences* (McDonald, 1993), before the critique of logical positivism and before postmodernism, science and social science as empirically based disciplines enjoyed a productive cohabitation not only with each other but with feminism; advocates of women's rights in the 19th century, and before, recognised the desirability of grounding their arguments in information about the ways in which women lived and were treated by men and society.

The argument put in this chapter – that feminism needs to reappraise the value of empiricism – is contrary to much popular opinion, and also to much of the received wisdom of feminism. For example, women's health groups have argued for extended access to cervical cancer screening, and for more doctors sympathetic to prescribing HRT, just as they have argued for more mammography, and just as, in the past, they have argued for technologies such as pain relief in childbirth as essential strategies for women's 'liberation'. Women's organisations today agree that "gender sensitive health care should be available, accessible, affordable, appropriate and acceptable" (Gijsbers van Wijk et al, 1996, p 708). The words *effective* and *safe* are missing from this list.

It is unethical for women not to appraise critically the costs and benefits of modern mythologies about health promotion and other forms of intervention. In order for this debunking to happen effectively, and for women to promote the right kind of research, it is necessary for women and feminism to reclaim science. Science, in this sense, can be reconceived as what we all do when we contribute to knowledge.

Gender as a system of crime and punishment

Denise Riley (1988) has argued that, while women 'do not exist', we should, in practice, behave as if they did. Much the same argument could be made about gender as an ideational category. The concept of gender as a major ideational and material device for discriminating against women has as much explanatory power as it did in the early days of second-wave feminism (Willmott, 1996). What gender successfully describes is a system of 'crime and punishment': "a relatively autonomous, hegemonic, ideological structure that divides the world hierarchically" (Grant, 1993, p 161). Abolishing the concept of gender from feminist discourse and analysis would have effects akin to those for Marxists of abandoning the idea of class.

Retaining *on some level* the capacity to distinguish between sex and gender is, moreover, a necessary tool for contending the 'essentialist' slant identifiable in some feminist theory. The mapping of women's approaches to knowledge (Belenky et al, 1986), emotion (Denzin, 1987), moral choice (Gilligan, 1982), and diverse forms of nurturance and altruism (Merchant, 1980; Finch and Groves, 1983), celebrates precisely that gender difference and gender ideology which is the enemy of feminism in the first place. Replacing the universal male subject with an essential female one is not an advance towards either an integrated understanding of the human condition, or the production of knowledge capable of enhancing women's welfare.

Conclusion

Nothing in this chapter is intended to suggest that modern scholarship on the complexities of both sex and gender does not contain important insights for feminism; nor does the chapter's argument promote a wholesale rejection of what modern medicine can do *for* (as distinct from *to*) women; nor does the argument recommend abandoning the powerful qualitative methodological strategies feminist researchers have developed. The scientific method, with its traditional quantitative and experimental approaches to knowledge, suffers from a contamination through association, because of its siting within the male academy. Much of the contemporary feminist critique of quantitative and experimental methods understandably reflects the way in which these have sometimes been used, as techniques for exploiting women or rendering them invisible as agents (Jayaratne and Stewart, 1991; Oakley, 1997). Similarly, 'gender' can be, and has been, used against women, but these contingent historical associations can be overcome in the interests of confronting the still unmet challenges of second-wave feminism.

If we took the admonitions of postmodern anti-quantitative theorists seriously, we would abandon altogether the interest a practical feminism must have in establishing how people's material resources, life chances and experiences are affected by their gender. When the postmodern critics of empiricism abandon objective criteria, they implicitly replace these with another kind of authoritarianism. Rejecting truth-claims is itself to make a truth-claim, the specious nature of which cannot be veiled by the curtain of feminist deconstructivism. While it is one thing to criticise science as often, in practice, exclusionary and embedded with values, it is quite another to reject altogether the possibility of arriving at forms of knowledge that minimise bias and are helpful to women in making everyday life decisions.

Part 2: Housework and family life

Behind the structural ambivalence of women's situation, with its emphasis on femininity and domesticity, stands the woman-as-housewife. Everybody in a sense knows what being a housewife is like; but in another sense, nobody knows.... (*Housewife*, 1974, p 91)

Introduction

Most of the world's domestic work is done by women. This is as true now as it was when I undertook the study which provides the main extracts for this part of the book. Housework was also what turned me into a social scientist. A transformative moment, which occurred during the dusting of my husband's books on the sociology of work some time in the late 1960s (see Oakley, 1984a), opened my eyes to the ways in which bias can masquerade as scientific knowledge. I was truly shocked to discover how not even a discipline as pre-eminently 'social' as sociology could be trusted to encapsulate the experiences of the majority. That women's housework is the typical and most globally important type of labour was certainly a well-kept secret in the 1960s. Thanks to several decades of work by sociologists, economists, anthropologists, psychologists, philosophers and social policy academics, the status of housework has now been elevated to a 'legitimate' and 'well-established' topic of study (VanEvery, 1997, pp 411, 419).

The first five extracts come from my book *The sociology of housework*, published in 1974, and containing the work undertaken for a PhD in sociology at the University of London. The core of the project was a small empirical study – interviews with 40 women with young children in a western suburb of London in 1971. Around this, I assembled a repertoire of sub-studies: How did sociology represent housework? What was the anthropological evidence about gender and domestic work? How did the modern position of women as houseworkers evolve historically? Why *do* women do housework? Each of these inquiries sent me to the library (which afforded some escape from my own housework), and resulted in partial answers, either tacked onto the housework study or published in its companion volume, *Housewife* (1974a). The historical and cross-cultural material is represented here in condensed form – a chapter from the later women's studies textbook, *Subject women* (1981b). There is also a brief extract from my later study of the transition to motherhood, on the timeless subject of whether men are willing to change babies' dirty nappies. Like later extracts from *Becoming a mother* (see Part 3, Chapters One and Two), the normal typesetting convention is reversed in these comments, with the women's words in normal font and mine, less intrusively, in *italics*. This seemed (and seems) only fair, given that the women's accounts form the bulk of the research 'findings'.

The sociology of housework was the first published study of women's experiences of housework as a gendered aspect of modern family life. It earned such epithets as 'pathbreaking' (VanEvery, 1997, p 411) and 'pioneering' (Delamont, 2003, p 43); and it became 'a standard source on the topic' (Bonney and Reinach, 1993, p 617), establishing a new genre of academic work, both empirical and theoretical.

The perspective I took was to regard housework as labour akin to other forms of labour, most of which are paid and publicly acknowledged to constitute work. I was particularly keen to establish a conceptual separation between housework and childcare. In this I was inspired by long-standing feminist critiques to the effect that much housework is not in children's best interests (Gilman, 1903), and housework and childcare have been conflated historically by a mythology of maternal love in which the best mothers are the economically inactive ones (Riley, 1983). So my original questions were: How do women's experiences of unpaid housework compare with those of other workers? What aspects of the work are important in shaping job satisfaction? How is the work defined? Who defines it?

These were unusual questions to ask at the time. The main interest in housework then was among political activists in the women's liberation movement, who asserted its importance as a cause of women's oppression (Wandor, 1973; Rowbotham, 1990). Feminist theorists were attempting to make this insight compatible with Marxist economic analysis. Women's household-based labour helps to reproduce capitalism as an economic system (Gardiner et al, 1975; Gardiner, 1995), but women are marginal in economic theories of all kinds (Ferber and Nelson, 1993), and the family has rarely been treated as an economic system with its own form of oppressive labour relations (Delphy and Leonard, 1992).

Significantly, housework remains an analytical challenge for both neoclassical and Marxian economists today (Jefferson and King, 2001). The arrival of the 'new household economics', spearheaded by US economist Gary Becker, treats households as mini firms in which rational choice leads to specializations producing greater efficiency (Becker, 1980). This is an argument very close to that of functionalist sociology (Parsons and Bales, 1955), which I found necessary to debunk at the start of my housework study (see Part 4, Chapter One). It is also mirrored in other more recent perspectives, such as 'preference theory' (Hakim, 1996), which restates gender inequality in the home as the outcome of women's rational choices not to prioritise the rewards of the marketplace. All these perspectives are dismissive of the evidence that, by and large, women do not feel free to choose either to take responsibility for, or to do, housework (Devine, 1994). The situation for motherhood and childcare is quite different.

The extracts from *The sociology of housework* included here reproduce its main themes: the basic ambivalence of women's feelings about housework (valued for its autonomy, disliked for its time pressures, monotony and lack of social interaction); the differentiation between household tasks (cooking the most, and ironing the least, liked); the practices of male domesticity (often a source of tension but also accepted as the lesser contribution). The calculation in *The sociology of housework* of the housewife's average working week of 77 hours was much quoted. The story of how women specify the standards and routines of housework got less attention, although to me it was one of the most important themes (see Pittman et al, 1999).

The heavy use of the term 'housewife' in these extracts seems a little outdated today, as does the emphasis on marriage as the context for doing housework, and the description of women in terms of their husbands' occupations. Living arrangements have changed and our vocabularies are more liberal now. Other key changes since the early 1970s are the structural growth in women's employment and the proliferation of household technology. Both of these might have revolutionised the pattern uncovered in *The sociology of housework*, but neither has done so.

The first conundrum is why a shift of women into the paid labour force has not been paralleled by a male takeover of housework. Between 1960 and 2000, there were apparently dramatic shifts in the ratio of breadwinner father/housewife mother to dual-earner, families in many Western countries: in the USA, for example, there were twice as many of the first sort in 1960, but in 2000 twice as many of the second (Coltrane, 2004). Nonetheless, as late as the 1990s, 'keeping house' was the largest occupation for women, and it was also a highly gender-segregated occupation: 97% female (Cohen, 2004). Time-budget studies show that women's housework has decreased and men's has increased somewhat with the growth in women's employment, but men's greater efforts do not fill the gap left by women doing less (Gershuny and Jones, 1987; McMahon, 1999). Most of the observed changes in the gender distribution of time between housework and paid work are accounted for by women's adaptation to the demands of their 'second shift' (Hochschild, 1989). Men create more housework than they do (Coltrane, 2004) and, in many households, children do as much housework as men (Manke et al, 1994; Robinson and Godbey, 1997). When women move into similar occupations in the paid labour force, these are less gender-segregated (for example, in the US in 1995 women did 74% of domestic cooking but only 45% of workplace cooks were women (Cohen, 2004). The impact of women's increased employment on gender equality is therefore much greater on paid work than it is in what has aptly been termed the 'gender factory' of the home (Berk, 1985).

Even in supposed paradises of gender equality, such as Sweden, 87% of couples do not share housework (Nordenmark and Nyman, 2003). This inequality is supported by the persistence of beliefs that 'fairness' in matters of gender nonetheless validates women doing the lion's share. This is a general finding (Baxter and Western, 1998). Family work remains women's work and a threat to masculinity (Arrighi and Maume, 2000); gender ideology is a powerful influence on the allocation of household tasks (Kroska, 2004), perhaps especially in professional households, where "... the symbolic significance of intensive mothers and breadwinner fathers [still] serves to reproduce unequal gender relations" (Coltrane, 2004, p 216). However, women *are* more likely than men to complain that the gender distribution of household work is *not* fair, and men doing more housework *does* increase women's perceptions of fairness (Nordenmark and Nyman, 2003). Women's perceptions of unfairness are related both to their higher chances of being depressed (Roxburgh, 2004) and to the risk of divorce (Frisco and Williams, 2003; Strazdins and Broom, 2004).

The story about technology, the second major change in housework since the 1970s, in *The sociology of housework* was that it made no apparent difference to women's satisfaction. Some of the forty housewives interviewed had much more technology than others; fifteen did not have washing machines, for example, and some had no running hot water. The evidence about the impact of household technology on people's attitudes to, and performance of, housework is not straightforward. A substantial body of work suggests that technology is a conservative force (see, for example, Vanek, 1978; Robinson, 1980; Cowan, 1983;

Bose et al, 1984): new products support gendered household structures, and time saved by mechanisation is expended in setting higher standards. Detailed histories of technologies such as the microwave oven (Cockburn and Ormrod, 1993) show the patriarchal slant of manufacturing design, development and marketing processes, which are, critically, *not* aimed at reducing housework time, but rather at elaborating the activity itself (Silva, 1995). In this and other ways, linear history and concepts of rationality cannot explain the cultural patterning of housework. Added to accounts such as the one reproduced here (see Part 2, Chapter Seven), we now have the benefits of new historical scholarship which has explored ideas such as modernisation (Reiger, 1985) and cleanliness (Hoy, 1995).

The sociology of housework was criticised for its focus on a small sample of married couple households which may have led to unrepresentative data (Bonney and Reinach, 1993) (see Part 2, Chapter One for other reactions to the study), but many of its conclusions have been supported by other studies. The modern study of housework is much more sophisticated than I was about such issues as measuring time budgets (Floro and Miles, 2003; Bryant et al, 2004), avoiding bias in assessing who does what in the home (VanEvery, 1997), undoing the conflation between gendered housework and heterosexual family arrangements (Natalier, 2003), and conceptualising housework in ways that avoid the polarisation of life into 'work' and 'non-work' (Himmelweit, 1995). It has confirmed and elaborated on the pattern of gendered preferences whereby men avoid cleaning and laundry (Stockman et al, 1995), and on the influence of social position, as marked, for example by education, which continues to shape both gender practices and beliefs (Van Berkel and De Graaf, 1999; Kitterød, 2002).

Housework is a topic that has generated much controversy, both inside and outside households, and will continue to do so. Women's stories about housework should be a source of inspiration for policy makers, whose traditional dismissal of gender practices in homes as too private for policy concern has meant many lost opportunities for gender-equitable social change (Bittman, 1999; Brinig, 1999). What women and men say about the most dominant form of labour on planet earth is also a rich and underused resource of theory for social science, explaining such fundamental, puzzling and disparate phenomena as the gender segregation of paid work (Cohen, 2004), the feminisation of 'caring' (Finch and Groves, 1983; Graham, 1984; Folbre, 2001), gender differences in morbidity and mortality (Stacey, 1988; Bartley et al, 1992; Thomas, 1995), the health-damaging neglect of basic hygiene in healthcare work (Teare et al, 2001) and many of the tribulations of feminine and masculine psychology (Miller, 1976). And the central characteristic of housework – its cultural undervaluation – still persists to prop up the popularity of androcentric models within social science (Waring, 1988; Ferber and Nelson, 1983).

On studying housework

The sociology of housework was one of the first published studies on that subject. It belonged to a long-established tradition of female commentary on the social value and material undervaluation of women's domestic labour. The study described in the book was carried out as a doctoral thesis, and the pursuit of both the thesis and the book took me on a lonely, depressing and enlightening journey: lonely, because in Britain the 'looking glass' insights of the radical revolt against postwar complacency with the status quo had not yet infiltrated the universities; depressing, because the force of tradition should never be underestimated; and enlightening, because greater knowledge of current ideologies and practices, and their enclosing structures, offers a glimpse of light at the end of the tunnel.

The reception given in academic and media circles to *The sociology of housework* was mixed. According to the *New Statesman,* the book represented "a devastating reappraisal" of the social-scientific myth that marriage is more egalitarian than it used to be. It was written in "the brusque, uncompromising, workmanlike [sic] prose of an author who, although capable of savage irony at times, strikes one as being a trifle humourless" (Naughton, 1975). The review's author did concede that housework and the position of women were hardly funny subjects. *The Daily Telegraph's* review, somewhat missing the point, complained that my book contained no useful tips on how to make husbands share housework (Edmunds, 1975).

Abroad, *The Sydney Morning Herald* printed a photograph of me standing nervously in the kitchen, and described the book as "hard but rewarding reading" (Allan, 1975). Like many other reviews, the *Herald* piece picked out three main conclusions of the study: that the working hours of housewives were long by anybody's standards; that a majority of the housewives in the urban sample I interviewed were dissatisfied with housework; and that the oft-attributed discontent of the working class woman was nothing but a tendentious myth.

In the academic press, *The Economist* in Britain noted quite rightly that *The sociology of housework* was only the beginning of a serious study of housewifery and commented, rather less accurately, that in it I had overlooked the positive features of homemaking (Anon, 1975). In similar vein, *The Times Literary Supplement's* reviewer observed my failure to mention that housework could be for women the price of social mobility – that high-earning husbands were able to provide a standard of living many women could not buy with their own efforts (Jackson, 1975). Logical the abolition of the division of labour in marriage might be, but surely the price to be paid was a little too high? Eileen Barker in *The Times Educational Supplement* came right out with the worm that was silently worrying away at the scientific facade of academia: "Dr Oakley", she said, "can hardly be called a disinterested observer. She is unashamedly a feminist" (Barker, 1974). But none of us is a disinterested observer in this world. Sociologists are not more pure than any other kind of person, and the whole question of the relation in academic work between the personal and the professional has, in recent years, been more healthily exposed to open discussion and scrutiny, instead of continuing to fester as an unacknowledged sore on the sociological body politic (Bell and Encel, 1978; Roberts, 1981a).

Reviews of the book in the sociological journals did draw attention to some valid criticisms of the study: the tendency for the vitality, individuality and integrity of the interview material to become buried in a morass of chi-square tabulations; the absence of inside information about the evolution of the rating scales; the rather poor differentiation between key concepts such as 'identification' and 'involvement' with the housewife role; and the enormously important underlying assumption that there *is* a single phenomenon called the 'housewife role' rather than − a distinctly more interesting but difficult possibility − many multiple interpretations in different social groups of what it means to be a housewife (Hurstfield, 1975).

Publishing *The sociology of housework* taught me something about myself, something about feminism and much about the practice of a feminist social science. About myself I learnt both the facility of securing approval from a male-dominated academic establishment ('nothing succeeds like success') and the very sterility and irrelevance of this approval. About feminism I learnt, it's alright to laugh; a sense of humour is one of everyone's most valuable assets and there is no human enterprise that is not improved by it − including, or maybe especially, the study of housework.

The lessons acquired about the practice of a feminist social science are a good deal more complex. In Chapter 1 of *The sociology of housework* [see Part 4, Chapter One], I took a rapid excursion through the minefield of sociology's treatment of women. Obviously, it was clear that sociology would not become less sexist simply by including the study of women in its various subject-areas; for androgyny to be realised, the separate domains of sociology, together with their conceptual and methodological kits, needed a total restructuring. But I do not think I, or anyone else, at the time understood just what that might mean, or what implications it might have for the whole reflexive enterprise of studying the human condition.

The study on which *The sociology of housework* is based was undertaken within a specific academic context. That context emphasised the role of social scientists as collectors and analysts of objectively verifiable data, and their duty to be as 'scientific' as possible in the pursuit of data, and in the interpolation of their conclusions between data and the domains from which the data had been gathered and to which these were issued as 'research findings'. This exercise carried a number of implications which are not spelt out within the pages of *The sociology of housework*. There is, for example, the difficult task of treating women who are interviewed as merely data-providers − an objection required by science, but disclaimed by feminists, and one, moreover, that undermines the very importance of subjectivity in the mapping of social experience. Although this conflict appears between the lines of *The sociology of housework*, it was not until some years later, after another research project, that I was able to articulate it [see Part 4, Chapter Four].

The feminist critique of sociology and social science research is now much more developed than it was in the mid-1970s, and some of the statements made in *The sociology of housework*, which appeared new and daringly radical at the time, now wear the guise of naïve or tentative formulations of the problem.

The knowledge of hindsight is a truly wonderful thing. I would not do, or write, *The sociology of housework* in quite the same way in 1984 as I did in 1974. But, in provoking others to take up a line of enquiry, the book had a certain historical value; and what it has to say about a sample of London women interviewed in the early 1970s is both still valid and echoed by many other studies. In this particular field of research and writing, much has happened since 1974: from histories of housework (McBride, 1976; Davidson, 1982; Strasser, 1982) to more detailed studies of housework and childcare (Luxton, 1980; Boulton, 1983); and from further investigation of the role of housework and childrearing in the domestic division of labour and institutionalised heterosexuality (McKee and O'Brien, 1983) to its incorporation into theoretical debates about the intersecting forces of class and gender oppression (Barrett, 1980; Coward, 1983; Gamarnikow et al, 1983; Porter, 1983). Much of this work is original and stimulating; some is arid, repetitive or confused. Within it, there is a healthy mix of agreement and disagreement. And, of course, it is all located within a tremendously expanded field – 'women's studies' exists now in a way it simply did not ten years ago. As Kate Millett said in her *Sexual politics*, the object of feminist work is "to retire sex from the harsh realities of politics by creating a world we can bear out of the desert we inhabit" (Millett, 1969, p 363). While the current political and economic context is making life for many women more difficult, at least the academic desert is a good deal more habitable now.

Images of housework

Two conflicting stereotypes of housework exist in popular thinking today. According to one, the housewife is an oppressed worker: she slaves away in work that is degrading, unpleasant and essentially self-negating. According to the other, housework provides the opportunity for endless creative and leisure pursuits. In this view, housework is not work but homemaking, and the home is a treasure house of creative domestic joys. But how does this argument – and its converse – measure up to the reality of the housework situation as perceived by housewives themselves?

Throughout the 40 interviews in my sample, a clear perception of housework as work emerges. The women experience and define housework as labour, akin to that demanded by any job situation. Their observations tie in closely with many findings of the sociology of work; the aspects of housework that are cited as satisfying or dissatisfying have their parallels in the factory or office world. This equivalence is emphasised further by the women's own tendency to compare their reactions to housework with their experience of working outside the home.

Housewife, July 1949, p 90

A number of interview questions in particular provided answers on which these generalisations are based. The first two of these are questions about the 'best' and 'worst' aspects of being a housewife. Over half the answers to the 'best' aspects question refer to what could be called the 'work' dimension of the role, as do almost all the answers to the 'worst' aspects question – even though these questions do not specify housework, but permit answers relating to marriage, motherhood and home life generally. The answers are shown in Tables 1 and 2.

Autonomy is the most valued quality of the housewife role; housework is the worst. Joanna Giles, an ex-computer programmer, described her feeling of autonomy thus:

> To an extent you're your own master ... you can decide what you want
> to do and when you want to do it ... it's not like being at work when

somebody rings you up and you've got to go down and see them or
you've got to do this and that within half an hour.

Many of the answers used the phrase 'You're your own boss' to describe the
housewife's feeling of being in control. Autonomy, in the sense of freedom from
supervision and ability to determine one's own work rhythms, is an important
dimension of employment work. Martin Patchen, in a study of 834 US government
employees, found that the factor of control over work methods consistently
emerged as most closely associated with high job motivation (Patchen, 1970).

However, in the housewife's case, autonomy is more theoretical than real. Being
'your own boss' imposes the obligation to see that housework gets done; the
failure to do it may have serious consequences. As itemised by these women,
such consequences include the wrath of husbands and the ill-health of children
(through lack of hygiene):

> Why do I clean the kitchen floor twice a day? Well, it's because she's all
> over it, isn't it? I mean it's not nice to let a child crawl on a dirty floor –
> she might catch something off it. (Lorry driver's wife)

**Table 1: Answers to the question 'What would you say are the best things
about being a 'housewife?'**

'Best things'	Number of answers mentioning
You're your own boss	19
Having the children	9
Having free time	5
Not having to work outside the home	4
Having a husband	4
Having a home/family life	3
Housework	1
Other	2
Total[a]	47

Note: [a] Total adds up to more than 40 because some housewives gave more than one answer.

**Table 2: Answers to the question 'What would you say are the worst
things about being a housewife?'**

'Worst things'	Number of answers mentioning
Housework	14
Monotony/repetitiousness/boredom	14
Constant domestic responsibility	6
Isolation/loneliness	4
Must get housework done	3
Being tied down	3
Children	2
Other	2
Total[a]	48

Note: [a] Total adds up to more than 40 because some housewives gave more than one answer.

What this means is that the taking of leisure is self-defeating; the fact that one is one's own boss adds to, rather than subtracts from, the psychological pressures to do housework. Joanna Giles, the ex-computer programmer, went on to make this point:

> The worst thing is I suppose that you've got to do the work because you *are* at home. Even though I've got the option of not doing it, I don't really feel I *could* not do it, because I feel I *ought* to do it.

Housework – the actual work involved – is the other side of the coin from the nominally high evaluation attached to autonomy. Twenty-eight replies to the 'worst things' question mentioned housework or its monotonous, boring quality as the most disliked dimension; a further six described negatively the women's feeling of being constantly responsible for home and children. To use Eleanor Driscoll's words:

> [What would you say are the worst things about being a housewife?] Having to get up *every* morning … you think 'Oh heck I've got to do the place today, and I've got to do the dinner' – that's something I can't stand, thinking I've got to do the dinner. (Shop manager's wife)

The housewife is 'free from' but not 'free to'. But, if housework is work, what kind of work is it? Answers to two other questions give information on this point. The first invited the women to compare their own work (housework) with that of their husbands. This is a sensitive issue on which many wax indignant. Deborah Keyes, an ex-typist, says:

> I think housewives work just as hard. I can't stand husbands who come home and say 'Oh look you've done nothing all day, only a bit of housework and looked after the child'. But I reckon that's tiring myself, well, not tiring, *it's just as hard as doing a job – I don't care what any man says*…. My husband says this – that's why I feel so strongly about it. (emphasis added)

Deborah Keyes has one child, is married to a central-heating fitter and lives in a 'high-rise' flat. She is dissatisfied and tends to comment apathetically on her dissatisfaction, but her observations at this point in the interview were very lively indeed:

> I say to him [husband], I'm going to clear off for the day and you can do it all one day, and you'll see what it's like.

Of the 40 women, 26 claimed that they worked harder than their husbands, seven said the men worked harder and seven said that it depended on the personality or on the kind of job the husband had. There are explicit comparisons of one set of work routines with the other:

> Housewives work harder. My husband's always coming home and saying
> 'Oh I sat down and talked to so-and-so today' or 'We had a laugh today
> with so-and-so...'. I don't do that, I never sit down. (Plasterer's wife)

> The husbands never look very tired do they? It's always the woman
> that's tired isn't it? When they've finished, they've finished.... Things like
> road digging might be harder [than housework] but there again, when
> they've finished, they go and have a drink and a cigarette and that's it.
> (Painter and decorator's wife)

Reference is made to the *unconstructive* nature of housework tasks, to the
emotionally frustrating sense of being on a treadmill that requires the same action
to be repeated again and again:

> Housewives tend to be busy all the time but they're not really doing
> anything constructive, are they? Well, I suppose it is constructive in a
> way, but you never really see anything for it and it's all routine.
> (Statistician's wife)

Miles are walked in exchange for a feeling of perpetual defeat. In the eyes of Jean
Bevan, an ex-nurse married to an office manager, housework is 'real' work and
employment work is not:

> [Do you think housewives work as hard, not so hard, or harder than
> their husbands?] Harder. He doesn't work you see – he just sits in an
> office and tells other people to work.

When asked how they felt about writing the occupation of housewife on a form,
21 housewives 'minded' and 19 did not see anything disadvantageous in it. A
journalist's wife makes reference to the social stereotype:

> I only think of myself as a housewife when I have to fill up a form.
> Sometimes I'd like to put something a bit more interesting. I think it's a
> *menial* sort of job – *people look upon it like that.* (emphasis added)

Mixed with low social ranking are the related notions of housework as 'dull'
work and the housewife as a 'dull, boring' person. A warehouse foreman's wife
says:

> I mind writing 'housewife' on a form. I'd like to put 'secretary' or
> something – it sounds better. The majority of people are housewives. It
> sounds dull – you've nothing else to do except clean and dust and cook.

The image of the housewife as a cabbage makes a number of appearances in
answers to the question about writing 'housewife' on a form; it is mentioned by

12 of the 40 women. A 'cabbage' housewife is someone entirely immersed in domestic affairs, a colourless personality, a drab, uninteresting automaton.

One woman resolutely described herself as a 'shrink wrapper' rather than a housewife. This is the definition of her part-time factory job, which consists of wrapping tins in cellophane paper. She gets a certain amount of amusement from describing herself in this way, but the verbal presentation of self has a serious purpose:

> I think of myself as a housewife, but I don't think of myself as a cabbage. A lot of people think that they're housewives and they're cabbages; I don't like to think I'm only a housewife.… I usually say 'I'm a wife and a mother and I've got a part-time job'. People look down on housewives these days.

'Only' or 'just' a housewife is the ubiquitous phrase. Elaine Cawthorne, another working-class housewife, expresses it splendidly:

> I'm not married to a house! I hate the word 'housewife' … they say to you 'What are you?' and you say 'I've got a baby. I'm a mother, a wife' and they say, 'Oh, just a housewife'. Just a housewife! The hardest job in the world … you're never just a housewife.… Into that category comes everything.

Housework is not a single activity. It is a collection of heterogeneous tasks that demand a variety of skills and kinds of action. Washing a floor contrasts with shopping for groceries; peeling potatoes contrasts with washing dirty socks and planning a week's meals. To call all these jobs by the same name is to disguise their differences, to reduce them all to the same common denominator. In fact, some are more liked than others, some are more repetitive, some less tiring, some more potentially creative and so forth. Each of the tasks that the housewife does – cooking, laundering the clothes, cleaning the house and so on – can, after all, constitute a paid work role in its own right. The role of chef is very different from the role of commercial laundry operator or the job of 'domestic help'.

The six core housework tasks – cleaning, shopping, cooking, washing up, washing and ironing – can be arranged in a kind of league table of likes and dislikes. Table 3 shows the percentage of the sample who say they 'like', 'dislike' or 'don't mind' each task. Two percentages are shown in each case: one relates to first responses to the question 'Do you like …?' and the other to all responses.

Of the six tasks, ironing is most disliked: three-quarters of the sample report a negative attitude. It is disliked because it is physically an exhausting activity: more than any of the other tasks, it consists of actions that have to be repeated time and time again with little variation.

> I loathe ironing. It's just standing there, and you take one [garment] from the pile and stick it on the ironing board and iron it, fold it, and

put it down, take the next one – and it's as though it's never going to end. (Plasterer's wife)

Ironing consists of repetitive actions that tire specific muscles without engaging the attention of the mind or the concentrated energy of the whole body. The obvious comparison here is with the assembly-line worker in a factory, tied machine-like to a mindless and endlessly repetitive task. No other aspect of housework presents quite this parallel. Those housewives who 'don't mind' ironing make it clear that they dislike the task itself, yet have found conditions under which it becomes bearable. Having the radio or television on is one such ploy.

Washing up is next in the 'dislike' section of the table: taking first responses together with later ones, seventy per cent of the women describe a negative attitude. Like ironing, it tends to have assembly-line aspects, although these are not so pronounced. One 'just stands there washing plate after plate', or 'it just tires one out'. It is also a *dirty* job; in an ex-fashion model's words:

I hate it. I dread it. I just can't bear mucking around with dirty greasy things.

The unpleasantness is stressed because it is usually preceded by an enjoyable activity – eating a meal. Every meal is followed by washing up:

It's never ending. You've no sooner done one lot of washing up than you've got another lot, and that's how it goes on all day. (Lorry driver's wife)

Those who say they like washing up do not like the task itself: one woman likes it because she has a dishwasher, one because she has just acquired a new stainless steel sink, and the third likes it merely 'to get it out of the way'.

Table 3: Answers to questions about housework tasks

| House-work task | Dislike | | Don't mind | | Like | |
	First answer[a] (%)	All answers[b] (%)	First answer (%)	All answers (%)	First answer (%)	All answers (%)
Ironing	75	75	20	33	5	15
Washing up	65	70	28	30	8	8
Cleaning	50	68	20	20	30	38
Washing	33	65	35	40	33	38
Shopping	30	60	20	20	50	55
Cooking	23	48	18	18	60	60

Notes: [a] To the question 'Do you like...?'

[b] With probing, for example, 'What do you like about it?' or 'Is there anything you dislike about it?'

Attitudes to cleaning – the third in the 'dislike' list – are a little less negative: 20 of the 40 women dislike or hate cleaning; eight 'don't mind' it; and 12 like or 'love' it. Typical responses are:

> I don't really mind it. It's something to do. I'd be bored if I didn't have it to do. (Carpenter's wife)

> I like cleaning – polishing, everything. I like to see a nice shine. (Wife of a driver's mate)

> Cleaning a house is just like working in a factory – you dust the same thing every day and it's never appreciated. I mean I could get this whole place so tidy and the kids come home from school and it's like a bomb's exploded and nothing's appreciated about it, whereas if you're decorating or teaching children there's something always gained out of it ... as far as actual housework goes, I don't see how anyone can like it. It's boring, just like a robot. (Shop manager's wife)

Unlike shopping, cleaning is a lonely duty. The felt need to get the cleaning done conflicts with the desire to be sociable; one can iron, or perhaps cook, while talking to a friend or neighbour, but one cannot wield a vacuum cleaner and carry on a conversation at the same time. The conflict is clearly illustrated in the interview with Marilyn Thornton, a plasterer's wife with five children. She does her own housework in the mornings and spends every afternoon cleaning the bedrooms in an overnight transport café belonging to a friend of hers. She takes her 18-month-old twins with her to work. While the point of the job is to make money, it is also to get out of the house and talk to other people. (When doing her own housework, Marilyn Thornton has the radio on constantly 'for company'.) Because she has this afternoon job, she must get through her own work in the mornings; but she gets her work done in the mornings in order to create time for a job.

The example of Marilyn Thornton emphasises sharply the association of housework with social isolation. The importance of this in relation to work satisfaction patterns is discussed in Part 2, Chapter Three. Another common reason for disliking cleaning concerns technical aspects of the work:

> I've been on at my husband to get a fitted carpet in this room because this lino drives me mad. It gets so dirty and it *looks* dirty if it's not polished every day. (Policeman's wife)

> This carpet's navy and it's terrible, it shows everything. You've got to do it again and again. Invariably if I leave it, someone walks in. So I feel happier in my mind if I do it every day. (Retail chemist's wife)

A frequent claim is that cleaning is only a bore when one's mood is out of tune with it; conversely, in the 'right' mood, cleaning is cheerfully and quickly done.

Connections can be traced with the imagery of advertisements which portray harassed housewives overcome by sudden headaches while coping with the demands of husband, home and children; the mood is corrected by the appropriate painkiller or vitamin pill, and then the housewife proceeds to go happily about her work. The housewife, in an important sense, *is* her job:

> I like housework. I'm quite domesticated really. I've always been brought up to be domesticated – to do the housework and dust and wash up and cook – so it's natural instinct really. (Supermarket manager's wife)

The indistinguishability of the housewife and her work provides, if anything, a motivation to be satisfied – whether with cleaning specifically or with the whole complex of housework activities generally.

So far as washing – the fourth most disliked task – is concerned, attitudes are more evenly divided between positive, negative and 'don't mind' categories. Thirteen housewives say they 'like' washing, 14 'don't mind' it and 13 'dislike' or 'hate' it. Although both washing and washing up are activities in which dirt is removed from objects, the pleasure inherent in washing seems to be greater. Possibly this is due to the personal associations that clothes have. The clothes that are washed belong to and are used by someone, normally the housewife, her husband and children:

> I like washing his [the baby's] clothes, but I hate washing his nappies. I find them tiresome ... It's not that they're his nappies and he wets them – it's nothing to do with that – it's just that they're endless. Whereas if you're washing his clothes, you're washing one jumper and it's not the same as the next jumper; nappies are one square after another, like a nightmare.... (Elaine Cawthorne)

A counterbalancing image is suggested by the next quotation from the interview with a supermarket manager's wife:

> Once the washing's on the line, I think that's *nice* – *nice* and clean. I suppose it's a satisfying thing – to know

Housewife, March 1950, p 35

> you've done it at last and it's all there, *nice* and clean. It's always a *nice*
> sight to see a line of washing blowing. (emphasis added)

Why is a line of washing a 'nice' sight? Mass media advertising reiterates the message of white clothes gently blowing in the wind, transmitting a feeling that 'whiteness' or 'cleanliness' is the housewife's moral obligation to her family. Perfect cleanliness is the ideal, but the clothes must also be *seen* to be clean. Public visibility is achieved when the clothes hang in the garden and the advertising image adds the alluring finishing touches to this picture with cloudless skies, matched only by the cloudless smile on the housewife's face. Seven of the 40 women specifically mention the pleasure they obtain from seeing a line full of clean clothes; some explain it is because they anticipate the silent admiration of neighbours at this visible (though short-lived) achievement.

Automation makes a difference here. Eleven of the working-class and 14 of the middle-class housewives had washing machines; use of a machine in one's own home lightens the task. As Eleanor Driscoll recollects:

> At one time I had this scrubbing brush and I used to spend the whole day scrubbing and I used to have a big pan and I used to boil my clothes up in it – it drove me round the bend…. I've got this washing machine now, thank goodness. A washing machine cuts housework really down.

'I don't know what I did without it' is the sentiment.

By contrast with these other tasks, the housewife's role as a consumer is a more public one; it requires an absence from her workplace – the home. Largely for this reason, answers to the question 'Do you like shopping?' are predominantly favourable; many women mention 'getting out of the house' or 'meeting people' as advantages of shopping.

> I like shopping. You see people when you go out – it's a change from the house. (Carpenter's wife)

> I like it because I'm out, I think, and I like looking in the shops and sometimes I bump into people I know and it just makes a little break…. (Policeman's wife)

The proliferation of shopping excursions – for most of the women, a daily event – as a relief from domestic captivity is recognised:

> I do my big shopping on Tuesday – but I go for odds and ends every day. I make these journeys just to get out of the house. Otherwise I'd be in the house all the time. (Policeman's wife)

> I go shopping nearly every day – although that's not really necessary. But I do because I combine it with taking her [the child] for a walk. And it does me good to get out of the house. (Journalist's wife)

Another merit of shopping is that it can be expanded to include (or even defined to consist of) window-shopping. This is self-consciously an escapist activity, its main value being that it avoids the careful budgeting and penny-counting which shopping itself entails.

Of course, a limited budget could be seen as a challenge. Only two housewives actually see it this way without reservations; Dorothy Underwood, a cinema manager's wife and the mother of three children under four, and Sandra Bishop, the wife of a painter and decorator and the mother of one child:

> I quite enjoy shopping. It makes a change from housework – getting out of the house – and it's a bit of a challenge too, budgeting and trying to get the cheapest of everything. (Dorothy Underwood)

> I like it. But I don't just go in one shop, and I never buy anything without looking at the price. I'm terrible with prices. Some people say 'You're mad – just go in one shop' but I can't. I usually go in at least three. Like tea – we have the same brand each week – but if I know it's cheaper in one shop I go into that shop, just to get that one thing – like I got it for 1/6 this week and it's usually 1/11 – I like to get the best, but cheaper. (Sandra Bishop)

Other complaints about shopping cite physical difficulties. Having to take children along imposes both a physical and a mental burden; there is the problem of managing children and shopping simultaneously, and the housewife's attention is distracted by the need to pacify a crying child or by the knowledge that a baby in a pushchair is parked out of sight. Consequently, she becomes a less efficient shopper and a more frustrated one. Queuing or having to wait in shops is disliked; so are certain kinds of shops – for some, the large supermarket, and for others, the small corner shop. The more shopping resembles work, the less it is liked. Small semi-serious shopping expeditions are valued as a relief from the social isolation and the work of housework. But major expeditions for food are disliked. All except two of these 40 women do their 'big' shopping once a week – that is, stocking up on goods like sugar, flour, etc. – and it is customary to combine this with shopping for the weekend. Virtually all dislike this kind of shopping. The mental strain of trying to concentrate on it with small children is considerable, and so is the physical strain of getting it all home. Only five of the 40 had the regular or occasional use of a car for shopping and other activities.

Of the six basic housework tasks, cooking is, according to these women, potentially the most enjoyable activity. It presents a challenge; it can be an art:

> Cooking doesn't bore me like cleaning does. I enjoy it – I enjoy trying new recipes. (Cinema manager's wife)

> I get fed up with cooking the same old thing – I like it if I can experiment. We [herself and the housewife in the next flat] try new recipes off the *Jimmy Young Show*, and see how they turn out. (Lorry driver's wife)

They say it can be creative, but is it, in practice?

> I do like cooking if I've got time to do it properly. But the way I'm doing it now, I don't like it. I used to love it. I used to love concocting meals … really love it. But now the quickest and most nourishing meal is the winner. (Lorry driver's wife)

Limitations of time (and money) act as brakes on the enjoyment of cooking. The housewife is not only a chef but also a washer up, a cleaner, a nanny and a childminder:

> I mean I can't get my hands covered with flour and egg and stuff if he's going to cry and I've got to pick him up, can I? (Lorry driver's wife)

> I think if I was left in peace to cook, then I'd get pleasure from it. But as it is … if I make pastry, there's usually pastry from one end of the house to the other, because the kids have got to have their little bits, and in the end you think, 'Oh was it worth it?'. (Food technologist's wife)

In reality, husbands demand meals at specific times, small children cry when their stomachs are empty, and the hour that might be spent cooking competes with the hour that ought to be spent washing the floor or changing the beds. 'Thinking what to eat' is an endless duty, however creative the actual task may be. Thus one latent function of the creative cookery ideal is the production of dissatisfaction. Standards of achievement exist of which the housewife is permanently aware, but which she cannot often hope to reach due to the other demands on her time.

To summarise, one could list certain properties of housework tasks, their context, or the housewife's approach to them, which make recurrent appearances in answers given to the section of the interview dealing with what is liked and disliked about the six core housework tasks. Attributes referred to as promoting a positive attitude include (in order of importance):

1) Being able to talk to other people while working
2) Being in the 'right' mood
3) Having enough time
4) Having the right work environment or tools of work
5) Having enough housekeeping money
6) Having one's work appreciated

The following factors are mentioned as associated with a negative attitude:

1) Monotony and repetitiousness
2) Having the wrong environment or tools of work
3) Being in the 'wrong' mood
4) Children getting in the way
5) Not having enough time

6) Social isolation
7) Having to think about work

Housewives approach housework as work, analogous with any other kind of job. Their comments about the 'best' and 'worst' aspects of housewifery refer predominantly to the work dimension of the role; freedom from supervision heads the list of positive qualities, while the work itself is the major negative aspect named. Housework is defended as 'real' and 'hard' work, a defence made all the more necessary because of the low status and value conventionally accorded to it. While the stereotyped image of housework treats it as a single activity, women see it as consisting of many disparate ones. Feelings about these different tasks do not seem to be dependent primarily on temperament or on personal background; rather they emerge as related to the kind of conditions under which the tasks are performed.

Work conditions

One preoccupation of the sociology of industrial work has been the *causes* of job dissatisfaction. What accounts for the fact that some workers are satisfied, while others are not? Certain patterns of job satisfaction or dissatisfaction seem to be associated with particular kinds of jobs. Thus jobs which involve social interaction with other workers are generally more satisfying than socially isolated work; monotonous, repetitive work is more likely to be linked with job dissatisfaction than more varied work; jobs which involve responsibility and the ability to organise work time and work methods are generally preferred over those which lack these qualities, and so forth (Parker et al, 1967). It would seem that one source of industrial discontent in the modern world is the structure and content of work itself.

This is a general conclusion. But does it apply to the case of the housewife? Answers given by the 40 women in the sample suggest that certain characteristics of housework may be more or less uniformly experienced as dissatisfying, while others are potentially rewarding. Hence it would seem both helpful and important to examine a number of aspects of work that industrial sociology has highlighted as critical in the explanation of job satisfaction. These are the experiences of monotony, fragmentation and excessive pace in work and social interaction patterns. Two other dimensions of work, which have been found less important in the case of the industrial worker, are also looked at in this chapter: working hours and the technical environment.

Monotony, fragmentation and excessive pace

A common charge levelled against housework is that it is inherently monotonous and repetitive. There is nothing more 'automatic' than the perfect housewife, mechanically pursuing the same routine day in and day out. The Peckham Rye Women's Liberation Group (1971) call housework:

> An endless routine; it creates its own high moments of achievement and satisfaction so as to evade ... futility. The bolt you tighten on the factory floor vanishes to be replaced by another: but the clean kitchen floor is tomorrow's dirty floor and the clean floor of the day after that. The appropriate symbol for housework (and for housework alone) is not the interminable conveyor belt but a compulsive circle like a pet mouse in its cage spinning round on its exercise wheel, unable to get off....

Thus monotony and fragmentation are intimately connected and, through the need to accomplish a long series of jobs each day, a feeling of always having too much to do may be added.

In their study of affluent workers' attitudes to work, John Goldthorpe and his colleagues asked three questions designed specifically to measure the extent to which industrial work is experienced as intrinsically unsatisfying: 'Do you find your present job monotonous?' 'Do you find you can think about other things while doing your job?' and 'Do you find the pace of the job too fast?' (Goldthorpe et al, 1968, p 17). On the basis of the answers they received to these questions, Goldthorpe and his colleagues concluded that monotony is a definite source of job dissatisfaction. Fragmentation and excessive pace were also found to be important variables bearing on job satisfaction, with many workers, who did not find their work monotonous, stating that it did not absorb their full attention or that they found the pace of it too fast. These three questions were used in an adapted form for housewives in the present sample.

When asked, 'Do you find housework monotonous on the whole?', 30 out of the 40 women said 'Yes':

> It's the feeling that, although you've done the job for today, you've still got to do it tomorrow. It's one of the things that gets me down about it. (Journalist's wife)

Dissatisfaction is higher among those who report monotony. Eighty per cent of the women who said 'Yes' to the monotony question are dissatisfied with housework, compared with 40% of those who said 'No'. Monotony is clearly associated with work dissatisfaction, and this is supported by the large number of housewives who mentioned monotony *spontaneously* at various points in the interview:

> I like cooking and I like playing with the children, doing things for them – I don't like the basic cleaning. *It's boring, it's monotonous.* (Cinema manager's wife) (emphasis added)

> It's the *monotony* I don't like – *it's repetitive and you have to do the same things each day.* I support it's really just like factory work – just as boring. (Toolmaker's wife) (emphasis added)

Fragmentation – the experience of work subdivided into a series of unconnected tasks not requiring the worker's full attention – is also a common experience. Thirty-six of the 40 women said 'Yes' to the question 'Do you find you can think about other things while you're're working?'. The women were on the whole surprised at the question, apparently assuming that a dispersal of concentration is intrinsic to housework. As Dawn Abbatt, a middle-class housewife, answered the question:

> [Do you find you can think about other things while you're working?] *Oh, of course.* Today I've been thinking to myself, I've only got the sleeves to put in that dress – when am I going to have the time to do it?

Perhaps for this reason, fragmentation is not associated with work dissatisfaction (Locke, 1969). Since women do not see housework as a coherent, meaningful structure of tasks demanding their full attention, they are not made dissatisfied by its fragmented nature.

What kinds of thoughts occupy the housewife while she works? The list of topics given in answer to the fragmentation question is as follows: fantasy (18 replies); leisure/social activities (17 replies); housework (14 replies) and childcare (12 replies). (These add up to more than 40 because some women mentioned more than one topic.)

The housewife's name for 'fantasy' is 'daydreaming': Sally Jordan, a dustman's wife, says:

> I daydream when I'm doing anything. I'm always going off into a trance. I don't hear people when they talk to me. I stare into space. I'm working at the same time.

Favourite topics for daydreaming are housing and holidays. The significance of fantasising about a new house or a new flat is that one is visualising a change in one's work environment. Pauline Cutts, a secretary who lives in a rented furnished flat with her husband and one child, says:

> Usually I dream about having my own house. I think about that most of the time. I think there's more reward in housework if you've got your own house – even with an unfurnished flat there is.

Although the desire to become a home-owner may represent a genuine social aspiration for these women and their families, there is no evidence that it guarantees satisfaction with housework: the housewives in the sample who did own their homes were no more satisfied than those whose homes were rented. The ideal of 'each woman in her own house' is certainly one fostered by advertising, and thus it may be, in part, a stereotyped response to the boredom of housework. The same holds true of holidays as themes of mental activity while working:

> [Do you find you can think about other things…?] Yes – a summer holiday in Ibiza! – No – seriously – I'm usually thinking about what Susan is up to, planning what to do. (Machine operator's wife)

Holidays are avenues of escape:

> I think about how I could get dressed up and go out somewhere, for a couple of hours, and just leave it all, because I get so sick of it sometimes…. I do get very irritable with myself very often. I often feel like I could pack up and go home for a holiday in Ireland. (Painter and decorator's wife)

As answers to the 'fragmentation' question, the category of leisure activities tends to merge into that of fantasy. 'Getting out for the day/away from the house' are ubiquitous topics; there is also a focus on social life:

> [Do you find you can think about other things while you're working?]
> Yes – what I've done the night before, the day before – thinking about parties and that. What people said, the things that happened, what we might do next Saturday night – that kind of thing. (Van driver's wife)

Although 14 answers to the fragmentation question concern housework, the housewife rarely thinks about the work she is *actually* doing. Instead, there are references to past and future performances:

> I think about the carpet that's got to be laid, and I must clean those windows tomorrow.... (Lorry driver's wife)

> I think about what I'm going to do next ... what I'm going to cook, the children, where I'll take them out ... this sort of thing. (Sales director's wife)

This is a crucial finding. Housework is such fragmented work that almost never does the housewife report thinking about the task in hand. Whatever the skills that are needed, complete mental concentration is not one, and the effect of having many different tasks to do is a dispersal of the housewife's attention in many different directions. Children amplify this fragmentation effect. They make perfect concentration impossible and are often the cause of breaks in work activity.

All these strands of thought fulfil the latent function of enabling women to get housework done:

> Daydreaming? That's what keeps me doing it [housework]. (Factory hand's wife)

Like fragmentation, the experience of time pressures in housework is not associated with work dissatisfaction. The women were asked 'Do you find you have too much to get through during the day?'. Roughly half of those satisfied and half of those dissatisfied with housework say they have too much to do. Neither do feelings of 'having too much to get through' relate to the number of children the housewife has, or to the kind of aids and amenities she possesses.

This finding is inconsistent with the conclusions of various surveys of job satisfaction in industry, according to which a feeling of excessive pace is a potent cause of dissatisfaction (Goldthorpe et al, 1968; Patchen, 1970). For the housewife, the situation is complicated. Apart from the deadlines created by husbands' and children's needs, she imposes her own time pressures; these follow from the way she organises her work and the kind of standards she sets herself. The interviews suggest that satisfaction or dissatisfaction are the prior conditions here, and that the feeling of having too much to do or not flows from these. A woman who is generally satisfied will organise her days so that she is not overcome by the many demands on her time. For example, Barbara Lipscombe, the wife of a car patrolman and the mother of three children aged four, two and one, says of ironing:

> I don't let the ironing build up too much. I wait until my husband's doing the late shift, and I wait until the children have gone to bed, and I sit down in front of the television. I find I can do it much easier if I've got one eye on the television. I seem to get through it easier and it doesn't worry me at all then.

Lack of organisation creates work and may be a consequence of feeling dissatisfied, as in Juliet Warren's case:

> My standards have definitely dropped since I've been at home with the baby. I suppose it's because I can't do anything uninterrupted and I still can't get used to that. It takes a lot of effort. I'm very aware there's lots of jobs I ought to do – I used to be pretty thorough – and there are things I haven't got the time to do. I might start off the day with lots of intentions and, by the end of it, I'm so fagged out I just collapse. I'm just badly organised. (Wife of a television documentary director)

Another facet of work is that of limits or deadlines. The need to complete a task within a set period may produce a negative attitude towards it. Cooking is especially subject to this limitation, although it is in theory one of the most liked activities. In one study of job motivation among industrial employees, Patchen (1970) sums up:

> The finding that those who more frequently work under time limits are *not* more interested in their work and take *less* pride in their job ... is arresting. It may be that ... while time limits may provide one standard of excellence, the attention which they focus on the speed of work diverts attention from the possibility of doing work which is creative or innovative, thereby reducing achievement incentive. (p 70)

So far as the housewife is concerned, time limits imposed by factors outside her control mean that the pace of her work is too fast for each task to get the attention she would like to give it. Unlike many jobs, housework can often be done in a very short space of time, without actually failing to be done at all. Cleaning may consist of a quick dust or 'whip round'. However, it is the housewife's ultimate responsibility to see that all tasks get done properly. Awareness of this fact causes time pressures to be felt possibly more acutely than they are in other kinds of work.

In Table 1, housewives' experiences of monotony, fragmentation and speed are compared with those of a sample of factory workers. Housewives experience more monotony, fragmentation and speed in their work than do workers in the factory. But, when a particular sub-group of workers is taken – assembly-line

Table 1: The experience of monotony, fragmentation and speed in work: housewives and factory workers compared

Workers	Percentage of the 40 women studied experiencing		
	Monotony (%)	Fragmentation (%)	Speed (%)
Housewives	75	90	50
Factory workers[a]	41	70	31
Assembly-line workers[a]	67	86	36

Note: [a] These figures are taken from Goldthorpe et al (1968, p 18).
The assembly-line workers are a sub-sample of the factory workers.

workers – the gap is narrowed. The inherent frustrations of assembly-line work are also to be found in housework. This gives substance to the contemporary feminist polemic which brands housework as 'alienating' work.

Social interaction

An aspect of work which many studies agree has possibly the strongest influence on a worker's satisfaction is social interaction. Research has shown that loneliness is an occupational hazard for the modern housewife, who is often cut off not only from community life but from family life – in the wider sense – also. According to Gavron's survey of 96 urban housewives, the feeling of being tied to the house and isolated from meaningful social contacts is a common one for both working-class and middle-class women (Gavron, 1966). Herbert Gans (1967), in his study of American suburbia, *The Levittowners,* reports that boredom and loneliness affect women more than men, because of the women's housebound role.

The 40 women interviewed were asked early in the interview to give an account of their daily routines. This enabled the topic of social relationships to be covered, although a direct question was also asked: 'Do you ever feel as though you're on your own too much in the daytime?' Of the 22 women who said 'Yes', 17 (76%) were dissatisfied with housework, while 11 (61%) of the 18 who said 'No' were also dissatisfied. The difference is in the direction of more dissatisfaction in the lonely group. The women vary a great deal in their patterns of social relationships. In some cases, only two or three people are seen in the course of a week; in others, there are two or three social contacts in the course of each day. Compare the description of her social life given by Linda Farrell, a delivery man's wife, with that given by Margaret Nicholson, the wife of the director of a publishing firm:

> Although I'm quite happy to be indoors and getting on with my work – I don't say I'd be outside gallivanting everywhere – it'd be nice to know people. I'd like just to pop round to my sister's – that sort of thing… The only person I really see is my neighbour next door. I suppose I see her once or twice a week – she comes in for a cup of tea, or I go to her. She's got one child at school. My other neighbour's working. I don't like this area at all – you just don't know people. My mother

comes once a week, for the day. She phones me every other day. I look forward to my husband coming home in the middle of the day – it makes a break, breaks the day up. Normally I don't see anyone till my husband comes in – it *is* lonely really When I first got married, I got terribly depressed, because coming from a big family there was always something going on at home. I somehow regretted getting married, at first. I couldn't get used to it at all. I used to hate coming home here. I'd wait till he came home, and then go to my mother's … it sounds childish, doesn't it? (Linda Farrell)

I suppose I have a friend in to tea nearly every afternoon – that is, a friend with children. We come back from fetching the children together, and then she'll stay till about 6.30. I get tea for all the children. Then there's a friend next door I see an awful lot – every day, certainly. My children play in her garden. About twice a week I go to lunch with a friend, and again about twice a week I have someone to lunch here. Monday afternoons I have to keep free because I like to take Mrs James – the domestic help – home and Friday afternoon Lucy has a dancing lesson. On Friday morning, I take my neighbour shopping. I do it because she relies on me, she can't get down there on her own. Oh, and I belong to a Young Wives' group; we meet once a fortnight and I see people from that quite often. (Margaret Nicholson)

Linda Farrell's social circle is much more restricted than Margaret Nicholson's. It is also more narrowly focused on the kinship group – relationships with her parents, brothers, sisters, in-laws and so on are the ones she most values.

The social relationships engaged in by Margaret Nicholson include a wide variety of friends and the stress on family ties is missing. This is much more the stereotyped picture of middle-class coffee mornings, flower-arranging and other 'feminine' cultural activities. There is more stress on the companionship of the husband-wife relationship: an ethic of 'being on our own together'.

There is an association between the number of 'social contacts' the housewife has during work time and work satisfaction patterns. A 'social contact' here is any individual, not a residential member of the housewife's family, with whom she experiences social interaction. What seems to be important is the number of people the housewife sees. Twenty-six of the 40 women have 19 or fewer social contacts a week; 13 have more. (I excluded the one woman who had a full-time job from this tabulation since this in this respect her housework situation was not directly comparable with that of the other women.) The relationship with work satisfaction patterns is shown in Table 2.

Some women expressly blame loneliness for their dissatisfaction. As a supermarket manager's wife put it:

[Do you ever feel you're on your own too much in the day-time?] Yes. The last couple of months it's been dragging: you feel 'I wish I could talk

Table 2: Work satisfaction and social contacts

Social contacts per week	Work satisfaction		Total
	Satisfied	Dissatisfied	
	Number (%)	Number (%)	Number (%)
19 or less	5 (19)	21 (81)	26 (100)
20 or more	7 (54)	6 (46)	13 (100)
Total	*12 (31)*	*27 (69)*	*39 (100)*

$p<0.05$

Note: The figures in this table add up to 39, not 40, since the one housewife who was employed full-time was excluded from this analysis; her housework routines were not comparable with those of the others in this respect.

> to somebody' … not knowing anybody else you tend to get this feeling that, unless you go out and talk to someone, you'll go stark raving mad.…

The general impression conveyed is that these women would not necessarily be *more satisfied* with work if they saw more people, but that they would certainly be *less dissatisfied*. It is interesting to note here that similar findings have been reported for employed workers. The quantity and quality of social interaction during work time can apparently act as a 'dissatisfier' but not as a 'satisfier' (Herzberg et al, 1959).

Working hours

The housewife's working hours are among the longest in contemporary society. Hours worked by housewives in this sample ranged from 48 (the one housewife who had a full-time job) to 105. The range of variation is shown in Table 3 in relation to number of children. Most of the women – 25 out of the 40 – work between 70 and 80 hours a week. Only ten work fewer than 70 hours, and five do 90 or more hours of housework a week.

These calculations of working time are taken from the accounts of daily routine obtained in the interviews. They include all time spent in housework, including shopping, and in childcare or supervision. Not counted as 'work time' are periods described by the housewife as spent in leisure occupations – watching television, reading and so on. Time away from home, visiting relatives, neighbours or friends, is not included in the total. The care or supervision of children, although not strictly speaking housework, is included because, in practice, it was impossible to make an adequate distinction between the two activities of housework and childcare. From these women's descriptions of their days, it is clear that rarely, if ever, is it possible for them to make this distinction either. (A distinction between *attitudes* to housework and childcare is a different matter from a temporal merging of the two activities.)

There are two exceptions to the inclusion of childcare in housework time. One is the counting of visiting as leisure which, from the viewpoint of childcare, it really is not. Wherever the housewife-mother is, she retains the responsibility

Table 3: Weekly[a] housework hours and number of children

Number of children	Weekly hours spent in housework							
	40-49	50-59	60-69	70-79	80-89	90-99	100+	Total
One	1	2	5	5	1	1	1	16
Two	0	1	1	5	4	0	1	12
Three or more	0	0	0	2	8	2	0	12
Total	*1*	*3*	*6*	*12*	*13*	*3*	*2*	*40*

Note: [a] 'Weekly' means a seven-day week.

for the care of her children. The other exception is time when children are asleep. Here again, the responsibility for children is maintained and the housewife must be prepared to interrupt whatever she is doing at a moment's notice if her children wake up and require her attention. Neither of these categories of time is included in the assessment of working hours unless, of course, in the latter case, the housewife is actually doing housework during the hours 'freed' by her children's sleep.

The average working week of housewives in this sample is 77 hours – almost twice as long as an industrial working week of 40 hours. This figure is in agreement with other information about housework hours gathered by other researchers (Wilson, 1929; Bryn Mawr, 1945; Stoetzel, 1948; Moser, 1950; Mass Observation, 1951; Cowles and Dietz, 1956; Girard, 1958; Girard and Bastide, 1959). These studies cover three countries and a period from 1929 to 1971. The figures indicate that there has been no decrease in housework time over this period. In the United States, in 1929, rural housewives put in a 64-hour week; in France, thirty years later, a 67-hour week. Comparing urban Britain in 1950 and in 1971, housewives have added seven hours a week to their working time during this period. This lack of change contrasts with the situation of employed workers. For example, between 1920 and 1953 in the United States in the manufacturing industry, the average hours of work decreased by ten: from 50 to 40 hours.

These various surveys use different methods and different kinds of sample for the computation of housework time, so precise comparisons are difficult. However, if one looks at the size of family, the findings are fairly consistent: in the 1948 French study, for instance, housewives with one child put in, on average, a 78-hour week; in the 1950 British study, a 67-hour week; and, in the present study, a 71-hour week was the average figure for housewives in this group. The French studies, which contain the most sophisticated breakdown of housework hours according to a number of variables, suggest that, on average, one child adds 23 hours to housework time; two children add 35 hours, and three or more add 41 hours. Of the twelve housewives with three or more children in the present sample, none works fewer than 70 hours a week, eight work 80 or more hours, and two 90 or more.

Somewhat surprising is the fact that the longest hours are *not* put in by the women with the largest number of children. In the group with one child, Elizabeth Gould works 84 hours, Clare Pullen 91 hours, and Elaine Cawthorne 104 hours. In the group with two children, Jill Duffy puts in a 105-hour week.

Is a long working week connected with work dissatisfaction? In this sample, there is no statistical relationship. What accounts for the absence of a relationship between work hours and satisfaction patterns? The interviews suggest two answers to this question. First of all, it seems that the housewife's resentment of her long working hours is located by her in the context of a comparison between her own and her husband's situation. The assertion that women work harder than men is part of a constant dialogue between husband and wife. A second answer is that long working hours are not a cause of housework dissatisfaction because they are an expected part of the housewife role. Like its fragmented nature, housework's 'never-endingness' is so much bound up with the idea of housework that the two are not conceived apart. Housewives simply do not expect to work the same hours in the home as they would in an office or factory.

The relative unimportance of extended work time as a determinant of dissatisfaction is confirmed by studies of industrial work. In one review of job attitudes research, working hours come out as less important than any other aspect of working conditions, and working conditions as a category come ninth in a ranked list of ten job factors. Not surprisingly, working hours are more important to employed married women than to employed men, since they have the double burden of employment work *and* housework (Herzberg et al, 1959, p 74).

The technical environment

Is the modern housewife's malaise due to deficiencies in her work environment?

The women interviewed were assessed on the number of amenities (running hot water, nearness to shops and so on) and the technological aids (vacuum cleaners, washing machines and so forth) they possessed. A score was then obtained by assigning a value to each item. The average score for amenities was 7.5 and for aids 3.1. As was expected, scores were higher for both aids and amenities in the middle-class group (8.0 and 3.8 as opposed to 7.0 and 2.4 in the working-class group).

A housewife with an average 'score' was Joan Hubbard, an ex-shop assistant married to a toolmaker. She has two children, aged four and two years, and lives in a privately rented unfurnished flat. It has two bedrooms, a kitchen, a bath and inside lavatory, and one living room, and is within five minutes' walk of the shops. The Hubbards have access to a small garden, but they have no running hot water; all water has to be heated on the gas stove. In the way of household appliances, Joan Hubbard has a single-tub washing machine (one that cannot rinse or dry the clothes), a vacuum cleaner and a fridge.

The highest score on amenities and aids was obtained by Sarah Maddison, an ex-office worker married to a food technologist, and the mother of three children. She lives in a house, owned on a mortgage, with four bedrooms and a large garden. In addition to such items as a fridge and a vacuum cleaner, she has a dishwasher, central heating, hired domestic help and the use of the family car in the daytime. In these last two respects, Sarah Maddison is unusual. Only three housewives had paid domestic help. (A further two normally had help in the house, but were temporarily without it when interviewed.) Of the 40 women, only five had the regular or occasional use of a car for domestic or leisure purposes.

Differential ownership of technological aids and differences in the possession of amenities may affect the *way* housework is done, and they may have some influence on attitudes to work tasks, but they do not appear to affect satisfaction with work. Neither scores for amenities nor those for aids are related to work satisfaction patterns in this sample, although, in the interviews, housewives sometimes expressed dissatisfaction with the aids and amenities they had:

> I hate cooking more than housework. I'm bored with food. I think it's partly because of my kitchen actually – it's down those two little stairs, it's with the bathroom and it's away from the living room. It's not the sort of room that anyone wants to come and chat to you in. I couldn't have the baby in there, for example. (Radio producer's wife)

> Washing is a drag because I've got nowhere to dry it ... these heating cabinets don't work.... I have to put it in the bathroom. At my mother's, I could dry it in the garden. (Lorry driver's wife)

Some of the most satisfied women were actually those with the smallest number of aids and amenities. Sandra Bishop, who lives in a new two-bedroomed council flat on a new estate with her husband (a painter and decorator) and one child aged 18 months, lacks several aids which many women would consider essential, including a vacuum cleaner and either a washing machine or access to a launderette. She says:

> I love housework. And yet some people come and say, 'Oh you have a hard time, with no washing machine and no hoover', but they're the ones who moan! I say I just get on with it ... my Mum's managed – she still manages without a washing machine, and she washes every day, and I think *it's really how you are*.... (emphasis added)

The absence of a relationship between differences on the technical dimension and work satisfaction patterns in the case of the housewife cannot be directly compared with the factory worker's situation, since factory work is defined in a total sense by its technology; housework is not. (This, of course, is partly because the level of technology applied to housework is a long way behind that in industry. Domestic technology affects particular tasks but not the job of housework as a whole.) However, the lack of a relationship between the technical dimension of work and housework satisfaction patterns may point to the relative unimportance of working conditions as factors shaping work satisfaction generally. For example, Arthur Kornhauser (1965, p 264) reports for his sample of Detroit car workers that the physical conditions of work appear "to have little or no explanatory value in accounting for poorer mental health at lower versus upper job levels".

In short, then, neither the technical environment of work nor the hours of work the housewife puts in at her job are linked with patterns of work satisfaction and dissatisfaction in the present sample. But a limited amount of social interaction is related to dissatisfaction with work, as also are feelings of monotony. The fragmented nature of housework is an accepted characteristic of it and, for this reason, is not a source of dissatisfaction. Feelings of excessive pace are symptomatic of the housewife who is generally dissatisfied and do not proceed directly from qualities of housework as work, although frequent time limits are intrinsic to housework and affect attitudes to work tasks.

Standards and routines

'Work' has no single definition or shared meaning for the individuals who do it; the meanings of work are as various as the kinds of job that exist. Nevertheless, for most people, the idea of work contains some notion of externally imposed constraint. Even if one's occupation is freely chosen, it usually carries with it a set of rules about what should be done, when, how and to what standards. A train driver follows printed schedules and rules controlling speed and safety; accountants are accountable to their clients and are governed by rules of 'professional' conduct, and so forth. But housewives are impressed by their freedom from the constraints of externally set rules and supervisions. The housewife is her own supervisor, the judge of her own performance, and ultimately the source of her own job definition.

The two dimensions of this job definition are *standards* and *routines*. In describing her daily life, every woman interviewed outlined the kind of standards she thought it important to stick to in housework, and the type of routine she used to achieve this end.

Barbara Lipscombe, a cheerful, warm woman, lives in a rented three-bedroomed house and has three children under five. She used to be a typist and is married to a car patrolman on shift work. Most of the Lipscombes' family life takes place in the room off the kitchen, at the back of the house, furnished with a table and chairs, a sofa and a television. Barbara's day goes like this:

> I get up when the children wake up about a quarter to eight. I get a cooked breakfast, then I always get myself and my little girl washed and dressed first, because I take her to school. I take her to school, I come back, and my husband shoots off – he minds the other two for me while I go to the school. I get the other two washed and dressed. Then I like to get the washing in the machine, because I can leave it doing while I'm down the shops. I go shopping every day, and by the time I come back it's usually time for the baby to have her food – at about twelve – and then she usually sleeps till about two, and then I cook lunch for him [the two-year-old] so that in the evening it's a tea, although it's usually a cooked tea.

> Usually we've finished with lunch by about a quarter past one. Then I tidy round. I make the beds first thing in the morning, but on Thursday I do enough shopping for Friday, so that on Friday I don't go out, I do all my housework. I go right through the house. Usually I start in my bedroom and I like to get to the top of the stairs by the baby's lunchtime, and then I stop and give them lunch and then I carry on and get on quite well. I go through the front room and then I get to this room [the 'breakfast' room] and I do the lunch washing up then, and I wait till they go to bed to put the hoover over this room and polish round. The

rest of the week I just sort of tidy round, dust, put the carpet sweeper over – that takes me till quarter past three, when I go to meet my little girl from school, and I don't very often get much done once she's home....

She goes to play with a little girl up the road, and then it's usually time for the baby's tea. I feed her and get her washed and undressed and ready for bed and then these two sit down to tea. If my husband's going to be in about that time we all have it together, but if he's going to be late they have theirs first. Then quite soon after tea I wash and undress them, so I've finished for the day. They play around for a bit, and he goes to bed about half past six, and the little girl between seven and half past – and then I can sit down! I do the washing up when the children are eating their tea.

Like the other women, Barbara Lipscombe was asked if she had 'particular ways of doing things' that she regularly kept to in housework:

I think I like particular standards, but I don't think I always keep them. I like everything to be clean – not particularly tidy – I like the washing and ironing to be nice – nice and clean and nicely ironed. If I've got a lot to do, I can't actually take as much time as I'd like over it. I like the beds changed often, which I find is hard to keep up with, because of drying the washing.

[Is it important to you to keep to these standards?] I find I've got to make excuses for myself if I don't, but I sort of think I've got this to do for the children, and that to do – and I'll have a grand old clean up next week, sort of thing. It's probably the wrong attitude but I feel if I can't keep up, I can't keep up, so it doesn't really worry me.

A journalist's wife with one child paints a different picture altogether. Catherine Prince is tall, athletic-looking, easy going and sociable. Her home, owned on a mortgage, is still in the process of being 'done up': some rooms gleam with newly stripped floorboards and pristine white walls, while others have barely been touched:

I get up about 8.30 – when the baby wakes up. My husband gets up earlier and makes his own breakfast I feed the baby and have something to eat myself and clear up a bit. About 9.30, I sit down with a cup of coffee to read the paper. After that I might do some washing – I'd rather do a little each day than a large amount at once. I tidy the beds. The baby sleeps for about an hour from 11 till 12 – I'm afraid I read a book then – I don't do very much housework!

When she wakes up we sometimes go shopping – though not every day, by any means; sometimes we don't go at all and sometimes we leave it till the afternoon. We have lunch between one and two and usually I cook, though if I don't feel like it, I don't bother. Then I play with the baby and we might go out for a walk or go and see friends – that sort of thing. From about 3.30 she plays quite happily by herself and I return to my book again! I give her supper about half past five and then she goes to bed. I tidy and vacuum the sitting room after she's gone to bed – I don't see any point in doing it in the morning because it'll only get messed up again. I can't spend much more than ten minutes a day cleaning altogether!

In the evening I get supper and we've eaten and washed up by eight. After that, I knit or do some dressmaking and watch television.

[Would you say you have particular ways of doing things…?] Yes, I've got very low standards! You see, I think housework is a waste of time. I don't do it, or I do a minimum. I do things like making the beds.

[How do you decide which things to do?] Well, as long as it doesn't make me feel uneasy, I'm a fairly tidy sort of person, so I do make the bed, and sort of tidy up in the bedroom, and I tidy up in here, when she's gone to bed. But if I don't think 'Oh God, that's dirty!' well then, it's alright. But if I suddenly think 'That's a bit dirty,' then I do it.

These are 'low' standards compared with those of many other housewives in the sample, and the routine is there, but it is not anchored nearly so securely to set times of the day as Barbara Lipscombe's.

The 40 women were all assessed on this dimension of their approach to housework. There are three categories: a 'high', a 'medium' and a 'low' specification of standards and routines. 'Specification' here describes a process of rule-definition to which housewives, either implicitly or explicitly, refer when describing their standards and routines; the dictionary definition of 'specification' is 'detailed description'. Table 1 shows the spread of these assessments in the whole sample. Over half the sample have a 'high' specification; about a third fall in the 'medium' category; and the rest are 'low'. There are no social class differences.

The specification of standards and routines has four identifiable functions. First, it provides a means of unifying the collection of heterogeneous tasks that make up housework; dissimilar tasks are knitted together, and some kind of coherent job structure emerges. Second, it serves as proof that housework is *work*: the spelling out of the rules to be followed places housework in the same category as other work – there are things that simply *have* to be done. Third, rule-specification is a means of job enlargement, a process of elaborating housework tasks so they take up increasing amounts of time. And, lastly, the definition of rules for housework establishes a mechanism whereby the housewife can *reward herself* for doing it.

The housewife receives no wage for her work. The husband is one potentially

Table 1: Specification of standards and routines and social class

Social class	Specification of standards and routines			
	High Number (%)	Medium Number (%)	Low Number (%)	Total Number (%)
Working class	11 (55)	6 (30)	3 (15)	20 (100)
Middle class	10 (50)	8 (40)	2 (10)	20 (100)
Total	21 (53)	14 (35)	5 (13)	40 (100)

appreciative figure in the housewife's landscape, but none of the 40 women referred spontaneously to their husbands' comments as a source of personal reward for doing housework. Eight women said their husbands never passed opinions about how the housework had been done:

> I think I ought to keep the house clean, but I don't do it for my husband – because quite honestly he doesn't notice whether it's clean or not. He just takes it for granted that it always looks like this. (Retail chemist's wife)

Most of the housewives – 24 of the 40 – said that their husbands *only* commented negatively, never appreciatively:

> I think if you *haven't* done something, it's noticed. If you *have* done something, it's not noticed. That's always true, isn't it? I mind. I once said to him, 'If you can't pay compliments, don't insult'. I think they should do both.

Some reward may be obtained from neighbours' or friends' comments, and some from a comparison of one's own work achievements with those shown in the media. But, in the end, the housewife has to encourage and reward herself. The existence of this self-reward mechanism is demonstrated by the women's answers to a question about how they felt when they had got their work done as they liked it:

> I'm more satisfied in my mind when I know it's clean. Then I can sit down and psychologically I feel relaxed.

> Well, proud, I expect.

> Happy. Once it's all finished, I can sit back and I think, 'Oh that's lovely'.

Psychological reward is derived from simple adherence to standards and routines which, although originally emanating from the housewife as worker, take on an *objective* quality. Of course, women do not define these housework rules entirely in isolation from other influences. Media advertising has an effect and so does the prior socialisation of women for domesticity.

The paradox is that, although standards and routines are, in the first instance, subjectively defined, they become curiously externalised. The housewife refers to them as external obligations to which she feels a deep need to conform. A second paradox follows. This process of objectification effectively robs the housewife of her much-prized autonomy. She becomes bound by the constraints of pre-set work rhythms:

> The top of the cooker *mustn't* look dirty, whatever happens. So I clean it after every meal. (Policeman's wife)

> One thing that *must* be done is that my place *must* look respectable by 11 a.m. so that, if anybody does come in, it looks tidy. (Accountant's wife)

A further implication is that, although standards and routines provide a basis for self-reward in housework, they also make possible less happy outcomes. 'Guilty', 'worried', 'miserable' and 'depressed' are the words which women use to express their responses to a situation in which they do *not* get their work done 'as it should be done':

> If I've got a routine, I like to try and keep to it, otherwise I get very disorganised and upset. I feel very inadequate if I can't live up to the standards that I have and I start to feel guilty as well. (Cinema manager's wife)

> If the floor needs washing, okay, I won't wash it, but I know it needs washing and it'll go on nagging me until I've washed it – so you can't win really. (Lorry driver's wife)

What, then, is the relationship between the specification of standards and routines and work satisfaction? Table 2 suggests that work satisfaction is more likely when standards and routines are highly specified.

Yet fewer than half of the women with a high specification *are* satisfied with work. One explanation is that a high specification of standards and routines is *symptomatic of the search for satisfaction*.

A high specification of housework rules can be seen as a common response to a common problem – the problem being how to make sense of work that is

Table 2: Specification of standards and routines and work satisfaction

| Work satisfaction | Specification of standards and routines | | |
	High Number (%)	Medium/low Number (%)	Total Number (%)
Satisfied	9 (75)	3 (25)	12 (100)
Dissatisfied	12 (43)	16 (57)	28 (100)
Total	*21 (53)*	*19 (48)*	*40 (100)*

$x^2 = 3.22$; $df = 1$; $p < 0.10$

Table 3: Housework hours and specification of standards and routines

Specifications of standards and routines	Weekly housework hours		Total
	40-69 Number (%)	70 or more Number (%)	Number (%)
High	2 (10)	19 (91)	21 (100)
Medium	4 (29)	10 (71)	14 (100)
Low	4 (80)	1 (20)	5 (100)
Total	10 (25)	30 (75)	40 (100)

$x^2 = 10.84$; df = 2; $p<0.01$

intrinsically unsatisfying under conditions where less and less of it *need* be done (through automation, 'convenience' foods, better housing conditions, etc), but where the structural pressures which assign women to the home remain as strong as ever.

One consequence of 'job enlargement' in the housewife's case is an increase in working hours. There is an association between the kind of standards and routines followed in housework and the amount of time spent doing it. The relationship between standards and routines and working hours in the sample as a whole is shown in Table 3. The principle that 'housewifery expands to fill the time available' was discovered by Betty Friedan (1963) in her tour of American suburbia in the 1950s. The trend towards rising standards provides an explanation of why housework hours have shown no notable decrease in recent years; pre-prepared foodstuffs, household machines and equipment, and cleaner more comfortable homes do not necessarily reduce the housewife's workload. Betty Friedan (1963, p 241) cites an apt illustration of this:

> The automatic clothes dryer does not save a woman the four or five hours a week she used to spend at the clothes line, if, for instance, she runs her washing machine and dryer every day ... As a young mother said, 'Clean sheets twice a week are now possible. Last week, when my dryer broke down, the sheets didn't get changed for eight days. Everyone complained. We all felt dirty. I felt guilty. Isn't that silly?'.

Silly it may be, but it is only by considering the way women define their job as housewives that the housewife's long working hours can be understood. This is one reason why standards and routines represent an important dimension of housework behaviour. The unique quality of housework as a job is precisely this dimension of self-definition. It explains why housework is apparently so different from, and yet is experienced by women as so similar to, other jobs. A lack of structure is intrinsic to housework; thus a psychological structure is imported to it. Women enter into a form of covert contract with themselves to be their own bosses, judges and reward-givers. Gaining coherence and self-reward in their work, autonomy is relinquished and creativity constrained.

Marriage and the division of labour

Legal definitions current in our culture tie the status of 'wife' to the role of unpaid domestic worker. The husband is legally entitled to unpaid domestic service from his wife, and this is a right that courts of law uphold. This cheerless picture of inequality is contradicted by a number of studies of marriage. Ronald Fletcher's *The family and marriage* (1966), *Husbands and wives* by Robert Blood and Donald Wolfe (1960), and Michael Young and Peter Wilmott's *The symmetrical family* (1973) are three works in this genre. In general, these books stress the *equality* of husband and wife in marriage today, compared with the situation in the 19th century. In the areas of housework and childcare, the consensus of opinion is that husbands now participate much more than they used to:

Housewife, March 1950, p 169

> the old pattern of male-dominated, female-serviced family life is ... being replaced by a new and more symmetrical pattern ... our domestic ideology is quietly modified and a bloodless revolution occurs, unnoticed, in millions of homes.... (Benson, 1960, pp 302, 310)

The vision is dramatic. Certainly the logic of the argument is on the side of the vision; it seems that one consequence of women's equality *should* be men's increasing domesticity. The only way to gauge the truth of these claims is to look at the facts. This chapter examines data on marriage obtained from the 40 women interviewed. It also looks at the values about men's and women's domestic roles which underlie sociological research on family life. Social science – at least in its popularised version – has played a large part in spreading the view that modern marriage is an egalitarian relationship. If this conclusion is based on false premises, then the weakness in the argument must be exposed.

Behaviour

The division of labour in the home

Interviews were conducted only with the housewives and not with their husbands, so that information on the husband's role comes from the women. It might be objected that women cannot be relied on to report their husband's domestic role accurately; dissatisfied wives might, for example, underestimate the extent to which their husbands help in the home. A careful study of this problem by Michael Rutter and George Brown (1966) concludes that the tendency for such bias to occur is insignificant, provided that the questions asked are aimed at the actual performance of specific tasks over a particular time period.

Husbands were assessed as 'high', 'medium' or 'low' on their participation in both housework and childcare. The criterion used was how much of a share the husband took in the total amount of domestic work and childcare done. Like the other ratings used in the research, these are *relative* assessments – a husband who has a 'high' level of participation simply does more domestic work/childcare than the men assessed as 'medium' among the husbands of the 40 women. The figures resulting from the assessments are shown in Tables 1 and 2.

Three main conclusions can be drawn from these tables:

- Only a minority of husbands give the kind of help that assertions of equality in modern marriage imply. Fifteen per cent have a high level of participation in housework and 25% in childcare.
- Patterns of husbands' participation are class-differentiated.
- There is a greater tendency for men to take part in childcare than in housework.

Table 1: Husband's participation in housework and social class

| Social class | Husband's participation in housework | | | |
	High Number (%)	Medium Number (%)	Low Number (%)	Total Number (%)
Working class	2 (10)	1 (5)	17 (85)	20 (100)
Middle class	4 (20)	9 (45)	7 (35)	20 (100)
Total	6 (15)	10 (25)	24 (60)	40 (100)

$x^2 = 11.233$; df = 2; $p<0.01$

Table 2: Husband's participation in childcare and social class

| Social class | Husband's participation in childcare | | | |
	High Number (%)	Medium Number (%)	Low Number (%)	Total Number (%)
Working class	2 (10)	8 (40)	10 (50)	20 (100)
Middle class	8 (40)	4 (20)	8 (40)	20 (100)
Total	10 (25)	12 (30)	18 (45)	40 (100)

$x^2 = 5.155$; df = 2; $p<0.10$

Jeremy Abbatt is one of the minority whose participation in housework and childcare is described by his wife as substantial (classed in the tables as 'high'). He has recently started his own business selling pre-packaged foods; his wife used to be an audio typist before she had a baby. She says:

Strange black ring © Jackie Fleming

I help with his work – typing, adding up, that sort of thing, and he helps me with mine. He's a good cook and he thinks nothing of coming in at the end of the day and cooking a meal. He cooked three meals last week. Or, if I was hoovering one room when he came in, he'd help me do the other one. He regularly cleans the windows, empties the rubbish and dries up the dishes. He helps me to get the housework done, because he likes us to sit down together in the evenings. He presses his own suits and trousers as well.

We look after the baby together when he's home. He bathes him in the evening. I dress him, and he gives him his bottle and puts him down.

[Does he ever change a dirty nappy?] He doesn't mind dirty nappies – he's never objected. At the weekend, he always gets him up in the morning so I can have a lie in.

By comparison, the picture painted by Eleanor Driscoll of *her* husband's behaviour is an inflexibly segregated one (his participation is assessed as 'low' in both domestic areas). She says he never does any housework, shopping or cooking. She adds:

He used to be a head chef and at one time he used to cook the dinner on Saturday. But he's a sod like his father and he doesn't like women to dominate him. He says 'I'm a working man, I come home from work, and I'm tired'.

Meals have to be ready at set times in the Driscoll household and the kettle has to be on the point of boiling when Larry Driscoll comes home at 6.20 every evening. Of Larry Driscoll's relationship with the children – two of his from a previous marriage aged 12 and 14, and two younger ones of two and three years – Eleanor says:

He won't look after his children. He loves children – he thinks the world of them ... but he won't look after them.... I wanted to go to a funeral the other day, and he wouldn't let me. 'I'm not looking after the children' he said. He never takes them out, he's never changed a nappy. He plays with them, but it depends on what mood he's in. Not when he comes home from work. I say he's good with children. He does think the world of them.

The last comment contrasts with Eleanor Driscoll's earlier complaints, suggesting an image of a 'good' father who plays with children, while taking very little routine responsibility for childcare.

Larry Driscoll's behaviour in the domestic area follows what is seemingly a recognised working-class tradition. Half the working-class husbands are low on their participation in both housework *and* childcare. The social class difference is greater in the case of housework than childcare, indicating a generalised preference for involvement with children as against the alternative of more washing up, shopping, cooking, washing or cleaning. A man's performance of housework tasks cannot be predicted from his record in childcare, and vice versa.

The figures given in Tables 1 and 2 show an overall level of masculine domesticity which is generally lower than that found by other researchers. One reason for this might be the type of interview question used. Hannah Gavron, in *The captive wife*, concludes on the basis of information obtained from 96 London housewives that 21% of the middle-class and 44% of the working-class couples "simply shared the housework between them" (1966, p 93). Gavron asked only one direct question on this topic: 'Does your husband help with the housework? (a) If yes, *would* he do: (1) cleaning, (2) washing, (3) ironing, (4) washing up, (5) shopping; (b) if no, why not?'. This is not a question about what husbands *actually* do, but about what they might be *prepared* to do.

Beliefs and attitudes

In this section, I discuss the beliefs about male and female roles held by the women in my sample and by sociological researchers who have studied the division of labour in the home.

Housewives

Two questions in the study of housework threw particular light on the function of gender role norms as organisers of marriage behaviour. The first question – 'Does (or did) your husband change the baby's dirty nappy?' – was planned as a question which would hopefully 'get at' the boundaries of the father's role in childcare. Here are three typical replies:

> No! He absolutely refuses. He says 'No thank you, goodbye, I'm going out!'. If I'm changing a nappy, he runs out of the room, it makes him sick. He thinks it's my duty. (Retail chemist's wife)

> He might do it under protest, but I think he tends to think that's not what he *should* do. (Radio producer's wife)

> You're joking! He says 'I'm not doing that – it's a woman's job'. (Shop manager's wife)

As Table 3 shows, slightly more middle-class than working-class men are prepared to change a dirty nappy.

Taken together with the responses given to other questions about the father's role, these answers build up a picture of the 'good' father. The physical side of child-rearing is the mother's responsibility. Fathers are there to play with children. This distinction between the hard/unpleasant work aspect of child-rearing and the 'pleasant' side is made explicitly by a policemen's wife:

> [Does your husband change the baby's dirty nappy?] I've asked him a couple of times when I've been busy and he's done it, but he's not too keen…. He likes to play with him – *he doesn't like any of the work involved.*

One husband refuses to change his baby's nappies because she is a girl. Another refuses because the child is a boy ('He's frightened of damaging something,' said his wife.) Fear is also cited as a reason for not bathing or feeding a baby, and for not holding her or him longer than a few minutes. Pram-pushing is another delicate subject:

> I wouldn't let him take the baby out – I don't mind when they turn two or three. I wouldn't like to ask him to push a pram – he wouldn't push a pram, oh God no! (Painter and decorator's wife)

A second question women were asked on the subject of gender role beliefs concerned a reversed roles marriage: 'What would you think of a marriage in which the wife went out to work and the husband stayed at home to look after the children?'. The answers to this show the existence of a firm belief in the 'natural' domesticity of women, and a corresponding belief that domesticity in men is 'unnatural'. Of the 40 women, 30 rejected the possibility of a reversed roles marriage for its transgression of gender role norms. (The remaining ten said

Table 3: Answers to question 'Does (did) your husband change the baby's dirty nappy?', by social class

| Social class | Answer to question | | Total |
	No/occasionally/ under protest Number (%)	Yes Number (%)	Number (%)
Working class	17 (85)	3 (15)	20 (100)
Middle class	13 (65)	7 (35)	20 (100)
Total	30 (75)	10 (25)	40 (100)

$x^2 = 2.133$; df = 1; $p < 0.20$

it depended on the couple as to whether or not such a marriage was appropriate; none of the women directly approved of this arrangement.) The replies given by Olive Brennan, a factory hand's wife, and Vera Rundle, a journalist's wife, are typical:

> [Reversed roles marriage?] Oh, that's ridiculous – it's up to the woman to look after the kids and do the housework. It wouldn't be my idea of a man. I think a man should go out to work and a woman should look after the house.

> I don't agree with men doing housework – I don't think it's a man's job – I certainly wouldn't like to see my husband cleaning a room up. I don't think it's mannish for a man to stay at home. I like a man to be a man.

Against the image of the real man is that of the real wife, described by Eleanor Driscoll in this commentary on her husband's previous marriage:

> His first wife was a *typical* wife – she was a *real* wife – she'd have his slippers there, she'd have a cup of tea in his hand. I get very annoyed at times to think why the hell should I have to compete with her? He doesn't say, she was this, she was that, but she was such a *typical good wife*. He often expects me to…. I mean, I think blinking heck, we're not under Hitler's reign.

> He's like his father. His mother wiped his father's backside practically – she'd walk miles to bring his drink home, take his shoes off. No one would eat till he came home.

A real wife is 'typical' and 'good'. She is the subservient female, dedicated to the satisfaction of her husband's needs.

But the belief in feminine domesticity is ultimately reduced to beliefs about motherhood. The mother-child relationship is a 'natural' unit. Women have a maternal instinct and are hence closer to children than men ever could be: children need their mothers more than their fathers:

> The only thing is, I think women are better at bringing up children than men. [Why?] I think it's an instinctive thing really, due to the fact that they've given birth to the child and they're more anxious and worried about it; therefore they're more likely to spot if there's anything wrong….

> There's an advertisement in our local newsagent that says 'student doctor available for babysitting'. Well, I suppose the fact that he's a doctor would be an advantage, but the fact that he's a man would mean I would never employ him because I don't think a man is quite as aware of what a

child means as a women, and I think it's a physical thing – it's not anything you could learn, or only a few men could learn. (Joanna Giles)

When women go out to work, men may help more; this is confirmed by various British and American studies of marriage and women's employment patterns. Lois Hoffman, an American specialist on women's employment and its effect on the family, reports that the tendency for men to help more when wives work outside the home holds true whether or not the couple profess egalitarian views about marriage (Hoffman, 1963). Women in the present sample of 40 back up this conclusion that increased male domesticity is a response to the fact of female employment:

> He was very good when I was working. He did an equal share. I said 'You're going to do this and this and this' and he said 'Alright'. (Toolmaker's wife)

> He just doesn't want to help in the house, and he doesn't enjoy doing it. He feels I'm at home all day and so I should do it, and I do feel he's right. If I was working, that would be different – he did help a bit more then. (Journalist's wife)

A striking aspect of these interviews was that none of the women questioned the assignment to women of the primary duty to look after home and children. This was reflected in the language they used. Housework is talked about as 'my work' ('I can't sit down till I've finished *my* work'); the interior décor of the home is spoken of as the housewife's own ('I clean *my* bedroom on a Monday'; 'I wash *my* basin every day'). The home is the woman's domain. When these housewives discuss their husband's performance of domestic tasks, they always use the word 'help': 'He *helps* me with the washing up in the evening'; 'On Sunday he *helps* me put the children to bed'. Husbands are housewives' aids. The *responsibility* for seeing that the tasks are completed rests with the housewife.

This question of responsibility is a critical one. As long as the blame is laid on the woman's head for an empty larder or a dirty house, it is not meaningful to talk about marriage as a 'joint' or 'equal' partnership. The same holds of parenthood. So long as mothers, not fathers, are judged by their children's appearances and behaviour (and, in dual career families, it is the mother's responsibility to find substitute childcare), symmetry remains a myth.

Sociologists

Turning to sociological researchers' own values about the domestic roles of men and women, it is immediately clear that the unequal responsibility factor is concealed or ignored in much existing research. For example, when Jennifer Platt discusses the criteria used in the 'affluent worker' study to distinguish between 'joint' and 'not-joint' marital activities, she says her procedure was to:

> regard all cases where an activity was done by both husband and wife
> together, or by either equally, as joint; and to regard all cases as joint
> where the husband did what would conventionally be regarded as
> woman's work (eg washing up, putting the children to bed). (Platt, 1969,
> p 288)

In classifying as joint all cases in which the husband does 'woman's work', Platt is effectively saying segregation/jointness measures only one kind of sharing or non-sharing – the extent to which couples adhere to, or deviate from, traditional distinctions between male and female roles. The same criticism applies to the assessment of segregation/jointness in other areas. For instance, a wife's ability to drive the marital car is taken by Platt as a sign of 'jointness' (whereas, of course, the significance of the husband's ability to drive the car merits no comment at all).

The only questions about household tasks used in Platt's survey were 'Who washes up?', 'Who does the main shopping?', 'Who takes the children out?' and 'Who puts the children to bed?' These are highly selective questions, leaving out, as they do, cleaning, daily shopping, washing, ironing, cooking and the routine care of children. A number of studies (including the present one) make it clear that of *all* domestic tasks, putting children to bed, taking children out, washing up, and doing the main shopping are the ones most likely to be engaged in by men.

In another study of marriage, Toomey (1971) obtained data from a sample of Kent couples. Toomey's method of assessing the relative roles of husband and wife in the division of labour was to ask the women questions about whether they ever did what counted traditionally as 'men's' tasks' ("painting inside the house, wall papering, lighter work in the garden"). The men's questions concerned 'women's work' ("cleaning the house, washing up, laundry, cooking, ironing, looking after the children"). Toomey's classification of answers is even more heavily biased by an idea about 'proper' gender role behaviour than is his choice of questions. Thus he counts as joint a wife's response to the effect that she 'very often' or 'often' papers the walls. For the husband's responses about women's tasks:

> The following replies were classed as 'joint': 'Very often' or 'often' for
> cleaning the house and washing up, 'very often' 'often' or 'sometimes'
> for ironing and cooking, 'very often', 'often', 'sometimes' or 'rarely' for
> doing the laundry and 'very often' for looking after children. (Toomey,
> 1971, p 419)

A husband who rarely looks after the children is not making a joint response. But a husband who rarely does the laundry *is* doing so. It is difficult not to conclude from this that it is Toomey's opinion that men ought to look after their children, whereas they ought not to do the laundry. This evaluative approach, as in other studies, extends beyond the domestic work sphere. Husband and wife were asked if the wife knew the husband's weekly earnings (an affirmative reply being classed as a joint response); the couple were not asked if the husband knew the wife's earnings.

In such studies as these, an assumption of gender role differences appears as a kind of baseline from which questions are asked and assessments made. The use of such a baseline is an obvious source of bias in the collection of data and the analysis of research findings. However, none of these researchers attempts to generalise their conclusions into broad assertions of egalitarianism in modern marriage. In *The symmetrical family,* Michael Young and Peter Willmott do precisely this.

Young and Willmott (1973, p 94) say of the men in their London sample:

> Husbands also do a lot of work in the home, including many jobs which are not at all traditional men's ones.... There is now no sort of work in the home strictly reserved for 'the wives', even clothes-washing and bed-making, still ordinarily thought of as women's jobs, were frequently mentioned by husbands as things they did as well.

On what information is the statement about men's domesticity based? The 113-question interview schedule contains *one* question on the division of labour. This was: 'Do you/does your husband help at least once a week with any household jobs like washing up, making beds (helping with the children), ironing, cooking or cleaning?' (Young and Willmott, 1973, p 331). Answers were coded as follows: None = 0, washing up = 1, making beds = 2, help with children = 3, ironing = 4, cooking = 5, cleaning = 6. The code appears to be partly based on the researchers' view of what is socially acceptable: washing up, being acceptable, gets a low code; cleaning, being more unusual, a high one. Of the men in the sample, 15% do no domestic work at all; a further 13% only do washing up, while 72% do vaguely and euphemistically termed 'other tasks' (Young and Willmott, 1973, p 95). This sounds impressive until one considers how it was arrived at. A man who helps with the children once a week would be included in this percentage; so would a husband who ironed his own trousers on Saturday afternoon. The degree of task-sharing shown by the answers to even this one poorly worded question hardly holds up a convincing image of male domestication.

Such, then, is the message of this chapter. In only a small number of marriages is the husband notably domesticated and, even where this happens, a fundamental separation remains: home and children are the woman's primary responsibility. Doubt is cast on the view that marriage is an egalitarian relationship. The important question is: what is meant by equality? Psychological intimacy between husband and wife, an intermingling of their social worlds, and a more equitable distribution of power in marriage, are undoubtedly areas in which marriage in general has changed. But the importance of women's enduring role as housewives and as the main rearers of children continues. Inequality in this area is often overlooked, and sociologists surveying family life are no exception to the general rule. They bring to their data their own values about the place of men and women in the home, values which repeat the popular theme of gender differences.

Helping with baby

Feelings about fatherhood

Our society defines fatherhood principally in economic terms. The only time that is available for fathers and children to be together is time left over from the job. One consequence of this is that a third of the sample fathers saw their five-month-old babies for an hour or less a day.

In many cases, it has become more acceptable for a husband to 'help' his wife; provided he doesn't help too much, it is regarded as probable that his masculinity will survive. 'Helping with baby' has become one index of a man's involvement with his children. The sample women were asked how much their husbands did for the baby at five weeks and five months, and what they (the mothers) felt about this[1].

Sophy Fisher, television producer, and Matthew Fisher, designer
Tiffany, aged five weeks

Sophy: I don't think Matthew knows quite what to make of having her. She's less real to him than she is to me. I think he's slightly less involved than I thought he would be.

Interviewer (I): Does he change nappies?

Sophy: He's *watched* me change her nappy, but I haven't forced it. You see it's usually part of the feeding process [*Tiffany is breastfed*] so I mean I just do it. And I think he feels a bit unsure about *dressing* her, so he doesn't do that. Really the only thing he does is wind her; he's terribly good at winding her when she's got bad wind.

I: Does he get up in the night to her?

Sophy: I take her into the bathroom to feed her in there. He slightly resents being woken in the night. I did try taking her into bed and feeding her one night but he got very upset about that and said he had to live a normal life even if I could sit around all day and other such-like unjust things!

When Tiffany is five months old

He gets more and more interested in her, but he is still on a fairly peripheral level with her. I mean he *plays* with her a lot and I think that's very important, but he

---

[1] The sample in this chapter differs from that referred to in the previous chapters, taken from *The sociology of housework* (first published 1974). This extract comes from *Becoming a mother* (first published 1979).

doesn't *do* anything practical for her – that's not to say he *won't* but he *doesn't*, and I have the responsibility for feeding her and looking after her. And if he wanted to do more of that, I wouldn't mind sharing it with him.

I: Does he change nappies?

Sophy: He has done. I've gone to have my hair cut and if she's needed a nappy change he's done it. But it's probably not been half dozen times.

I: What about bathing?

Sophy: He's never bathed her. I've shown him how to and said he ought to because it's such fun, but he never actually has. I think he's a little bit frightened, but he wouldn't admit it.

I: And feeding?

Sophy: I've said do you want to give her her supper a couple of times but he's said no, you do it. [To Tiffany] We'll have to get him to, won't we darling?

I: Why doesn't he want to do these things?

Sophy: I don't even know that it's really that he doesn't. I suppose it must be that he doesn't want to, or he probably would. I don't think he's particularly interested; I think he gets the pleasure from her from the playing times. He thinks I'm quite happy to look after her – as I am. He's got more involved with her personality-wise; he finds her much more interesting now; she responds to him, plays games and so on. I don't know; it doesn't worry me at the moment.

Maureen Paterson, ex-library assistant, and Henry Paterson, shop manager
Thomas, aged six weeks

Maureen: He's very good: he's *marvellous* with him. First of all he was a bit frightened to hold him; he kept saying, am I doing it right? Am I doing this right? But he's really good with him.

I: Does he feed him?

Maureen: He gives him a bottle. Only a couple of times he's done it. He usually does something else while I feed him. But he gets up, if I have to get up early in the morning, he'll get up with me. He gets up and he makes a cup of coffee. He's very good. He mixes all his feeds up, he mixes them all up for the day for me and puts them in the fridge.

I: Does he change nappies?

Maureen: Yes, he has done that. Only a couple of times. But he knows *how* to do it,

I: Does he bath Thomas?

Maureen: No. He's *helped* me sort of thing.

When Thomas is five months old

Maureen: He thinks the world of him. He's proud of him and that.

I: Does he feed him?

Maureen: Not very often, no. Not that he doesn't *want* to, it's just usually that I do it. But he will. He still mixes his milk, he always has done. And he changes the steriliser.

I: So how often does he feed him – once a week?

Maureen: Not that often. Normally I'll feed him and Henry'll probably get on, if it's tea time he'll get on with the tea while I see to him.

I: Do you prefer to feed him?

Maureen: It wouldn't worry me. I think it worries him a little bit still, I mean he'd *do* it but I think he gets a bit panicky. And now especially you have to hold him down because he wants to put his hand in the dish.

I: What about nappies?

Maureen: Oh yes, he'll do that. Sometimes if I'm doing something, he'll start him off.

I: And washing his clothes?

Maureen: Sometimes, if I've boiled the nappies, he'll rinse them out for me. He doesn't *wash* anything, you know. The hand washing, I wouldn't like to see him standing there doing that anyway.

I: What do you feel about the amount he does for the baby?

Maureen: Oh he's good. Sometimes I think he does *too* much … I don't know how some girls manage really if their husbands don't help them.

In the two tables below, some figures are shown that give an idea of fathers' participation and mothers' satisfaction with this.

Fathers' help with babies[a]		Satisfaction with fathers' help	
A lot	11%	Satisfied	54%
Some	24%	Dissatisfied	46%
A little/none	65%		

Note: [a] As described by their wives five months after the birth.

The most favoured paternal task, as Sophy Fisher's account makes clear, is playing with the baby. The least favoured task is changing a dirty nappy.

Dirty nappy stories

I: So has he ever changed a dirty nappy?

Catherine Andrews: No. He'd never changed a nappy for quite a while and I said it's about time you did, just to show that you can. He said, of course I can do it. I said, show me. So he proceeds to undress her, to the nappy, undid the pins and everything else, then he said oh it's dirty. I said well go on then. He said um ah well, do I *have* to? So I did it....

Michelle Craig: I mean we went swimming a long time ago, about two months ago. We was only out two hours and I told him where everything was and when I come back I said I bet you haven't changed his bum? He said well no I haven't changed his bum, I don't want to change his bum. He changes nappies unless they're messy ones, and then he won't, I'll have to do it.

Jane Tarrant: He does moan about it sometimes if it's dirty. On Easter Sunday, he took him upstairs and it was dirty and he called me up to see what he should do about it.

Unlike most other couples, Jo Ingram and Steve are trying to share the work of bringing up the baby, who at three weeks is breastfed.

Steve: All I ever do is wash and change him.

I: So do you do about half?

Steve: No I think I probably do less than half.

Jo: Right, right.

Steve: I get all the shit work.

Jo: That's the sad thing. He was changing nappies in the hospital, which made them quite cross.

Steve: Especially when I stood at the end of the ward and shouted. where do you put the shitty nappies then?

Jo: At night, Steve gets up and changes him so all I've got to do is just feed him. It really is helpful actually to have this baby handed to you. That's one of the biological myths, isn't it? It's very much a biological myth that's thrown at you isn't it, that if you breastfeed a baby you've got to do housework; all the nappy-changing and everything. You want someone who can perform the services of a lover *and* a nanny.

Steve: I went to a benefit the other day and there was a play on and, in the middle of it, I had to go and change him, which meant I had to go down to the men's toilets. I started getting things out, and he'd really shitted and it was all at the back of his clothes as well. There wasn't an incinerator there or anything. So what I did was I took his pad off first and threw that into the toilet – the urinal part, not the other toilet; then I had to clean him up with these little cotton buds, and I started throwing them in all the sinks. And there was shit and everything all over the place. And I thought well fuck them, that'll show them!

A typical man

There are few facilities for changing babies in men's toilets because men are not supposed to change babies. In part, the issue is one of public versus private behaviour: what a man does in the privacy of his own home does not have to live up to the same standards of masculinity as what he does outside it.

Anne Bloomfield: We had an argument last week, a really bad argument, and I stormed out. And I came back about an hour and a half later and she was screaming for food and I didn't have any clean nappies and I didn't have any disposables. I was going to buy them but I forgot, and he was just going to buy some with her and he was going to push the pram then. But he doesn't when I'm with him. He wouldn't do that because of his friends. I don't expect

'Mammy, what's a daddy for?' © Spellbound Postcards

him to. I mean, you know, when he's in here and no one can see him, he's lovely with her, but when he's out, he's a typical man.

Rachel Sharpe: The only thing I don't like is the fact that he won't walk down the street with a pram. I mean he won't walk with me when I'm pushing it. When he saw the pushchair, he said that's very nice. I don't know if it'll make any difference. He just says he hates prams. He just doesn't like to walk down the street with one. When we were at his parents at Christmas time, his mother had a big pram she'd got from someone, and we were going into town one day. They live about a mile out of town and there were three of us going, the two of us and his sister. He said you go ahead with Mary and I'll come later. It was just because he didn't want to walk with the pram.

Tanya Kemp: Since we've got the buggy, he'll push that, whereas he wouldn't push the pram.

This liberated response to the buggy on the part of fathers was reported by many mothers – a real case of technology bringing about social change?

Housework in history and culture

Calculations of the importance of housework in relation to other industries set the figure at more than a third of the GNP: 39% in Britain, 35% in the USA (Wickham and Young, 1973). These figures are based on time-budget studies of housework and calculate the total market value of the housewife's services in her various capacities as cleaner, cook, laundress, nursemaid, etc. However, the exercise of adding up the hourly rates for these jobs to see what housework is 'worth' is an academic one only. For the first characteristic of women's work as housewives is that it is not paid. All over the world in the late 1960s and early 1970s, feminists rediscovered what earlier feminists knew: that the question of women's equality with men cannot be restricted to the world of paid employment and public power, but resides firstly in their domestic relationships.

What is housework?

An all-consuming function of production

According to J.K. Galbraith, housework exists to service the consumption function of the economy. The rising standards of consumption made possible by advanced capitalism are only attractive economic goals, if they do not mean the loss of labour power. A gourmet meal is enjoyable when not preceded by long hours in the kitchen; a well-furnished house soothes the eye as long as its maintenance has not already worn one out. It is the conversion of women into a 'crypto-servant class' that renders consumption pleasurable to the dominant economic group. 'True' servants are available to only a minority of the population, but

> … the servant–wife is available, democratically, to almost the entire present male population… If it were not for this service [of women as housewives] all forms of household consumption would be limited by the time required to manage such consumption – to select, transport, prepare, repair, maintain, clean, service, store, protect, and otherwise perform the tasks that are associated with the consumption of goods. The servant role of women is critical to the expansion of consumption in the modern economy. (Galbraith, 1974, p 33)

Before the establishment of industrial capitalism, housework had the character of manufacture rather than service. In the southern colonies of America in the 17th century, for example, the housewife's duties included the gathering, drying and distilling of herbs for curing the sick; the making of conserves, syrups, jellies, pickles and wines; and the construction of 'Oyles, Oynments and Powders to Adorn and add Loveliness to the Face and Body' (Spruill, 1972, p 210). The

18th-century Purefoy family of Shalstone Manor in Buckinghamshire in England recorded their domestic organisation in a series of letters (Purefoy, 1931; quoted in Davis, 1966). Mrs Purefoy and her adult son Henry produced the basic food consumed by themselves and their six servants at home. They had several cows, sheep, asses, goats, pigs, poultry, a dovecote and three well-stocked fishponds. They brewed their own ale and made their own bread. Clothes and household extras – tea, fancy spices and herbs, sugar, coffee-berries – had to be purchased, either in London or in the local shops, usually by letter. More of these commodities were bought than a generation before as rising living standards allowed them to be redefined as necessities, instead of luxuries.

Most British and American homes before and during industrialisation were not places where much housework – in the modern sense of cleaning, dusting, tidying and polishing – could be done. Rooms did not have individual uses and were plainly and sparsely furnished as places of work – in the undifferentiated sense of production for use and for exchange:

> The labor needs of the household defined the work roles of men, women and children. Their work, in turn, fed the family. The interdependence of work and residence, of household labor needs, subsistence requirements, and family relationships constituted the 'family economy'. (Tilly and Scott, 1978, p 12)

The architecture and furnishing of homes reflected this: beds and spinning wheels or other tools of the family's trade shared rooms; cooking, eating, 'working' and relaxing were activities all housed in the same place. The idea of the kitchen as a special room, where women prepared food, started to emerge among the upper class in the late 16th century but was not a general feature of working-class homes until the early 20th century (Chapman, 1955; Henderson, 1964). Margaret Plant (1952) describes the typical 18th-century rural home in Scotland as follows:

> There was normally one main living-room where the family had their meals, slept, did their work and chatted with the neighbours who dropped in for the evening. Its social centre was the common fireplace, which … was large and open and surrounded, beneath the great wide chimney, with seats for family and guests…. Roughly hewn boughs formed a not unattractive ceiling, and the space between them and the roof proper was floored with brushwood covered with dried moss or grass. The resulting attic made a useful storeroom; or, if the main living-room would hold no more beds, an extra bedroom, the entrance to it being by way of a ladder and a trap-door.

> Behind the living room was the 'spence', or parlour, where the housewife put the best furniture and kept the Sunday clothes, and, on great occasions, received company. A passage known as the 'through-gang' joined the living-room to the cow-house and stable (a rather doubtful advantage). (pp 24-5)

'Carpet' meant a tablecloth and what went on the floor was turf. People tended to eat out of the same wooden dish and share a single glass, and those attending meals elsewhere were well-advised to take their own knife and fork; it was the custom for the diner to wipe and reuse utensils between courses.

Housekeeping is also a simple activity in pre-literate societies where women's (and men's) energies are concentrated on the production of food. The African Nyakyusa, considered among the most well-to-do of all 'primitive' cultures, live in permanent well-built houses, but these are still one-room dwellings made of traditional wattle and daub (Hammond and Jablow, 1976). There is little in the way of household furniture in such cultures, few pots and pans, and no complicated recipes to absorb a cook's time.

As the level of material possessions rises and definitions of women and work change, a radical transformation is brought about in women's relationship to their work. Production for family use is converted into consumption for family use. Commodities become available on the market that require little of the housewife even in the way of preparation. At the same time, more energy and hours are needed in home-maintenance activities – dusting, polishing, carpet-shampooing, curtain-washing and so forth. These may be, in Galbraith's terminology, "the crypto-servant functions of consumption administration", but such language hides the chief significance of the housewife's invisible and unpaid work from the viewpoint of the maintenance of the economy. The housewife's work remains productive, for what she produces is workers for industry: her husband with his clean clothes, well-filled stomach and mind freed from the need to provide daily care for his children; the children fed, clothed, loved and chastised ready for their own adult gender-specific roles as workers or worker-producers.

In the early years of the women's liberation movement, when feminists began to grapple with the theoretical problem of how women's subordination might be explained, it was the situation of women as unpaid workers in the home that came to be seen as the central enigma. Margaret Benston (1969), in one of the first analyses, stated that housework

> is pre-capitalist in a very real sense. This assignment of household work as the function of a special category 'women' means that this group *does* stand in a very different relation to production than the group 'men'.... The material basis for the inferior status of women is to be found in just this definition of women. In a society in which money determines value, women are a group who work outside the money economy. Their work is not worth money, is therefore valueless, is therefore not even real work. And women themselves, who do this valueless work, can hardly be expected to be worth as much as men who work for money. In structural terms, the closest thing to the condition of women is the condition of others who are or were also outside of commodity production, i.e. serfs and peasants. (pp 15-16)

The disadvantage of this argument is that it allows housework to be seen as some kind of incongruous historical relic; its advantage is that it shifts women's labour from a marginal to a central economic position: it thus "completely changed the terms on which a discussion of women's work had to be carried on" (Malos, 1977, p 7).

Since Benston wrote, a great deal of discussion both in and outside the women's movement has been devoted to the thorny question of the exact meaning of the term 'productive labour' as applied to the housewife's work. The central point in the Marxist domestic labour debate is "that the housewife works for the maintenance of capitalism rather than simply being a worker for her family" (Glazer-Malbin, 1976, p 919). Industrial capitalism as an economic system requires *somebody* to buy the food, cook the meals, wash the clothes, clean the home, and bear and bring up the children. Without this back-up of domestic labour, the economy could not function – or, at least, enormous and profit-handicapping resources would have to be devoted to catering for these personal and reproductive needs.

It is part of the conventional wisdom of family life that, just as 'the' family has historically lost its function (of production to industry, of reproduction to the hospital, of child socialisation to the educational system), so women within families have lost their function to household technology – it is the washing machine, not the vote, that is the true liberator of women. However, it is nearer the truth to see mechanical household aids as rather like the Marxist model of women's emancipation: theoretically, both ought to free women from housework, but in practice neither does so.

The machines-liberate-housewives view ignores, as Cowan (1974) has pointed out, the possibility that the component activities of housework are merely profoundly transformed when they undergo mechanisation. Technological innovation always occurs in a social context. Leonore Davidoff (1976) has described how the hierarchical structure of the household (master versus mistress, mistress versus servant) acted against the 'rational' application of science and technology to household work from the very beginning:

> For example, it must have been known by experience that soaking very dirty pans in water overnight made it both much easier and much quicker to clean them, but it was the rule that every single pan had to be scoured and polished and put away before the servants were allowed to go to bed, no matter how late the hour, and young scullery maids could be hauled out of bed to scrub the pans if they had neglected this duty.

To assume that domestic technology liberates housewives is to ignore all that is known about the social impact of technology on work. Increasing division of labour and increasing routinisation are the almost inevitable products of general technological 'improvements' in the work process, and what *these* lead to for the worker is an intensified sense of powerlessness, not a feeling of freedom from the bondage of work.

One mechanism for the elaboration of housewifery is the advertising industry, which sells to housewives through the sexist messages of the media, not only X brand of carpet shampoo and Y brand of washing powder, but an immensely powerful imagery of virtuous womanhood. The image is constructed and propagated through the use of stereotypes: "A particular reality is presented as if it were the only reality. A particular idea of what life is like is presented as if it were the only, or at least the best, way of life" (Millum, 1975, pp 51-2). The most invidious message is that the hardworking housewife is at one and the same time the calm, satisfied, attractive woman; housework is a labour of love performed with scarcely a hair out of place and a permanently unruffled, cosmetically enriched grin. The message "this product takes the hard work out of housework" appeals to the very notion of femininity that got women into their present predicament: the idea that real femininity is incompatible with real work. At the same time, it most sympathetically acknowledges that housework *is* work, hoping to win the hearts of its female customers by taking their side in the sexual politics of marital domesticity: housework is the hardest work of all.

Who does the housework?

Definitionally speaking, a housewife is "the person wholly or mainly responsible for running the household" (Hunt, 1968, p 25): 85% of women aged 16-64 in this survey were classed as housewives.

Current European and American preconceptions about housework originated in the domestic hygiene movement that developed in the late 19th century. In America, Ellen Swallow Richards, a 'firm-jawed, heavy-browed, confident' ex-chemist, was an early populariser of the message of domestic science. This was a direct result of discrimination against women in her chosen profession: at the Massachusetts Institute of Technology, she had been forced to study apart from the male students and was commandeered by her professors to sort their papers and mend their suspenders. But not even suspender-mending could qualify her for a graduate degree or for a job in the male world of chemistry. What she did instead was to teach people "the science of right living": a mixture of chemistry, biology and engineering geared to the practical tasks of housekeeping. The idea was, as a colleague of Richards put it, that "Nature has assigned to her [woman] special duties which man has deemed safe to be trusted to her instincts, yet in reality need for their performance the highest scientific knowledge" (Cotten, 1897, p 280).

Biochemistry could reform cooking and economics would revolutionise shopping. But, behind it all, was the magnificent Germ Theory of Disease, whose foundations were laid when Pasteur discovered micro-organisms in 1857. Pasteur's discovery had the advantage that disease could be reclassified as, in principle, under man's control – or, more specifically, as controllable by means of the cleanliness and common sense of women. It had the disadvantage that germs, being invisible to the human eye, might be anywhere. By the 1890s, an epidemic of public anxiety about contagion was in full swing. When the typhoid epidemic of the 1870s nearly killed the Prince of Wales, wealthy householders began to confront their problems of indoor sanitation. In America, the case of 'Typhoid Mary' an Irish-American cook who communicated typhoid to 52 people in the homes of her employers, was seen to raise in an especially urgent form the question: who is responsible for the public health?

For various cogent reasons, the answer seemed obvious: women. In the first place, women were already defined by their domestic function – if not as housewives in the modern sense, then at least as the moral guardians of the home and as domestic servants. In the second place, the domestic science and sanitary reform movements were seen as relevant to an issue that was of direct biological concern to women: the question of infant mortality. Germs played a large part in the diarrhoeal diseases of infants responsible for a quarter of all infant deaths. (One in six babies died in their first year in 1899.) Diarrhoea was diagnosed as a 'filth disease' to be prevented only by 'scrupulous domestic cleanliness':

> infant mortality, it became clear, was a matter not so much of environmental hygiene, but of personal hygiene. It was more a social problem ... the mother was evidently the factor of paramount importance. (McCleary, 1933, p 35)

Mothers were taught not only how to feed babies artificially without giving them gastroenteritis, but also how to eliminate germs from their homes. The penalty of a dead baby for careless maternal housework provided an immensely powerful moral justification for the zealous housewife: bad housekeeping equals child abuse.

While the intrusion of 'science' into housekeeping was argued as a strategy for *reducing* housework, its overall effect was undoubtedly to *increase* it. Instead of mindless routine, housework became a quest for new knowledge, became white collar work (analysing, planning and consulting with the experts). The education of consumers eventually became their manipulation into the belief that good housewives had to employ a wide range of expensive products to achieve a clean home and a satisfied family. And the moral imputation that proper womanhood is a state of grace only gained when everyone's health and domestic comfort has been cared for, was, of course, presented in such a way as to be quite irresistible.

Yet a third reason why women were seen as guardians of the public health has to be dredged out of the buried subsoil of cultural attitudes. Pollution and purity rituals, such as housework, are attempts to impose cultural patterns on the natural world, and, in particular, to maintain boundaries between people, activities and places that are felt to be antithetical: the kitchen versus the dining room; poor people versus rich people; urination versus conversation. Because women can more easily be construed as natural creatures than men (only they have the body products of menstrual blood, babies and milk), their social position is more readily defined as marginal than that of men. As Douglas (1970) has shown, it is people at the margins of society – not only women, but little children, ethnic minorities, and lower castes and classes – who are felt to be most potentially dangerous and polluting. The paradoxical consequence of this is that they are required to act as the agents of other people's purity, in order to guarantee their own. Ideas of physical cleanliness as communicated by the 19th-century domestic economy movement in Britain and America are mixed with ideas about social and moral purity. A belief in the threatening contamination of femaleness struggled with an intransigent vision of women's inherent goodness to produce a situation in which women can never be just ordinary, but must be either angels or devils.

It is not, of course, the case that only women do housework. In many pre-literate societies, what we call 'housework' is turned over to small children or old people of both sexes who are not able to do other kinds of work. In colonial societies, as Davidoff (1976) points out, native men in preference to native women have provided most of the domestic labour for the foreign dominant group. Table 1 shows the division of domestic and childrearing tasks among the Tanulong and Fedizilan people of the Phillipines. Of the 29 tasks in Table 1, 12 are shared equally; 15 are shared, but less equally; and only cloth-weaving (feminine) and pig-killing (masculine) are one-sex activities.

Table 1: Domestic household tasks and their performers in Tanulong and Fedilizan

Task	Performer
Cooking	B
Washing dishes	B
Feeding animals	B
Skinning sweet potatoes	FM
Pounding rice	B
Keeping floors clean	FM
Gathering sweet potato leaves for pigs	FM
Waking up to cook in the morning	B
Splitting wood	MF
Cutting wood from the forest	MF
Preparing pig's food for cooking	B
Preparing cotton thread for weaving	FM
Weaving cloth	F
Washing clothes	FM
Sewing/mending clothes	FM
Washing dishes and pans	FM
Dressing and sacrificing chickens	B
Killing pigs	M
Distributing meat	MF
Cutting up meat for meals	MF
Fetching water	B
Babysitting	B
Keeping the child clean	FM
Feeding the child	B
Washing the child	FM
Cutting the child's hair	MF
Seeing the medium when child is sick	B
Taking care of sick child	FM
Counselling children	B

Note: B = tasks performed equally by females and males; F = tasks performed by females only; M = tasks performed by males only; FM = tasks performed usually by women; MF = tasks performed usually by men.

Source: Adapted from Bacdayan (1977, p 282)

In some cultures, men regularly do the cooking (Firth, 1965), or they may participate only on ritual occasions (Little, 1954). In others, who cooks what is determined by the division of labour in procuring food. Among the Tiwi of Northern Australia, foods are divided into men's and women's, with men hunting the products of the sea and air, and women those of the land (Goodale, 1971); for the Ilongots of the Phillipines, the division is between rice, which is provided, cooked and allocated by men (Rosaldo, 1974). Malinowski, discussing *The family among the Australian aborigines* (1963), noted that Kurnai men's work was confined to hunting opossums and making rugs and weapons, a strange combination from a Western point of view. Among the Tungus of Siberia, men who are too old to hunt share with women their work of caring for reindeer herds, dressing and preparing skins for clothing, and managing tents and their belongings (Forde, 1957). Men of the Mbum Kpau tribe in Africa fetch water and sweep the courtyards of houses, weave mats and baskets, and dress skins; but they will not pound grain, make beer or oil or render salt (O'Laughlin, 1974).

In Western societies, the psychological effect of housework combines with women's economic dependence to mould a certain opportunity structure. Housework remains an incredibly important limit on what women are able to do and become.

Part 3: Childbirth, motherhood and medicine

Beyond the presumptions of knowledge and value-neutrality that medical and social science project, lies unveiled a repertoire of patronizing moral precepts about women's nature; but the nature of women must also be described by women themselves.... Having a baby is essentially a kind of social transition, one source and cause of life change.... Tracing the connections between women's reactions to birth and their social circumstances in this way suggests a new interpretation of the manner in which women become either victors over or victims of their childbirth experiences. (*Women confined,* 1980)

Introduction

The bodies of women give birth to children, anchoring motherhood firmly in what we think of as nature; but both women and motherhood are subject to the complex formulations of culture. This makes the experiences of women bearing children a fascinating topic for academics to study: how do women experience childbirth and motherhood? How do biology and social representation interact? Why is culture, in the form of the medical profession and other 'experts', so apparently intent on defining what motherhood is and how childbirth must happen? Such questions are crucial to any project of feminist social science, and they have featured prominently in work over the last 30 years (see, for example, Leifer, 1980; Roberts, 1981b; Rothman, 1982; Martin, 1987; Rothman, 1988, 1989; Kahn, 1995).

The extracts in Part 3 come from two books: *Becoming a mother* (1979, later reprinted as *From here to maternity*) and *Women confined: Towards a sociology of childbirth* (1980). Together these report on a study I did which focused on the experiences of 66 women having their first babies in London in 1975-76. The women, mainly young and middle class, were interviewed twice in pregnancy and twice after birth, and I also attended some of the births. Before this, I carried out an observational study of antenatal clinics in the hospital in which the women were booked to have their babies. This generated transcripts of hundreds of encounters between women and doctors, some of which are drawn on in Part 3, Chapter One.

I wrote two books about the transition to motherhood project, rather than one, because there were a lot of important things to say about women becoming mothers. Also, dividing the material into two seemed to be one solution to the endemic methodological problem of social science: how to represent people's individual social experiences faithfully, at the same time as critically analysing these. *Becoming a mother* is mostly made up of women's own accounts. The central chapters of *Women confined*, on the other hand, are more standard academic fare: they present in fairly dense format a new analytic model for childbirth within the context of other sociological work on life events and transitions.

The basic argument of the two books is simple: having a first child is a key event in women's lives because, even in modern Western cultures, women continue to be defined as mothers and carers; childbirth is heavily medicalised and far from 'natural'; becoming a mother is a process with losses as well as gains. Some people said the picture conveyed in the women's accounts was too bleak, a contraceptive device, perhaps, to put other women off motherhood (Jenkins, 1979)? The response of the *British Medical Journal*, was, more optimistically, to see the mothers' "frank remarks" as guiding doctors to a better understanding of pregnancy and motherhood (Anon, 1979).

That better understanding was on its way, in any case. The 1970s saw the birth of an influential 'consumer movement' in maternity care which continues today (see, for example, Haire, 1972; Arms, 1975; Kitzinger, 1979; Edwards and Waldorf, 1984; Oakley, 1984b, Chapter 10; Oakley, 1984c). This has contested the medical stereotyping of women as unreliable and incompetent patients; has argued for choice and diversity in patterns of maternity care; and has provided an ongoing critique of the rising tide of medical intervention in pregnancy and childbirth. Some of this research has crept into government policy, which now iterates a philosophy of woman-centred care very different from the authoritarianism of the 1960s (DH, 1993).

The transition to motherhood project proved to be a catalyst for a new tradition of research in this area (Crouch and Manderson, 1995, p 7). Research by social scientists and others has expanded on many themes of the original study: for example, the deficiencies of assembly-line antenatal care and the historical development of these rituals (Garcia, 1982; Oakley, 1984; Hall et al, 1985; Carroli et al, 2001); effects of the medical 'management' of childbirth (Macintyre, 1977; Cartwright, 1979; Romney, 1980; Romney and Gordon, 1981; Garforth and Garcia, 1984); the ambivalent position of midwives (Hunt and Symonds, 1995); the extent and impact of medical attitudes towards women (Scully, 1980; Romalis, 1981; Roberts, 1985; Fisher, 1986; Sherwin, 1992), and the placing of childbirth within the broader framework of the sexual politics of reproduction (Homans, 1985) and the politics of women's healthcare (Doyal, 1998). There is impressive evidence of substantial cultural differences in patterns of obstetric and midwifery care (Oakley and Houd, 1990; Stephenson et al, 1993), and surprisingly *little* evidence that most of the technologies used in childbirth are effective and safe (Chalmers et al, 1989; Wagner, 1994; also see www.cochrane.org).

The escalating use of technology is the most striking medical aspect of changes since the 1970s. When the transition to motherhood study was done, for example, ultrasound scanning was only just beginning in antenatal clinics, and, in the figures I cited for the childbirths of the women in the study, I did not think it necessary to mention Caesareans at all. Today, ultrasound is a routine part of antenatal care and more than one in five mothers in the UK have their babies cut out of their abdomens in an operation euphemistically known as Caesarean 'section' (Royal College of Obstetricians, 2001; also see Richards and Oakley, 1990).

As with housework, the study of technology and motherhood is full of complex plots. Both stories exemplify a bigger cultural shift towards a world in which there is less nature than there used to be (Lie, 2002). Technologies alter the relationship between nature and culture, and this is especially true of motherhood, where the overall effect is to control and commodify women's bodies (Rothman, 1989; Duden, 1993). This makes women's labour in bearing children invisible, just as their labour at home is discounted as not being 'real' work. But the technologies applied to childbirth and motherhood have another covert function: they suggest that women can only be women with expert (mostly male) professional help. When I studied the transition to motherhood in the 1970s, the advice manuals for mothers then current stressed women's almost childish dependence on medical care and control, although at the same time, oddly, as 'normal' mothers with an instinctual drive to mother (Oakley, 1982). These, and related themes, appear in more recent analyses, which foreground a gendered ideology of child-centred, expert-guided intensive mothering (Marshall, 1991; Hays, 1996). The tone of the advice literature for pregnant women remains "patronizing" and "hectoring" (Gross and Pattison, 2001, p 515), and is full of banal and/or contradictory messages, especially about the impact of work. Employment, which is now commonplace for mothers, is portrayed as essentially hazardous, with its protective effects ignored (Romito, 1993, 1997), and women are overtly or covertly urged to a life of feminine passivity with motherhood as their key life experience. Their unpaid work in the home is scarcely mentioned. Over time, it seems that the accompanying typifications of women in obstetrics and gynaecology texts have got hardly less sexist: notions of women's essential achievements deriving from their uteruses and pictures of motherhood as unfortunately destabilising, but inherently fulfilling, continue to dominate medical discourse (Scully and Bart, 1973; Koutroulis, 1990).

In *Becoming a mother*, many women used the language of shock to describe their experiences, and many felt that the realities of pregnancy, childbirth and motherhood conflicted with over-romanticised expectations. These early revelations in the social science literature of what the American writer Adrienne Rich (1977) called "motherhood as experience", as distinct from the *institution* of motherhood, have been confirmed in other studies. For example, in a synthesis of 18 qualitative studies, Beck (2002) identified four themes in data supplied by mothers: lack of congruence between expectations and reality; low emotional wellbeing after giving birth; pervasive feelings of loss; and eventual realisation of gain. Mothers' frameworks of meaning relating to pregnancy and labour are often qualitatively different from those of the doctors who 'manage' childbirth (Graham and Oakley, 1981). The language of shock is common (Apter, 1993; Richardson, 1993; Parker, 1995). Within the literature on the transition to *parenthood,* difficulties and tensions are also frequently reported, and more often by women than by men (LaRossa and LaRossa, 1981; Andersen, 1984; Michaels and Goldberg, 1988; Nomaguchi and Milkie, 2003). The transition to parenthood is the most stressful of all adult transitions, especially for women (Gauthier and Furstenberg, 2002).

One major consequence of childbirth for women, much explored in the post 1970s literature, was and is termed 'postnatal depression'. Despite its appearance, this is a deeply unscientific label: it lacks any clear definition, aetiology or treatment, and has no apparent link to the hormonal mechanisms which are often said to produce it (Romito, 1989; Whiffen, 1992; Nicolson, 1998; Boath and Henshaw, 2001). But postnatal depression has a key function as ideology. It is part of the way in which mothers and others talk about motherhood, and it was an important focus for my own study, for this reason. 'Depression' after childbirth was a normal experience for most of the women, and their accounts stressed such aspects of the transition to motherhood as hospitalisation, surgery, body and career change, fatigue, overwork and social isolation as making them feel less than joyful as new mothers. Subsequent research has shown both the widespread prevalence of distress after childbirth (Romito, 1989; Green et al, 1990; Brown et al, 1994; Bashiri and Spielvogel, 1999;) and its relation to social factors (Paykel et al, 1980; Mauthner, 1995; Swendsen and Mazure, 2000; Des Rivières-Pigeon et al, 2003). Fatigue seems especially undervalued and important as an explanation (Bozoky and Corwin, 2002; Elek et al, 2002; McQueen and Mander, 2003).

The model of postnatal depression arrived at in *Women confined* was built round such previously ignored 'causes' of women's unhappiness. It was a radical departure from existing explanations because it emphasised the nature of childbirth as a *human* life event, with women's accounts of depression interpreted as *human* responses to difficulty, rather than as deviations from normative femininity. This aspect of my work is probably the one that has received the least recognition (Nicolson, 1998, p 37). As a contribution to a burgeoning feminist social science, it may have seemed off-beam in stressing women's status as human beings rather than as women. It could simply have come too early in the history of second-wave feminist concerns, which were initially directed at repudiating, rather than embracing, motherhood (Maroney, 1986). But there may be more fundamental explanations. The transformation of women's unhappiness into a medical condition has a long history which is deeply embedded in patriarchal cultural thinking (Astbury, 1996). The ideology of postnatal depression plays a powerful role in tying mothers to a socially useful mode of production. Society trades on, and therefore has to help to construct, a definition of motherhood in which women do not behave like good capitalists, bent on raising the best children with the least effort and for the most profit (Hays, 1996). And, as some have argued, 'the mask of motherhood' is put there by a conspiracy of silence about the power that mothers have over all of us (Maushart, 1999).

As with other areas of gender research, the 1990s and 2000s have brought more recognition of cultural diversity: class and ethnicity affect women's expectations and experiences of childbirth and motherhood in complex ways (Fox and Worts, 1999; Katbamna, 2000; Templeton et al, 2003). It is important to remember that, globally, the transition to motherhood is a perilous trajectory with a lifetime risk of maternal death as high as one in seven in some countries (Macfarlane et al, 2000).

The debate about the experience of childbirth technology which started in the 1970s continues today. Is the 'dissatisfied consumer' just a middle-class construct? Does technology damage women's health, not only by making mothers unhappy (Green et al, 1990; Brown et al, 1994), but by physically damaging their bodies in lasting ways (Macarthur et al, 1991; Hemminki, 1996; Johnstone et al, 2001)? Are doctors themselves a risk for normal childbirth (Romito and Hovelaque, 1987)? How can we trust research when a condition of normal motherhood is the inability of women to talk honestly about *all* their experiences (Brown et al, 1994)? Procedures such as episiotomy may be routine, but they are also a form of genital mutilation. Motherhood can scar women for life. But children are intensely lovely and rewarding, perhaps the more so precisely for their contrast with the labour of a commodified capitalist world. Not for nothing did medical experts try to abolish breastfeeding – a very untechnological activity and a great resource for mothers and babies – and then reluctantly discover and start reminding women of its health benefits (Jelliffe and Jelliffe, 1978).

Life for many women has changed since the 1970s, with more employment and less motherhood, but these pulls of nature and culture remain. As I wrote at the end of *Becoming a mother*, "Motherhood is a handicap but also a strength; a trial and an error; an achievement and a prize" (Oakley, 1979, p 308).

The agony and the ecstasy

Introduction

How can the experience of childbirth be described? Does it defeat words? Or is it twisted by being trapped within words so that an event powerfully experienced is reduced to a technical account, a recitation of medical manoeuvres? Some people find it easier than others to put their feelings into words. Questions provoke answers, but the answers may only be clues, signposts. Statistics sketch another kind of picture; to know how many women had what kind of pain relief during labour is not to know how much pain was relieved; to be told how many babies were tugged or persuaded into the world with forceps, is not really to know much more than that.

Certain themes run through the accounts of birth gathered in this research: the problem of recognition – is this labour, is this a contraction; the clash of expectations and reality – now I know how it feels, I know how I expected it to feel; the question of control – am I doing this myself, or are other people doing it to me? How to recognise symptoms of impending birth and how to square these with the images collected from mothers, antenatal classes, television programmes, Victorian novels and so forth – these are the classic dilemmas of women having a first baby. But the issue of who controls birth is part of childbirth today in a more general sense. In entering hospital to give birth, a woman becomes part of that great and growing debate about who is having the baby: the mother, the medical profession, the hospital, the family, the state. In the role of patient, a mother is vulnerable, but she is vulnerable twice over, for she has not only her own interests to defend but her baby's. Hospitals are made up of rules and set procedures; certain things must be done in certain ways at certain times and in certain places. This proper way to give birth may seem improper, but, as a patient, it is not the reasoning behind the rule that matters, only the existence of the rule itself.

These statistical statements about the sample women set the birth accounts that follow in their technological context:

- *79 per cent of the women had epidurals (with or without other analgesics).*
- *20 per cent had other analgesics only.*
- *Only one woman had no analgesia at all.*
- *52 per cent of the women had forceps or ventouse deliveries.*
- *98 per cent of women had episiotomies.*

- *41 per cent of women had induction or acceleration of labour with syntocinon.*
- *59 per cent of women had their membranes artificially ruptured.*
- *69 per cent of women said they did not feel in control of themselves or what was going on during the labour.*

Birth passages

Alison Mountjoy, 27, fashion designer. Labour accelerated, 16½ hours, epidural, forceps delivery

I'd better tell you the whole story. Do you want to know the whole story? Right. The doctor had said at the hospital that, if nothing happened, I might as well come in after the weekend to be induced. Which was alright, because I thought by then I'll be two weeks late and I can't keep hanging onto it forever. But you know when you've finished at the clinic, and you have to see the nurse and get more iron pills? Well, this nurse and a woman doctor who was also sitting at the desk, when they heard that I was going to be induced – having the membranes broken – which I hadn't been nervous about previously, but the way those two went on – they were sort of half joking, saying ugh how uncomfortable it was, and I was getting a bit worried, I said well you are joking aren't you? Well, it's not *too* pleasant, you know! So you can imagine what I felt then. And of course it got worse as the days went on, as Tuesday approached and nothing happened, and then Tuesday morning I woke up with piles. Just the day I had to go into hospital. That just about *finished* me. I was *terrified* of going into hospital, *terrified* of just about everything, and with this bloody pain up my backside.... I couldn't even get any toilet paper anywhere near my backside.... I mean, why did they have to come the day I had to go into hospital?

I went into hospital in the afternoon, and I was *so* terrified. Luke stayed with me, he went home for supper and he came back and they let him stay. I asked the sister what it was going to be like, whether it was going to be as bad as everyone made out, and *she* didn't put my mind at rest at all. Yes, well, it *is* a bit uncomfortable. You know, when doctors say something's going to be a bit uncomfortable, you know it's going to be bloody awful. Anyway, the doctor who was going to do it came to see me about ten o'clock at night and he could see I really was in a state by then, and he said, if you can relax, it's nothing. So I said well how the hell can I relax? He said, well look, if you really are this worried, I can give you an injection and you'll just be nice and woozy – you won't *care* what we're doing to you. So I said well why didn't anybody tell me that before? So we arranged for me to have this injection at about six o'clock in the morning, because they wanted to do it [*rupture the membranes*] at about six thirty.

They came and gave it to me at six o'clock and I drifted off feeling absolutely wonderful ... and while I was lying there feeling wonderful, I started feeling these wonderful twinges starting and I thought no, no, nothing's happening – too good to be true. They couldn't take me up then, because the delivery rooms were so crowded; they'd had a busy night. So there I was starting off by myself. I felt so proud of myself, and I didn't tell anybody for about an hour. I can't *tell* you how pleased I was that I started off myself: I was *so* chuffed. And eventually I thought I'd better tell somebody because I had a show and everything started happening, and they came and timed the contractions and they said yes, you actually *are* in labour. And I was so pleased: that set the day off right!

So when they did take me upstairs, they didn't do anything. Until about twelve when they decided they wanted to monitor the baby which apparently they do *routinely* there. And the bag [*membranes*] hadn't broken by then so they had to do it – I said why, what for? But of course they didn't listen. By then, these pains were coming quite fast and they were pretty painful. You're not allowed to call them pains, are you? They're contractions. It always made me laugh when I read that because I *knew* they bloody well hurt. Everybody kept asking me every ten minutes whether I was going to have an epidural. And I had been in such a state the night before that I was in no mood to be firm about anything. Also the breathing wasn't working – it's a load of old codswallop, that breathing, so when the tenth person asked me if I wanted an epidural, I said yes. They did it just after the membranes – that wasn't that bad, it's no worse than an ordinary internal.

The worst thing about the whole of the day, the only bad thing, was that, at the same time they did the epidural, they wanted to put me on a glucose drip. I wouldn't have the other – the drip that speeds it all up. They wanted to do that straightaway when they broke the membranes. I don't know why, I suppose because they didn't want me to be in labour for very long, for their own convenience probably. But I said no: I'm doing alright, aren't I, I said: I'm having good strong contractions aren't I, so you're not going to do it, are you? I had one nurse to start with who was on my side. She talked two doctors out of putting me on the drip. She said this patient is *in* labour. She doesn't want to go on a drip and there's no need to, is there? I think because I'd gone into hospital to be induced they hadn't really worked themselves round to the idea that, in fact, things were a bit different.

If you count from when I started having contractions, which I suppose was seven o'clock in the morning, and I had her at eleven thirty at night – sixteen and a half hours. At four o'clock, they did put me on the other drip. They said, look, you're doing very well, but it doesn't seem to be progressing much, so do you mind if we do this? So I said, no. Well as I had the drip in, I said you're not going to put another needle in are you? No, no, we just attach it to the same tube. Anyway I had so many tubes coming out of me by then – the two down there, the epidural, the drip – so it was the fifth thing altogether. You feel so strung up, you think, well what's one thing more?

It was what I *feared* was going to be the case. I think they have actually gone round the bend there. And I think that was why, knowing that hospital was so keen on sticking tubes into you and injections and all sorts of things, I think that was one of the reasons I had the epidural. Because, to be honest, when I asked for the epidural, when I finally decided to have it, it wasn't *totally* the pain, it was also the fear of – they're so used to doing all these things to people who've had epidurals and who are completely numb – what's it going to be like when they start doing things to me, forgetting maybe that I can actually *feel* everything?

Having said that, I definitely didn't want an epidural before going into hospital and then deciding eventually to have one to make life easier – for them as well as me – it was actually super; I mean I don't regret having had it. I mean, having decided to have a baby at that hospital, the best thing to do was to have done what I did.... It's terribly unlikely that I'll have a baby there again, because we'll be moving out of London, so presumably I will be somewhere where they will have the attitude of encouraging you and helping you to get over the pain, instead of saying why put up with it, we can give you something for it. [*And this in fact was what happened – her second child was born twenty months later without an epidural in a small country hospital.*]

And I had a forceps delivery. That was a bit unfortunate because the last time they topped up the epidural was about nine o'clock in the evening, and about two minutes later they were due to do another internal, and they did it and all hell broke loose because they suddenly realised that I was completely dilated, whereas before I'd been only about four centimetres, and they rushed off and got a doctor and it was this nice doctor that I'd liked who'd been on duty again by this time which was rather nice, so he also had a look and said, right, okay, start pushing! And the unfortunate thing was that this last top up left me *completely* numb from the waist down, whereas I'd been topped up about four times and each time it'd left me with *something*. But this time I really did have to look at the machine to know when I was having a contraction.

I was *very* disappointed that I couldn't feel to push. I suppose the most disappointing thing about the whole procedure was not being able to feel her slither out ... I would *love* to have felt her slither out or whatever the feeling is that you do have when they come out. I really would have liked to have felt that. I was furious that they topped me up. I was never shouting to be topped up, they topped me up without even asking me: I said what are you doing? I don't need it, I don't want it. They just put it in: I mean you can't really move away. He let me push for an hour which is quite a long time for them because normally it's ten minutes and that's it. And eventually he said you just can't get the head round the corner. So he said you're going to push it out, but I'm just going to ease it at the same time – good psychology! I mean I don't know whether that's a typical forceps delivery.... It was one pull, one push, and out she came; she didn't have a mark on her. And then suddenly everybody was saying oh you've got a little girl and all the rest of it, and I said I can't see it, I can't feel, where? And Luke had to pull me up and she was only half out and she was already crying and I was so relieved to see her: she was so obviously all in one piece and crying and … I just felt immense relief. She looked totally *right* when she came out: the right size, the right length. I held her all the time they were stitching me up. They just plonked her on my chest. It was totally amazing. Looking at her and thinking – well I suppose it was terribly difficult to believe that she'd come out of *me*. I sort of half thought that she must have come from under the table somewhere, because having *not* felt but seen the direction she was coming out of, I sort of wanted to go and look under the table to see what was going on under there. It felt very strange. I mean yes: it was *my* baby, and I loved her, but I think I was just so shattered by then that, whatever I was feeling, I couldn't feel much of. I mean I was totally aware that she was my baby and I loved her and I wanted to hold her but I felt so sick I couldn't react to *anything* by then. I could hardly believe that she'd come out of me.

Sharon Warrington, 21, audiotypist. Labour 18½ hours, epidural

It was six o'clock on the twenty-third and I got backache, not a bad backache, but it was annoying. It went on all night and I woke up at four in the morning. It got worse, but not that bad; I didn't know, I'm not ignorant, but I just didn't know: I got up, and started pottering around, I didn't know what was going on really. My mum said I don't want to frighten you, but I think you've started labour, and I laughed. She said, right: you wait and see. She said my face was so flushed. I didn't think I was in labour, I expected it to be painful. It was right at the bottom of my spine, as though someone had got their knuckles into it. My mum got up and sat making tea and coffee and seven o'clock came and I felt tired, so I got back into bed about seven fifteen. I just moved in bed and, as I moved, I got a terrible thud in the back and the waters broke. So up I jumped, ran from the bed into the kitchen, gets to the toilet, and finds what's happened. I told mum what had happened and by this time my tummy had started to tighten and that. So I got washed and dressed and my mum rang the hospital and said I was on my way. I said to Alan, would you get up, and he looked at me out of one eye and said why, what's wrong? He didn't know what I meant. So I said my waters have broke and the baby could come at any time, and he said you are joking, and I said I am not; he thought I was joking. And within five minutes we were off. He didn't even have a wash.

Got to the hospital and from the reception they took me up to the admission place. I was upset: I cried when I said goodbye to my mum. I was alright going in the car, but once you are in that delivery room and you see all these things ... I was thinking, oh God, if when the baby is born it has to go on that machine or this has to be done ... then I got a little bit scared. I got examined and then I went straight into the delivery room because I'd already started to dilate. Then the doctor came in and then the pain started really to come about lunchtime and I wanted that epidural so I had it done, and it didn't work. Alan went out for his lunch and he said, what time did they think the baby was going to be born, so they said about four. Anyway up comes four and I am still there, so they gave me an epidural again and it still didn't work, so I gave up. They examined me quite a few hours after I was admitted and I was still only about three and a half to four centimetres, and then they examined me again about half nine and it was completely open.... When they examine you, they write in the file and give a special stamp and I asked her what it was and she said I can't tell you. She said all I can tell you is that you are progressing. She said what is written in the file is strictly confidential.

He had this thing on his head [*an electrode to record the baby's heart-rate*]. I was worried in case it could harm him, and they don't ask your permission to do it which I think is all wrong. But when it came off – it took long enough to be put on, and it darn well hurt, because the girl who had done it hadn't before, and it took quite half an hour to get it properly in place; anyway, within half an hour of being put on it fell off, because you have got about four tubes going inside and they keep turning you from side to side and each time you turn you pull. You can't help it, and I said I don't want it again, because I said it might damage his head when he is born, and they said it doesn't harm him, they said if you look at this, this records his heart, this records your contractions. So, well, you can't really say no to them and yet they say that they only do it with your approval. But they don't ask.

He was the only baby born at Christmas. The only one, all Christmas Eve day and all Christmas Eve night, and all Christmas day and night. There was only me, and this other woman having a race. About half nine, they said that I was ready to push, so the nurses and all that come in. I started pushing about nine forty five and he was born at twenty past ten, it was all over. I was propped up, but you've got your legs on the table and you have a foot on each nurse's shoulder, so you have to rick your neck to look down and you can't do it, because you are trying to breathe at the same time. Alan see it. When the actual birth came, they went and got him from the room and they brought everything in and got all ready and I started to push and push and push and his head sort of got stuck; it just wouldn't come out.

You feel like your whole bottom half is going to split, literally, you can feel this bulge and as they say the urge to push is terrible. They say don't push, don't push, and they tell you when to push. I always thought you could push when you wanted to push, but you don't: you have to wait for their command. They feel your tummy and your face is all crinkled up with agony and they say oh you've got a pain, you can push now, and you push and then you relax.

Anyway the sister who was on duty came in and said how was I doing sort of thing, and I didn't know what they was doing, but they got this big blue sterile pad and I knew she had something in her hand, because she kept her hand down there, but Alan could see, because she was on the same side as him and she said right push, push really hard. And as I pushed I hear snip, snip and Alan went white, and they cut me down and across like a hot cross bun, and then his head was born and another push about a minute later and he was completely out, and Alan was half way up the corridor, gone. It was a darn shame that he had to go, but if he hadn't have gone, he would have been out on the floor. He saw the head, it was about half out, and he said that all he could see was like the back of his head, and then he said they cut you and I said to him, how did you know, and he said, well I see didn't I? And the nurse ran after him and got him and he came straight back in again, and the baby was just lying in between my legs at the bottom of the bed. They wrapped him up and put him in his crib and Alan just went straight over to him. He didn't want to know me!

Now I am glad the epidural didn't work, at the time I wished it had done. I think I appreciate what I done, I am pleased with myself, that I could do it. I think some people have that just for the sake of having it. Ninety per cent before their pains even start have it, and even a couple of days after I was so pleased to say I had it but it didn't work, that I took the full brunt of it, whereas these people who had had it said they couldn't feel a thing. Well to me that isn't having a baby. What's the point? I said it was awful. But it's not awful really. What you suffer for an hour or two is all gone. What you suffered for the whole nine months and the last few hours is sheer hell really. But it is all worth it, once they give you the baby, it's absolutely marvellous.

I held him for a couple of minutes and they asked Alan if he wanted to hold him and he said no, and that upset me. Then not long after a nurse from the ward came up and took him down, and that was all I saw of him … I would have liked him exactly as he was born, for them to have cut the cord and given him to me. But they've held him first, that's the way I look at it. You are not the first. I think a mother should be the first one to hold it. A couple of days after we was talking about it in the ward and one of the women was saying that she didn't hold hers for about twenty minutes and they were mucking around with it and that, and I said I had him about five minutes after, so she said I don't think it is fair, I think you should have them raw sort of thing, just as they are, and I said yes. He was such a sweet little thing, he was wide awake with his eyes open looking at me, and looking at Alan, and although they can't see, he was staring all the time, he didn't blink once. They commented about that; he still does it now, he still stares.

I had thirty stitches, I had thirteen inside and all the rest were outside. It was about one o'clock before he came along, he was singing to me 'God rest ye merry gentlemen'. It was Christmas Eve. It was funny, as the contractions were getting bad they came in and they turned all the lights off and I thought what on earth are they doing? And they moved me and all these machines and everything into the door and I got this pain and I'll never forget it as long as I live. I was swearing under my breath and there was this whole mob of doctors and nurses singing 'Away in a manger' and I'll never forget that as long as I live. I cried my eyes out. I hadn't cried all the way through. I'd bitten my lip, but that really broke my heart.

Louise Thompson, 30, law student. Labour 4½ hours

I tell you, I almost had her at home. That was the funniest thing. I had a show at six thirty in the evening, but the contractions came every five minutes or so. I phoned the hospital and they said, oh don't worry; it's your first child, it'll take twenty hours or something. Eat dinner, stay calm, and come in, you know, tomorrow morning. So I actually was cooking dinner – it was about seven – but they just got worse, they didn't hurt that much, they were just coming very often. And I said, well you know, maybe I should pack my suitcase. But we'll stay calm: right? Oh and also we were moving that Monday so the flat was such a mess. Then at seven thirty I was starting bleeding, like a period, and I said I'd better phone the hospital. And they said, yes, you'd better come in. But if I hadn't started bleeding I surely would have had her at home. Because I got there at eight fifteen and then I had her at ten to eleven. When I came in, after they examined me, I was put into the labour room. I was five to six fingers dilated. But it didn't hurt at all – not at all – until right before I was in the second stage of labour. I tell you, if I hadn't started bleeding I would have waited till the pains got really bad and it would have been half an hour. They got quite bad at the end of the first stage. I mean I didn't have any drugs or anything. It wasn't terrible.

When they said, oh it's a girl, I said oh good, I am so happy!... I held her after a while. Actually she fed right away. Oliver said – let her feed, let her feed.

It was just amazing. It was like a miracle. It could be a religious experience. Now I *know* it's superior to be a woman.

Vera Abbatt, 28, canteen worker. Labour 16 hours, epidural, forceps delivery

Well, it was a Sunday, we were just sitting here and I had pains in my stomach.

Mother-in-law (MIL): She always laid about, didn't do anything, just laid about. But this Sunday morning, she was just the same. She kept laying about, didn't you? Frank said to her, don't you feel well? She said, I'm alright, I'm alright. He said, shall I make a bed for you over there? She did lay on a bed. This was the day time.

Vera: No, it was night time, six o'clock.

MIL: This went on all day, this palaver with her. About seven she goes upstairs and she tells him she's had a show. He called me upstairs and, when I saw their bed, straightaway I said phone for the ambulance; it had been there all day.

Vera: I lost it during the night, and I didn't realise it. And yet I went up and I went to the toilet and I had a show then and I called Frank and I said – because his cousin was running us up – I said you'd better go and get Dave, I think we have a bit of a problem here. Anyway, I was taken to hospital. But when we got up there we didn't have any problem – they took me right into the labour ward. Then they took me into another ward and they gave me two sleeping tablets. Because apparently they thought I was going to go on till next morning. And, just as she gave me the tablets, she said she was going to test the contractions, and as soon as she put her hand on my tummy she said, oh never mind the tablets. By this time, I'd taken them. She said, get her down to the delivery room. So I was in there about eleven o'clock and he was born at half past four.

I mean I was all that time in labour, all day, and I didn't know anything about it. I felt pains in me stomach but it didn't dawn on me that's what it was. I thought it was wind actually. That's what it felt like to me. I thought I was full of wind.... It was about an hour after we got to hospital it started to get really bad. And then they gave me the epidural for the birth. So I felt nothing during the birth at all. In fact I slept during most of the delivery. It was terrific.

I had a forceps delivery. He was stuck in the neck of the womb, he got stuck coming round the corner. They told me that. And, of course, as soon as they told me they were going to have to do a forceps delivery, I was up in arms again: what's wrong with him? She said there's nothing wrong with him, he's just stuck. It was a bit degrading.

I didn't even know he was out – he was crying his eyes out and I thought – there was another lady in the next room having a baby – and I thought it was hers. I didn't know he was out! She picked him up and said, you've got a baby son! Oh God – is he mine? Where did he come from? I didn't really feel anything, I was so tired: I was glad it was over, that was it. I couldn't think of anything else.

Elizabeth Farrell, 28, publisher's assistant. Labour 3 hours

It was unpleasant. I felt more pain than I've ever felt in my life before. I really know now that I was expecting it to be virtually painless; I think I was. And oh my goodness, it wasn't.

Afterwards I thought about it a lot. I mean I remember thinking, I wonder if I shall ever want another baby. I wrote it all down: here it is: 'It was like Richard or Edward II – I can't ever remember which it is – they wanted to kill him without it looking like murder, so they stuffed a red hot poker up his rectum and the screams could be heard all over Gloucestershire!'

It woke me up from a deep sleep – such a sudden, strong pain. Robert and I had just had an awful row, that was another thing; that was the only reason he stayed [at the birth], I'm sure. I went to sleep in tears. We hadn't made it up and so, when I woke up, I had these great swollen eyes from crying. I woke up at 2 a.m. and she was here by five. I woke up with a stabbing pain as the waters broke and from then on the contractions were more or less continuous. I could hardly get dressed. In fact, the way I woke up *shocked* me. I was suffering from shock after it and I didn't really know what to do in spite of all the preparation So, of course, I mechanically thought I should have a bath. But I couldn't move. I was standing in a plastic bowl dribbling, so I woke Robert up and he said, wake me up when it's all over, and I said no, you'll have to get up and put some newspaper on the floor from here to the bathroom. So he did that and I had a bath which was completely pointless, because I was still dribbling away. Got dressed and put on endless disposable nappies and sanitary towels and two pairs of knickers. And it came all the way through all these disposable nappies I had on to my dress. And Robert took me in and they examined me and I think it was two fingers dilated when they first examined me and so they wheeled me straight into the delivery room.

My goodness, that was a struggle: when I said I don't want anything [*that is, no analgesia*] the midwife, she got, well, not exasperated with me, but I could read what was going through her mind. She thought I was stupid. And I hate to inconvenience people and have them ill-disposed towards me so then I sort of said, well maybe I'm being silly; then she was getting it [*an injection of pethidine*] ready and I said, no, I don't think I will. I suppose that must have been a gap between contractions; I definitely decided *not*. And then I mean I didn't get a chance to get into the breathing rhythm at all. It seemed to be meaningless – I didn't have enough time to think myself into it. The contractions weren't, the build up wasn't *gentle* enough, they were just too sudden.

Time meant nothing. It could have been one hour or twenty-four hours, I don't know. And then there was that awful stage when they were telling me not to push and I couldn't. You can't prevent yourself. One minute they're telling you that your uterus is an involuntary muscle and the next minute they're telling you not to push. I don't know whether you push with your uterus. I don't suppose you do. To me, if the uterus is pushing, it's nature working properly. I don't know *how* you can damage your cervix. I wonder whether that's not a fashion as well.

I couldn't help it; I couldn't *believe* how strong they were. And well they'd given me that enema thing and I hadn't been to the lavatory – I hadn't had a chance. And that was another thing I now realise – that was sort of coming out along with everything else, which must have been awful for everyone else. I didn't feel embarrassed at the time – I couldn't think of anything else except the contractions! And I do like to be helpful and cooperative and do what they say and it really distressed me at the time that I couldn't prevent myself from pushing.

From the researcher's notes

Elizabeth (E): What's the time?

Pupil midwife (PMW): I don't think you'll be long.

Robert (R) to Elizabeth: Is it painful?

E: I can't describe it.... Can I have some water?

PMW: Can I listen to the baby, please?

E: How much longer till I can push?

PMW: I don't think you'll be very much longer now. Right, over on your back, let's see if I can see the baby's head.

E: No, no [*she's in the middle of a contraction*]. No, not yet.... I'm sorry.

PMW: That's alright. You're doing very well.

E: Am I in the transition stage?

PMW: Yes, you are, that's why it's so difficult.

E to R: I'd like you to stay, but if you don't feel you want to....

E to PMW: Keep shouting at me, it helps me to remember what I'm supposed to be doing.

PMW: Are you hoping for a boy or a girl?

E: I don't mind.

PMW: Don't push.

E: You've no idea how hard it is, it just happens, I can't control it.

PMW: I just want to have a look, lift your leg up.

E: Am I making progress?

PMW: Yes, I think I'll get staff. I can just see a few strands of hair.

[*Elizabeth is propped up ready for pushing.*]

PMW: There's going to be a time when I tell you not to push, just to pant, alright?

Staff midwife (SMW) to R: Are you going to stay?

R: Yes, alright.

SMW: Can you sign this form please?

PMW: Now, push down towards your back passage.

E: At the classes, they said push down towards your stomach.

SMW: No, that's wrong, you want to push down into your back passage, as if you're constipated and you're dying to go to the loo.

E: But at the classes, they said that was wrong.

SMW: No, it's no good pushing into your stomach ... you've got to give some longer pushes, short ones are no good … if you give us some nice long pushes, it'll be out in half the time.... That's it, a nice long push. Down to your bottom.

E: Is that right?

SMW: Yes, yes. Another deep breath … that was better.

E: I'm beginning to get the hang of it. Can you touch it yet? Is its head on the outside?

SMW: Yes, it's got lots of dark hair.... No, put your bottom on the bed, love. That's it, push.... We're just doing a little injection now, alright?

E: Oh I want to push.

SMW: Okay, push, put your bottom on the bed.

E: Are you going to cut me?

PMW: We're going to have to give you a little cut – you shouldn't feel it too much because we'll do it during contractions and you've had an injection. [*Episiotomy done*] Now push, push.... Keep your pushing up now, nice and long – with the next contraction the head'll be out.

E: Really?

SMW: Okay, stop pushing now.... Just a small push, a little one again.... I'm just feeling for the cord, right there's no cord … there we are: the baby's head is out.

E: What do I do?

SMW: Push down.

PMW: It's a little girl.

E: Gosh.

PMW: [*looking at clock*] Not bad: from two till five, just three hours in labour.

E: It's long enough. [*Watching PMW and SMW handling baby*] What are you doing to my little girl? What are you doing to it? [*Is handed baby*]

E: Oh Robert she's *huge*.... Do you want to hold her?

R: No, I don't think so.

E: Oh Robert, I'm sorry you haven't got a son.... [*To PMW*] You'd better wash my bosom [*undoes delivery gown, puts baby to breast, baby very mucousy, won't suck*].

PMW: Don't be disappointed, Mrs Farrell, if the baby doesn't suck – she will later.

E TO BABY: Well, feel my skin anyway [*holds baby very close, strokes her cheek*].

Asking women to summarise their feelings about birth reduces these narratives to a standardised response. But it is useful to see how the individual fits into the general picture:

- *42 per cent of women said the birth was better than they expected.*
- *47 per cent of women said the birth was worse than they expected.*
- *49 per cent of women said they felt more pain that they expected.*
- *34 per cent of women said they felt less pain than they expected.*

What were the best aspects of the labour and birth from your point of view? And the worst?

There weren't any best bits at all. It was just no fun. It was a right drag from start to finish: a smelly horrible experience in a smelly horrible room. (*Kate Prince*)

A nice feeling was him coming out. I took it that I'd passed the head and now it was the body twisting round. I thought: that's nice. The worst bit was all the time I was shivering and being sick. I was like jelly all the time. And me husband come in: he said what's the matter, try and relax – I couldn't, couldn't keep calm. I put it down really to me being nervous. (*Michelle Craig*)

The best bit, well there weren't any best bits. Well the best bit was my husband being there. I liked that, that was nice. The worst bit was just the pain of it all I suppose. The first hour before I had the epidural. (*Pauline Diggory*)

The best bit was when he was born really. The worst bit was the bit after, just waiting to be stitched up. That was the most boring. (*June Hatchard*)

When she was born and when they cut me. (*Ellen George*)

There were no best bits. That catheter was horrible. I think I could feel it. She said, you won't feel it, but I'm sure I could feel something, and then the bloke coming round to stitch me up and *that* is embarrassing. That's more embarrassing than having a baby as well. (*Anne Bloomfield*)

The details of what happened coalesce into a memory. Part of this memory is weighing images versus reality.

In general, was having the baby anything like you expected it to be?

No. I mean yes. No, it wasn't really. I'd never imagined it like that. You read things about what it's going to be like but words can't convey what birth is like; it's just something completely different from anything you've ever done before. (*Jo Ingram*)

Well, I knew it was going to be pretty painful, but in fact I think it was worse than I thought it was going to be, I don't think that I've experienced anything quite like it. It was quite incredible. (*Clare Dawson*)

Yeah. It wasn't bad. That's what it had in this book – how every woman is afraid of the pain of labour, but I wasn't afraid. This crazy friend, she has a child, two years old. And she had a forceps delivery. It was very painful, and she had about a thirty-hour labour. She said: Yeah, you have a natural childbirth – you have it once, and you'll see, ha ha. (*Louise Thompson*)

It was what I expected really. I mean it was what I'd been waiting for, for nine months. Because when you see this baby, if you were cut all over you wouldn't think about it. (*Dawn O'Hara*)

Do women forget the pain of childbirth? That is one of the legends, passed down from mother to daughter. Is this how the labour of women in childbirth is disposed of – the suffering, for suffering it must be, is forgotten?

Kate Prince, four months later

I think that it isn't a question of women forgetting about the pain of having a baby. I think that you forget about the actual sensation of *any* pain. You can't describe pain because, I mean, if I pinch myself now, I know it bloody hurts. But then I've forgotten about it; that's all there is to it.

How much do you think about the actual labour and delivery now [five weeks afterwards]?

I do think about it. I often do. I thought one would forget about it. But I often find myself – in fact I dreamt about it the night before last. Really horrible, worse than it was: I *keep* rerunning it. I sit in the bath; I always think in the bath, and I find myself thinking about it without meaning to. I just find myself going through it again. (*Janet Streeter*)

I did have nightmares afterwards about having her, about the forceps. I had quite a few nightmares, horrible dreams about these forceps. I kept thinking, I don't know, it was just horrible, you know; a jumbled nightmare, and always at the end a baby was dead or something was wrong with her. Never anything clear-cut. It felt like a huge suction – as though everything had come out: as though I was all *empty*. Like everything had come out with it. I certainly think my brain was born at the same time. I said to Nick for days I was like a lunatic. (*José Bryce*)

Right at the very end when they'd sort of gone away and somebody was coming to wash me down I remember thinking, gosh I don't want to go through this again in a hurry. But now, six weeks later, I look back on it with interest. You forget the unpleasant bits: well you don't forget them, but I think the thrill of giving birth to a baby and everything doesn't strike you at the same time, but now it does. (*Jane Tarrant*)

I try to push the birth out of my mind. It's over and it's done with, and I don't think it's the be all and end all of... I mean he's growing now and he's smiling and he's doing things – the fact that he was born, I mean he obviously *was*, but I'm not going to hold it against him that he tore me or anything like that: that would be ridiculous. No, the birth wasn't this great emotional experience. (*Gillian Hartley*)

When I think about it. I think about them actually giving the baby to me and then Keith nursing it... But as far as thinking about the pain, no I don't: I've forgotten the pain. I look back on it with – nostalgia is not the word but I feel quite sentimental about the birth. The scenes that I remember are pleasant scenes. (*Sarah Moore*)

Suddenly to see her there and to see her head coming screaming out, you know it was super... In a way I wish I could do it again. If I could sort of watch it again, or do it again, and really take notice of what – remember it detail by detail. It fades away, you don't quite remember all you would want to remember. (*Clare Dawson*)

Lessons mothers learn

Expectations

Looking back on the process of becoming a mother, women come to understand the visions they had – of motherhood as a bed of roses, of birth as agony or ecstasy, of pregnancy as a flowering or a burden. After the event, these images are brought sharply into focus by the contrast medium of reality, which exposes the outline of what was, too often, a romantic dream.

More than a third of women said they found becoming a mother a difficult experience. Eight out of ten said it had been different from what they had expected. The same proportion thought the pictures of pregnancy, birth and motherhood conveyed in antenatal literature, women's magazines and the media in general were too romantic, painting an over-optimistic portrait

© Christine Roche

of happy mothers and fathers, quiet contented babies, and neat and shining homes that bore little resemblance to the chaos, disruption and confusion of first-time motherhood.

Becoming a mother (%)

Was difficult	36
Was different from expected	84
Is too romanticised	84

Fairy stories

Nina Brady, ex-shop assistant

What's romantic about changing that nappy down there? What's romantic about it? I think people should be told about the hard life it is to be a mother. It's not easy to be a mother. I don't think it is, I think it's very difficult. It takes all your energy out of you. The responsibility and the work: because you are kept going. If that child cries at three o'clock, you have got to get up and feed it if it continues to cry, haven't you? Isn't that a responsibility? Well you can't dial nine nine nine and tell them to come, the baby's crying: you've got to do it. I think they should be *warned* more: because when you go to those classes, they tell you about your baby and they make it sound so nice, like the adverts on television, they make everything sound so nice. But it's not. When your baby is born in hospital, it took me a long time to get to want to see it at all. I'm telling you the truth; it took me about four or five days before I wanted to look at that child; I didn't want to know.

Rachel Sharpe, ex-copywriter

I suppose it's quite a difficult thing to convey to people who don't have the experience, but I think it *is* far too romantic the way they portray it. Especially those *sickly* booklets they give you in the hospital; they're *disgraceful*, they really are. You know, everybody looking sort of starry-eyed. I think they should do something to correct that image: that the only time you spend with the baby is whenever he needs to be fed, and that's at ten and two and six and on and on like that. Just things like that. And also I think you're under the impression too that a newborn sleeps twenty hours a day which I didn't find was true.

José Bryce, ex-manicurist

I think they don't say much, in anything I've read, about how you get depressed. They just sort of say this is perfectly natural and you might feel a bit weepy for a couple of days when you're in hospital and that's about all that anyone seems to say. If you knew how long it was going on, you'd feel alright. But it was just the fact that day after day after day I felt the same. That was the worst thing. Every morning that sort of dread: another day. And then I used to say, now tomorrow I'm really going to make the effort, I can't do it now, tomorrow will be better. And I did make myself go out just to stop crying really. I mean I just used to walk around the streets pushing her just so I wouldn't cry.

Gillian Hartley, illustrator

No, I don't think it's too romantic. I mean it's not the whole picture, obviously, but it *is* romantic and sentimental to be a mother in many respects. The feeling you have for the child is a very romantic one. With all the realism, you do love the child and that's a very romantic thing – just the way romantic novels do not present a very *accurate* picture of love, but they present a *portion* of it. I think they might do well to tell you more about the realities and then let you find out about the nice things which will come.

Ellen George, ex-health visitor

They treat you like a person with the lowest possible intelligence I think. I think they should tell you more of the sheer hard facts of the whole business – of the whole process from start to finish. They tell you bits that they choose to tell you, but they leave out quite a lot. They don't tell you about the aftermath, and they don't tell you enough about breastfeeding.

Sasha Morris, ex-air hostess

You always see mothers and babies looking terribly happy. They look collected and together. But it's not the case at all. In the photographs of me and the baby in the beginning, I always looked haggard and the baby looked marvellous. I was the haggard one.

The reality of motherhood

Would you say becoming a mother has been pretty much as you expected it to be?

Pat Jenkins, ex-shop assistant

It's very hard work. Well I knew it was hard work, because I've looked after a lot of kids, you know. But I mean you could always hand them over. It's different with your own. If you're tired, there's no one you can give him to . You know he's your own and you've got to put up with it. That's not right, put up with it, but you know what I mean: you can't hand him over when you feel, oh I've had enough.

Sarah Moore, ex-civil servant

There haven't been any nasty shocks. It's been much more rewarding than I thought it was going to be, and much more pleasurable. Everybody knows that, when you're at home looking after a baby, you tend to get very bored. I think maybe I had a very jaundiced view of it, and I didn't take into account the pleasure that a baby can give.

Pauline Diggory

They do assume, you see, because these hospitals are male-dominated, they do assume that the minute you have a baby you know what to do. I don't believe in the maternal instinct. I wish there was a book that tells you that it's *common* that some of them are sick or that half of them don't wind, and don't be frightened of it. I mean I feel like saying to some mothers, if I was writing for them – maybe they're not as frightened as I was? – don't be frightened of the baby as long as it's eating and sleeping, that's a good rule of thumb. You seem *incompetent* you see if you moan to outsiders; this is why mothers do talk to each other, because they can let the barrier down. But people, they do tend to expect – *I* expected – that once you have a baby you know it all. I *suspected* that you didn't, but everyone behaved as though they knew it all once they'd had one, and nobody *said* it. And then I thought, well I'm just as intelligent as most mothers, why aren't I managing? Maybe I'm not maternal enough. This is another fallacy I think that exists. Those books, it's all don't worry, everything's fine. That annoys me; they don't allow for the unusual, which is always happening as far as I can tell. Like that she brings up so much milk, that she didn't take to the breast: I thought that was uncommon until I realised that half the ward were having the same trouble. All those sorts of things. It annoys me because you go through all those worries to find out that you needn't have gone through it at all. I get angry with that.

Joining the club

Life is changed because motherhood is a new job: a baby transforms a private relationship between man and woman into 'family life' with all its traps and trappings; economically a woman with a baby is dependent in a way that a woman without a baby is not. But the job of mother has other, more pervasive consequences. Women's views about themselves, their ideas about themselves as people, also change. One in three of the sample women had distinctly stronger notions of themselves as mothers five months after the birth than they did earlier.

Angela King

It' made me feel more fulfilled. It's given me something in life; I feel that I've *achieved* something now. Whereas before, I mean work and everything, maybe it was the jobs I had, but I always felt like I was in a rut and was never *achieving* anything. But I feel as though I've done something *useful*; and if I can turn her into a nice person and put her into the world I'll feel that I've really achieved something.

Emma Buckingham

Apart from feeling awfully proud, you feel terribly *important*. I think I feel much securer having her. In many ways, life's more relaxed. Well, you really feel *proud* of your baby: it's something you've done together. I'm more contented.

Jane Tarrant

I suppose you've got a slight mystique about you once you've had a baby, which I think people had for me before I had one. And to people who *have* got babies you've joined the club so to speak – excuse the pun!

José Bryce

I didn't think I could feel so *passionately* about something. I'd always assumed that, if I had a baby, I'd love it, but I never thought I would actually feel like I do about it. If someone said, cut your arm off otherwise something would happen to her, you'd do it. It's a different sort of love from, say, you feel for your parents or your husband. I didn't realise I could feel so *deeply* about something. I look at her sometimes and think – I don't know how to describe it really. But how can people get over something like if their child dies or something? I don't know how anyone can get over a thing like that.

I'm more *emotional* now. Like I can watch the news now and if I see anything to do with children or babies, whereas before I'd think how awful, how sad; now I feel a real *twist*.

Sandy Wright

The miracle of it: I look at her and I think you're *mine*, you're nobody else's, or you're *ours* rather. We produced her and it's a wonderful feeling. I don't think you can understand it until you've actually had one, no matter how much someone tells you. And how that also affects other things; when you hear something awful's happened to a child you think, oh God, that could be you. Before, when I heard about baby battering and so on I would discuss it and feel terrible about it, but it didn't affect *me*. Now when I hear about I have a *pain* almost.

Gillian Hartley

I think when you're a parent you're conscious of so many good things. I think what struck me particularly since the baby's been born is – I really have wondered how men can kill each other: I've wondered how there could be wars. I can't understand how people can kill each other.

Living through the babyhood of one's own child is reliving one's own babyhood: through the actions and emotions of oneself as a mother, the experience of being mothered is reawakened. So bridging the generation gap is another unanticipated consequence of first-time motherhood.

Rosalind Kimber

I feel closer to my mother: I identify with her much more now. I feel I understand an awful lot more about her, and I feel much more sympathy for her now. Sometimes I look at the baby and I think my goodness my mother must have thought that about not just me, but all my brothers and sisters. And then I will make an effort to telephone her and that sort of thing. How much she must miss not having us at home, and how hurt she must be if we don't telephone her. Because I mean it's very easy to just forget and not bother. I find I bother much more now: I write to her and send her photographs of the baby.

Lily Mitchell

I think it's the closest I've felt to her, if you know what I mean. Because now you can sort of half-understand, really, some of her feelings. Because I used to say, why do you worry about John [*her brother*] even though he's 24? I said, why do you worry about him? But mothers worry about their children until they die because they're still their children no matter what age they are. And this is what we're like now with William. You know what I mean: you're still going to worry about him, even after he's got married. And I think it's made me see that a little bit more now.

Vera Abbatt

The last time I saw her I didn't feel it was my mother, she was more like a friend. I can see all the things that used to rile me with her now, I can see why she did them all now, whereas I could never see it before. I could never understand why she had to tell me to do this and why she had to tell me to do that. But sometimes I sit here and think what I would do if he did something like that: didn't go to school, stayed out all night at a party, fell off a train.

Juliet Morley

I certainly understand far better than I used to things that happened when we were children. I can certainly remember as a child thinking my mother wasn't very easy to please and was always being *cross* – this sort of thing. Well now I can understand it. Four children and a large house and going out to work.

Louise Thompson

I think she must have been a good mother – she was never angry, she was always loving and we were close, and I feel the same way to Polly: that's why I assume she was like that.

Pat Jenkins

I think it's because I've experienced the same as my mum, you know, and when we're talking we know what we're talking about, because she knows that I've gone through it as well. I've always been close to my mum anyway. But it's nice; because we can talk about it more. I tell her what I went through and things like that. Mum went through a terrible time with us, having us. I don't know – I said I don't know how she did it!

Mothers and daughters share the secret society of those who are guardians of future generations: they are united in their protectiveness, in that special sort of anxious devotion that is the birthright of children in our culture. Yet, in becoming a mother, a woman acquires a new kind of citizenship, or is deprived of one. When she is childless and out at work, she can pretend (or believe) that everything in the garden is lovely. When she is 'just a housewife', the vision of equality fades a little and motherhood, deeply rewarding as it is, become an imperfect occupation.

Women of the world

Since you became a mother, have your views about the position of women changed at all?

Sarah Moore

My views have changed, become more radical. I do think that women are – oppressed is a very emotive word, isn't it? But they are to a certain extent. I mean I *do* work twelve hours a day; I've *never* worked twelve hours a day: I never thought I would. And I'm buggered if I like it! I mean I *do* it because the work's got to be done, and I try to do the housework so I haven't got any to do at weekends. I realise that my twelve hours isn't nearly as hard as other women; I've got a washing machine, I've got carpets which are a darn sight easier to clean than scrubbing floors and polishing them. I realise that the work I put in is far less than my mother did or hundreds of other women do, but nevertheless you *are* working. I mean I don't think *anybody* should have to work twelve hours a day.

My views are changing towards society as well. I mean I knew that society was definitely anti-children; I knew that before he was born. But there are so many things now that you can't do because you've got a child. Shopping, for example. I mean I don't like shopping – I don't mean food shopping, that's *got* to be done – but window-shopping, that never used to appeal to me, I didn't go very often; but now I know I *can't* go, even if I want to, because I've got a kid.

I do think you're thought of as a second-class citizen. You're described as a housewife. Oh well, you've got plenty of time on your hands, you can sit down and knit all day. I mean I *work*!!! I don't think you should be paid, but I think that national insurance contributions, we should get those, so that then you can claim benefit when you're sick. I went down with gastric flu, that really brought it home to me. I felt so ill. Dick, it happened, couldn't take a day off from work that day; he had a lot on. And I was sort of running to the loo, being sick – oh God, you haven't got time to be ill when you've got kids, and this is what *really* brought it home to me. I mean I thought, if you go out to work, you take a day off and you don't even lose your *pay* if you take a day off, if you're sick. You can't take a day off when you've got kids.

It's taken Jonathan for me, and for me to be at *home* for me to realise this. It's strange, isn't it, because before when I was working, I wouldn't say I was a liberated woman by any means, but I was certainly holding my own at work and running a home. And so I should have then been in favour of women's lib. Let's be honest, once you've got an education behind you, you're not discriminated against as much as other women, are you? And you don't *experience* it: it's all very chatty, you go down to the pub at lunchtime with the fellows from work and what's this women's lib all about. My God.

Jo Ingram

It's been a consciousness-raising experience for me; it's shown me tremendously that I'm just one of millions.

I just feel I understand the difficulties women have. I was thinking the other day about how I'd never totally accepted what some people said – that, even if women are working, their main interest is still going to be the children and the housework and all the rest of it – and I never *really* took that too seriously, although I sort of half-accepted it; I never really knew what it *meant*. But now I think it's probably true for the majority of women. I mean the thing that's most likely to turn them on is something to do with kids, that's my personal experience; that's what worries *me* far more than my job conditions – what sort of chance he's getting, nursery facilities and so on.

Juliet Morley

I miss having an independent life, that's the thing. I don't miss the work I was doing particularly, it's having an independent life: something outside the home, something that's mine as opposed to something I share with Paul. Well I don't *have* an independent life at the moment, really.

But things like women not getting to the top in their careers just don't seem as important at the moment as they used to be. Things to do with the position of women in that sense don't seem so important. I think things could be made a lot easier for *mothers*. Even in the sense of providing access to buildings: I've certainly thought about people in wheelchairs a lot more since I've had a pram to push. Shopping could be made a lot easier and, when new buildings are designed, people ought to think about prams and wheelchairs a great deal more. I never realised, I thought these bloody people with prams: I wish they'd get out of the way!

Louise Thompson

I think I've become a feminist. I really get annoyed at men's roles – like in school [*she's a law student*] lots of men are married and you never see their kids; they have this total freedom. To Oliver, she's like a little toy; he can play with her.

Caroline Saunders

I tend to favour female politicians more than I did before and I respect them more; I think because I tend to think of women being stronger now, able to cope more. Because I'm sure if I was left in a position now where I had to cope, I probably would.

Gillian Hartley

Having experienced childbirth, the potentialities of being a woman are so much greater. Women are so lucky to have been the ones able to give birth, to have a child: that's marvellous.

Sophy Fisher

The disadvantages are the same as with being a housewife. I don't like being categorised, because people then generalise about categories. I say I don't think of myself as a mother; of course I do, but not in the social category sense. I must have had about eight million things through the post saying, wouldn't I like to do my shopping at home with Janet Frazer or somebody else's catalogue. No I *wouldn't*. And because I've had a baby, I'm no more likely to do my shopping through Janet Frazer's catalogue than I ever was.

Josephine Lloyd

I think probably more and more I've realised how women do get taken for granted. For example, when Howard and I go out shopping and he wants a drink on the way home, we sit in the pub and he might meet a couple of friends and sometimes I get the feeling that they're not interested in me: I'm just his wife and I've got a baby, and I'm not a person. I think that women definitely get taken for granted.

We don't get a lot of money anyway, but it does annoy me, because before, when I was working, I always had my own money. Howard gets the money on Monday, he gets about £28 social security [*he is unemployed*] and he gives me about £13 and keeps the rest. And he forgets that the money that he's given me isn't for me. He says, if there's some money left, he says oh spend it on yourself: but I've never had enough housekeeping to do that. I went to the social security and said, look, we've had so many arguments over money, he's been borrowing and borrowing, he goes into the pub for some cigarettes and then when he's got the money on Monday he'll repay it, and I don't have anything, and I've drawn out all my savings to spend on food. So I asked, if I can have half, just for the food, but they didn't want to know: they said no, we can't do that. So I have to rely on him giving me the money.

Power lies where the money is. The birth of a first child divides the sexes. Emotional dependence matches economic dependence: bringing up a child in our culture is socially isolated work. Most first-time mothers have few friends in the community. The stereotype of middle-class mothers' coffee mornings is at odds with even middle-class reality: how to break down the isolation of each housewife locked behind her own front door is the problem. For working-class mothers, the range of contacts is even narrower. One or two childhood friends, a married sister with children, mothers or other relatives – these may be the only available confidantes. People, strangers, peer into the pram as it is wheeled down the street and make noises at the baby, but this breach in social manners is not the beginning of a beautiful friendship. The world shrinks to the size of the home: mother, father and baby.

Deborah Smyth was married at 18 and she was 19 when Dominic was born. She used to work as a checker in a factory; her husband works in a greengrocer's:

My friend was getting married last Saturday. And she saw the baby – it was the first time she'd seen him, and she said oh I want to start a family. And I said to her: don't start a family yet.

I: Why did you say that?

Deborah: I don't know. [*long pause*] We did it quickly. I like him – I like having him at home, you know. And I like looking after him and everything else. I don't know why I said that.

Sometimes I think about before we got married and that, you know: I think about going to work every morning. I never want to do it again, you know: I just *think* about it.

Janette Watson, an ex-factory machinist, was also married at 18 and a mother a year later:

Well, I always think of what I'm missing. You know, before I was married I used to go out with friends; I don't do it any more. They all go out in crowds. I miss that really, because I don't get out much. I miss that a lot, I suppose.

They're all going abroad for their holidays – that's what I miss, I think: I've never been abroad. Mind you, when I started going out with Dan, I always wanted to be with him more than with them. So I suppose you can't have everything.

I think sometimes I've thought I should have waited for a little while to get married and have a baby. But we both wanted to get married. I think of what I'm missing – going abroad and everything.

But I like it: I like being married now. I mean I'll still be young when he grows up. I hope.

Medical maternity cases

Nature and culture

Childbirth stands uncomfortably at the junction of the two worlds of nature and culture. Like death and disease, it is a biological event, but the defining feature of biological events in human life is their social character. The way people are born and die, their assignations with illness and health, cannot be explained and predicted purely on the basis of knowledge about the biological functioning of the human organism. Bodies function in a social world and the parameters of this world supply an influence of their own.

But the components of nature and culture are more potently and ambiguously mixed in the case of reproduction than in other physiological states. Having babies must be deeply natural, since the architecture of the female body fits women for this role, the production of children follows naturally from that other human occupation, heterosexual congress, and the replacement of the population is necessary for human survival. Yet, at the same time, and because of these features, reproduction is a cultural activity: it has far-reaching consequences for the life of a society. Particular childbirths create or break families, establish the ownership of property and entitlements to poverty or privilege; they may alter the statuses, rights and responsibilities of persons, communities and nations.

The other paradox is that only women are the true *dramatis personae* of childbirth. They thus personify the union of nature (biological reproducer) and culture (social person) directly. The association between a biological emptying of the uterus and the social character of its product, a child, poses a cultural dilemma, but so also does the very existence of women. Levi-Strauss (1969) argued that the demarcation of boundary lines between nature and culture is the crux of the human social order: in such a manner is the territory in which human beings may fully experience their humanity marked out. But the division is fragile, and the core difficulty is that women are culturally anomalous, tied as they are by their reproductivity to a continuing and necessary natural function (Ortner, 1974).

It can be argued that the cultural subjection of women derives from the fact that, because they have wombs, they are caught in the trap of a collective need to control the natural forces of reproduction. Where the social order is ruled by men, women become the embodiment of an alternative government, which must be avoided at all costs. Two modes of avoidance are historically evident: separation and incorporation. According to the logic of the first, the business of reproduction is given over exclusively to women. Its practice and control are divided off from the rest of social life, so that no pollution of one by the other is possible. But, according to the logic of incorporation, women must give up their reproductive autonomy, their own right of control over reproduction, which is then 'mastered' by members of the dominant social group: the social, professional and gender elite of male-dominated medicine. In this way, reproduction comes to be the legitimate subject matter of medicine. Medicine diagnoses, prescribes and prognosticates about women as maternity 'cases' and the reproductive experiences of women are shaped by medical messages. Yet, in becoming a repository of 'knowledge' about reproduction, medical science is not some kind of ultimate truth. It hides an ideological face. The products of science in general can be regarded as specific cultural representations, as theoretical strategies arising in distinct cultural milieux (Kuhn, 1962). Such an approach to medicine is necessary if the aetiology and influence of medical paradigms about reproduction and women as its agents are to be exposed.

Medical mastery

Doctor knows best

Obstetrics, like midwifery, in its original meaning describes a female province. The management of reproduction has been, throughout most of history and in most cultures, a female concern; what is characteristic about childbirth in the industrial world is, conversely, its control by men. The conversion of female-controlled community management to male-controlled medical management alone would suggest that the propagation of particular paradigms of women as maternity cases has been central to the whole development of medically dominated maternity care (Verbrugge, 1976). The ideological element, as would be expected, is not part of the agenda in conventional medical histories chronicling the rise of male obstetrics (see, for example, Spencer, 1927).

In such histories, the achievements of male obstetrics over those of female midwifery are rarely argued empirically, but always a priori, from the double premise of male and medical superiority. More recent investigations of this argument reveal a different picture, in which the introduction of men into the business of reproductive management brought special dangers to mother and babies. The easier transmission of puerperal fever in male-run lying-in hospitals is one example; the generally careless and ignorant use of technology another (Oakley, 1976). In Britain, in the 18th and early 19th centuries, many of the male midwives' innovations were often fatal for both mother and child. The forceps, in particular, which are frequently claimed to be the chief advantage of male medicine, were not used in more than a minority of cases attended by male midwives, and had little effect on infant mortality, except, perhaps, to raise it further. In the 1920s in America, where female midwifery was to be most completely phased out, doctors had to contend with the fact that midwifery was obviously associated with less mortality and morbidity than the interventionist character of the new obstetrical approach (Barker-Benfield, 1976).

Improvements in knowledge and technique do not in retrospect justify male participation in midwifery during the 18th and 19th centuries and, if they did so at the time, it was the ideological power of the claim to greater expertise that had this effect. The success of the claim seems to have had a great deal to do with the propagation of certain notions of womanhood.

"It is almost a pity that a woman has a womb", exclaimed an American professor of gynaecology in the late 1860s (Wood, 1974). This statement neatly summarises the low regard in which the medical profession held its female patients; through its ideological construction of the uterus as the controlling organ of womanhood, it effectively demoted reproduction as woman's unique achievement to the status of a pitiable handicap. Such a construction presented women essentially as reproductive machines, subject to a direct biological input. It enabled physicians to assert a role in the mechanical management of female disorder, thus justifying the particular techniques of drastic gynaecological surgery and obstetrical intervention, and therefore establishing the 'need' for a male medical ascendancy over the whole domain of reproductive care.

How and why male medicine came to assume control over the care of women in childbirth in Britain and America over the last hundred years is, of course, a complex question. There are important parallels between medical and social ideologies of womanhood, yet medicine plays a particular role as social ideology. The reason for this is that the theoretical foundations of patriarchy lie in the manipulation of women's biology to constitute their social inferiority. Medicine, as the definer of biology, holds the key to its 'scientific' interpretation, and thus its cultural consequences. The power of medical ideology stems from the incorporation of social assumptions into the very language of physiological theories.

The conflict between reproducer as expert and doctor as expert may have five outcomes: the reproducer may accept the doctor's definition of the situation; the doctor may accept the reproducer's; the reproducer may challenge the doctor's view; the doctor may challenge the reproducer's; or the conflict between them may be manifested in a certain pattern of communication between doctor and patient that indicates the presence of unresolved questions to do with what has been termed "intrauterine neocolonialism" (Swinscow, 1974, p 800). In a large series of doctor–patient encounters observed for the 'Transition to motherhood' study, this latter outcome was much more common than direct confrontation. The woman's status as an expert may be accorded joking recognition:

Doctor: First baby?

Patient: Second.

Doctor [*laughing*]: So you're an expert?
Or:

Doctor: You're looking rather serious.

Patient: Well, I am rather worried about it all. It feels like a small baby –
I feel much smaller with this one than I did with my first, and she

weighed under six pounds. Ultrasound last week said the baby was very small, as well.

Doctor: Weighed it, did they?

Second doctor [*entering cubicle*]: They go round to flower shows and weigh cakes, you know.

First doctor: Yes, it's a piece of cake, really.

But frequently, patients concur in the doctor's presentation of himself (most obstetricians are male) as the possessor of privileged information:

Male doctor: Will you keep a note in your diary of when you first feel the baby move?

Patient: Do you know – well, of course, you would know – what it feels like?

Doctor: It feels like wind pains – something moving in your tummy.

At the same time, a common feature of communication between doctor and patient is a discrepancy between their labelling of significant symptoms. The medical dilemma is that of discerning the 'presenting' symptoms of clinically significant disorders; the patient's concern is with the normalisation of her subjective experience of discomfort. Of 677 statements made by patients, 12 per cent concerned symptoms of pain or discomfort which were medically treated either by being ignored, or with a non-serious response, or through a brief and selective account of relevant physiological/anatomical data:

Doctor: Feeling well?

Patient: Yes, but very tired – I can't sleep at all at night.

Doctor: Why is that?

Patient: Well, I'm very uncomfortable – I turn from one side to the other, and the baby keeps kicking. I get cramp on one side, high up in my leg. If I sleep on my back, I choke myself, so I'm tossing and turning about all night long, which isn't very good.

Doctor: We need to put you in a hammock, don't we? [*Reads case notes*] Tell me, the urine specimen which you brought in today – when did you do it?

****

Patient: I've got a pain in my shoulder.

Doctor: Well, that's your shopping bag hand, isn't it?

****

Patient: I get pains in my groin, down here, why is that?

Doctor: Well, it's some time since your last pregnancy, and also your centre of gravity is changing.

Patient: I see.

Doctor: That's okay. [*Pats on back*]

Such abbreviated 'common-sense' explanations are one mode in which doctors talk to patients. The contrasting mode is to 'technicalise' – to use technical language as a means of keeping the patient in her place. In maternity consultations, this interactive pattern particularly characterises those encounters in which a patient contends equality with the doctor:

> Doctor: I think what we have to do is assess you – see how near you are to having it. [*Does internal examination*] Right – you'll go like a bomb, and I've given you a good stirring up. So what I think you should do is, I think you should come in.
>
> Patient: Is it possible to wait another week, and see what happens?
>
> Doctor: You've been reading *The Sunday Times*.
>
> Patient: No, I haven't. I'm married to a doctor.
>
> Doctor: Well, you've ripened up since last week and I've given the membranes a good sweep over.
>
> Patient: What does that mean?
>
> Doctor: I've swept them – not with a brush, with my finger.

[*Writes in notes 'give date for induction'.*]

> Patient: I'd rather wait a bit.
>
> Doctor: Well, we know the baby's mature now, and there's no sense in waiting. The perinatal morbidity and mortality increase rapidly after 42 weeks. They didn't say that in *The Sunday Times*, did they?

A second classic area of dispute between reproducers and doctors is the dating of pregnancy. Six per cent of the questions asked and 5% of statements made by mothers in the antenatal clinic concerned dates, mothers usually trying to negotiate the 'correct' date of expected delivery with the doctor, who did not see this as a subject for negotiation – as a legitimate area of maternal expertise. The underlying imputation is one of feminine unreliability:

Doctor: Are you absolutely sure of your dates?

Patient: Yes, and I can even tell you the date of conception.

[*Doctor laughs.*]

Patient: No, I'm serious. This is an artificial insemination baby.

****

Doctor: How many weeks are you now?

Patient: Twenty-six-and-a-half.

Doctor: [*Looking at notes*]: Twenty weeks now.

Patient: No, twenty-six-and-a-half.

Doctor: You can't be.

Patient: Yes I am. Look at the ultrasound report.

Doctor: When was it done?

Patient: Today.

Doctor: It was done today?

Patient: Yes.

Doctor: [*reads report*]: Oh yes, twenty-six-and-a-half weeks, that's right.

[*Patient smiles triumphantly at researcher.*]

Perhaps it is significant that increasingly the routine use of serial ultrasound cephalometry is providing an alternative medical technique for the assessment of gestation length. A medical rationale for the inflation of medical over maternal expertise is thus provided. It is important to note that, although the efficacy, safety and technical superiority of ultrasound is widely assumed within the medical frame of reference, this does not rest on a 'scientific' basis. No randomised controlled trials have, for example, been conducted that evaluate the usefulness of ultrasound examination and maternal report in assessing gestation length and fetal wellbeing. [There are now a number of trials which show that routine ultrasound is no better in preventing baby deaths and may be associated with long-term effects on children's development (Neilson, 1998; Bricker and Neilson, 2000).] Laboratory investigations of the physiological effects of ultrasound on developing embryonic and fetal cells are limited and contradictory. Longitudinal follow-up of children subjected to ultrasound while in the womb is sparse and restricted to a six-year period, the kind of time span known to be inadequate in showing up the long-term effects of other procedures inflicted on fetuses, such as X-rays and the administration of hormones.

Similar kinds of scientific caveats can be levelled at other medical techniques generally used in the treatment of women as maternity cases (see, for example, Richards, 1975; Stewart and Stewart, 1976; Chalmers and Richards, 1977). Unbridled medical enthusiasm for new techniques is a general feature of modern medicine.

Medicalisation

> Normally patients come to the hospital because they're ill. Pregnant women aren't ill and illness is a reason for *not* coming to the hospital.

The consultant who made this statement did so to make his colleagues laugh, but it is not really a laughing matter. This paradoxical situation – in which a large number of healthy people are treated with a barrage of medical and pharmacological techniques in surgeries, hospitals and clinics for a 'natural' and 'normal' condition – has to do with the general social function of medicine, as well as with its specific management of reproduction. The obstetrical claim to expertise is an aspect of the medicalisation of life: the ascendancy of doctors as arbiters of human concerns. As Eliot Freidson puts it, it is characteristic of our culture that "The medical profession has first claim to jurisdiction over the label of illness and anything to which it may be attached, *irrespective of its capacity to deal with it effectively*" (1970, p 251; my emphasis). The medicalisation of reproduction as a potentially abnormal activity is the theme of much medical writing and practice. It is only by a ideological transformation of the 'natural' to the 'cultural' that doctors can legitimate reproduction as a medical speciality. For example:

> Patient: I'm a hairdresser, I only do three days a week – is it alright to go on working?

> Doctor: Up to twenty-eight weeks is alright on the whole, especially if you have a trouble-free pregnancy as you obviously have. After that, it's better to give up.

Patient: I only work three days a week. I feel fine.

Doctor: Yes, everything is fine, but now you've got to this stage it's better to give up, just in case.

****

Doctor: It'd be difficult to get you off now – I think you ought to come in for rest and to do some more water tests, and then we can start you off. The baby isn't growing as fast as it was.

Patient: What do you mean, 'Come in'?

Doctor: Really it's a matter of when you come in. Sunday, I should think, and then stay in.

Patient: Stay in until it's born, you mean?

Doctor: Yes.

Patient: I don't fancy that very much.

Doctor: If you'd been ready, I would have started you off today. You see, on the ultrasound, it's not growing as well as it was, and on the water tests the oestriols are falling. It's not bad, but you should come in and have some water tests, get some rest, and then we can start you off sometime next week probably, when you're ready.

Patient: If my husband wanted to come and talk to you about inducing me, can I make an appointment for him?

Doctor: I don't think anything your husband said would affect our decision one way or the other.

Patient: No, but he would like to talk to you.

Doctor: Yes, well, he can talk to whoever's on duty, but there's nothing he can say that will affect us; it's a medical question.

****

Doctor: This is Mrs Taylor. She's due in four weeks. Very scientific, aren't we – she used to be a botanist. Did we do an alphafetoprotein for the previous spina bifida?

Patient: Yes.

Doctor: The risk is about one in twenty of the same thing happening again, but in fact we know it's alright, and she's not going to have one, don't we?

Patient: Yes, they said it was normal.

Doctor: Four weeks to go. You last had ultrasound – today? When are you going to have it again?

Patient: They said it was up to you.

Doctor: I think you'd better have another. We'll make you an appointment.

Patient: Does it seem alright?

Doctor: Yes, it's fine.

Patient: It's just routine?

Doctor: It isn't that we suspect anything abnormal; we're just being cautious.

Patient: I see.

Doctor: Come here next week and then in two weeks you can go to ultrasound before the clinic – that'll save you another visit.

Patient: Thank you, doctor.

Other signs of medicalisation are that, in the sample of 'normal' primigravidae I interviewed in the 'Transition to motherhood' study, 100% took drugs of one kind or another in pregnancy; 100% had blood and urine tests; 68% were given ultrasound; 19% had X-rays and 30% other tests; the average number of antenatal visits was 13. Of a series of 878 questions asked the researcher by the women in this study, 24% concerned medical procedures – about which women felt deprived of information or in need of reassurance. In nearly half the doctor–patient encounters observed in the research hospital, there was at least one reference to technology – to one testing procedure or another. Of the questions asked by patients, 29% concerned technology (ultrasound, induction, blood tests and so forth), as did 17% of the statements they made to doctors.

These are some aspects of the medicalisation of women as maternity cases; they are reinforced by the later treatment of women in the delivery room, where a birth without medical intervention is now virtually unknown in many industrialised countries. But obstetricians must also come to terms with the self-evident fact that childbearing *is* natural – most women are able to deliver babies safely and without problems. Much of the antenatal literature in British use illustrates this ambivalence. Pregnant women are told that pregnancy is a 'natural function' or a 'perfectly normal event' during which mothers enjoy 'the best of health'. They are nevertheless instructed to visit the clinic or doctor regularly, pay careful attention to medical advice and follow the doctor's orders, with the implicit message that the 'natural' function of childbirth can only be accomplished within a circumscribed medical context (Graham, 1977).

The importance of the medical context is established by the *routinisation* of technological, pharmacological and clinical procedures during as many stages of the reproductive process as possible and in as many patients as possible. To reserve such procedures for a small proportion of maternity cases would emphasise the probability of normality; to use them for the majority of patients stresses the probability of abnormality, and the need for women to be dependent on medical care. Mary Cousins is a comptometer operator, married to a greengrocer; she had had a termination of pregnancy in the past and had been (unknowingly) included in a research project designed to see whether regular vaginal examinations are of any use in preventing abortion due to cervical incompetence following a termination:

> Doctor [*Entering examination cubicle*]: Okay, dear, pop up on the couch. [*Patient does so.*]
>
> Doctor [*Consulting case notes*]: Mrs Cousins?
>
> Patient: Yes.
>
> Doctor [*Palpating abdomen*]: I want to do an internal examination now. Open your legs and relax.
>
> Patient [*Begins to obey instructions, then suddenly realizes what the doctor intends to do and closes her legs*]: Oh no, please doctor, no doctor.
>
> Doctor: Why not?
>
> Patient: The doctor last time, he hurt me and I had a lot of bleeding afterwards – he promised he wouldn't do it again.
>
> Doctor [*Visibly angry*]: I don't care a damn what the doctor promised last time. If you lose the baby, it's up to you. Do you know why we do these examinations?
>
> Patient: I thought it was to tell the size of the baby.
>
> Doctor: No, it's nothing to do with that. You've had a termination, and this can damage the neck of the womb and cause prematurity, and we look to see if the womb is opening up. If it is, we put a stitch in.

Patient: I'd rather not, doctor.

Doctor [*Still evidently cross*]: Okay. Well, everything else appears to be alright. We'll see you in two weeks.

The purpose of the regular internal examinations had obviously not been explained to Mary before, and it was only through a direct challenge that the covert character of the examination was revealed.

One important norm within the culture of the medical profession is that judging a sick person well is more to be avoided than judging a well person sick (Scheff, 1963). This 'medical decision rule' is applied to obstetrics as it is to other branches of medicine; the doctor views reproduction as a potentially problematic condition, reserving the label 'normal' as a purely retrospective term. Every pregnancy and labour is treated as though it is, or could be, abnormal, and the weight of the obstetrician's medical education acts against his/her achievement of work satisfaction in the treatment of unproblematic reproduction. Thus doctors in the research hospital openly declared their preference for working in the 'special clinic' where high risk cases are seen, as it 'makes life a bit more interesting'. The consequence of this attitude is of course that 'normal' reproduction becomes an anachronistic category:

Consultant: Interesting, very interesting, most unusual.

Registrar: You mean it was a normal delivery?

Consultant: Yes – pushed the baby out herself!

The equation of 'normal' with 'unusual' illustrates the medical rationale, for if this equation did not hold, obstetricians would presumably have no valid role in managing reproduction. A further device that labels women as medical maternity cases is the *fragmentation* of reproductive care through the separation of obstetrics from paediatrics and its alignment with gynaecology, the *diseases* that women, by virtue of their special biology, exhibit.

Indices of success

'Successful' reproduction in the medical frame of reference is measured in terms of concrete statistical indices: perinatal and maternal mortality rates. Certain limited indices of morbidity are also used: for example, the physical condition of the baby in the immediate postpartum period. But the prevention of death remains the chief yardstick by which the obstetrician judges the value of his/her work, being particularly concerned with the concept of 'avoidable' death, the most prominent meaning of which is death for which the practitioners of reproductive medicine could hold themselves, or be held, responsible.

It might seem obvious that only mortality statistics can offer any objective base for judging the success of reproductive management. But, in fact, the form this argument has taken has generated two basic errors. In the first place, the reproductive 'performance' of women deduced from the mortality statistics has often been directly attributed to the impact of obstetric medicine. In the second place, the limited notion of success entailed by statistical criteria has not always reflected success from the reproducer's point of view.

Taking the point about the relationship between obstetric medicine and mortality statistics first, it is evident that this is an example of a general tendency within medical history – to pre-empt the primacy of non-medical influences by asserting the exclusive right of doctors to improve health (see, for example, Poynter and Keele, 1961).

Contemporary obstetric medicine has its roots in the 'scientific' and technological domination of male midwives over the empiricist and 'natural' methods of traditional female midwifery. What has consequentially followed is a style of medicine that decisively emphasises the physical rather than the social or psychological. This type of medical ideology and practice fits very well the notion that success can be judged quantitatively via mortality statistics, rather than (or as well as) through the medium of the *quality* of life that mothers and babies experience during and after the medical manipulation of reproduction. The restricted meaning of successful reproductive outcome in the medical model implies (i) that a woman's own satisfaction with her childbirth experience should be complete if she emerges from childbirth alive and with a live, healthy infant, and (ii) that other more broadly based indices of health (the woman's emotional reactions to the experience of childbirth and its management, the way in which motherhood is integrated with a woman's life-style, her satisfaction/dissatisfaction with the baby and with the mother–baby relationship) are not relevant measures of reproductive success.

Again, this concern should be placed in the general context of medical care, where keeping people alive has become the primary medical goal and the quality of the lives thus extended has seemed a secondary consideration. Live babies who are brain-damaged or have had their health impaired in other ways through the circumstances of their birth present particular problems to their mothers, and may alter their capacity to 'adjust' to motherhood. In some cases, a mother may feel it would have been better for all concerned had the child not survived. One such case history stands out in the series observed for the 'Transition to motherhood' study. A single woman had an intrauterine contraceptive device (IUCD) fitted before having intercourse with her boyfriend and immediately became pregnant with twins. She was told by the doctor to give up work in order to allow the babies to grow more satisfactorily, but because she had no income aside from her employment, did not intend to get married and was planning to have the babies adopted, she saw the advice to devote herself exclusively to the task of gestation as quite counter to her own interests.

This is an extreme instance of clash between the index of statistical survival and mothers' own assessment of reproductive success; in most cases, the goal of a live baby is, of course, one that mother and medical staff share. But achievement of this goal is not necessarily equated by mothers with reproductive success.

Other negative experiences may intrude: a 'bad' birth, a difficult baby, severe postnatal depression. Doctors and mothers may have different views of whose achievement the birth is. For mothers, successful childbirth is often contingent on certain ideas being realised about how birth should be accomplished. If obstetricians block the realisation of these ideas, they may prevent maternal feelings of success and make more likely a pervasive sense of personal failure in the act that is culturally held out to be the primary achievement and proof of womanhood. Most women evaluate the success of their childbirths in a more holistic way than the medical frame of reference allows.

Pregnant patients

The medical control of reproduction assigns a specially limited status to the pregnant woman, whose career as a patient begins with the medical confirmation of her pregnancy and ends shortly after the delivery of her child. During this reproductive phase, being a patient is the only relevant role in medical eyes, an aspect of the medical frame of reference that is illustrated in the following encounter between a shop assistant and a houseman:

Doctor: Mrs Bates?

Patient: Yes.

Doctor: This is your first visit in this pregnancy?

Patient: Yes.

Doctor: You were on the pill?

Patient: Yes.

Doctor: Was that period in May the only period you had?

Patient: What?

Doctor: You haven't had a proper period since that one?

Patient: No, but I've had a brownish discharge since then.

Doctor: When?

Patient: Well, more or less all the time.

Doctor: Recently?

Patient: Yes.

Doctor: Do you wear a pad?

Patient: No.

Doctor: Does it itch?

Patient: No.

Doctor: Have you felt the baby move?

Patient: Oh yes.

Doctor: Why have you left it so long [*Patient is about 22 weeks pregnant*] before coming here?

Patient: Well, I didn't go to the doctor for ages. I was so depressed. I didn't want the baby. I wanted an abortion.

Doctor: Have you ever had diabetes, tuberculosis, rheumatic fever, kidney diseases, high blood pressure?

Patient: No.

Doctor: Has anyone in the family ever had any of those?

Patient: No.

Doctor [*Reading notes*]: So you've just got two babies alive – you had a couple of miscarriages?

Patient: Yes. Well, I had three.

Doctor: And you had a blood transfusion?

Patient: Yes.

Doctor: And you had twins? [*Two of the miscarriages were of twin pregnancies, one at 12 and one at 24 weeks.*]

Patient: Yes.

Doctor: Let me have a look at you. [*Proceeds to palpate abdomen*]

Patient: I fell down the stairs with this one.

Doctor: Did you? [*Looks in mouth*] Are they all yours?

Patient: No, I've got dentures with six on.

Doctor: Do you go to the dentist regularly?

Patient: I do.

Doctor: When was the last time you went?

Patient: Two weeks ago.

Doctor: And you don't breastfeed your babies?

Patient: No.

Doctor: You're not going to breastfeed this one? [*Examines breasts*]

Patient: No.

Doctor: Have you noticed any lumps?

Patient: No.

Doctor: They just feel heavier than usual?

Patient: Yes.

Doctor: I want to have a look at this discharge of yours. Bend your knees up for me. [*Patient moves to side*] No, on your back please. That's right. Can you let your knees go floppy and just relax? This'll be a bit cold [*inserts speculum*]. Okay, just stay as you are, I've nearly finished. I just want to examine you. [*Withdraws speculum and does bimanual examination.*] Okay. All finished. That's fine. Everything's alright. The brownish discharge is from a sore place you've got on the neck of the womb. That's quite common in pregnancy. You're about right for dates, but because you were on the pill, I want you to go to ultrasound.

Patient: Is that date – the third of March – right?

Doctor: When you've been to ultrasound, we'll know more accurately.

Patient: Do I have to go there now?

Doctor: No, nurse will make an appointment for you.

The patient's attitude to the pregnancy is ignored by the examining doctor, who instead focuses his and the patient's attention narrowly on its medical management.

In the main, antenatal consultations are managed so that there is no place for mention of social/emotional factors. The relevance of a woman's other roles is considered only where employment or marital status (i.e. working, being unmarried) are perceived as in conflict with the goal of the production of a live, healthy full-term infant. In other cases, the intrusion of 'personal' considerations into medical decision making transgresses the prevailing norm of reproduction as a medical process:

> Doctor: We want you to come into hospital today.
>
> Patient: Today! I can't possibly come in today. I've got some furniture arriving. I can't come till Monday at least.
>
> Doctor: Who's at home, then?
>
> Patient: No one. My husband's out at work.
>
> Doctor:: Well, it's time this baby was delivered. Your blood pressure's up and you've got some protein in your urine, and you need to rest in hospital until we can start you off.
>
> Patient: But it's not due until the 27th [*two weeks' time*].
>
> Doctor: I know, but we've been watching the baby's growth at ultrasound and it's quite big enough now.
>
> Patient: There's nothing wrong with it, is there?
>
> Doctor: No, but your blood pressure's up and there's protein in your urine and we feel that the baby ought to be delivered. If we leave it longer, the baby might be affected. I would object anyway, if I knew you were going home to have furniture shifted. That's not good for you, or the baby.
>
> Patient: I can't get hold of my husband today.
>
> Doctor: When will he be home, then?
>
> Patient: Twenty past six.
>
> Doctor: Well, could you come in this evening?
>
> Patient: I suppose so.

The outcome is negotiated – but only minimally so. Irritation is the typical medical reaction to patients' mentions of attitudinal factors or their other social-role obligations. Ninety-three per cent of patients' questions/statements concerning social factors met this response. In these two examples, conflict between medical and maternal frames of reference is very evident.

A registered baby minder and a senior registrar:

Patient: Can you give me some sort of idea as to when my operation's [*a Caesarean*] going to be done?

Doctor: Well, it's very difficult to say.

Patient: It's very difficult for me too. My husband's got to take time off work and I've got two kids to make arrangements for.

Doctor: Yes, I see. Well, sometime in the last week of your pregnancy, I imagine.

Patient: No.

Doctor: What?

Patient: Thirty-eight weeks, Mr Hawkins said.

Doctor: Well, I'm not Mr Hawkins.

Patient: It's a bit thick, this is. If it's not done till forty weeks, my husband'll go mad. Mr Hawkins promised faithfully it'd be done at thirty-eight weeks.

Doctor: Well, then, there's no point in asking me, is there?

Patient: I've got to ask. I've got two kids to look after.

Doctor: Well, I can't decide for Mr Hawkins. I don't know what his work commitments are.

Patient: I can't ask Mr Hawkins, can I? He's not here.

Doctor: There's plenty of time to ask him. Ask him next week.

Patient: I want to know now. I need to know to make arrangements.

Doctor: Why will you husband go mad?

Patient: Because of what happened last time. I'm not waiting for the selfsame thing to happen again, am I?

Doctor: What happened last time? [*Reads notes: an intrapartum haemorrhage and fresh stillbirth*] Oh, I see. Right, I'll give you a date now. Right, I'll work it out. [*Writes in notes: 'Patient very keen to know date of admission to hospital, and has many arrangements to make. Can't wait until Mr Hawkins returns …'*]

A receptionist and a senior registrar:

Doctor: Mrs Carter? How are you getting on?

Patient: Horrible.

Doctor: Why?

Patient: I feel horrible.

Doctor: Have you had any more bleeding?

Patient: No.

Doctor [*Palpates abdomen*]: Yes, that's alright.

Patient: Was the test [*urinary oestriols*] alright?

Doctor: Yes. And they're expecting you at ultrasound today.

Patient: I feel so depressed.

Doctor: Why?

Patient: I don't know.

Doctor: So, why aren't you well?

Patient: I feel it's so difficult to walk.

Doctor: You shouldn't be walking much at this stage of pregnancy.

Patient: I don't. But I have my housework to do and I've got my in-laws staying.

Doctor: They should be doing your housework for you, shouldn't they? Isn't that what they're for?

Patient: They're not females. It's my father-in-law staying. Things aren't very good at home at the moment.

[*Doctor says nothing and continues to palpate abdomen.*]

Patient: What are the chances of a Caesarean?

Doctor: It's early days yet. We'll wait and see. Good-sized baby, that, isn't it! That's a good size.

Patient: It's the tightening I keep worrying about.

Doctor: It's normal in pregnancy. Your womb is supposed to tighten.

Patient: I didn't have it with the other three.

Doctor: Every pregnancy is different. Let's see you in one week. [*Reading notes*] You do seem to have put on a bit of weight.

Patient: What does that mean?

Doctor: It doesn't necessarily mean anything, but you must take things easy.

Patient: That's what my husband says. It's easy for men to say that.

Doctor: You shouldn't blame us.

Patient: I'm not blaming you, it's not your fault.

Doctor: It's your set up at home. You should have organised things better.

Patient: Well, I've got three kids to look after.

Doctor: Yes.

[Doctor, later, to researcher: It's her silly fault; she should have made arrangements. Now my wife, I left her without the car the other day, and she had to walk the three-year-old three miles to school, and she complained. I said ring up a friend, and she did, and they were only too delighted to help. It just takes a bit of organising, that's all.]

Behind this medical emphasis on clinical judgement and decision making lies an underlying concern with social typification. This includes a division of the patient population into 'special' and 'ordinary' cases. Whereas clinical data would predict a concentration of working-class women in the special clinic, because of their higher risk of obstetric problems (Illsley, 1967), the association in the observational data is, in fact, in the opposite direction: middle-class women were more likely to attend the special clinic ($p<0.01$). Patients with any kind of medical status – being doctors, nurses, midwives or (especially) the daughters or wives of doctors – were particularly likely ($p<0.001$) to be seen in the special clinic. The implications of special clinic attendance are greater privacy and more space in the examination cubicle, more doctor time and more chance of seeing a higher status doctor. In both clinics, working-class patients and white, as opposed to brown, patients were given more time by the doctor (though the differences are not statistically significant, $p<0.14$ and $p<0.08$ respectively).

Medical understanding of the concept of social class is limited. In one study of an obstetric unit, the researcher asked the staff how to assess social class. The replies were randomly distributed between intelligence, money, education, occupation, accent, personality, clothes and hairstyle. Most attributions in clinical practice were in terms of intelligence; in 68 cases over the twelve-month study 'intellectually deficient' was written in the case notes, while in only one case was there any evidence for this statement. One obstetrician observed had two methods of conducting an examination. Either he would read the notes at length and then turn to the patient, or he would begin to talk to the patient immediately on entering the examination cubicle. The first method was reserved for patients whose notes recorded a manual occupation, and the second for those with non-manual occupations (Fish, 1966).

Of course, such discrimination against working-class, ethnic minority group and non-medical patients is not exclusive to the maternity care field. Other researchers have noted it in other areas of medical practice. But so far as maternity cases are concerned, such designations are peculiarly mixed with ideological constructions of the feminine character.

Medical typifications of women

Two paradigms of women jostle for first place in the medical model of reproduction. In the first, women are seen not only as passive patients but in a mechanistic way as manipulable reproductive machines. In the second, the mechanical model is replaced by an appeal to notions of the biologically determined 'feminine' female.

The 'reproductive machine' model has informed much of the technological innovation in obstetrics that has taken place since the colonisation of reproductive care by medicine. This style of obstetrics is known as 'the active management of labour'. It embodies a physicalist approach to childbirth: "To put the matter rather crudely, obstetrics treats the body like a complex machine and uses a series of interventionist techniques to repair faults that may develop in the machine" (Richards, 1975, p 598). A mechanical model directly opposes the natural model; it is 'man-made' and requires regular servicing and maintenance to function correctly. Thus antenatal care can be interpreted as maintenance and malfunction-spotting work; obstetrical intervention in delivery as repairing mechanical faults with mechanical skills. Concretely, as well as ideologically, women appear to become machines, as machines are increasingly used to monitor pregnancy and labour, to initiate and terminate labour itself. One machine controls the uterine contractions, which are recorded on another machine; regional analgesia removes the woman's awareness of her contractions so that these must indeed be read off the machine; and keeping all the machines going becomes what 'looking after' a patient in labour means.

The mechanical metaphor sharpens into an analogy with a computer; it is only by the careful selection and coding of information that computers can be made to function correctly (to produce the desired result). The main vehicle for the programming of women as maternity patients is antenatal advice literature. The evolution of this literature in Britain in fact reflects very closely the chronology of expanding medical jurisdiction over birth. Today the emphasis is on the need for women to be informed about the physiology of pregnancy and labour, and to a smaller extent to be cognisant of the rationale behind the medical management of these. Yet a very clear dividing line is drawn between desirable and undesirable information: the first two sections in Gordon Bourne's widely read *Pregnancy* (1975) are called 'Importance of information' and 'Don't read medical textbooks'.

The necessary contentment of necessary motherhood

Doctor: This is twins. They're growing well, but you need more rest. I'd advise some good books and a quiet life for three months. You're not working?

Patient: No.

Doctor: Just normal exercise – I want you to have a walk every day, but no gardening, no heavy work, postpone moving or decorating the house. If you do rest, you'll grow yourself slightly bigger babies. After all, it's this [*pats her abdomen*] that's your most important job, isn't it?

Women, mothers, housewives

Doctor: Does it make you want to wee when I press there?

Patient: It does slightly – I spend more and more time in the loo than anywhere else.

Doctor: Moved the cooker in there, have you?

Doctor [*To pupil midwife*] She can't rest at home, and if she doesn't rest, she'll have tiny babies – like kippers. No, she can't rest at home, I wouldn't listen to arguments, not unless she's the Queen or the Duchess of

Malborough. There's a good case for telling her that now, so she can get granny over from Limerick or wherever.

The marriage symbol

Patient: When I wake up, my fingers and ankles are so swollen.

Doctor: And I see you haven't got your wedding ring on.

Doctor [*To researcher*]: And she's got some oedema – fluid retention. [*To patient*] Is your ring tight?

Patient: I don't wear it.

Doctor: Why don't you wear it?

Patient: It's tight.

Doctor [*To researcher*]: You see, when they get embarrassed not wearing a ring in pregnancy, they borrow someone's – their mother's or grandmother's.

Patient: I'm not embarrassed.

A proper family

Doctor [*Palpating abdomen*]: Ah, a nice-sized baby.

Patient's two-year-old son: Yes.

Doctor: So you want a little girl, I suppose?

Patient: No.

Women never know, do they?

Doctor [*To researcher*]: Mrs Connell hasn't got a clue about her dates. I bet you don't know when your last period was?

Researcher: Yes, I do.

Doctor: I don't believe you. Women never know.

****

Doctor: Have you felt movements, yet?

Patient: Yes.

Doctor: When?

Patient: They started on March 18th.

Doctor: That's a good girl, a very good girl, that's what we like to see, someone who knows the date.

****

Doctor [*Reading case notes*]: Ah, I see you've got a boy and a girl.

Patient: No, two girls.

Doctor: Really, are you sure? I thought it said ... [*checks in case notes*] oh no, you're quite right, two girls.

Doing what comes naturally, or you shouldn't believe all that

Doctor [*To audience of pupil midwives*]: I don't agree with husbands being there when women are in labour. After all, cows and bitches kick the stallion away.

Pupil midwife: Yes, but women aren't cows, are they?

****

Doctor: How old are you?

Patient: Eighteen.

Doctor: Do you want an epidural, dear?

Patient: What?

Doctor: Do you want an injection to take the pains away?

Patient: No, it's dangerous.

Doctor: There's nothing dangerous about it. You mustn't believe all you hear, you know. I've just done an epidural for a friend's wife, and he's an anaesthetist.

****

173

Patient: Last week Mr Mitchell said he'd have me in at term to be induced. I'd rather not be induced – unless there's a reason.

Doctor: Well, we won't induce you if there's no indication. We don't do social inductions.

Patient: Okay, fine. The other thing was, I've heard you do routine epidurals.

Doctor: Yes, on request.

Patient: Do you have to have them?

Doctor: Oh no.

Patient: That's alright then.

Doctor: You want it au naturel?

Now then, sweetie

Doctor: Have you had a smear test from the neck of the womb recently?

Patient: No.

Doctor: Well, I want to do one today. Could you turn over and face the wall, move your bottom over, and put your feet forward, so you don't kick me in the chops. I'll just go and get the equipment I need, I'll be back in a tick. [*Leaves cubicle, returns with speculum*] Now then, sweetie, I have warmed it for you under the tap, so that's nice of me, isn't it?

Patient: Thank you, doctor.

This feminine paradigm of women is presented in parallel with two other ideological tendencies: a hostility to female culture and an identification with masculine interests. Diana Scully and Pauline Bart carried out a study of women in gynaecology textbooks and found that they "revealed a persistent bias toward greater concern with the patient's husband than with the patient herself" (1973, p 1045). The same tendency is evident in obstetrics, where, for example, concern with the role of husbands in labour is associated with the promotion of types of analgesia that make the *husband's* experience of childbirth more pleasant. Alternatively, the doctor becomes the husband; a well known popular treatise on the treatment of infertility proposes medical students as the ideal donors of sperm to women with unfertile husbands:

Who are the donors?… My own preference is for medical students, and other doctors who engage in AID [artificial insemination by donor] tend to use the same source. Medical students are generally acceptable to the recipients as being intelligent young men who have gained a place in a medical school. They generally are emotionally stable people and are frequently good all-rounders who take part in the sporting and social activities of their hospitals. (Newill, 1974, p 165)

The merging of doctor and husband roles through the identification of doctors with husbands is one device used to 'desexualise' the intimacy of the obstetrical encounter. The registrar in the following case was seeing a childless woman in her late twenties for a follow-up appointment after an emergency hysterectomy. This was preceded by an emergency Caesarean section for fetal distress in premature labour: the baby was stillborn and, in the early puerperium, the patient sustained an uncontrollable haemorrhage and was admitted to hospital in acute shock.

Doctor: Hello, how are you? [*Reading case notes*] You came to see Mr Mitchell again?

Patient: Yes [*Smiles*] but it's proving rather difficult to see him. [*The consultant failed to turn up to take his clinic.*] You took some urine tests because it hurts a bit when I go to the toilet, and they thought there might be an infection there.

Doctor: I can't find the result [*Looks in notes*]. You brought some urine in today, did you?

Patient: Yes.

Doctor: Ah, here it is; no, there doesn't seem to be an infection.

Patient: Do you know if it's healed up inside?

Doctor [*Obviously reluctant to examine patient*]: I thought Mr Mitchell had done all that.

Patient: He did, but he said it wasn't quite healed and he'd like to look again.

Doctor: Turn on your left side, will you, and I'll have a look. How long has it been now?

Patient: Six weeks.

Doctor [*Inserting speculum*]: And how is your poor husband bearing up all this time?

Patient: Alright. I don't think it worries him, really. He's more worried about how I am.

Doctor [*Looking inside the vagina*]: Poor chap. How long altogether has he been without his rights?

Patient: I don't think he minds. I think he's worried something else might happen to me – all that bleeding upset him.

The doctor's concern for what he sees as her husband's sexual deprivation, a concern expressed significantly at the exact moment he inserts a speculum into her vagina, contrasts with the patient's calm insistence that lack of intercourse is not a problem for her husband. She refers to the trauma of what happened to her medically – after all, her husband saw her nearly die. The doctor repeats the same point: "poor chap…".

Medical work in obstetrics and gynaecology is characterised by these two themes of sexuality and gender. Through stereotypical visions of female parenthood, doctors exercise a social control function over women's lives that has little to do with the ostensible medical rationale of disease diagnosis and treatment:

Doctor [*To researcher, discussing second doctor*]: How do you rate him, then?

Researcher: What do you mean?

Doctor: I don't think he'll ever have any sexual impact on the patients, that chap.

The typical obstetrical encounter is between a man and a woman. Moreover, through the intimacy of the 'clinical' procedures that are medically defined as necessary, the encounter has strong sexual connotations. These provide a base for many of the communicative patterns characterising doctor–patient interaction as, for example, in the following episodes:

Doctor: Hello, how are you?

Patient: Alright.

Doctor [*Reading case notes*]: This isn't our first rendezvous, is it? We can't go on meeting like this, you know.

****

Doctor: I think you'd better go to ultrasound – it might be twins. I'm sure they'll tell us the answer one way or the other.

Patient: There aren't any twins in the family. But I'd like it.

Doctor: There's a first time for everything, as the archbishop said to the actress.

****

Doctor: Hello.

Patient [*Taking pants off*]: Sorry.

Doctor: Touting for business?

Patient [*Smiling*]: Yes.

****

Doctor: I'll give you some tablets for the tingling – the only thing is, you shouldn't take them too late or they'll make you pee all night: they increase the water flow, you see. What time do you go to bed?

Patient: Oh luxuriously early – about 9 o'clock, and I have an orgy of TV watching.

Doctor: An orgy of what?

Patient: TV.

Doctor: Oh yes, well [*exiting from cubicle, talking loudly*], I should cut out the orgies at this stage, if I were you.

Significantly, sexual joking of this type is restricted to the beginning (first and third examples) and ends (second and fourth examples) of the encounter. Examination of the patient's body, especially a vaginal examination, brings doctor and patient into greater intimacy, which must be denied if the encounter is to retain its overtly clinical purpose. Many manoeuvres are used to achieve this end, but the main one is making sure a nurse is there to 'chaperone'. Every doctor in the series of antenatal encounters observed was selective about this procedure, for instance: "It isn't the youngsters I worry about, but the thirty to forty year old woman: I always insist on a chaperone" (registrar, early forties). Talking about something else is also a mode of distracting attention from the sexual embarrassment of the situation:

Doctor: I'd like to examine you down below to do what we call pelvic assessment, to see if the pelvis is the right size.

Patient: Okay.

> Doctor: Can you bring you knees up for me? [*Inserts gloved hand into vagina*] Right now, we don't have a clinic next week, because of Easter, so you'd better come next in a fortnight's time.

And the sexual embarrassment itself is occasionally given overt recognition:

> Doctor: Right, could you turn on your side, put your bottom over here, and pull your legs up?

> Patient [*Doing so*]: I'm sure I didn't have this last time.

> Doctor: Did you have it on your back?

> Patient: Yes, I think so. Is it better this way?

> Doctor: Well it is, because I don't have to stare you in the face.

> Patient: Oh, I see. It's better for you, not for me.

Technical words for the woman's genitals are significantly not used, 'down below' being the most common euphemism, although 'inside' and 'tail' are also prominent. Such parlance contrasts with doctors' tendencies to 'technicalise' during other parts of the consultation. Both manoeuvres are distancing techniques, the requirements of keeping the patient in her place and of desexualising the episode calling for different strategies on the doctor's part (see also Emerson, 1970).

Clinical behaviour is shaped by moral judgements in which culturally normative paradigms of femininity abound: such investigations of physicians' beliefs as J. Aitken-Swan's *Fertility control and the medical profession* (1977) give ample evidence of the interaction between attitude and practice. A truly horrific and terrifying revelation of how medical behaviour can exemplify the most 'criminally negligent' aspects of social ideologies that degrade women is Ian Young's *The private life of Islam* (1974), an account of a London medical student's midwifery training in Algeria, where obstetricians are "unhappy executioners, working in the blood, excrement and death of the most respected attitudes" (p vi).

In the less overtly sexist tableau of modern industrialised society, the feminine paradigm has been clothed in a more subtle veil. The ideological appeal is to sexual *difference* rather than sexual inferiority. Paradigmatically, women are just different sorts of people from men, and the matrix of the argument is that their reproductive behaviour and attitudes can only be understood against this background of cultural femininity.

Mistakes and mystiques of motherhood

Veiled by the mystiques of feminine psychology and deterministic biology, mothers' reactions to motherhood have been regarded by medical and social science as in a class of their own. Science, responding to an agenda of basically social concerns, has provided the label 'postnatal depression' as a pseudo-scientific tag for the description and ideological transformation of maternal discontent. Thus labelled, maternal difficulties remain impervious to scientific understanding; it is only the alternative approach of considering responses to childbirth as a species of a larger genus, human reactions to life events, that their intrinsic character can be mapped out.

Any analysis of women's 'adjustment' or 'non-adjustment' to motherhood must proceed on a number of levels if it is to avoid the feminine paradigm mistakes of male science. In the first place, how women feel about their childbirths is not the same as how they feel about their babies, and neither of these is coterminous with their attitudes to the social role of mother – the 'institution' as opposed to the 'experience' of motherhood. Furthermore, the kind of 'depression' women may undergo after childbirth has a number of different components: a short-term relief/reaction syndrome (the 'blues'); a state of heightened anxiety on first being alone with, and responsible for, the baby; a condition of fluctuating depressed mood in early motherhood; and a more disabling and clinically definable 'depression' whose characteristic feature is a tendency to interfere with physical wellbeing and to block feelings about being able to 'cope'. Taking these different ways of measuring reactions to childbirth, it is clear that it is normal to experience difficulties. A quarter of the women in the 'Transition to motherhood' sample had depression; four out of five reported the 'blues', three quarters anxiety and one third depressed mood. A third had less than' high' satisfaction with the social role of mother, and two thirds less than 'good' feelings for the baby five months after the birth. Only two of the 55 women experienced no negative mental health outcome, had 'good' feelings for their babies and 'high' satisfaction with motherhood; the reactions of the other 53 did not follow this pattern.

The data suggest a model of influences on these six measures of maternal reactions to first birth. This model stresses the interconnections between depression and postnatal blues and a technological experience of birth; between depressed mood and current social environment (not going out to work, having housing difficulties and not sharing interests with the baby's father); between feelings for the baby and the baby's behaviour, the mother's isolation, overwork, restriction and capacity to view herself as a mother; and between women's satisfaction and their ideas about themselves as mothers and as women. Particular kinds of 'vulnerability' increase the risk of depression after childbirth: not being employed, having a segregated marital role relationship, housing problems, and little or no previous contact with babies. All the women with all four of these factors became depressed, compared with 70% of those with three, 53% of those with two, and 20% of those with one. Given a birth marked by high or medium levels of technology, vulnerability factors are able to discriminate between victims and victors more clearly: all 13 women who had depression were in the high/medium technology, two or more vulnerability factor group. Finally, if women's own feelings about labour are added to the analysis, it is clear that not enjoying and not experiencing achievement in labour constitute a further deprivation that, cumulatively with high technology and social vulnerability, provides a hazardous start to motherhood.

Reproduction is one instance of stress and change occasioned by life events, and it is in this framework that maternal difficulties are best understood. The social transitions of achieving adult femininity, acquiring the status of mother, retiring from work, changing one's career, undergoing physical (body-shape) transformation, becoming a medical and surgical patient, experiencing a 'disaster' and being institutionalised, are all common aspects of the transition into motherhood. What is characteristic of childbirth and becoming a mother today is the tendency for women to feel they have lost something, rather than simply gained a child. What is lost may be one's job, one's life-style, an intact 'couple' relationship, control over one's body or a sense of self, but the feeling of bereavement cannot be cured or immediately balanced by the rewards of motherhood – just as the bereaved person will not cease to feel anguished if offered alternative relationships and occupations.

The primary loss of women in becoming mothers is a loss of identity. The fragility of self-esteem, the tangentiality of the idea and feeling that women can 'master' their own fate – these are contours of female personality as it develops in a male world; they are characteristics of women and their induced subordination to men, and they constitute the special vulnerability of women to the stress of life events. Childbirth is no exception to this general rule; it needs to be understood in terms of the psychological trauma to women as human beings.

Medical definitions of women as maternity cases are coloured by the theme of hostility to female culture. This engenders an antagonism between doctors' 'knowledge' and that of women who have already had babies. The identification of women with other women promotes a wish to share the insights of reproduction, since these have a protective value in immunising against shock. Male society idealises motherhood: it is this idealisation of motherhood and its ramifications that constitute the greatest problem for women in becoming and being mothers today. This idealisation is linked with the fostering of romantic expectations of childbirth: it is part and parcel of the feminine image of women that has been shown empirically to militate against satisfying childbirth and motherhood.

Two facets of masculine culture make a special contribution to women's difficulties as mothers. There is the widespread belief that a maternal instinct qualifies women for childbearing and childrearing alike. This places women on the same level as animals and exposes them to the devastating discovery that, as is the case with male humans, 'instinct' plays an insignificant part, or even no part at all, in human social life. There is also the peculiar pervasive ambivalence about motherhood that is expressed in the combination of ideological glorification and actual social-economic discrimination.

Bringing up children is held out to be women's greatest achievement; but mothers are a socially and economically impoverished group. However, the male idealisation of motherhood proceeds by representing mothers as higher in the scale of core human values than men. Mothers' lives are seen as geared to the production of love and the facilitation of growth in a way that is contrary to the values of the rest of (male) society, which occupies itself in the aggressive pursuit of self-aggrandisement. Mothers are also, and partly for these reasons, the social group that is most different from men: most quintessentially feminine and 'other'. In their femininity, mothers thus stand for the purest kind of selflessness; they are symbols of, and carriers for, the motive of altruism in human social organisation (Miller, 1976).

All the findings of the 'Transition to motherhood' study relate to these themes of the idealisation and male medical control of motherhood. For example, the coexistence of depressed mood with depressing social circumstances maps out the vulnerability of mothering in the nuclear family context. Undoubtedly most impressive of all these connections are those between the medicalisation of birth and depression, for here is summed up an account of the manifold injuries imposed on women through the chauvinism of men's ambivalence to motherhood.

These characteristics of the definition of motherhood today point to the influence of a culture where (from women's point of view) the mistake has been to link women's biological reproduction with the social 'mothering' of children. The mistake gives rise to the mystique of childbearing and childrearing as (feminine) self-fulfilling occupations. As the hands that rock the cradle are not those of the people who rule the world, the axiom that it is mothers who oppress women is perhaps not fair – but it is, nevertheless, true. By mothering their daughters, women induce in other women the desire to be mothers and the relational capacities and psychic structures that match this goal. By mothering their sons, women participate in their own subjugation; turning their male children towards masculinity, they turn them away from women and towards a lifelong campaign on behalf of patriarchy. This paradox has a different formulation, however: it could also be said that the capacity for loving children is what ensures women's continuing oppression, because the cycle of mothering is constantly reproduced, and with it the gender-divisive consequences of maternal love, from men's desire to control the 'giving' of birth to their reluctance to cede to women full citizenship in the male world.

One final paradox: all that has been said derives, in a sense, from a male perspective. I have been describing how women are not the same as men and how not being so and being confined by male images of women has imposed certain limitations on their development. I have not given equal (or any) attention to the pleasures women have, despite or because of this, managed to obtain from motherhood. I have ended on the most apparently paradoxical and confused point of all – by saying that women are oppressed because they love children; or (alternatively put) that, if they didn't have children, women would no longer be oppressed.

This is, in fact, the logic of the male perspective on motherhood carried to its most extreme formulation. It strikes me, as a woman who has enjoyed having children, as a reductio ad absurdum in much the same way, I imagine, as Karen Horney found herself unable to come to terms with the role accorded the penis in the Freudian account of feminine personality development (1974, p 10). What these contradictions point to is the considerable task women confront in designing a psychology (not to mention a society) that authenticates a female point of view. Reproduction is not just a handicap and a cause of second-class status. The problem is to reconcile the feminist political programme of women's advancement with the subjective logic of reproduction stripped of its masculine ideological transformation: childbirth as seen through women's eyes, without the obfuscation of masculine ambivalence.

Part 4: Doing social science

Sociology has been changed by women's studies, but the two have not achieved integration, largely because sociology's resistance to central precepts of women's studies work has been, and remains, too great to allow this to happen. It is rather like what has happened in the domain of the family ... small changes at the last minute.... ('Women's studies: theory or practice', 1989, p 283)

Introduction

Studying the social sciences is a way of studying ourselves. Many challenges since the 1960s, most prominently that of feminism, have exposed the highly situational character of social science theory, methodology and social 'facts': what we know is always conditional, hinged on the politics of personal biography. Social science's responses to this allegation are a tale of shifting landscapes, geographical hesitations and partially redrawn maps. Although sociology, in particular, is widely understood to be undergoing a 'crisis' of confidence and coherence (Gouldner, 1971; Giddens, 1973; Davis, 1994; Imber, 1999), there have been no world-altering earthquakes as a result of the injection of a feminist perspective into the discipline (Wallerstein, 1999; Delamont, 2003; and also see Part 4, Chapter Three).

Chapter One in this final section of the book was commissioned by the farsighted publisher of *The sociology of housework*, who saw in my contention that social science had ignored housework a much more fundamental charge to be levelled against the discipline as a whole. Surely the treatment of women as houseworkers was a symptom of a much more pervasive disorder? My jibes about the private lives of sociology's founding fathers – Durkheim, Marx and Weber – were poorly received in some quarters (it is rude to make personal remarks about famous men), but the point was probably nonetheless adequately driven home - that the culture of sociology mimics the culture of the Euro-American world in which it was born. Both impose the limitations of a patriarchal legacy (Walby, 1990; Johnson, 1997). So, today, the original trio of founding fathers has been joined by a supporting all-male cast, and histories of sociology continue to set aside female achievement in the interests of a "simplistic and uncritical all-male grand narrative" (Delamont, 2003, p 159).

Chapter One, 'The invisible woman: sexism in sociology', talks about the mismatch between sociological visibility and social presence. Why did sociologists of marriage and the family uniformly see women as wives, rather than as workers and citizens in their own right? Why were girls only studied in relation to boys' gangs, not their own? How much real power went on in the interstices of female gossip, compared, for example, with male voting behaviour, and why was this not seen as a respectable and important subject to study? Given the explosion of gender scholarship since the 1970s, it is hard now to understand how iconoclastic these questions were then. There *was* something terribly unsettling for social science in being told that what determines the representation of women's experiences is not these experiences *per se*, but how they are seen (or not seen) by a male-dominated and epistemologically masculine profession. One index of lack of movement here is that 20 years later 'The invisible woman' was still cited as "the most fully developed" critique of masculine bias in social science (Stanley and Wise, 1993, p 27).

Sylvia Walby (1988) cites an impressive marker of sociological sexism as Lipset's (1963) designation of societies as democratic, even when women in them lacked the vote. The examples I took in 'The invisible woman' – deviance, power, social stratification, the family, industry and work – all yielded fairly straightforward evidence of discrimination against women. Anyone writing the same chapter now might pick different examples ('deviance', for instance, reflects a political incorrectness of which we were not aware at the time), but examples of sexist faultlines remain relatively easy to find. Theorising social inequality, for example, is still heavily dependent on a concept of social class which is weighted towards male employment, and the intersections with gender as a system of 'crime and punishment' (Grant, 1993) are treated as a side issue. In 1983, the sociology of social mobility – a major focus of British social science – still had "virtually no female dimension" (Payne et al, 1983, p 61); the first full defence of stratification theory's omission of gender appeared in the same year (Goldthorpe, 1983). The unoriginal point this made, that families, not individuals, are the units of stratification, ignored the evidence I cited in 'The invisible woman', that many people do not live in families and many families are 'cross-class' (McRae, 1986). Inequalities within households are the norm, and the parameters of women's social position go far beyond the income and status of the men with whom they live. Demographic change since the 1970s has, of course, given these points even more cogency. The problem is that mainstream social science continues to regard gender inequality as an epiphenomenon. But gender relations are *not* derivative of class relations; they form a primary stratification system of their own (Wright, 1997; England, 1999). In this sense, the preoccupation with Marxist theory has been something of a disaster for the feminisation of sociology. It has imposed impossible constraints on the redefinition of all forms of household labour in a theoretical framework which *depends* on the separation between production and reproduction (Grant, 1993).

The first onslaughts in the 1970s on the sexism of social science were followed by much partial and some tokenistic door-opening in the late 1970s and 1980s. Thus, for example, the sociology of work became more thoughtful about the errors of assuming the unisex worker – that worker being a man (Brown, 1991). Researchers took on board the challenge of understanding women's experiences of part-time and temporary employment (McNally, 1979; Beechey and Perkins, 1987) and of both 'feminine' (Howe, 1977) and 'masculine' (Kanter, 1977) occupations; they clarified patterns of occupational segregation (Dex, 1985), and later the impact of these on the economics of male-female wage differentials, the labour market and equal opportunities (Humphreys and Rubery, 1995). A critical move was the reconceptualisation of gender and gendering as properties of *institutions*, not just individuals, an essential step in the theorisation of patriarchy (Acker, 1992; Pierce, 1995; Hawkesworth, 1997; Wharton, 2000).

As part of this process of 're-seeing', sociologists looked at their own work with a new consciousness of how behaving like 'godlike authors' did the subject no good at all when it came to providing democratic representations of people's lives. One place where the distance between representation and reality was acute was the famous tradition of British community studies. Here the focus on men's lives in such occupations as coalmining (Dennis et al, 1956) 'lovingly' described the relations of production at work, while ignoring those at home, or treated families as units of consumption with wives occupying much the same non-essential place as dogs (Young and Willmott, 1973; see Frankenberg, 1991, p 109). However, the core of social science's responses to the challenge of feminism has come from feminist scholarship. Here there has been much less tinkering at the edges and much more of a fundamental reworking of the structure of the discipline. This includes sociology (Smith, 1988, 1999; Delphy and Leonard, 1992; Ollenburger et al, 1992), social policy (Callender, 1988; Pascall, 1997; Charles, 1999), psychology (Morawski, 1994; Crawford, 2003) and economics (Ferber and Nelson, 1983; Waring, 1988; Cook et al, 2000). The extent of change over two decades can be gauged by the organisation of Sara Delamont's two books on *The sociology of women* (1980) and *Feminist sociology* (2003). Not only was the notion of a sociology 'of' rather than 'for' women discarded between the two volumes, but the organisation of the material was quite different. *The sociology of women* follows conventional categories – 'Childhood', 'Adolescence', 'Adulthood', 'Work, deviance [again] and leisure', 'Community and class', and so forth. In *Feminist sociology*, there are chapter titles such as 'When the patriarchy gets worried', 'The brotherhood of professors' and 'Neither young, nor luscious, nor sycophantic: developments in feminist sociology, 1968-2002'. It is in this colourfully titled chapter that Delamont defines feminism as one of five 'anti-functionalist', 'anti-positivist' sociologies (the others are postmodernism, 'the cultural turn', and critical race and queer theory) which have collectively dislocated the discipline's identity.

The development of a distinctively feminist methodology, theory and epistemology is certainly one of the most important consequences of the feminist challenge (see, for example, Bowles and Duelli Klein, 1983; Belenky et al, 1986; Harding, 1987; Crawford and Gentry, 1989; Garry and Pearsall, 1989; Fonow and Cook, 1991; Harding, 1991; Barrett and Phillips, 1992; Reinharz, 1992; Antony and Witt, 1993; Stanley and Wise, 1993; Rose, 1994; Goldberger et al, 1996), although views are divided as to whether the 'anti-positivist' strand in this work is a service or disservice to the goal of making social science a more useful emancipatory tool. Chapter Two was commissioned as a commentary on A.H. Halsey's *A history of sociology in Britain* (2004). Written 30 years after Chapter One, it takes the view that anti-positivism is more of a problem than a merit; reflects that changes in sociology have been more cosmetic than structural; and makes some observations about current failures of British social science. These are also taken up in Chapter Six, 'Paradigm wars: some thoughts on a personal and public trajectory'.

Chapters Three to Six are part of the general debate about social science research methods. Chapter Four, 'Interviewing women: a contradiction in terms?', one of my most quoted works, is about the theory and practice of interviewing. It grew out of the 'Transition to motherhood' study, which involved me in an emotionally absorbing series of interviews and other contacts with women at a critical time in their lives. The short Chapter Three, which precedes this, is from the 'Endnote: being researched' to *Becoming a mother*, and contains some of the comments the women made about taking part in the study.

'Interviewing women: a contradiction in terms' acquired a life of its own in the literature on feminist research methods as "emblematic of the new approach of emphasising subjectivity and qualitative perspectives" (David, 2003, p 78). It was actually written as a riposte to the unworkable mechanistic and masculine invocations about how to interview which were current in the methods books at the time. Hilary Graham (1983) provided the same kind of commentary for the survey method. Such observations about the gendering of social science methods led me later to a much fuller exploration of the ways in which modern paradigm warfare about qualitative and quantitative methods intersects with the cultural construction of gender both inside and outside social science (Oakley 1998b, 2000).

Current methodological warfare throws up three main issues for an emancipatory social science. Firstly, the automatically laudatory designation of qualitative methods within feminist social science and other 'anti-positivist' sociologies is a cause for concern, since such methods are no guarantee of equal power relations between the researcher and the researched (Stacey, 1988), nor of reliable truths about people's lives (Oakley, 2004). In qualitative research, there is simply more room than in quantitative research for the knower's own world-view. The second problem relates to the description of quantitative research, and especially experimental research, as downright exploitative and generally inappropriate, on the grounds that 'manipulating' variables (and, by implication, people) has to be disrespectful of subjective experience.

Chapter Five, 'Who's afraid of the randomised controlled trial?' takes up this issue of experimentation in social science. It argues that many important research questions concern the impact and effectiveness of forms of social action. For example, do sex education programmes actually prevent sexually transmitted diseases and unintended pregnancy, and help young people negotiate positive sexual health? Do anti-social behaviour orders reduce anti-social behaviour? What strategies might be effective at the local level in combating environmental change and the causes of global warming? Answering such questions demands well-designed controlled experiments which have not featured much in British social science. Other methodological approaches to such questions are both unscientific and unethical because they cannot provide reliable answers. 'Who's afraid of the randomised controlled trial?' draws on my own experience in carrying out a trial of social support for childbearing women (Oakley, 1992), an experience since added to with other similarly designed studies (Toroyan et al, 2003; Stephenson et al, 2004; Wiggins et al, 2004). All these have shown how the use of random allocation is not regarded as exploitative by research participants (Oakley et al, 2003), and also, importantly, how essential (and possible) it is to combine quantitative/experimental research design with the use of qualitative methods (Wight and Obasi, 2003; Oakley et al, 2004). The latter precept holds true for systematic literature reviews, another important device for minimising researcher bias, where the insights from qualitative research are absolutely invaluable (Thomas et al, 2004).

What we are left with, then, is the problem of the *discourse* about ways of knowing – the paradigm war itself. The final chapter in the book, 'Paradigm wars: some thoughts on a personal and public trajectory', focuses on this directly. Combining the personal with the political, it asks why my work is increasingly

187

being represented as suffering from some kind of split identity: from a starting point in qualitative research (the early studies of housework and motherhood), I am caricatured as ending up as a convert to some ill-defined disease called 'positivism'. But, actually, I have always been a positivist in the polite sense that the point of doing social science seems to me to be the generation of reliable knowledge about social systems which can serve a practical purpose in helping us to improve life on planet earth. This is the third problem about the gendering of methodology: that the defence of 'anti-positivism' is a form of 'veriphobia' (Bailey, 2001) which will destroy social science's long-established and valuable contribution to a practical understanding of the world in which we all live.

I have been privileged to work as an academic social scientist in a period of fascinating intellectual history. Universities are not comfortable sites for feminist struggle, and they remain relatively inhospitable to women and other outsiders (Bannerji et al, 1992; Goetting and Fenstermaker, 1995; Hague, 2000; David, 2003). The fit between what is regarded as 'cutting edge' research and scholarship, on the one hand, and the products of masculine social science, on the other, remains uncomfortably close (Forbes, 2003). But the freedom to think and criticise established patterns of thought still receives some protection as a core value. In this sense (but probably *only* in this sense), academia removes human beings' efforts to understand themselves from the constraints of the marketplace. Like women standing in the kitchen doing housework, we can use our imaginations and the inspiration of our everyday lives to know many things that might otherwise not enter the realm of knowledge at all.

The invisible woman: sexism in sociology

A growing body of literature is drawing attention to the disadvantaged position of women in society. Despite legal changes, smaller families and improved educational and employment opportunities over the last century or so, marked inequalities remain between the social and economic roles of men and women. The revival of organised feminism, in the form of the women's liberation movement, has attached a powerful polemic to these differences. It seems that the situation we are witnessing is neither the effect of a biological underpinning of sex roles, nor can it simply be seen as the persistence of institutional inequalities. Discrimination against women is still to be found in law, and it is codified in other institutional practices determining sex-differentiated rights and opportunities; but a more fundamental source of discrimination lies in the realm of social attitudes and beliefs. The reality of women's situation is daily constructed out of these attitudes: women are, in part, the way they are because of the way they are thought to be.

Thus one finds discrimination against women not only in society at large, but in the academic domain. This is particularly true of sociology, the 'science' that studies social reality. The counterpart to discrimination against women in society is sexism in sociology. In much sociology, women as a social group are invisible or inadequately represented: they take the insubstantial form of ghosts, shadows or stereotyped characters. This issue of sexism has a direct relevance to the main topic of *The sociology of housework*, a survey of housewives and their attitudes to housework which I carried out in London in 1971. The conventional sociological approach to housework could be termed 'sexist': it has treated housework merely as an aspect of the feminine role in the family – as a part of women's role in marriage, or as a dimension of child-rearing – not as a work role. The study of housework as *work* is a topic entirely missing from sociology.

Sociology is sexist because it is male-oriented. By 'male-oriented', I mean that it exhibits a focus on, or a direction towards, the interests and activities of men in a gender-differentiated society. The social situations of men and women today are structurally and ideologically discrepant, and the dominant value-system of modern industrialised societies assigns greater importance and prestige to masculine than to feminine roles. This bias is reflected within sociology, which tends to adopt the values of the wider society. Attempts at 'objectivity' – a major premise of the sociological method – may reduce many obvious biases, but they do not seem to have affected the deeply ingrained bias of sexism.

The question of sexism raises the question of feminism. Is not feminism just as much of a bias as sexism? To answer this question, it must be noted that in sociology (and elsewhere) a feminist perspective appears to be polemical because it runs counter to the accepted male-oriented viewpoint – a viewpoint which is rarely explicitly articulated. The word 'feminist' – like the words 'sexist', 'male-biased', or 'male chauvinist' – carries heavy polemical implications. Although these are highly political words, we use them because they are the only available ones: conceptually, the area of gender-differentiation in sociology is very poorly developed. For these reasons, feminist values stand out like a sore thumb. Conventional male-oriented values are buried in the very foundations of sociology and have to be dug up to be seen (but not believed). Wright Mills (1959) talks of 'biases' rather than 'orientations' or 'perspectives', but his point stands:

> My biases are of course no more or less biases than those I am going to examine. Let those who do not care for mine use their rejections of them to make their own as explicit and as acknowledged as I am going to try to make mine. (p 21)

Essentially, feminism is a perspective rather than a particular set of prescriptive values. A feminist perspective consists of keeping in the forefront of one's mind the lifestyles, activities and interests of more than half of humanity – women. Many different arguments or blueprints for a sexually egalitarian society can be, and have been, constructed on this basis. Institutional sex equality (Myrdal and Klein, 1956), the overthrow of the capitalist system (Rowbotham, 1973), the abolition of the family, and the revamping of our entire ideology pertaining to gender roles (Firestone, 1972), have been variously identified as prerequisites for women's 'liberation'. These are all different strands of thought, but their common focus is on making visible the invisible: bringing women 'out from under' into the twin spheres of social reality and cultural belief-systems.

Manifestations

The concealment of women runs right through sociology. It extends from the classification of subject areas and the definition of concepts through the topics and methods of empirical research to the construction of models and theory generally.

The broad subject divisions current in modern sociology appear, at first sight, to be eminently logical and non-sexist. Social stratification, political institutions, religion, education, deviance, the sociology of industry and work, the family and marriage, and so on: these are, surely, just descriptions of different areas of human social life. To examine whether or not this is so, one needs to ask three questions. First, to what extent are the experiences of women *actually* represented in the study of these life areas; secondly, how does this representation compare with the empirical role of women in social life; and, thirdly, do the subject categorisations *themselves* make sense from the perspective of women's particular situation? These represent different criteria of visibility. The third criterion is more problematic than the other two. Male-orientation may so colour the organisation of sociology as a discipline that the invisibility of women is a structural weakness, rather than simply a superficial flaw. The male focus, incorporated into the definition of subject areas, reduces women to a side issue from the start. For example, a major preoccupation of sociologists has been with the cohesive effect of directive institutions through which power is exercised – the law, political systems, etc. These are male-dominated arenas; women have historically been tangential to them. The more sociology is concerned with such areas, the less it is, by definition, likely to include women within its frame of reference. The appropriate analogy for the structural weakness of sociology in this respect is the social reality sociologists study: sexism is not merely a question of institutional discrimination against women, but the schema of underlying values is also implicated.

Taking the major subject areas of sociology, such as those listed above, it should in theory be possible to chart the areas in which women are most invisible. The procedure would be to identify discrepancies between the extent to which women are studied in each subject area, and their actual role in the sphere of social life that the subject category represents. For example, in the case of housework, the omission of this topic from both family sociology and the sociology of work clearly conveys a distorted impression of women's situation. No account is taken of the importance of housework to women, either in terms of the simple amount of time women spend on domestic care activities, or in terms of the personal meaning of housework to women (which may, of course, vary with different social locations). Using such a critical procedure, two indices could be constructed: an index of women's *sociological visibility* and an index of their *social presence*. Lack of correspondence between the two indices would suggest a failure of sociology to take into account women's experience. It might also point to more appropriate ways of re-classifying subject areas so that the perspectives of both genders are represented. The value of taking this kind of critical stance to the subject classifications of sociology can be illustrated by taking a brief look at five areas: deviance, social stratification, power, the family and marriage, and industry and work.

Deviance

Patterns of deviance in women are 'lonely, uncharted seas' of human behaviour (Heidensohn, 1968). Very little of the empirical data collected by sociologists relates to women and, of that which does, a main focus concerns sexual offences. Theories of deviance may include some passing reference to women, but interpretations of female behaviour are uncomfortably subsumed under the umbrella of explanations geared to the model of masculine behaviour (Cohen, 1955). Even where there is some attempt to account for female/male differences in deviant behaviour, the explanation may simply resort to the simplistic notion that sex roles are generally differentiated. One reason why women are under-represented in this area is undoubtedly that the sociology of deviance has, until recently, concentrated specifically on *criminal* behaviour. Since far fewer females than males commit crimes, this preoccupation has been one main source of sexism.

There is no doubt that women *are* less deviant than men, according to various criteria, such as official crime statistics, suicide figures, data on vagrancy, and so on. Eight or nine men are convicted of crimes for every single female (CSO, 1973a). [In 2000, 81% of offenders found guilty or cautioned were men (Dench et al, 2002, p 182).] Some of this lower deviance in women may be an artefact of the definition or administration of the law. There are some crimes for which women cannot be convicted (eg homosexuality, rape); courts may deal more leniently with females, and a proportion of female crime may remain undetected because the police are less sensitive to it. Nevertheless, even allowing for these factors, women are more 'conformist' than men.

But the invisibility of women in the sociology of deviance is not simply a mirror of reality. Women's social presence in this area, as shown by crime statistics, is far greater than their sociological visibility would suggest. For example, in 1970 there were 15,623 occasions on which British women aged between 17 and 20 were found guilty in court. Over the decade from 1960 to 1970, the rate of all offences committed by females in this age group doubled, while the comparable male rate increased by less than a half (Davies and Goodman, 1972). [The rate of increase in female criminality has slowed: between 1990 and 2000, the proportion of all offenders who were women rose from 17% to 18.7% (Dench et al, 2002, p 182.)] There is a well-established pattern of gender-differentiated criminal behaviour. Female shoplifting offences exceed those of men, but women commit only a small percentage of sexual crimes and crimes of violence. The feminine pattern of crime has the uniformity and degree of constancy that usually attracts the attention of sociologists, yet despite the fact that the sex difference far outweighs any other variable associated with criminal behaviour:

> No one seems to have any idea why; but hardly anyone seems to have thought it worth while to try to find out.... While there have been few studies of women offenders, investigators have generally looked upon the difference between masculine and feminine criminality merely as a reason for eliminating female subjects from their researches on the ground that they provide insufficient material. (Wootton, 1959, p 318)

The situation is a little better today than it was when Barbara Wootton wrote these words in *Social science and social pathology*. There has still been no systematic attempt to relate female deviancy to women's situation.

But, aside from the question of their own delinquency/criminality, there is the important question of women's influence over masculine patterns of criminal and delinquent behaviour. To what extent do girls act as brakes on, or motivators of, delinquent behaviour in masculine adolescent gang culture, for example? This question has not been taken up in any serious way. Girls may form a small part of the whole complex of gang behaviour, but the evidence is thin. David Downes, in *The delinquent solution* (1966), refers to a study of Chicago gangs carried out 30 years previously for support on this point. He also asserts, although giving no evidence for the claim, that "the delinquent's girl is a force for conforming behaviour, as opposed to acting as provocateur for delinquent activity" (Downes, 1966, p 251). Research on adolescent girls in South Wales indicates that patterns of social relationships in girls do differ from those of boys; in particular, the 'best friend' phenomenon seems more important (Ward, 1974). As this researcher points out, the backdrop to women's invisibility in the deviancy literature is the lack of attention paid to girls in sociological studies of adolescence. Quite simply, a sociology of adolescent boys exists, while a sociology of adolescent girls does not.

A major way in which women *are* represented in the study of deviance is through the theory of 'feminine identification', which is a common one in explanations of delinquency and criminality (see Cohen, 1955). The relative absence of the husband-father from modern family life supposedly leads boys to over-identify with their mothers, so that in adolescence 'compulsive masculinity' develops as a protest against femininity. Women also appear as 'invisible deviants', 'causing' delinquency through going out to work (Rutter, 1972). Such theories at least attempt to cope with the reality of the female presence, even if they do not do so accurately.

Finally, does the traditional definition of deviance make sense from a female perspective? Perhaps the rejection of marriage and the espousal of a profession represents a 'deviant career' for women, or perhaps the phenomenon of the obsessive, house-proud housewife could be usefully seen as a form of gender role-related deviance. If the contention of Pollak (1950) and others is correct, that the roles of women reduce the public display of deviance, then it is indeed in such 'private' areas that one would expect female forms of deviance to be located.

Social stratification

In social stratification theory and its application in research, a number of assumptions made about the role of women serve to guarantee women's invisibility. These assumptions make up a set of interrelated hypotheses about the processes and criteria of class membership. They are theoretically testable, but in practice remain untested. Three main ones are as follows:

1) The family is the unit of stratification.
2) The social position of the family is determined by the status of the man in it.
3) Only in rare circumstances is the social position of women not determined by that of the men to whom they are attached by marriage or family of origin.

The first of these is the lynchpin of the argument. One can offer three principal objections to it, which constitute general criticisms of stratification theory, but relate specifically to the issue of whether women's situation is adequately represented in the theory (or its practice in research). Firstly, not everybody lives in a family. In the British Census data for 1966, about one in 12 of the population do not live in families (General Register Office, 1968). A second objection is that stratification theory rests on the assumption of a 'normal' unit of male, female and child/children in which the father is the breadwinner. How normal is this?

Fifty-eight per cent of all British households are not of the nuclear family type according to 1966 data, and one in 20 of all households is a single-parent family (General Register Office, 1968). [In 2002, the figure for non-nuclear family households had risen to 79% (www.statistics.gov.uk, accessed 17 November 2004).]

Thirdly, while members of the same family are held to share identical degrees of status, privilege, power and wealth, simply by virtue of their common membership of this unit, differences of role, position and status within the family are not themselves considered to be criteria of stratification. This implies (a) that females have no resources of their own, and (b) that the family is an entirely symmetrical status structure. Both these implications are false. Apart from the question of wealth, married women have personal resources of education and sometimes occupational training; many are also employed during their marriages and are in receipt of income and status from this source. The assumption that women's own resources become inoperative on marriage means that abrupt alterations to the class structure are liable to occur every time someone gets married. An occupationally based class categorisation of married women would put many in a different class from their husbands. This is shown, for example, in the British 1971 Sample Census data (Table 1).

On the status dimension, husband–wife equality cannot merely be assumed, either. The Finnish sociologist, Elina Haavio-Mannila (1969), set out to test the assumption that wives share the same status ranking as their husbands. Some of her findings are set out in Table 2; this compares the ranks of men and women employed in certain occupations with the ranks assigned by a sample of respondents to the wives of men in these occupations. The data suggest that gender role is influential. Women are generally ranked lower than men, and wives lowest of all.

These criticisms of stratification theory derive from the known importance of gender as a criterion of social differentiation in modern society. Sociologists have paid very little attention to the significance of gender – much less attention than has, for example, been paid to age or ethnicity. Gender differentiates; it may also stratify – that is, the attributes of femininity and masculinity may be systematically ranked differently. Although there are scattered suggestions in the stratification literature that gender forms a criterion of stratification (Lenski, 1966), such a statement tends to be either treated frivolously, or rebutted by a neat process of tautological argument. Hence (to take the former method of dismissal first) Randall

Table 1: Married couples with both partners economically active, by social class of husband and wife

Husband's social class	Percentage of wives whose social class is different from husbands
I	93.8
II	66.2
III non-manual	48.7
III manual	87.8
IV	63.5
V	77.6

Source: Adapted from the 1971 Census, 1% sample, summary tables, Great Britain (Table 36)

Table 2: Mean ranks of male and female representatives of modern occupational groups, and wives of men in these groups (ranks ordered on an 18-point scale)

		Male	Female	Wife
2.4	Male architect	1		
2.8	Male psychologist	2		
3.7	Female architect		1	
4.2	Female psychologist		2	
6.6	Male advertising agency secretary	3		
7.2	Female advertising agency secretary		3	
8.9	Male student	4		
8.9	Wife of architect			1
9.3	Wife of psychologist			2
9.4	Female student		4	
10.6	Male furniture salesman	5		
11.6	Female furniture saleswoman		5	
12.8	Wife of advertising agency secretary			3
13.1	Male office messenger	6		
13.5	Wife of student			4
13.9	Female office messenger		6	
15.1	Wife of furniture salesman			5
16.3	Office messenger's wife			6

Source: Data from Haavio-Mannila (1969, Table 6)

Collins' account of 'A conflict theory of sexual stratification' claims that stratification by gender is based on 'sexual property' – the notion of exclusive sexual rights (Collins, 1972). Men are bigger and sexier than women; every encounter between them is a sexual encounter; the only important market is the sexual market, and therefore women's resources, lifestyles and class position are ultimately determined by the 'biological facts' of female sexual attractiveness and male sexual aggression. The argument is frivolous, firstly because conceptually it is full of elementary mistakes, the primary one being the equation of 'sexuality' with 'gender'. Social classification as masculine or feminine (gender) is not the same as biological maleness or femaleness, nor is 'sexuality' a synonym for it. Sexuality may be a component in stratification by gender but it cannot be assumed a priori by a process of projection in which the male sociologist, himself accustomed to thinking of women in these terms, imposes his own preoccupations on the data he is analysing. Secondly, Collins' argument is deficient on the level of empirical evidence. For example, the description of different sexual stratification systems, on which the theory rests, makes an appalling number of generalisations which can be falsified by a random search through the ethnographic literature (see, for example, Campbell, 1964; Henry, 1964).

In *Class inequality and political order*, Frank Parkin (1971) unwittingly provides an illustration of how stratification by gender can be tautologically argued away. The steps in his argument are summarised as follows:

1) The family is the unit of the class system: hence people are wrong in saying that sex or gender stratification exists.
2) Women are certainly oppressed, but these sex-based inequalities do not constitute a stratification system: for most women, social and economic rewards are determined by the position of the male head of the family.
3) Only if the disabilities associated with female status were 'felt' to over-ride class differences would sex/gender represent an important dimension of stratification.
4) Women see themselves as members of a kin group rather than as women.
5) Because the major unit of reward is the family, most women do not feel that their interests conflict with those of men.
6) Therefore gender is not the basis of a stratification system.

Parkin asserts that only if women see themselves in non-family terms is stratification by gender meaningful, but he presents no *evidence* as to what women actually feel in relation to their family or class position. He simply asserts that their perceptions are congruent with his own view that the family is the important unit.

In the end, there has to be some way of restructuring the mode of analysis to take account both of gender differences in role, status and resources within the family, and also outside it. This is a major task, but its importance is affirmed by the attention feminists in general, and Marxist-feminists in particular, are giving to the problem of women's place in the class system.

Power

The phenomenon of power is closely allied with that of stratification. Rather than examining the visibility of women in all the various types of sociological analyses of power, I am going instead simply to draw attention to an area in which the undoubted social power of women has not been considered at all.

Women have power as housewives, wives and mothers, and as members of the community. As the "degree of control a person or a collectivity of people exercises over the actions of others" (Giner, 1972, p 145), the sociological examination of power is conventionally linked with male-oriented stratification analysis, and with the analysis of formal institutions, such as government. This line of thinking presupposes that there is only one kind of power. Attention is thereby diverted from another variety: informal or unarticulated power. This kind is more often exercised in private than in public places, the concept of 'legitimate authority' tends to be irrelevant to it, and it is less visible and less easily amenable to sociological analysis.

An example of the difficulties associated with the analysis of informal power in the case of women is given in a footnote to Katz and Lazarsfeld's study of *Personal influence*:

> In the study of voting behaviour during a presidential campaign, it was found that while wives frequently referred to discussions with their

husbands, the latter rarely returned the compliment. The husbands apparently did not feel that they were 'discussing' politics with their wives. Rather, they were telling their wives what politics was all about. (Katz and Lazarsfeld, 1964, p 160)

Were the women influencing the voting choices of their husbands or not? Katz and Lazarsfeld's own study delineates the crucial role of women in the shaping of everyday decisions to do with consumption patterns, fashions, public affairs and cinema attendances in a mid-western American community. Female influence was greatest in consumer decisions, and least in public affairs; however, as in the above example of voting choices, the researchers say that the latter finding may be due to the men's unwillingness to admit to having serious political discussions with women.

Katz and Lazarsfeld found 'gregariousness' to be an important factor associated with the role of women in the formation of public opinion. Gossip, defined as "idle, unconstrained talk especially about persons or social incidents" (*Oxford English Dictionary*) is a function of many gregarious rituals. As a means of controlling other people's behaviour, it meets the essential criterion of power, but is largely unanalysed. British and American community studies give the phenomenon of gossip some attention, but there is no systematic study of gossip as a form of unarticulated female power. While both sexes gossip, the literature suggests that they gossip differently. Where opportunities for controlling situations and events in a more organised sense are constricted – as in the case of women at home – it is logical to assume that power to exert control through gossip becomes relatively more important.

Gossip has received some attention in anthropology. According to Max Gluckman (1963), gossip and scandal are "among the most important societal and cultural phenomena we are called upon to analyse" (p 307). Although Gluckman does not consider the variable of gender, he describes some of the functions of gossip: the unification and affirmation of community values, the control of aspiring individuals and cliques within society, the selection of leaders and the maintenance of group exclusiveness. Gossip may not be a female prerogative, but it certainly is so in the social stereotype of women. For example:

> Few would dispute that women excel at gossiping…. In the seemingly endless, and to male ears repetitive, chatter that goes on among women … a massive and encyclopaedic confidence is built up in the gossipers … gossip serves exactly the same grooming functions for the women as poker for the men…. As gossip is to ladies and gambling to gentlemen, flirting is to both together. (Tiger and Fox, 1971, pp 200-1)

There are intimate ideological connections between women's gossip, on the one hand, and sorcery and witchcraft, on the other. Gluckman quotes one example of this from the ethnographic literature, an analysis of African village life in which gossiping between one lineage and another is believed to introduce a risk of sorcery. The fights of women (held to be the main culprits) who take their grumbles to outsiders provide an opportunity for these outsiders to bewitch the entire lineage. Another example, much closer to home, relates to the persecution of witches in pre-industrial Britain. A cursory glance at the literature in this field reveals the importance of suspicions concerning gossiping groups of women (Hole, 1957). Witches were also often midwives and healers, and it is interesting that their persecution coincided with the beginning of a 'takeover' process in which the (predominantly) male medical profession acquired control over the care of women in childbirth – an area in which women were originally autonomous. In other words, one form of power was challenging another (Oakley, 1976).

The family and marriage

If women have no place of their own in much of sociology, they are firmly in possession of one haven: the family. In the family, women 'come into their own'; they *are* the family. By far the largest segment of sociological literature concerning women is focused on their roles as wives, mothers and housewives – but not on the housewife's role as *houseworker*. Major topics in this literature are marital happiness, the division of labour and the general patterning of husband–wife roles; the combination of women's employment with marriage, and its consequences for husband–wife and mother–child relationships; the inter-relationships between the nuclear family and the wider kinship system; and the 'captive wife' syndrome – the socially isolated situation of women with young children. These topics are often looked at in an historical context: changes in the patterning of family life with industrialisation and urbanisation are examined. The general consensus of opinion among sociologists is that, compared with the state of affairs in the 19th century, the modern marriage relationship is happier, more egalitarian, more important, and therefore certainly more stressful (Fletcher, 1966). Disputes wage over the issue of whether or not nuclear families today are isolated from their kin (Edwards, 1969). It seems to be generally agreed that young mothers run a far higher risk of isolation and loneliness than their Victorian counterparts (Gavron, 1966).

Where are women in all this? They appear to occupy the centre of the stage, but in what guise? A favourite word is 'role', and the dramaturgical metaphor is highly appropriate. In family and marriage literature, women are entirely encapsulated within the feminine role. The psychoanalytic view has been very influential, leading to an implicit definition of women as wives and mothers to the virtual exclusion of any other life area. In addition, the literature has a definite 'social problem' orientation, which is shown most clearly in the vast number of studies of the 'working mother' (Nye and Hoffman, 1963). The focus on the child-rearing implications of women's employment has led to such detailed considerations as the relation between the employment status of mothers and their children's health (Cartwright and Jefferys, 1958), and the possibility of an association between employment and the nutritional adequacy of pre-school children's diets (Methery et al, 1962). The problem of disturbances in the traditional pattern of domesticated wife servicing employed husband is also implied. As one of the earliest studies in the field expressed it:

> ... many people see it [the employment of women] as a challenge to society, because it breaks with long-established patterns of family life, and with the values and beliefs supporting them.... It involves two of the most intimate personal relationships, that of husband to wife, and of parent to child.... (Jephcott, 1962, p 19)

Almost none of this literature is woman-focused. While considering the advantages and disadvantages to other family members of new patterns of domestic life, the consequences for the woman are often omitted. 'Role conflict' is talked about, but this is not quite the same thing.

None of these criticisms of course implies that marriage and family life are not important to women today; indeed, the evidence suggests that these areas of experience are still critical. But do we know *how* critical? Where is a sociological account of the relative importance attached to these areas in the totality of women's experience? The family and marriage are areas in which sociological visibility exceeds social presence; certainly the presence of men as fathers is not matched by an equal visibility in the discipline. A sign of the over-exposure of women in this area is the low status of family and marriage sociology. As a radical young female sociologist asked the feminist sociologist Alice Rossi in a moment of unguarded chauvinism: "How did you manage to get stuck in a low status field like marriage and the family?" (cited in Bart, 1971, p 736). The status of this area is low, because the status of its subjects – women – is also low, and because attitudes prevailing among sociologists towards the position of women as an academic subject serve persistently to trivialise its importance.

Another consideration is whether conceptual distinctions and classifications in family and marriage sociology are appropriate to a female perspective. These are the areas in which sexuality, reproduction, child socialisation and housework are carried out, yet rarely is an adequate distinction made between the four kinds of experience. Popular idiom has it that the four themes are very imperfectly combined in the family: 'children ruin a marriage', 'sex and family life simply don't go together', and so forth. There is a need to make this kind of distinction in sociology also.

Industry and work

By comparison with marriage and family sociology, women are conspicuous for their absence as data in the sociology of industry and work. This is in striking contrast to the important role they play in the occupational structure: currently [1974], some 36% of the labour force is female (CSO, 1973a). Despite this fact, studies of employment are almost wholly male-oriented. There is a notable paucity of studies analysing (from the viewpoint of work attitudes) the occupations in which women workers have traditionally been concentrated – food and clothing manufacture, retail sales work, clerical work, teaching, nursing and domestic work. The employment of women tends to be studied as a deviation from the norm – that is, when combined with marriage. (The fact that this pattern is yearly becoming less of a deviation is brushed aside: according to the Central Statistical Office [1973b], 43% of all married women in Britain were employed.) [In 2002, the employed rate of 'partnered' (married or cohabiting) women was 74%, higher than the rate for single women (Duffield, 2002, p 610).]

Married women are asked 'Why do you work?', a question whose equivalent in the study of men's work attitudes is 'Why aren't you working?'. The invisibility of women in the sociology of work is guaranteed by the choice of predominantly masculine jobs in research design. For example, the automobile industry, described as "the most intensively studied industrial situation" (Parker et al, 1967) has a largely male workforce. Whatever the specific features of the occupations chosen for study, samples tend uniformly to be male, or mostly male. This fact is hidden through the use of titles which purport to be describing work in general and the worker irrespective of gender; Arthur Kornhauser's *Mental health of the industrial worker* (1965), Herzberg, Mausner and Snyderman's *The motivation to work* (1959), Walker and Guest's *Man on the assembly line* (1952) and Hughes' *Men and their work* (1958) are examples. (In the latter two cases, 'man' and 'men' are generic terms.) Theoretical or descriptive surveys not based on empirical research commonly make no reference to women at all, or allot them a specific section on 'work and the family' or some such title.

Since women's place in the sociology of work is very much a secondary one, it follows that we do not have enough empirical data to determine the relative importance to women of their experiences in the occupational sector. The prevailing treatment of women workers defines them as a particular and different sub-group of the general category 'workers'. Robert Blauner (1964) in *Alienation and freedom*, an analysis of job conditions in four factory technologies, provides an excellent example of this traditional approach. He dismisses the women who make up almost half the workers in the textile industry he studied as "a major safety valve against the consequences of alienating work conditions". The high concentration of women in jobs which are, in Blauner's words "the least skilled, the most repetitive, and the least free" makes it possible for men to have jobs with the opposite attributes. "Women in the industry are not dissatisfied with such work", asserts Blauner, without giving his evidence for this statement: "Work does not have the central importance and meaning in their lives that it does for men, since their most important roles are those of wives and mothers" (Blauner, 1964, p 81).

There may well be gender differences in attitudes to paid work, but these are not adequately demonstrated by the reiteration of the old adage that women's primary role is a family one. A study which adopts a critical attitude to this conventional axiom is Wild and Hill's analysis of job satisfaction and labour turnover among women in the electronics industry (Wild and Hill, 1970). They show convincingly that the belief in women's capacity for boring and repetitive work is part of industrial folklore: if it were true, turnover rates should be no higher in industries which offer such work than in those where the work is more intrinsically interesting. However, this is not so. In the electronics industry that Wild and Hill studied particularly, female turnover rates showed a high relationship with job satisfaction/dissatisfaction: many women, like many men, express a need for personally satisfying work, and the failure to find it is often a reason for changing one's job.

****

These brief and incomplete excursions through five subject territories of sociology provide some examples of how male orientation may be manifested. In exposing this, it is possible to begin to see how and where the female perspective might usefully be introduced. Other areas which call out to be critically re-evaluated in this way are methodology and theory. For the former, Jessie Bernard (1973) has suggested an underlying distinction between two types of procedure that reflect traditional gender stereotypes. 'Feminine' methods – such as participant observation, small sample in-depth interviewing, and concentration on qualitative rather than quantitative variables – have less academic prestige and acceptability than their 'masculine' counterparts. This deserves further consideration.

Reasons

I propose three main reasons for the present bias against women in sociology: the nature of its origins, the sex of its practitioners, and the ideology of gender roles, borrowed from the wider society, which is reproduced uncritically within it.

Origins

The 19th century in Euro-American culture was one of the historical periods in which women have been most oppressed. Institutionally, they were deprived of most individual freedoms, rights and responsibilities, and ideologically they were little more than chattels, slaves or decorative ornaments (depending on their class position). This was also the period in which the foundations of sociology were laid. The so-called 'founding fathers' (an appropriate phrase) lived and wrote in an eminently sexist era.

Of five such founding fathers – Marx, Comte, Spencer, Durkheim and Weber – Marx (1818-83) and Weber (1864-1920) alone held what could be described as 'emancipated' views about women. Marx provided the bones of an analysis of marriage as female domestic slavery, although he was personally something of a rearguard romantic (Draper, 1971); Weber argued for sex equality within marriage (Mitzman, 1970). Herbert Spencer (1820-1903) protested that marriage was an unequal institution, and that women should have equal rights of competition with men, but in his later writing he reversed this opinion and declared that "if women comprehended all that is contained in the domestic sphere, they would ask no other" (cited in Schwendinger and Schwendinger, 1971, p 784). Auguste

Comte (1798-1857) was a doctrinaire sexist and his philosophy about women is most clearly shown in his utopian "positivist scheme of social reconstruction". Every social class except women was to be ranked on a hierarchical scale of importance and specialisation of function. Women were to be in charge of domestic morality and their moral influence was to be ensured by the rule of indissoluble monogamous marriage. Ultimately, his view amounted to a belief in the constitutional inferiority of women, whose maturation Comte considered to have been arrested in childhood.

The perspective Durkheim (1858-1917) held on women was also shaped by a biological doctrine: women belonged 'naturally' in the family. His analysis of the structure of the modern conjugal family was phrased solely from the point of view of the man. He regarded it as essential that men become more deeply committed to their work through the formation of professional/occupational groups, since for them an involvement in the family did not provide a sufficiently sound moral basis for continued existence: "Men must gradually become attached to their occupational or professional life.... In the hearts of men, professional duty must take over the place formerly occupied by domestic duty" (cited in Lukes, 1973, p 185). Meanwhile, the family (as the province of women) would continue to be a centre of moral education and security.

This axiom was one that Durkheim carried out in his private life. Indeed, the intellectual achievements of these men rested in a personal way on the basis of women's domestic oppression. (The Webers' marriage is, to some extent, an exception here: Marianne Weber was a feminist and a writer in her own right. Of the five, Herbert Spencer never married.) It was said of Comte that "the woman he chose as his wife was nothing more than a means for the immediate gratification of his crude sexuality" (Becker and Barnes, 1952, p 570). The prototype of many a wife, before and after, was Marx's wife Jenny, who

> dedicated her whole being to his life and work. It was an entirely happy marriage. She loved, admired and trusted him and was, emotionally and intellectually, entirely dominated by him. He leaned on her unhesitatingly in all times of crisis and disaster, remained all his life proud of her beauty, her birth and her intelligence.... In later years when they were reduced to penury, she displayed great moral heroism in preserving intact the framework of a family and a household, which alone enabled her husband to continue his work. (Berlin, 1939, pp 78-9)

Similarly, Durkheim's marriage

> could not have been happier, both personally and in creating an atmosphere conducive to his work ... the domestic ideal that is evident in his writings (the family being his favourite subject of study and lecturing) was most clearly represented by his own home life ... his wife created for him the respectable and quiet familial existence which he considered the best guarantee of morality and of life. She removed from him every material care and frivolity.... (Lukes, 1973, p 99)

It is perhaps reasonable to question the assumption of female happiness these comments make. Jenny Marx's life was at times appallingly wretched and difficult. Durkheim was a very austere man who led a rigidly timetabled existence and refused to talk to his family except at mealtimes.

Such points could be made repetitively. Domestic sexism does not guarantee sexism in public affairs, although one is often a symptom of the other. Both can be presumed to matter most when and where they are most influential – as in the charting of the interests, concerns and methods of analysis that make up a new academic discipline. The early sociologists established a number of traditions that have subsequently moulded the place of women in sociology. These include a biological reductionism applied to gender roles; a presumption that women belong in the family but hardly anywhere else; and a 'functionalist' analysis of the family and its connections with the rest of society. The American school of sociology had no less sexist beginnings. In particular, Lester Ward and W.I. Thomas took over themes from Comte and Spencer and developed their own form of biological dogma and social prescription applied to women's place. Their view of women as solutions to the Hobbesian problem of order repeated values dominant in America in the early years of the 20th century, according to which oppression by sex, colour or class could be justified in a laissez-faire, utilitarian philosophy of human relationships.

A male profession

As Wright Mills (1967) observed in his critique, 'The professional ideology of social pathologists': "If the members of an academic profession are recruited from similar social contexts and if their backgrounds and careers are relatively similar, there is a tendency for them to be uniformly set for some common perspective" (p 527). This applies both to the origins of sociology and to the characteristics of its practitioners since the beginning. Gender was not a variable that Wright Mills considered in his analysis of the social backgrounds of social pathologists (thus indicating his own low level of awareness about such matters). Systematic data on the sex of sociological personnel now exist. An American report, *The status of women in sociology* (Hughes, 1973), documents the existence of tokenism – in 85% of sociology departments, there is at least one woman. It shows the pattern of the gender hierarchy: 5% of full professors, 16% of assistant professors, but 30% of lecturers in 1972 being female. It demonstrates the under-representation of women in sociological publications and in editorial positions. Similar inequalities are to be found in British sociology. [In 2000, 90% of professors in UK universities were men (Hague, 2000).] Such facts are highly relevant to the continuing message of sexism transmitted by all aspects of the discipline.

The ideology of gender

"Perhaps the most enlightening part of the Committee's investigation was the discovery that many able sociologists ... abandon the empirical stance and rely upon folk myth and stereotype" (Hughes, 1973, p 26). This observation from the American *Status of women in sociology* report draws attention to the underlying ideology of gender roles which is responsible for all the various manifestations of sexism. Ideology in this context may be defined as "a set of closely related beliefs or ideas, or even attitudes characteristic of a group or community" (Plamenatz, 1970, p 15). This ideology relating to gender roles underpins the structure of sociology much as it does the structure of social life.

A multitude of *particular* interrelated notions about women may be identified as shaping research and theory in all areas of sociology, but a *general* set of axioms is responsible for the place of women in the two areas of family and marriage, and industry and work. The neglect of housework as a topic is also anchored in these axioms. They can be stated thus:

1)   Women belong in the family, while men belong 'at work'.
2)   Therefore men work, while women do not work.
3)   Therefore housework is not a form of work.

What is 'work'? According to one definition (Vroom, 1964, p 31), a work role has five properties. It requires the expenditure of energy; it permits a contribution to the production of goods or services; it defines patterns of social interaction; it provides social status for the worker; and, lastly, it brings in money. The only difference in this definition between employment work and housework is housework's lack of pay. But, because work is not a component of the female stereotype, housework lacks any conceptualisation in sociology *as* work.

The 'dual role' concept which is in common currency validates the denial of housework's status as work. Again, the two worlds are work and home. Alva Myrdal and Viola Klein's *Women's two roles* was one of the first studies to adopt this concept: its focus is the position of women in the labour force and the problems of combining home and work (Myrdal and Klein, 1956). In this analysis, housework is a side issue. The American habit of referring to housework as 'homemaking' neatly cements the ideological division between home and work.

A way of seeing is a way of not seeing. One example is functionalist theory, a school of sociology which, as a distinct 'way of seeing', has had a pervasive influence. Other feminist critics have pointed out how functionalist theory effectively presumes that the domestic oppression of women is necessary for the stability of the social order (Erlich, 1971; Laws, 1971). According to functionalist theorists, the role of 'task leader' in the family involves 'instrumental' activities, such as decision making, earning money and 'manipulating the external environment'; and the role of 'sociometric star' carries 'expressive' duties, such as the expression of emotional warmth and the integration of internal family relationships. Men perform an instrumental role, women an expressive one. Put in plain language, the women stay at home and provide *emotional* support while the men go out to work and provide *financial* support. The gender division is reducible to biology. According to Zelditch (1950), "a crucial reference point for differentiation in the family ... lies in the division of organisms into lactating and nonlactating classes" (p 313).

In functionalist theory, as in most family and marriage literature, women are over-visible. This is because the areas of women's greatest visibility in sociology tend also to contain examples of the most rampant sexism. The ideology of feminine passivity not only runs right through sociology, but is the cornerstone of that zone within it where women are least hidden. A correction of this distorted male-oriented perspective involves going back to women themselves and looking through their eyes at the occupation of housewife.

Reflections thirty years on

Many people wrestle with a sense of being caught between two worlds. This is particularly true of women and other migrants and asylum seekers. It is also the hallmark of the history inherited by sociologists brought up in the twin British traditions of well-meaning empiricism and privileged academic obscurantism. Is sociology a socially useful activity? Should it be? What is the role of the academic professor, confined in the narrow spaces of 'his' university and deeply committed to the value of ideas?

Having decided I wanted primarily to be a creative writer, I went to Oxford in 1962 to study Philosophy, Politics and Economics in the mistaken belief that these subjects constitute a form of social science which, as we all know, is close to fiction. Over the ensuing 40 years, I have been successively impressed by four aspects of British sociology. The first is its masculinity. The second is its addiction to theory for theory's sake; the third is the impressive neglect by British sociologists of well-designed experiments as an aid to sociological understanding; and the fourth, linked, issue is that of methodological warfare, which has been (and remains) a major distraction.

Masculinism

The key founding fathers, mentors and practitioners introduced to me as a student were all men; and masculine names, theories and positions have continued to dominate. A.H. Halsey's survey supports this view: the important mentors and key 20th-century sociologists named by 216 living British sociology professors (themselves 81.1% male) are also all male (Halsey, 2004, pp 169-71). But, of course, who does sociology and who is remembered for doing it is only one index of its character. What matters much more is the systematic and sustained way in which sociological theory, research and teaching is informed by the perspectives of the socially powerful, who therefore lack any incentive to understand or amend the distortions that may be consequent on this process. To put it differently, the problem noted by feminists and other ethnomethodologists, that knowledge is reached through *everyone*'s experience of everyday life, is not a perspective which has been incorporated into modern mainstream sociology.

An account of women's studies in British sociology I offered in 1989 ended with Sylvia Walby's (1988) four stages of the response of sociology to feminism: neglect of women's position; recognition of fallacies and gaps; adding women in; and full integration of gender analysis into the discipline (Oakley, 1989). Thirty years on, we remain fixed at stage two.

Theory

One important reason for this stasis is an over-attachment to theory. Too often theory is just speculation; definitions are arbitrary; subjectivity is extolled tokenistically; and we never know what difference a good theory might make. Postmodernism and other post-isms have brought a newly suicidal relativism to the sociological preoccupation with theory, and this has effectively closed off the attention of the sociological community from pursuing a scientific understanding of society. The 'flight from universals' – the view that human beings and their ways of being are fictions, and all that sociology can do is tell stories (Assiter, 1996) – decisively removes sociology from the field of practical public policy.

When positivism becomes a form of abuse, and anti-realism fosters the position that statements about being are always contingent, conditional and partial, the danger is that sociology will disappear down the plughole of theory and philosophy instead of contributing to the intellectual housekeeping of the policy-making process. In the face of global poverty, inequality, murderous aggression and environmental collapse (Oakley, 2002), this retreat from reality is more worrying than merely protracted self-abuse.

Evidence and experimentation

The malaise of anti-realism is aligned with a third feature of British sociology which increasingly preoccupies me and other social scientists interested in the rise of the 'evidence' movement as a new moment in the complex relationship between social research and policy making. 'Evidence-based' or 'evidence-informed' policy and practice is a child of mixed parentage, its father the evidence-based healthcare movement which, since the 1980s, has inspired doctors to consider a sounder basis than expert judgement for professional action (Maynard and Chalmers, 1997), and its mother the Blair Labour government's invention of the mantra 'what matters is what works' as a cover for discarding the old politics of identity and class (Solesbury, 2002). Reliable evaluations of public policies have not been the forte of British sociology, despite the clarion calls of some early social scientists, such as the Webbs and Barbara Wootton, for sociologists to engage in controlled experiments capable of yielding sound and cumulative knowledge. The need for such practices across sectors as diverse as criminal justice, housing, social care, transport policy and education is being very clearly articulated by many social scientists today (see, for example, Davies et al, 2000). Controlled experimentation is distinct from the uncontrolled experimentation that constitutes the normal social policy process. It remains a puzzle, as Martin Bulmer (1991) has noted, as to why British social scientists have so ignored the possibilities for large-scale social experimentation, especially when the history of sociology elsewhere is littered with successful examples (see Oakley, 2000).

Of course, the rejection of experimental methods is part of (British) sociology's old identity crisis: science or literature? An inventive response to this would outline a new conceptual framework for the activity of science itself. Such a framework would privilege the highly contextualised knowledge which has traditionally been sociology's forte and which is probably increasingly going to be a requirement of good non-social science (Nowotny et al, 2001).

Methodological wars

The fourth notable aspect of British sociology – that of general methodological warfare – is one with which my own work has been particularly aligned. Disputes about the relative values of 'qualitative' and 'quantitative' methods have enhanced many CVs over the last half century, but what they have not done is contribute much of lasting value to the sociologist's toolkit. What matters most is the fit between the research method and question, and the steps researchers take to minimise the chances of their research findings simply reflecting their own selective perception. Systematic reviews – another giant leap for sociology (Boaz et al, 2002) – are currently revealing how poorly designed and/or reported much British social research is (see, for example, Oakley, 2003). An enormous, as yet unmet, challenge concerns 'qualitative' research, whose parallels with fiction can be truly frightening. All of this is a serious indictment of professional sociology and it cannot just be rebuffed by epistemological excuses.

In *The scientific merit of the social sciences*, Cho-yee To (2000), a Professor of Education at the Chinese University of Hong Kong, identifies three obstacles in the path of improvement: uncritical attachment to theory; the entrapment of methodology; and unsystematic poorly executed social research. To this I would add reluctance to entertain in anything other than a rhetorical fashion the prospect of an emancipatory sociology which is for, rather than about, its subjects. What sociology has got right in the past is, I suggest, what it needs most to nurture for the future: an extension of the Enlightenment project from the natural to the social world; an engine of moral progress; and an intellectual aid to the young, capable of helping them to understand the changes, continuities and challenges of living on planet earth.

On being interviewed

Becoming aware

José Bryce

I've enjoyed it. I remember when you went the first time, I thought she must have thought, my God, that woman went on talking and how boring to have to listen – you know, not just to answer your questions, but to go on to other things; when you asked a question, I wouldn't say yes, so-and-so, that's how I feel about that, I'd go on: like a conversation after each question. I thought maybe she only wanted to be here for an hour or something. And she was here for *hours*.

Elizabeth Farrell

First of all, I enjoy talking. I think perhaps not quite so much *now* [*baby crying*]. I'll probably enjoy this afterwards, in retrospect, but it's difficult, because you're not so free. But before the baby, I really enjoyed talking.

Just as a person to talk to – yes, I've enjoyed it.

How much is what you would like to find or what you think anyway going to influence your selecting material from the tape-recordings? If somebody else listened to your recordings and wrote a book about it, they would interpret it completely differently, wouldn't they?

Sophy Fisher

I don't think it's affected the *experience*. I think it's possibly affected my *evaluation* of it: the fact that you make me articulate my responses, or rake about in my memory, or try to rationalise and explain; it makes me more aware of it as an outside experience. You see, questions you've asked me I might not ask myself. I don't think you *change* what I think, but you make me *look* at it.

Kate Prince

You come so rarely that it's not as if we're all in a goldfish bowl being observed with a camera. I think it's very good, actually, because it's put one's thoughts together. And it's interesting to hear you say what I said before, which I'd forgotten about: that's *very* interesting. But it is in a way a monologue. I rabbit on. I suppose you feel everyone's doing you a favour, but really it's a huge ego trip.

Clare Dawson

It's made me think about things I've never thought about before. For instance, when you said to me does it matter to you if you don't see the same doctor? And I began to think: I wonder if it does? At the time, I said no. And then I thought about it more. And I suppose it made me assess *more* what happened. I think I've found it helpful, actually. To talk about it: it's been good to talk about it.... I think it would be interesting to see what other people thought or felt. I can't see what *can* come out of it, in a way, because everybody's so different. I can't see how you can compare....

Feeling normal

Pauline Diggory

It's been very, I've really *enjoyed* it. Yes, it has helped me because I probably would have been even more worried. I mean, I think you know a lot. I mean, there you are with all these different mothers and I mean all I've got to say is, do you think Hannah's a bit sick, and you say, oh no, I've seen about so many.... Now that just helps, just to say you've seen a few.

Interviewer (I): But of course I'm not a doctor.

Pauline: Oh, I know. But I mean a doctor's not interested in a baby being sick anyway.

Us against them

I: Do you think that my being at the birth made any difference to the way you felt?

Steve Ingram: I don't know. It was their general attitude, I think they treated Jo better. That doctor....

Jo: Oh yes, I'm sure that doctor was behaving differently. It was much, much better. It was really nice you being there, I think. It was just really good. It made it more of a social event, not something I was on my own doing with a couple of nurses and Steve. More a social thing than a private family affair, which was nice. It made it an awful lot better I'm sure, the fact that you were there: another friendly face.

Steve: Yes, it did for me.

Jo: Not just familiar, friendly: somebody who you felt was on your side.

Steve: Yes. It was good that you were there, because I don't know how the fuck I would have coped if you hadn't been there.

Elizabeth Farrell

I know I felt so pleased you were there, because I'd expected Robert not to stay. And it made me feel much more secure that you were there. I felt they wouldn't try to pull any fast ones or anything like that if you were there. And so it had a good effect on me. But I forgot you were there, because I couldn't see you.

A case of change?

Lois Manson

It's the Hawthorne effect question isn't it? [*Lois is a sociology graduate.*] I don't think it's affected me, save that sometimes there are things you've asked me which I've thought about later. For instance, when you asked me about Jane's personality, I think perhaps immediately you'd gone I thought more about that particular question than I would have done otherwise. But I don't think it's affected my *behaviour*. Except, do you remember when you asked me if I went to the upstairs clinic or the downstairs clinic? [*A complete division: the 'special' clinic (upstairs) was for medically problematic, but also socially special, patients (ie doctors' wives).*] And I immediately asked a doctor. I'm sorry if I got you into any hot water. But I suppose that was obviously an effect, wasn't it? And there might be people I suppose that hadn't thought about looking at the hospital in any kind of critical light who might perhaps start thinking, well perhaps there *is* something to criticise.

Christina Lynch

I think it's made me more critical. I suppose it's really someone who I can air my criticisms to, who is not just – I mean, I've said it all to my friends and parents … I feel that you would take more notice of me because you are who you are and this is all going in a little book…. But I know I shall be just another statistic!

Talking it out

Angela King

I mean I talk a lot, I suppose. It puts a lot of things clearer in your mind. Questions that you ask me that I've never thought about: it does help in a way. To think about it, and to talk about it. It's a sort of relief sometimes to talk about things, especially nasty things, because it puts it all into perspective. Nobody else has really got the time, have they? I spoke to Tony's cousin that had a baby two or three weeks ago, and she was full of it: you could tell that she really wanted to talk about it. I think most women do, after a birth; although it might be boring to some people, they really want to tell you everything that's happened. And I think it's a relief to them in a way because it's really an emotional thing, and I think your nerves are at their highest pitch and when it's all over it's a kind of relief to talk about it. It makes you *feel* better. Because most people have a bit of a – well I wouldn't say *nasty* – time, but it's a *shock* I think, and it's never what you expected it to be … and it really helps for people to talk about it and there's not always somebody there *to* talk to about it, is there, because a lot of husbands find it a big bore, don't they? And it changes you emotionally, whereas it doesn't really affect them at all.

Sandy Wright

I think it's *useful*: it helps to get things off your mind. I *needed* to talk to people those first weeks – I really needed *desperately* to talk to somebody about it: somebody who'd been through the experience. Yes I think it *is* therapeutic. I think it helps to get it out of your system.

Gillian Hartley

I think it's improved it if anything. I thought it was marvellous. I really enjoyed being part of the project. I think it's made me more positive about it, because if this kind of research is being done about pregnancy and motherhood, it certainly means that things will probably get better in the future. At least *you'd* have to believe that, or you wouldn't be doing the project in the first place. I think it probably has made me more positive about the experience altogether.

Those lovely long discussions about the baby, and the whole process. Getting things out into the open – questions that I'd had that I felt I really didn't want to bother other people with – those kind of questions. Maybe in a sense middle-class mothers, educated middle-class mothers, suffer in not really having outlets to talk about their feelings. No, I think that's being very biased. Maybe everybody needs a chance to talk about their feelings about pregnancy, and there really isn't anybody who asks them the kind of questions that you do, that you have, rather, in the survey, which acts positively psychologically. You really have asked personal questions about myself that nobody else has – sexual, personal, physical – bringing to the surface things that should have been brought to the surface and not let lie. And there's really no outlet for pregnant and postnatal mothers to talk about these things if they're not going, say to a psychiatrist, who isn't often interested in those things anyway. I think that's one way healthcare could be improved. If there could be ways for social workers or what have you to talk about it. Or perhaps it's something that women's groups ought to be doing something about – in the same way as rape counselling: it belongs on that level. Your feelings about the experience: getting things out.

Dawn O'Hara

Dawn: Thank you very much. I really mean it.

I: Do you feel that being involved in this research … has affected your experience?

Dawn: It has, because I regard you as a friend, you know what I mean? Somebody to speak to. I mean I don't look on you as a doctor, you know, that kind of way? Or a health visitor. I feel I can talk more freely to you.

Nina Brady

If I'd known you were coming, I would have made a cake; I was looking forward to your coming, dear. I was wondering about you the other day, and I thought maybe I'd missed you…. Oh it has helped to talk, it has, and it does help you. Turn that thing off, now!

Interviewing women: a contradiction in terms?

Interviewing is rather like marriage: everybody knows what it is, an awful lot of people do it, and yet behind each closed front door there is a world of secrets. Despite the fact that much of modern sociology could justifiably be considered "the science of the interview" (Benney and Hughes, 1970, p 190), very few sociologists who employ interview data actually bother to describe in detail the process of interviewing itself. The conventions of research reporting require them to offer such information as how many interviews were done and how many were not done; the length of time the interviews lasted; whether the questions were asked following some standardised format or not; and how the information was recorded. Some issues on which research reports do not usually comment are social/personal characteristics of those doing the interviewing; interviewees' feelings about being interviewed and about the interview; interviewers' feelings about interviewees; quality of interviewer–interviewee interaction; hospitality offered by interviewees to interviewers; attempts by interviewees to use interviewers as sources of information; and the extension of interviewer–interviewee encounters into more broadly based social relationships.

I argue in this chapter that social science researchers' awareness of those aspects of interviewing which are 'legitimate' and 'illegitimate' from the viewpoint of inclusion in research reports reflects their embeddedness in a particular research protocol. This protocol assumes a predominantly masculine model of sociology and society. The relative undervaluation of women's models has led to an unreal theoretical characterisation of the interview as a means of gathering sociological data which cannot and does not work in practice. This lack of fit between the theory and practice of interviewing is especially likely to come to the fore when a feminist interviewer is interviewing women (who may or may not be feminists).

Interviewing: a masculine paradigm?

Let us consider first what the methodology textbooks say about interviewing. First, and most obviously, an interview is a way of finding out about people. "If you want an answer, ask a question.…The asking of questions is the main source of social scientific information about everyday behaviour" (Shipman, 1972, p 76). According to Johan Galtung (1967, p 149):

> The survey method … has been indispensable in gaining information about the human condition and new insights in social theory.

The reasons for the success of the survey method seem to be two: (1) *theoretically relevant* data are obtained, (2) they are amenable to *statistical treatment*, which means (a) the use of the powerful tools of correlation analysis and multi-variate analysis to test substantive relationships, and (b) the tools of statistical tests of hypotheses about generalizability from samples to universes.

Interviewing, which is one means of conducting a survey, is essentially a conversation, "merely one of the many ways in which two people talk to one another" (Benney and Hughes, 1970, p 181), but it is also, significantly, an *instrument* of data collection: "the interviewer is really a tool or an instrument" (Goode and Hatt, 1952, p 185). As Benny and Hughes (1970, pp 196-7) express it:

> Regarded as an information-gathering tool, the interview is designed to minimise the local, concrete, immediate circumstances of the particular encounter – including the respective personalities of the participants – and to emphasise only those aspects that can be kept general enough and demonstrable enough to be counted.

An interview is "a pseudo-conversation. In order to be successful, it must have all the warmth and personality exchange of a conversation with the clarity and guidelines of scientific searching" (Goode and Hatt, 1952, p 191), which means that "extraneous material" must be eliminated (Kahn and Cannell, 1957, p 16).

The contradiction at the heart of the textbook paradigm is that interviewing necessitates the manipulation of interviewees as objects of study/sources of data, but this can only be achieved via a certain amount of humane treatment. If the interviewee doesn't believe he/she is being kindly and sympathetically treated by the interviewer, then he/she will not consent to be studied and will not come up with the desired information. A balance must then be struck between the warmth required to generate 'rapport' and the detachment necessary to see the interviewee as an object under surveillance; walking this tightrope means, not surprisingly, that "interviewing is not easy" (Denzin, 1970, p 186).

Claire Selltiz (1965) and her colleagues give a more explicit recipe. They say:

> The interviewer's manner should be friendly, courteous, conversational and unbiased. He [sic] should be neither too grim nor too effusive; neither too talkative nor too timid. The idea should be to put the respondent at ease, so that he will talk freely and fully…. [Hence] A brief remark about the weather, the family pets, flowers or children will often serve to break the ice. Above all, an informal, conversational interview is dependent upon a thorough mastery by the interviewer of the actual questions in his schedule. He should be familiar enough with them to ask them conversationally, rather than read them stiffly; and he should know what questions are coming next, so there will be no awkward pauses while he studies the questionnaire. (p 576)

C.A. Moser (1958), in an earlier text, advises of the dangers of 'overrapport':

> Some interviewers are no doubt better than others at establishing what the psychologists call 'rapport' and some may even be good at it – the National Opinion Research Centre Studies found slightly less satisfactory results from the ... sociable interviewers who were 'fascinated by people'....What one asks is that the interviewer's personality should be neither over-aggressive nor over-sociable. Pleasantness and a business-like nature is the ideal combination. (pp 187-8, 195)

'Rapport', a commonly used but ill-defined term, does not mean in this context what the dictionary says it does ("a sympathetic relationship", *Oxford English Dictionary*) but the acceptance by the interviewee of the interviewer's research goals, and the interviewee's active search to help the interviewer in providing the relevant information. The person who is interviewed has a passive role in adapting to the definition of the situation offered by the person doing the interviewing. The person doing the interviewing must actively and continually construct the 'respondent' (a telling name) as passive. Another way to phrase this is to say that both interviewer and interviewee must be 'socialised' into the correct interviewing behaviour:

> It is not enough for the scientist to understand the world of meaning of his [sic] informants; if he is to secure valid data via the structured interview, respondents must be socialised into answering questions in proper fashion. (Sjoberg and Nett, 1968, p 210)

One piece of behaviour that properly socialised respondents do not engage in is asking questions back. Although the textbooks do not present any evidence about the extent to which interviewers find in practice that this happens, they warn of its dangers and in the process suggest some possible strategies of avoidance: "Never provide the interviewee with any formal indication of the interviewer's beliefs and values. If the informant poses a question ... parry it" (Sjoberg and Nett, 1968, p 212). "When asked what you mean and think, tell them you are here to learn, not to pass any judgement, that the situation is very complex" (Galtung, 1967, p 161). "If he [the interviewer] should be asked for his views, he should laugh off the request with the remark that his job at the moment is to get opinions, not to have them" (Selltiz et al, 1965, p 576) and so on. Goode and Hatt (1952, p 198) offer the most detailed advice on this issue:

> What is the interviewer to do, however, if the respondent really wants information? Suppose the interviewee does answer the question but then asks for the opinions of the interviewer. Should he give his honest opinion, or an opinion which he thinks the interviewee wants? In most cases, the rule remains that he is there to obtain information and to focus on the respondent, not himself. Usually, a few simple phrases will shift the emphasis back to the respondent. Some which have been fairly

successful are 'I guess I haven't thought enough about it to give a good answer right now', 'Well, right now, your opinions are more important than mine', and 'If you really want to know what I think, I'll be honest and tell you in a moment, after we've finished the interview'. Sometimes the diversion can be accomplished by a headshaking gesture which suggests 'That' a hard one!' while continuing with the interview. In short, the interviewer must avoid the temptation to express his own views, even if given the opportunity.

Of course the reason why the interviewer must pretend not to have opinions (or to be possessed of information the interviewee wants) is because behaving otherwise might 'bias' the interview. 'Bias' occurs when there are systematic differences between interviewers in the way interviews are conducted, with resulting differences in the data produced. Such bias clearly invalidates the scientific claims of the research, since the question of which information might be coloured by interviewees' responses to interviewers' attitudinal stances and which is independent of this 'contamination' cannot be settled in any decisive way.

The paradigm of the social research interview prompted in the methodology textbooks does, then, emphasise the following:

1) its status as a mechanical instrument of data collection
2) its function as a specialised form of conversation in which one person asks the questions and another gives the answers
3) its characterisation of interviewees as essentially passive individuals
4) its reduction of interviewers to a question–asking and rapport-promoting role.

Actually, two separate typifications of the interviewer are prominent in the literature, although the disjunction between the two is never commented on. In one, the interviewer is "a combined phonograph and recording system" (Rose, 1945, p 143), and the job of the interviewer "is fundamentally that of a reporter not an evangelist, a curiosity-seeker, or a debater" (Selltiz et al, 1965, p 576). Both interviewer and interviewee are thus depersonalised participants in the research process. The second typification of interviewers in the methodology literature is that of the interviewer as psychoanalyst. The interviewer's relationship to the interviewee is hierarchical and it is the body of expertise possessed by the interviewer that allows the interview to be successfully conducted. Most crucial in this exercise is the interviewer's use of non-directive comments and probes to encourage a free association of ideas which reveals whatever truth the research has been set up to uncover. Indeed, the term 'non-directive interview' is derived directly from the language of psychotherapy. One implication is that interviewees are like patients:

> the actor's [interviewee's] mental condition [is] ... confused and difficult to grasp. Frequently the actor himself [sic] does not know what he believes; he may be so 'immature' that he cannot perceive or cope with

> his own subconscious thought patterns ... the interviewer must be
> prepared to follow the interviewee through a jungle of meandering
> thought ways if he [sic] is to arrive at the person's true self. (Sjoberg and
> Nett, 1968, p 211)

Both psychoanalytic and mechanical typifications of the interviewer and, indeed, the entire paradigmatic representation of 'proper' interviews in the methodology textbooks, owe a great deal more to a masculine social and sociological vantage point than to a feminine one. For example, the paradigm of the 'proper' interview appeals to such values as objectivity, detachment, hierarchy and 'science' as an important cultural activity which takes priority over people's more individualised concerns. The errors of poor interviewing comprise subjectivity, involvement, the 'fiction' of equality and an undue concern with the ways in which people are not statistically comparable. This polarity of 'proper' and 'improper' interviewing is an almost classical representation of the widespread gender stereotyping which has been shown, in countless studies, to occur in modern industrial civilisations. Women are characterised as sensitive, intuitive, incapable of objectivity and emotional detachment, and as immersed in the business of making and sustaining personal relationships. Men are thought superior through their own capacity for rationality and scientific objectivity, and are thus seen to be possessed of an instrumental orientation in their relationships with others. Women are the exploited, the abused; they are unable to exploit others through the 'natural' weakness of altruism – a quality which is also their strength as wives, mothers and housewives. Conversely, men find it easy to exploit, although it is most important that any exploitation be justified in the name of some broad political or economic ideology ('the end justifies the means').

Feminine and masculine psychology in patriarchal societies is the psychology of subordinate and dominant social groups. The tie between women's irrationality and heightened sensibility on the one hand, and their materially disadvantaged position on the other is, for example, also to be found in the case of ethnic minorities. The psychological characteristics of subordinates

> form a certain familiar cluster: submissiveness, passivity, docility, dependency, lack of initiative, inability to act, to decide, to think and the like. In general, this cluster includes qualities more characteristic of children than adults – immaturity, weakness and helplessness. If subordinates adopt these characteristics, they are considered well adjusted. (Miller, 1976, p 7)

It is no accident that the methodology textbooks refer to the interviewer as male. Although not all interviewees are referred to as female, there are a number of references to 'housewives' as the kind of people interviewers are most likely to meet in the course of their work (see, for example, Goode and Hatt, 1952, p 189).

Interviewers define the role of interviewees as subordinates; extracting information is more to be valued than yielding it; the convention of interviewer–

interviewee hierarchy is a rationalisation of inequality; what is good for interviewers is not necessarily good for interviewees.

Another way to approach this question of the masculinity of the 'proper' interview is to observe that a sociology of feelings and emotion does not exist. Sociology mirrors society in not looking at social interaction from the viewpoint of women. While everyone has feelings, Hochschild (1975) writes:

> Our society defines being cognitive, intellectual or rational dimensions of experience as superior to being emotional or sentimental. (Significantly, the terms 'emotional' and 'sentimental' have come to connote excessive or degenerate forms of feeling.) Through the prism of our technological and rationalistic culture, we are led to perceive and feel emotions as some irrelevancy or impediment to getting things done. [Hence their role in interviewing.]

> Another reason for sociologists' neglect of emotions may be the discipline's attempt to be recognized as a 'real science' and the consequent need to focus on the most objective and measurable features of social life. This coincides with the values of the traditional 'male culture'.... (p 281)

Women interviewing women: or objectifying your sister

Before I became an interviewer, I had read what the textbooks said interviewing ought to be. However, I found it very difficult to realise the prescription in practice, in a number of ways which I describe below. It was these practical difficulties which led me to take a new look at the textbook paradigm. In the rest of this chapter, the case I want to make is that when a feminist interviews women:

1) the use of prescribed interviewing practice is morally indefensible;
2) general and irreconcilable contradictions at the heart of the textbook paradigm are exposed; and
3) in most cases, the goal of finding out about people through interviewing is best achieved when the relationship of interviewer and interviewee is non-hierarchical.

I have interviewed several hundred women over a period of some ten years, but it was the research project concerned with the transition to motherhood that particularly highlighted problems in the conventional interviewing recipe. Salient features of this research were that it involved repeated interviewing of a sample of women during a critical phase in their lives. (In fact, 55 women were interviewed four times; twice in pregnancy and twice afterwards and the average total period of interviewing was 9.4 hours.) It included, for some, my attendance at the most critical point in this phase: the birth of the baby. Although I had a research assistant to help me, I myself did the bulk of the interviewing – 178 interviews over a period of some 12 months. The project was my idea and the analysis and writing up of the data was entirely my responsibility.

My difficulties in interviewing women were of two main kinds. First, the women asked me a great many questions. Second, repeated interviewing over this kind of period, and involving the intensely personal experiences of pregnancy, birth and motherhood, established a rationale of personal involvement I found it problematic and ultimately unhelpful to avoid.

Asking questions back

Analysing the tape-recorded interviews I had conducted, I listed 878 questions that interviewees had asked me at some point in the interviewing process. Three quarters of these (see Table 1) were requests for information (for example, 'Who will deliver my baby?', 'How do you cook an egg for a baby?').

Fifteen per cent were questions about me, my experiences or attitudes in the area of reproduction ('Have you got any children?', 'Did you breastfeed?'); 6% were questions about the research ('Are you going to write a book?', 'Who pays you for doing this?'), and 4% were more directly requests for advice on a particular matter ('How long should you wait for sex after childbirth?', 'Do you think my baby's got too many clothes on?'). Table 2 shows the topics on which interviewees wanted information. The largest category of questions concerned medical procedures: for example, how induction of labour is done, and whether all women attending a particular hospital are given episiotomies. The second largest category related to infant care or development: for example, 'How do you clean a baby's nails?', 'When do babies sleep through the night?'. Third, there were questions about organisational procedures in the institutional settings where antenatal or delivery care was done; typical questions were concerned with who exactly would be doing antenatal care and what the rules are for husbands' attendance at delivery. Last, there were questions about the physiology of reproduction; for example, 'Why do some women need Caesareans?' and (from one very frightened mother-

Table 1: Questions interviewees asked (%) (total = 878)

Information requests	76
Personal questions	15
Questions about the research	6
Advice questions	4

Source: Transition to Motherhood project

Table 2: Interviewees' requests for information (%) (total = 664)

Medical procedures	31
Organisational procedures	19
Physiology of reproduction	15
Baby care/development/feeding	21
Other	15

Source: Transition to Motherhood project

to-be) 'Is it right that the baby doesn't come out of the same hole you pass water out of?'.

It would be the understatement of all time to say that I found it very difficult to avoid answering these questions as honestly and fully as I could. I was faced, typically, with a woman who was quite anxious about the fate of herself and her baby, who found it either impossible or extremely difficult to ask questions and receive satisfactory answers from the medical staff with whom she came into contact, and who saw me as someone who could not only reassure but inform. I felt that I was asking a great deal from these women in the way of time, cooperation and hospitality at a stage in their lives when they had every reason to exclude strangers altogether in order to concentrate on the momentous character of the experiences being lived through. Indeed, I *was* asking a great deal – not only 9.4 hours of interviewing time but confidences on highly personal matters, such as sex and money, and, 'real' (that is, possibly negative or ambivalent) feelings about babies, husbands, etc. I was, in addition, asking some of the women to allow me to witness them in the highly personal act of giving birth. Although the pregnancy interviews did not have to compete with the demands of motherhood for time, 90% of the women were employed when first interviewed and 76% of the first interviews had to take place in the evenings. Although I had timed the first postnatal interview (at about five weeks postpartum) to occur after the disturbances of very early motherhood, for many women it was nevertheless a stressful and busy time. And all this in the interests of 'science' or for some book that might possibly materialise out of the research – a book which many of the women interviewed would not read and none would profit from directly.

The transition to friendship?

As Laslett and Rapoport (1975) note, repeated interviewing is not much discussed in the methodological literature: the paradigm is of an interview as a 'one-off' affair. Common sense would suggest that an ethic of detachment on the interviewer's part is much easier to maintain where there is only one meeting with the interviewee (and the idea of a 'one-off' affair, rather than a longer-term relationship, may also be closer to the traditional masculine world view).

In terms of my experience in the childbirth project, I found that interviewees very often took the initiative in defining the interviewer–interviewee relationship as something which existed beyond the limits of question asking and answering. For example, at 92% of the interviews, I was offered tea, coffee or some other drink; 14% of the women also offered me a meal on a least one occasion. As Table 1 suggests, there was also a certain amount of interest in my own situation. What sort of person was I and how did I come to be interested in this subject?

In some cases, these kinds of 'respondent' reactions were evident at the first interview. More often, they were generated after the second interview. On this occasion, I gave them all a stamped addressed postcard on which I asked them to write the date of their baby's birth so I would know when to re-contact them for the first postnatal interview. This card was usually placed in a prominent position (for example, on the mantelpiece), to remind the woman or her partner to complete it and it probably served in this way as a reminder of my intrusion into their lives. Some of the women took the initiative in contacting me to arrange the second or a subsequent interview, although I had made it clear that I would get in touch with them. Several rang up to report particularly important pieces of information about their antenatal care – in one case, a distressing encounter with a doctor who told a woman keen on natural childbirth that this was "for animals: in this hospital we give epidurals"; in another case, to tell me of an ultrasound result that changed the expected date of delivery. Several also got in touch to correct or add to things they had said during an interview – for instance, one contacted me several weeks after the fourth interview to explain that she had had an emergency appendicectomy five days after my visit and that her physical symptoms at the time could have affected some of her responses to the questions I asked.

A feminist interviews women

Such responses as I have described on the part of the interviewees to participation in research, particularly that involving repeated interviewing, are not unknown, although they are almost certainly under-reported. Some of the reasons why they were so pronounced in the research project discussed may have related to my own evident wish for a relatively intimate and non-hierarchical relationship. I certainly set out to convey to the people, whose cooperation I was seeking, the fact that I did not intend to exploit either them or the information they gave me. For instance, if the interview clashed with the demands of housework and motherhood I offered to, and often did, help with the work that had to be done.

The pilot interviews, together with my previous experience of interviewing women, led me to decide that, when I was asked questions, I would answer them. The practice I followed was to answer all personal questions and questions about the research as fully as was required. For example, when two women asked if I had read their hospital case notes I said I had and, when one of them went on to ask what reason was given in these notes for her forceps delivery, I told her what the notes said. On the emotive issue of whether I experienced childbirth as painful (a common topic of conversation), I told them that I did find it so, but that in my view it was worth it to get a baby at the end. Advice questions I also answered fully, but I made it clear when I was using my own experiences of motherhood as the basis for advice. When asked for information, I gave it if I could or referred the questioner to an appropriate medical or non-medical authority. Again, the way I responded to interviewees' questions probably encouraged them to regard me as more than an instrument of data collection.

There were three main reasons why I decided not to follow the textbook code of ethics with regard to interviewing women. First, I did not regard it as reasonable to adopt a purely exploitative attitude to interviewees as sources of data. My involvement in the women's movement in the early 1970s and the rebirth of feminism in an academic context had led me, along with many others, to reassess society and sociology as masculine paradigms and to want to bring about change in the traditional cultural and academic treatment of women. 'Sisterhood', a somewhat nebulous and problematic, but nevertheless important, concept, certainly demanded that women re-evaluate the basis of their relationships with one another.

The dilemma of a feminist interviewer interviewing women could be summarised by considering the practical application of some of the strategies recommended in the textbooks for meeting interviewees' questions. For example, these advise that such questions as 'Which hole does the baby come out of?', 'Does an epidural ever paralyse women?' and 'Why is it dangerous to leave a small baby alone in the house?' should be met with such responses from the interviewer as 'I guess I haven't thought enough about it to give a good answer right now', or 'a head-shaking gesture which suggests "that's a hard one"' (Goode and Hatt, 1952, p 189). Also recommended is laughing off the request with the remark that "My job at the moment is to get opinions, not to have them" (Selltiz et al, 1965, p 576).

A second reason for departing from conventional interviewing ethics was that I regarded sociological research as an essential way of giving the subjective situation of women greater visibility, not only in sociology, but, more importantly, in society, than it has traditionally had. Interviewing women was, then, a strategy for documenting women's own accounts of their lives. What *was* important was not taken-for-granted sociological assumptions about the role of the interviewer, but a new awareness of the interviewer as an instrument for promoting a sociology *for* women, that is, as a tool for making possible the articulated and recorded commentary of women on the very personal business of being female in a patriarchal capitalist society.

A third reason why I undertook the childbirth research with a degree of scepticism about how far traditional precepts of interviewing could, or should, be applied in practice was because I had found, in my previous interviewing experiences, that an attitude of refusing to answer questions or offer any kind of personal feedback was not helpful in terms of the traditional goal of promoting 'rapport'. A different role, that could be termed 'no intimacy without reciprocity', seemed especially important in longitudinal in-depth interviewing. This involves being sensitive not only to those questions that are asked (by either party) but to those that are not asked.

On the success of this approach in the 'Transition to motherhood' research, I offer the following cameo:

> AO: Did you have any questions you wanted to ask but didn't when you last went to the hospital?

> MC: Er, I don't know how to put this really. After sexual intercourse I had some bleeding, three times, only a few drops and I didn't tell the hospital because I didn't know how to put it to them. It worried me first off, as soon as I saw it I cried. I don't know if I'd be able to tell them. You see, I've also got a sore down there and a discharge and you know I wash there lots of times a day. You think I should tell the hospital; I

> could never speak to my own doctor about it. You see I feel like this but
> I can talk to you about it and I can talk to my sister about it.

The quality and depth of the information given to me by the women I interviewed can be assessed in *Becoming a mother* (Oakley, 1979), the book arising out of the research which is based almost exclusively on interviewee accounts.

So far as interviewees' reactions to being interviewed are concerned, I asked them at the end of the last interview the question, 'Do you feel that being involved in this research – my coming to see you – has affected your experience of becoming a mother in any way?'. Table 3 gives the answers.

Nearly three quarters of the women said that being interviewed had affected them, and the three most common forms this influence took were in leading them to reflect on their experiences more than they would otherwise have done; in reducing the level of their anxiety and/or in reassuring them of their normality; and in giving a valuable outlet for the verbalisation of feelings. None of those who thought being interviewed had affected them described this effect as negative. There were many references to the 'therapeutic' effect of talking: 'getting it out of your system'. It is important to note here that one of the main conclusions of the research was that there is a considerable discrepancy between the expectations and the reality of the different aspects of motherhood – pregnancy, childbirth, the emotional relationship of mother and child, the work of childrearing. A dominant metaphor used by interviewees to describe their reactions to this hiatus was 'shock'. In this sense, a process of emotional recovery may be endemic in the normal transition to motherhood, and there may be a general need for some kind of 'supportive listening' that is not met within the usual circle of family and friends.

On the issue of cooperation, only two out of 82 women contacted initially about the research actually refused to take part in it. Once the interviewing was under way, only one woman voluntarily dropped out (because of relationship problems); an attrition from 66 at interview 1 to 55 at interview 4 was otherwise accounted for by miscarriage, moves, and so on. The sub-sample of women who were asked if they would mind me attending the birth all agreed and they all got in touch either directly or indirectly through their husbands when they started labour. The postcards left after interview 2, for interviewees to return after the birth, were all completed.

Table 3: 'Has the research affected your experience of becoming a mother?' (%)

No	27
Yes:	73
Thought about it more	30
Found it reassuring	25
A relief to talk	25
Changed attitudes/behaviour	7

Note: Percentages do not add up to 100 because some women gave more than one answer.

Is a 'proper' interview ever possible?

Hidden among the admonitions on how to be a perfect interviewer in the social research methods manuals is the covert recognition that the goal of perfection is actually unattainable: the contradiction between the need for 'rapport' and the requirement of between-interview comparability cannot be solved. For example, Dexter (1956), following Paul (1954), observes that the pretence of neutrality on the interviewer's part is counterproductive: participation demands alignment. Selltiz and colleagues (1965) say that, "Much of what we call interviewer bias can more correctly be described as interviewer *differences*, which are inherent in the fact that interviewers are human beings and not machines and that they do not work identically" (p 583). Richardson and his colleagues (1965) in their popular textbook on interviewing note that:

> Although gaining and maintaining satisfactory participation is never the primary objective of the interviewer, it is so intimately related to the quality and quantity of the information sought that the interviewer must always maintain a dual concern: for the quality of his [sic] respondent's participation and for the quality of the information being sought. Often ... these qualities are independent of each other and occasionally they may be mutually exclusive. (p 129)

It is not hard to find echoes of this point of view in the few accounts of the actual process of interviewing that do exist. For example, Zweig (1949), in his study of *Labour, life and poverty*,

> dropped the idea of a questionnaire or formal verbal questions ... instead I had casual talks with working-class men on an absolutely equal footing....
>
> I made many friends and some of them paid me a visit afterwards or expressed a wish to keep in touch with me. Some of them confided their troubles to me and I often heard the remark: 'Strangely enough, I have never talked about that to anybody else'. They regarded my interest in their way of life as a sign of sympathy and understanding rarely shown to them even in the inner circle of their family. I never posed as somebody superior to them or as a judge of their actions but as one of them. (pp 1-2)

Zweig defended his method on the grounds that telling people they were objects of study met with 'an icy reception' and that finding out about other people's lives is much more readily done on a basis of friendship than in a formal interview.

More typically and recently, Marie Corbin (1971), the interviewer for the Pahls' study of *Managers and their wives* (1971), commented in an Appendix to the book of that name:

Obviously the exact type of relationship that is formed between an interviewer and the people being interviewed is something that the interviewer cannot control entirely, even though the nature of this relationship and how the interviewees classify the interviewer will affect the kinds of information given ... simply because I am a woman and a wife I shared interests with the other wives and this helped to make the relationship a relaxed one.

Corbin goes on:

In these particular interviews I was conscious of the need to establish some kind of confidence with the couples if the sorts of information required were to be forthcoming.... In theory it should be possible to establish confidence simply by courtesy towards and interest in the interviewees. In practice it can be difficult to spend eight hours in a person's home, share their meals and listen to their problems and at the same time remain polite, detached and largely uncommunicative. (pp 303-5)

Another illustration of this point is Dorothy Hobson's account of her research on housewives' experiences of social isolation:

The method of interviewing in a one-to-one situation requires some comment. What I find most difficult is to resist commenting in a way which may direct the answers which the women give to my questions.

It is impossible to tell exactly how the women perceive me but I do not think they see me as too far removed from themselves. This may partly be because I have to arrange the interviews when my own son is at school and leave in time to collect him. (Hobson, 1975, pp 80-1)

As Bell and Newby (1977, pp 9-10) note, "accounts of doing sociological research are at least as valuable, both to students of sociology and its practitioners, as the exhortations to be found in the much more common textbooks on methodology". All research is political and this is one reason why social research is not "like it is presented and prescribed in those texts. It is infinitely more complex, messy, various and much more interesting" (Bell and Encel, 1978, p 4). The 'cookbooks' of research methods largely ignore the political context of research, although some make asides about its 'ethical dilemmas': "Since we are all human we are all involved in what we are studying when we try to study any aspect of social relations" (Stacey, 1969, p 2); "frequently researchers, in the course of their interviewing, establish rapport not as scientists but as human beings; yet they proceed to use this humanistically gained knowledge for scientific ends, usually without the informants' knowledge" (Sjoberg and Nett, 1968, pp 215-16).

These ethical dilemmas are generic to all research involving interviewing, but they are greatest where there is least social distance between the interviewer and interviewee. Where both share the same gender socialisation and critical life experiences, social distance can be minimal. Where both interviewer and interviewee share membership of the same minority group, the basis for equality may impress itself even more urgently on the interviewer's consciousness. Mamak's comments apply equally to a feminist interviewing women:

> I found that my academic training in the methodological views of Western social science and its emphasis on 'scientific objectivity' conflicted with the experiences of my colonial past. The traditional way in which social science research is conducted proved inadequate for an understanding of the reality, needs and desires of the people I was researching. (Mamak, 1978, p 176)

A poignant example is the incident related in Elenore Smith Bowen's *Return to laughter* when the anthropologist witnesses one of her most trusted informants dying in childbirth:

> I stood over Amara. She tried to smile at me. She was very ill. I was convinced these women could not help her. She would die. She was my friend but my epitaph for her would be impersonal observations scribbled in my notebook, her memory preserved in an anthropologist's file: 'Death (in childbirth)/Cause: witchcraft/Case of Amara'. A lecture from the past reproached me: 'The anthropologist cannot, like the chemist or biologist, arrange controlled experiments. Like the astronomer, his [sic] mere presence produces changes in the data he is trying to observe. He himself is a disturbing influence which he must endeavour to keep to the minimum. His claim to science must therefore rest on a meticulous accuracy of observations and on a cool, objective approach to his data'.

> A cool, objective approach to Amara's death?

> One can, perhaps, be cool when dealing with questionnaires or when interviewing strangers. But what is one to do when one can collect one's data only by forming personal friendships? It is hard enough to think of a friend as a case history. Was I to stand aloof, observing the course of events? (Bowen, 1956, p 163)

Professional hesitation meant that Bowen might never see the ceremonies connected with death in childbirth. But, on the other hand, she would see her friend die. Bowen's difficult decision to plead with Amara's kin and the midwives in charge of her case to allow her access to Western medicine did not pay off and Amara did eventually die.

A feminist interviewing women is by definition both 'inside' the culture and participating in that which she is observing. However, in these respects the behaviour of a feminist interviewer/researcher is not extraordinary: all research involves the political considerations which flow from the researcher's own identity.

A feminist methodology of social science requires abandoning the mythology of 'hygienic' research with its accompanying mystification of the researcher and the researched as objective instruments of data production. Personal involvement is more than dangerous bias: it is the condition under which people come to know each other and admit others into their lives.

Who's afraid of the randomised controlled trial? Some dilemmas of the scientific method and 'good' research practice

This chapter focuses on the nature and uses of the methodology of the randomised controlled trial (RCT) in the light of recent critiques of science, including the feminist concern with the social structure of science as representing an inherently sexist, racist, classist, and culturally coercive practice and form of knowledge. Using the example of one specific RCT aimed at promoting women's health, the chapter outlines some of the dilemmas thus raised for the pursuit of 'good' research practice.

Origins and problems of the RCT as a tool for researching women's health

The RCT is essentially an experimental test ('trial') of a particular treatment/ approach (or set of treatments/approaches) comparing two or more groups of subjects who are allocated to these groups at random (that is, according to the play of chance).

The prerequisite for any RCT is *uncertainty* about the effects of a particular treatment. If something is known to work (and to be acceptable and without harmful effects), then there is no reason to put it to the test in the form of a trial. It is, however, this very issue of certainty/uncertainty that constitutes one of the central problems of the contemporary debate about RCTs. People can be certain that something (for example, streptomycin, social workers) *is* effective but have no 'real' basis for their certainty; conversely, unless they are able to admit uncertainty, 'real' knowledge can never be gained.

The RCT has been increasingly promoted over recent years as *the* major evaluative tool within medicine. Over the same period, a new critical perspective has emerged, particularly within feminism (see, for example, Rose, 1986), towards what counts as 'knowledge' and the methods and techniques appropriate to its accumulation.

The starting point of this chapter is Davies and Esseveld's observation that the problem about the feminist rejection of quantitative methods as necessarily alienating is that it bars discussion both of the ways in which these methods are used, and of those in which they could be used to generate knowledge relevant to the exercise of improving women's situation (Davies and Esseveld, 1986, p 9).

Existing published work and the experience drawn on in this chapter suggest that RCTs pose three particular problems for feminist researchers. First and most obviously, there is the principle of *random allocation*, which uses chance – "the absence of design" (*Oxford English Dictionary*) – to determine the treatment received by participants in the research. The extent to which individuals are able to choose the form of their participation in the research is thereby limited. Linked with this is the much debated issue of *informed consent*. What is the meaning of consent, and how much of what kind of information is required by whom? The third problem concerns the epistemology, ownership and distribution of *certainty*. As already noted, the rationale for undertaking an RCT is uncertainty about the effectiveness/acceptability of a particular procedure. But the professionals may be certain and the lay public not; or the lay public may be convinced about the benefits of a procedure which meets with professional scepticism. This issue in particular has provoked a good deal of unclear thinking among those concerned with the promotion of women's health.

These issues were highlighted in a study of social support for childbearing women, conducted in 1985–89 (Oakley, 1992).

Who cares for women? An RCT of social support

The broad aim of this study was to establish whether social support provided as a research intervention has the capacity to make things better for women and their babies. Most previous work on this topic is problematic, on account of the repetitive methodological problem that, although better health is generally associated with more support, it is impossible to rule out the explanation that healthier, more supported mothers are different in other ways from less supported, less healthy mothers and babies (Oakley, 1985, 1988). Over a 15-month period, a total of 509 women agreed to take part in the study. Random allocation was used to determine who was offered the intervention, and social support was given by four research midwives who visited women at home during pregnancy, offered a listening ear for individual problems, provided various forms of practical and emotional help when required, and were available 24 hours a day to be contacted in case of need. The 'effectiveness' of this social support intervention in terms of a range of outcomes, including women's satisfaction and infant birthweight, was evaluated after delivery, using obstetric case note information from the four hospitals where the study was done, and by sending the women long and detailed postal questionnaires.

Methods used in this study fit more closely within the medical model of controlled evaluation of therapeutic strategies than with the social science model of qualitative research, in which in-depth interviewing is used to build up interpretative accounts of social processes. However, the study began life as a desire to test the idea that in-depth social science interviewing can *itself* have a supportive effect for those interviewed (Oakley, 1981a; Finch, 1984).

234

Chance or causation? The role of random numbers

The first of the three problems referred to earlier in combining a feminist research consciousness with the technique of an RCT concerns the process of random allocation itself.

As a research technique, randomisation is said to offer three principal advantages. First, each study unit (plot of earth, person, institution, etc) has an equal chance of being or not being in the experimental group. Estimates of chance variability are consequently much easier to come by. Second, assignment on the basis of a table of random numbers eradicates the potential for *bias*: researchers are unable to influence their results by choosing to load their experimental group with 'favourable' factors – 'good' seeds, middle-class women, well-resourced institutions. Third, the method allows the researchers evenly to distribute both those factors *known* to be associated with different outcomes and those which may be, but are *unknown*.

The advantage of random allocation is predominantly *scientific*. It improves the *design* of a study, in part by ensuring that the basic premise – of truly random sampling – underlying the use of statistical tests of significance is correct; in part by clearing the field of unknown 'biases', including those of both researchers and the researched. This removal of the human, subjective element is in line with what Reinharz (1983) and others have described as the 'conventional' or 'patriarchal' research model: research design is laid down in advance, research objectives are concerned with testing hypotheses, units of study are pre-defined, the researcher's attitude to research subjects is detached, data are manipulated using statistical analyses, replicability of the study findings is stressed, research reports are cast in the form of presenting results only in relation to preset hypotheses, and for approval in an academic community where neither researcher nor researched are allowed identities or personal values. It is, however, worth noting that one of the attributed weaknesses of RCTs – their concern with quantity, rather than quality, of life measures – is not a weakness of the method itself, but of its application (see Laing et al, 1975, for a counter-example).

As the study progressed, we had many discussions about how everyone felt about the procedure of random allocation. The midwives were sometimes unhappy about both the process and the results of the randomisation. They considered it a problem that random allocation was being used to determine which women were offered additional social support, as this meant that the women themselves could not choose their fates; it also meant that, in agreeing to participate in the study, they were agreeing to a 50% chance of either being offered additional social support or not. Second, the midwives worried because sometimes women they thought were in need of social support were allocated to the control group (standard care) or those they considered had enough of it already were allocated to receive it. One midwife wrote compellingly in a questionnaire we gave them halfway through the study about the conflict between random allocation and the principles of her midwifery training:

It's very strange in that, if this was practice and not research, you would evaluate each woman and decide if she needed the extra care for various reasons.... It's hard if you recruit someone who obviously has major problems and is desperate for extra help, and then she becomes control. I can feel guilty at showing them that extra care is available, and then not offering it to her – even more so if she eventually has a poor outcome to her pregnancy. Conversely, if she becomes intervention and has obvious major problems, I may wilt a little at finding the extra time and stamina to help her!

It can be a shame if, at first interview, you feel that a woman has no problems, is well-informed and supported, and yet you know you will keep on visiting, when you could spend that time with someone who would benefit more. But it's often not until you visit two or three times that problems become apparent.

Another midwife amplified this last point:

I went to a lady the other day. On the first visit, everything seemed fine. We were talking away and I got to the section on major worries. She said, well, yes, I suppose I have, and it turned out that her older son and her husband, who was not his father, had never got on, which could have had a bearing on the pregnancy in which she'd had a small baby. He'd been in trouble with the police, writing cheques, and so had her son; she brought out all these problems existing in her family since she'd remarried, and she said she can see such a difference in her life now. But I mean that sort of thing doesn't come out at first, does it?

The midwives tried various ploys to control the randomisation process. These included attempting to spot a pattern in the allocations, so that the order of intervention and control allocations could be predicted, and women entered in accordance with what the midwives thought would suit the women best; and good-humouredly trying to persuade the study secretary to tell them in which order to enter different women. (They were quick to realise that the secretary would have the pre-set allocation order in front of her when they telephoned with a new recruit to be randomised.) As well as the factor of women's own needs for social support, the four midwives openly confessed concern about distances they had to travel to carry out the home visits, and about other aspects of their work conditions, such as having to visit possibly dangerous ill-lit housing estates late in the evening. They understandably hoped their intervention group women would live close to home in places which were comfortable and safe to visit. Professional discussions of RCTs are replete with precisely these sorts of stories about people's natural human attempts to control the randomisation process (see, for example, Silverman, 1980, p 140).

Consenting adults?

The issue of randomisation is closely bound up with the question of to what extent participants in a research project (either an RCT or any other) consent on the basis of full information to take part in it.

In most, if not all, research studies in the social sciences and the market research/opinion survey domain, the people from whom, or on whom, information is gathered are given the opportunity not to take part. This convention accounts for the citation of what, perhaps revealingly, are called 'refusal' and 'non-response' rates: high refusal or non-response rates are considered to call into question the validity (generalisability) of the research findings, whereas low refusal or non-response rates are generally hailed as an achievement for the researchers.

Consent to participate in research is not necessarily the rule in medical research and the practice of informing people about their inclusion in RCTs is uneven. Until the late 1950s, there was almost no discussion, either in Europe or North America, of informed consent in medical or health research. The term itself seems to have been created in legal circles in 1957, and this legal base has been a continuing important pressure on doctors and medical researchers, particularly in the US, to consider the issue of what patients should know.

There is the issue of *what* patients are told, but there is also the issue of *which* patients are told, *when*, and on *whom* data are collected. From this point of view, it is customary to design RCTs in a number of ways. The differences between the designs centre on two issues: (1) the relationship between randomisation and consent, and (2) whether or not the trial analysis is done on 'an intention to treat' basis (so that data are collected on all randomly allocated subjects) or only on those who *were* treated. Figure 1 shows three variations on the possible combinations of these practices. In Design A, which has been in common use, informed consent is sought only after randomisation from the experimental group. However, data are collected on all randomised subjects whether or not their consent to take part in the research was requested and obtained, so that the sub-group of subjects randomised to the experimental group, who do not give their consent, none the less involuntarily contribute data. In Design B, consent is sought before randomisation, but, because data collection and analysis proceed on the 'intention to treat' principle, once again data on all patients are collected. In Design C, consent is also solicited before randomisation but, unlike Design B, only people who agree have information collected on them; those who refuse, either initially or subsequently, are excluded from data collection and analysis. We used Design C in our study.

The implications of the different designs for *what* people are told are also quite different. In Designs B and C, as opposed to Design A for example, what people are asked to consent to is not either to receive a particular intervention or not to receive it. They are asked to agree to putting themselves in a position where they have a fifty-fifty chance of receiving a particular treatment, or not receiving it. In our study, using Design C, the midwives were asked to follow a text prepared by us, explaining this when asking those women to take part in the study. Those women who agreed to take part were randomised and then informed of the

237

Figure 1: Alternative procedures for random allocation and informed consent

Design A

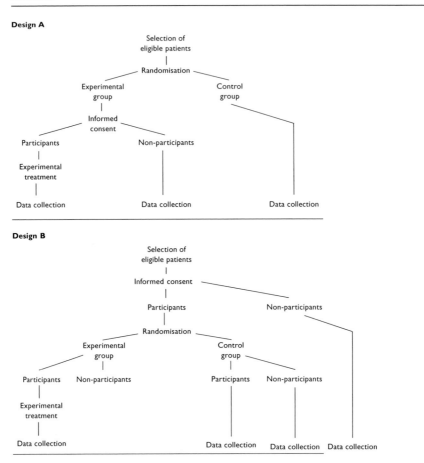

Design B

Design C

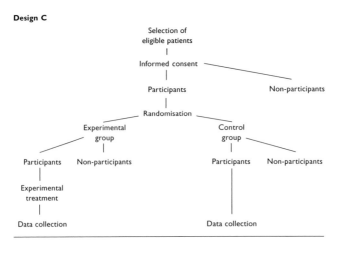

result. Twenty-five women out of the sample of 534 said they would rather not take part in the research. After randomisation, two women changed their minds – one in the control and one in the intervention group.

Design C is not in common use in RCTs of medical care carried out in Britain. The reasons why we chose to use it can be deduced from some of the arguments advanced in favour of the other methods, particularly Design A. These include the notion that asking for consent is a ritual that may itself damage health, and that consent is best left to "ethical committees who are in a better position to make such judgements on behalf of patients" (Papaioannou, 1982).

In the debate about informed consent, the question as to what patients want is rarely constituted as an empirical question, to be settled by appropriate inquiry. Dissatisfaction with the amount and kind of information they are given is the most common complaint patients make about medical care in both the UK and the US (see King, 1986).

In an interesting account of a 'failed' RCT, concerning methods of delivering very low birthweight babies in Australia, Lumley and colleagues (1985) describe how women's reluctance to subject their obstetric care to the play of chance on the basis of informed consent was anticipated by professionals as a problem before the trial started; however, the reason why it proved impossible to carry out in practice turned out instead to be the unwillingness of professionals to subject their behaviour to systematic evaluation. But it is, none the less, true that research on people's attitudes to information and consent in both healthcare generally and health research specifically is astonishingly limited.

In a chapter advocating the use of RCTs in perinatal research, Bracken (1984) introduces two further favoured medical reasons against informing patients when he says that:

> Patients are blinded in clinical trials for two major reasons. First, if blind, they are unlikely to withdraw from an RCT after being randomised into what they believe to be the less effective treatment. Such selective withdrawal would be extremely serious for the success of a trial. Second, blinding the patient avoids placebo effects. (Bracken, 1984, p 406)

Not telling people they are part of a research project thus unsurprisingly results in the advantage (for the researcher) that they cannot refuse to cooperate. But what are 'placebo effects' and what are they doing in this argument?

People's belief in the efficacy of what is being done to them has measurable effects on their health (see Brody, 1977). From a research point of view, however, the placebo effect is a problem, since it needs to be distinguished from that of the intervention itself. The logic of 'double blind' RCTs, in which researchers and researched remain unaware of who has been allocated to intervention and control groups, is threatened by the notion that those who agree to take part in research deserve this knowledge.

We encountered various difficulties with the method and content of the informed consent procedure we used in our study. Much the most important of these was the extent to which our informing women who were subsequently allocated to the control group what the study was about may have resulted in their feeling deprived. One example is this experience described by one of the midwives:

> Dawn Benn (Control). She was absolutely desperate to be intervention and she was so upset when I phoned her because of her social circumstances that, when she asked me if I knew the address of any mother and toddler groups, NCT groups, anything, because she's just moved into the area, I gave her a couple of phone numbers before I'd even got her allocated. She was heartbroken.

In other instances, control group women got in touch with the midwives for help even though they knew they had been assigned to the no-support group. We asked the midwives to respond minimally in such situations, conscious that responding fully would be to jeopardise the aims of the study. It is interesting to note that control group women were only able to request this help because the midwives felt it was unethical for them not to give all women in the study a contact address and telephone number. They did so, although this was not part of the study design, and partly in response to our discussions about the informed consent issue.

Evidence of a 'deprivation' response was also gleaned from a few of the women who took part, in the questionnaires they filled in after delivery: for example,

> Pleased to help. I would have welcomed home visits from a midwife.

> I was very pleased to help, but would have enjoyed the visits....

> Happy ... [to take part in the research] if it can help anyone in the future. Would have preferred to be in group visited.

For other control group women, the desire to feel included took such a form that they felt they had been. One of the sections of the questionnaire asked women to tick a list of possibly helpful people, including the research midwife ('if she visited') and 13 control group women ticked this, although they had not in fact been visited at all. One woman in the control group even went so far as to say she felt special as a result of taking part in the research: it was 'like belonging to an elite group'.

Because we gave information to all the women the midwives identified as eligible for the study, the women in the control group *were* part of a research project in which they had *chosen* to participate. In this sense, rigorous testing of the hypothesis that social support can improve pregnancy outcome may be at odds with the principle of informed consent. A further complication is that the standard scientific model of RCTs presupposes that there is no 'contamination' of the control group by the experimental group; the purpose of the control group is, after all, to act as a 'control' for the experiment. (In French, the term for 'control group' is 'le groupe témoin', literally 'witness' group, which carries an interestingly different connotation.) Again, the actual practice, as opposed to theory, of research reveals the chimerical nature of this model. It is assumed, for instance, that people do not talk to one another. In our study, had we not told the control group women about the study, we would have needed to rely on the intervention group women remaining silent about their receipt of social support – at home, with friends and neighbours, in antenatal clinics. But women are not silent.

A second problem we encountered with our informed consent procedure was in deciding how to present the aims of the study to the women we asked to take part in it. The standard procedure for an RCT involves the researcher setting out to test something affectionately known as 'the null hypothesis'. Adoption of the scientific method requires that one begins from the standpoint that there is no difference between the treatment and the lack of treatment, or between the treatments that are being compared. But, since we had designed our study to test the hypothesis that social support might affect the baby's weight, as well as to investigate other factors such as the type of delivery mothers had, and how they felt about their experiences, the dilemma was whether we should say so; or, if we said 'We want to see if social support can make babies grow better' (for example), were we somehow biasing the study from the start? Might we turn the study into a self-fulfilling prophecy, the results of which would never be believed except as such? This formulation of the question is interesting, for it leads to the next question, which is, if the hypothesis is that a *social* process may be therapeutic in a *clinical/physical* sense, what sensible arguments are there for concealing the purpose of the exercise from those taking part in it? The reason why researchers are wary about the placebo response is, after all, because of the possible beneficial impact on someone of feeling they are being cared for: it is the very presence and effect of the social process that is counted as disturbing. But for us the social process was of central concern. It was for this very reason that we decided to enlist the midwives' confidence in the aims of the study from the start; not to have done so would, we felt, not only have been unethical, but also intuitively counter to its aims. For the same reason, we were conscious of the tension with the principle that women allocated to the control group should not feel deprived. Thus, we also stated what we also believed, that we did not *know* whether social support could improve the health of all women and their children in this sense.

The importance of being (un)certain

Third, we come to the last of the issues being raised at the beginning of this chapter as especially problematic in this type of research – the question of uncertainty.

Much of the literature on informed consent refers to an uncomfortable prerequisite for the seeking of consent, which is that of researcher or practitioner uncertainty (our not knowing whether social support works). Certainty can be a consequence of very different political and ideological positions. It is not the prerogative of medical professionals, but also possessed by lay people and by women. In the childbirth field, for example, many attempts systematically to evaluate different modes of care have been shipwrecked on the rock of women's certainty about the effectiveness of apparently natural and innocuous methods, such as childbirth education, vitamin supplements, or raspberry leaf tea. The point is that, whatever form it takes and whoever professes it, certainty blocks progress towards greater understanding of the role of chance versus causation in the patterning and human experience of events and processes, including those responsible for health or its absence.

The issue of certainty was complicated in our study. None of us was prepared to say that we did not know whether social support was a good thing (in the same way as we would have been prepared to say, for example, that we did not know whether it is helpful for women prone to premature labour to be admitted to hospital during pregnancy). But, while it may seem axiomatic that social support, like love, is something we all want, what is at issue is the range and type of event/ process social support is capable of affecting, and the mechanism by which it does so (see Madge and Marmot, 1987, for a discussion). Assumptions about the inevitably therapeutic effects of social support may prove unfounded when subject to systematic evaluation. This was the case, for example, in the Cambridge-Somerville Youth Study, an early attempt initiated in 1935 to evaluate the long-term effectiveness of social work help in preventing delinquency and other 'undesirable' outcomes, in which it was found that the intervention of social workers was associated with more problems rather than fewer later on (McCord, 1981, 1982).

Conclusion

The RCT is a method of *experimental* research, and the term 'experiment' has been linked with what Chalmers (1983) has called the 'Auschwitz' view of scientific inquiry, according to which all experimental research is inherently suspect. The view of experimental research as inherently unethical is central to the feminist critique (Birke, 1986; Spallone and Steinberg, 1987) but also comes from other quarters (see Silverman, 1985). Much of it misses the absolutely crucial point that the condemnation of experimentation under the heading of 'research' allows a great deal of experimentation to pass unnoticed under the heading of standard practice. The frequency with which doctors impose on patients experiments of an uncontrolled nature has been one of the strongest objections to professionalised medicine made by the women's health movement over recent years in Europe and North America (Ruzek, 1978). For this reason, women have been, and continue to be, important beneficiaries of the advocacy of randomised controlled evaluation within medicine.

What our experience with an RCT of social support in pregnancy has shown is the need to subject every precept of the traditional scientific method to scrutiny. Is it necessary? Do its benefits outweigh its hazards? It is as important to ask these questions of a trial of something as apparently harmless as social support as it is of trials of other more obviously ambiguous therapies. The argument against 'methodolatry' is then transformed into the case for an *appropriate* methodology which, like its namesake, appropriate technology, requires that individuals involved in it be treated with sensitivity and respect, and *that there be no division between this ethical requirement and other requirements of the method.*

The use of feminist research principles to rehabilitate scientific method should thus result in a new paradigm of 'good' research practice.

Paradigm wars: some thoughts on a personal and public trajectory

Arguing about method: introduction

In his classic *The sociological imagination* (1959), C. Wright Mills takes a fairly dim view of method as self-conscious procedure. "Serious attention should be paid to general discussions of methodology only when they are in direct reference to actual work", he instructed (p 122). *The sociological imagination* is famous for its attack on the twin evils of grand theory and abstracted empiricism. Wright Mills' passion for a creative, lateral-thinking, problem-oriented social science did not go down well among some of his methodological colleagues. In a dialogue with Paul Lazarfeld, Wright Mills reputedly opened the conversation by quoting the first sentence of his book (p 3): "Nowadays men often feel that their private lives are a series of traps". Lazarfeld's response was: "How many men, which men, how long have they felt this way, which aspects of their private lives bother them, when do they feel free rather than trapped, what kinds of traps do they experience, etc etc?" (cited in Elcock, 1976, p 13).

This exchange sums up different positions in the long-running argument between so-called 'quantitative' and 'qualitative' methods. It is hard to say quite when this battle got off the ground, but there is little sign of it in the general methodological and professional literature before the 1960s. After that time, and partly infused by radical critiques of science, dissatisfaction with 'quantitative' methods generated increasing appeal to other forms and methods of collecting social science data (Cicourel, 1964; Rose and Rose, 1976; Bryman, 1988). These built, of course, on earlier work, including that of Weber (1947; see Platt, 1985), Schutz (1932) and Blumer (see Hammersley, 1989). But one highly significant driving force behind the paradigm war from the 1970s on was nothing to do directly with developments in social science. The arrival of feminism as a political and social movement underscored the importance for political reasons of using 'qualitative' research methods, and gave an altogether new gloss to anti-science critiques of quantification.

The old and new Oakleys

My own early work developed a reputation for 'qualitative' research (see, for example, Reid, 1983; Spender, 1985). More recently, however, much of my work has been seen as more easily fitting the 'quantitative' mould, with a particular stress on methodologies of rigorous evaluation. This has gained me another kind of reputation – what the informants in one recent case study called "this

Oakleyesque view" of "gold-standard-copper-bottomed-man(sic)-in-a-white-coat-randomized-control-trial evaluations" (Bonell, 1999). These contrasting reputations suggest a shift of position, which is the source of a certain amount of puzzlement. In a seminar I gave in a Swedish department of sociology in 1997, the commentator on my talk desperately produced evidence from my previous writings of 'the old Oakley' – a persona she much preferred – which she then contrasted with 'the new Oakley', asking me to account for the difference. I have been accused of some sort of strange conversion experience, of being brainwashed by medics, of letting the 'qualitative' and feminist sides down; at the very least, it has been important for people to stress that, while my methodological repertoire has seemingly expanded, a primary allegiance to the 'qualitative' tradition must remain (see, for example, Brannen, 1992; Leavey, 1997).

This chapter provides a brief account of my personal methodological trajectory. What it emphasises are the misconstructions involved in the asking of the question – why the change in methodological position? I argue, instead, that there has been little 'real' change: my position has been co-opted to fit various paradigm arguments.

Interviewing and other trials

In the late 1960s and early 1970s, I interviewed women about housework (Oakley, 1974b). The housework research, in the course of which I myself became a feminist, was followed by another project on women's transition to motherhood (Oakley, 1979, 1980). Both projects employed in-depth interviewing as a way of generating personal narratives about experiences which, at the time, were viewed within mainstream social science (and society more generally) as unimportant, because they are private, domestic and belong to women's lives. One of my most quoted publications, 'Interviewing women: a contradiction in terms?' (Oakley, 1981a; see Part 4, Chapter Four) came directly out of the transition to motherhood research. All this work fed into an emerging and highly vocal literature on social science and women, within which 'qualitative' research came to be highlighted quite unambiguously as the preferred paradigm, with 'quantitative' research being earmarked as the work of the patriarchal devil (see, for example, Mies, 1983; Stanley and Wise, 1983). The feminist case against quantification focused on 'the three ps: positivism, power and p values' (see Oakley, 1998a). Experimental research methods represented the apex of the quantitative paradigm as criticised by many feminists, who saw these as synonymous with an approach to knowledge which intrinsically violates the agency and autonomy of those who are known about (see, for example, Donovan, 1990; Reinharz, 1992).

In 1979 I moved from a department of sociology to a healthcare research unit specialising in maternity services research. Social science was in a minority position in this unit and I found myself exposed there to a different research tradition in which quantification, and especially prospective experimental studies, dominated the scene. A main driving force behind the unit's work was evidence that healthcare practices are more often based on guesswork, personal preference, tradition, professional modelling and fear of litigation than on convincing and reliable data about their appropriateness, effectiveness and safety. As a consequence, many lives are damaged. Exposure to this evidence drew my attention to the difference between 'controlled' and 'uncontrolled' experimentation (see Chalmers, 1986). Uncontrolled experimentation is what usually happens in professional practice. Controlled experimentation, on the other hand, happens within the context of a formal research study, whose design is capable of providing an answer to the question: does this treatment/intervention work or not?

The point was/is, that what applies to the practices of doctors and other health care professionals also applies to any social group which sets itself up as possessing expert knowledge about the best way to intervene in other people's lives. Teachers, social workers, criminologists, volunteer 'do-gooders', politicians and other promulgators of public policy are all guilty of choosing to do what they believe in, rather than what has been demonstrated to be the best thing to do. Medicine's prime way of knowing, the randomised controlled trial (RCT), evolved as an alternative to the uncontrolled experimentation of 'normal practice'. In this sense, it is just as relevant to the evaluation of social interventions. Indeed, and for this reason, early developments of the method took place in social science not, as is usually believed, only in medicine (see Oakley, 1998b).

By 1984, I had started work on just such a study, an RCT of social support and pregnancy. The study used socially supportive interviewing as an intervention, and evaluated the effects of this on women and babies by having a 'control' group of women who were not interviewed (see Oakley, 1992). Since then I have also been involved in RCTs of other social interventions. In the early 1990s, I embarked with colleagues on another programme which set out to look critically at the evidence base of health promotion, as a particular kind of social intervention. In a series of systematic reviews (Oakley et al, 1995a, 1995b, 1996; Oakley and Fullerton, 1995; Harden et al, 1998), we were surprised to discover how inadequately the effects of many of these interventions have been assessed, and how often their proponents argue that they work, when the evidence is either non-existent or consistent with the opposite being the case. For example, an intensive health visitor intervention aimed at decreasing falls among older people actually increased them (Vetter et al, 1992); another, of social work services for older people, succeeded in raising mortality and institutionalisation rates (Blenkner et al, 1974); social work counselling for boys at risk of becoming 'delinquent' made this more, not less, likely (Powers and Witmer, 1951; McCord, 1981); and advising parents about the dangers to children's health of passive smoking made them less likely to stop smoking (Irvine et al, 1999).

Mixing methods

What I have described is undoubtedly a process of methodological development, but it is not a revolution. For example, in the housework study, the women's accounts of their lives jostle for attention with 2 x 2 tables and tests of statistical significance. An important motive was an attempt to calculate the length of housewives' working weeks in order to put domestic labour in the language of the paid labour market and the economics of the gross domestic product; this required much painstaking counting. When I published the study, I was slated in certain quarters both for using tests of significance and percentages, and for being a feminist, although the same people who made one sort of criticism usually did not make the other. One of the volumes which reported the transition to motherhood study (Oakley, 1980) also made much use of statistical tests as a way of arriving at a model of childbirth as a human experience – one which challenges the human capacity to respond unprepared, immediately and constructively to new and often painful experiences. In this book, I argued the opposite of what people probably expected me to argue: I suggested that women's reactions to childbirth could best be understood by seeing them as people rather than as women. As this is my most neglected book, I have often speculated that my use of the 'quantitative' mode was what put people off. Many simply found it jarred with the 'softer' style they expected from a feminist social scientist.

Similar caveats could be applied to the labelling of my later work as 'quantitative'. For example, while the prospective experimental design of the social support and pregnancy study was clearly that of a randomised controlled trial with its traditional emphasis on the power of numbers, the study was prompted directly by experiences of interviewing as both a social relationship and form of action. It was 'qualitative', in the sense of using in-depth interviewing as a means of encouraging narratives from research participants about their experiences, and also because we collected a great deal of information about the processes of developing and implementing such an intervention. The challenge as we saw it – and this applies to RCTs more generally – is to integrate the collection and analysis of 'qualitative' and 'quantitative' data so as to arrive at an interpretation which makes productive use of both.

Quantification and experimentation for women (and other people)?

Insofar as I can be said to have undergone any 'conversion' experience, this has been limited to understanding four things. The first is the requirements imposed on a socially responsible social science by professional arrogance. It is *because* doctors, teachers, social workers and others are so prone to launch interventions without knowing their effects that social science is obliged to use the best tools at its disposal to scrutinise such activities. Method here is (as Wright Mills advised) properly harnessed to the service of the social problem itself, rather than the other way around.

Secondly, I learnt that well designed and ethically conducted RCTs offer an elegantly simple approach to assessing the effects of such arrogance, as well as yielding answers to questions about the impact of all sorts of interventions. If the term 'randomised controlled trial' upsets people (which it undoubtedly does), then 'socially equitable comparison test' offers an equally truthful but less offensive description (Oakley, 1998c). Thirdly, I discovered that, in our excitement to dismantle patriarchy, other feminist social scientists and I had mistakenly thrown at least part of the baby out with the bathwater. Women and other minority groups, above all, need 'quantitative' research, because, without this, it is difficult to distinguish between personal experience and collective oppression. Only large-scale comparative data can determine to what extent the situations of men and women are structurally differentiated. And, as targets of the healthcare industry in particular, women also need well-designed experimental studies, which are capable of reliably evaluating the increasing numbers of medical procedures encountered over a lifetime (Foster, 1995; Oakley, 1998d). Without such studies, many of the harmful effects of such routine procedures as hormone treatment for miscarriage, ultrasound scanning in pregnancy, induction of labour and hormone replacement therapy would remain unknown.

The fourth thing I learnt (and am still learning) is less straightforward. It concerns the question: what are research methods *for*? In an era dominated by postmodernism, postfeminism and a general acceptance of multiple meanings, it is obviously unfashionable to suggest that the aim of research methods is to provide some sort of approximation to what is 'really' going on. Yet this is, I think, what drives and should drive most social scientists, just as most of us live our everyday lives as though reality exists and can be known about. Put the other way round, this concern becomes one about the extent to which different research methods offer protection against bias, against the possibility that we will end up with misleading answers. Much 'qualitative' research is simply too unsystematic, too masonic in nature, too cavalier about appeals to 'triangulation' and/or analysis using computerised software packages, to establish serious credentials for being trustworthy. For example, in four lists compiled by different researchers of criteria for judging the trustworthiness of qualitative research, there are 46 different criteria, of which only two are common to all four lists; terms capable of varying interpretations, such as 'clear', 'adequate', and 'careful' abound (Cobb and Hagemaster, 1987; Mays and Pope, 1995; Boulton et al, 1996; Medical Sociology Group, 1996; see also Oakley, 2000). Of course it is the case that research methods must fit the question being asked and this means that 'qualitative' methods are undoubtedly sometimes the most appropriate choice. But *all* methods must be open, consistently applied and replicable by others.

On labelling

Sociologists are in a better position than most people to understand the social processes involved in labelling. The above brief excursion through one methodological career demonstrates some changes in direction prompted by the arrival of new understandings, but what it illustrates most of all is the way in which the labelling of work as 'qualitative' or 'quantitative' proceeds from the context and the culture, and may have little to do with the intentions of the individual. I have never presented myself as a single-minded advocate either or 'quantitative' or 'qualitative' methods. I have certainly stressed the need for adopting methods appropriate to research questions, for choosing methods which are sensitive to power relations, and for the ethical conduct of research (which also means well-designed research able to answer the questions it is set up to answer); but all these precepts apply right across the methodological board.

One disadvantage of labelling is that it introduces an artificial problematic which then has to be explained. A more fruitful line of inquiry is to consider the problematic itself. The alignment of feminism with 'qualitative' methods, at one extreme, and the association of experimental methods with medical science, at the other, speak to, and of, a long drawn out process of gendering which has informed the development and use of ways of knowing across the sciences. Semantic attacks and other activities distract attention from what Paul Meehl (1986, p 317) has identified as the central question: "To what extent does this discipline contain knowledge that brings some sort of credentials with it?". A secondary question is whether there is any kind of credentialed knowledge that is not, in some sense, 'scientific'. This takes us back to the very origins of social science, which is where we need to be in order to understand, not just one person's journey through the space and time of paradigm wars, but their institutionalisation in a more global, and thus ultimately more interesting, sense.

General bibliography

Acker, J. (1992) 'Gendered institutions', *Contemporary Sociology*, vol 21, pp 565-9.

Adams, P. and Cowie, E. (eds) (1990) *The woman in question, m/f*, Cambridge, MA: MIT Press.

Aitken-Swan, J. (1977) *Fertility control and the medical profession*, London: Croom Helm.

Allan, J. (1975) 'Abolish the role of housewife', *The Sydney Morning Herald*, 6 February.

Andersen, I. (1984) 'Transition to parenthood research', *Journal of Psychosomatic Obstetrics and Gynaecology*, vol 3, pp 3-16.

Anon (1975) 'Including the kitchen sink', *The Economist*, 8 February.

Anon (1979) 'In brief', *British Medical Journal*, 5 May, p 1208.

Antony, L.M. and Witt, C. (eds) (1993) *A mind of one's own: Feminist essays on reason and objectivity*, Boulder, CO: Westview Press.

Apter, T. (1993) *Why women still don't have wives: Professional progress and motherhood*, Basingstoke: Macmillan.

Ardener, E. (1971) *Social anthropology and language*, London: Tavistock.

Ardener, E. (1977) 'The anthropologist as translator of culture', Paper delivered to the Wenner-Gren Symposium on *Focus on linguistics*, Burg Wartenstein, Austria.

Ardener, S. (1978) 'Introduction: the nature of women in society', in S. Ardener (ed) *Defining females*, London: Croom Helm.

Arms, S. (1975) *Immaculate deception*, New York, NY: Bantam Books.

Arrighi, B.A. and Maume, D.J.J. (2000) 'Workplace subordination and men's avoidance of housework', *Journal of Family Issues*, vol 21, no 4, pp 464-87.

Assiter, A. (1996) *Enlightened women: Modernist feminism in a postmodern age*, London: Routledge.

Astbury, J. (1996) *Crazy for you: The making of women's madness*, Melbourne: Oxford University Press.

Bacdayan, A.S. (1977) 'Mechanistic co-operation and sexual equality among the Western Bontoc', in A. Schlegel (ed) *Sexual stratification: A cross-cultural view*, New York, NY: Columbia University Press.

Bailey, R. (2001) 'Overcoming veriphobia – learning to love truth again', *British Journal of Educational Studies*, vol 49, no 2, pp 159-72.

Bandura, A. (1973) *Aggression: A social learning analysis*, Englewood Cliffs, NJ: Prentice-Hall.

Bandura, A. and Huston, A.C. (1961) 'Identification as a process of incidental learning', *Journal of Abnormal and Social Psychology*, vol 63, pp 311-18.

Bannerji, H., Carty, L., Heald, S. and McKenna, K. (1992) *Unsettling relations: The university as a site of feminist struggle*, Boston, MA: South End Press.

Barfield, A. (1976) 'Biologic influences on sex differences in behaviour', in M. Teitelbaum (ed) *Sex differences*, New York, NY: Anchor Books.

Barker, E. (1974) 'Housewives' choice', *The Times Educational Supplement*, 13 December.

Barker-Benfield, G.J. (1976) *The horrors of the half-known life*, New York, NY: Harper and Row.

Barrett, M. (1980) *Women's oppression today*, London: Verso.

Barrett, M. and Phillips, A. (eds) (1992) *Destabilizing theory: Contemporary feminist debates*, Cambridge: Polity Press.

Barrett, M. and Roberts, H. (1978) 'Doctors and their patients: the social control of women in general practice', in C. Smart and B. Smart (eds) *Women, sexuality and social control*, London: Routledge.

Barry, H., Child, I.L. and Bacon, M.K. (1959) 'Relation of child training to subsistence economy', *American Anthropologist*, vol 61, pp 51-63.

Bart, P.B. (1971) 'Sexism in social science: from the gilded cage to the iron cage, or, the perils of Pauline', *Journal of Marriage and the Family*, vol 33, pp 735-45.

Bartley, M., Popay, J. and Plewis, I. (1992) 'Domestic conditions, paid employment and women's experience of ill-health', *Sociology of Health and Illness*, vol 14, pp 313-43.

Bashiri, N. and Spielvogel, A.M. (1999) 'Postpartum depression: a cross-cultural perspective', *Primary Care Update for OB/GYNS*, vol 6, no 3, pp 82-97.

Baxter, J. and Western, M. (1998) 'Satisfaction with housework: examining the paradox', *Sociology*, vol 32, no 1, pp 101-20.

Beck, C.T. (2002) 'Postpartum depression: a meta-synthesis', *Qualitative Health Research*, vol 12, no 4, pp 453-72.

Becker, G. (1980) 'A theory of the allocation of time', in A.H. Amsden (ed) *The economics of women and work*, Harmondsworth: Penguin.

Becker, H. and Barnes, H.E. (1952) *Social thought from lore to science*, Washington, DC: Harren Press.

Beechey, V. and Perkins, T. (1987) *A matter of hours: Women, part-time work and the labour market*, Cambridge: Polity Press.

Belenky, M.F., Clinchy, B.M., Goldberger, N.R. and Tarule, J.M. (1986) *Women's ways of knowing*, New York, NY: Basic Books.

Bell, C. and Encel, S. (eds) (1978) *Inside the whale*, Oxford: Pergamon Press.

Bell, C. and Newby, H. (eds) (1977) *Doing sociological research*, London: Allen and Unwin.

Bell, C. and Roberts, H. (eds) (1984) *Social researching: Politics, problems, practice*, London: Routledge.

Belotti, E.G. (1975) *Little girls*, London: Writers and Readers Publishing Cooperative.

Benney, M. and Hughes, E.C. (1970) 'Of sociology and the interview', in N. Denzin (ed) *Sociological methods: A source book*, London: Butterworth.

Benson, L. (1960) *Fatherhood: A sociological perspective*, New York, NY: Random House.

Benston, M. (1969) *The political economy of women's liberation*, Boston, MA: New England Free Press.

Berger, B. and Berger, P. (1983) *The war over the family*, Harmondsworth: Penguin.

Berger, J. (1972) *Ways of seeing*, Harmondsworth: Penguin.

Berk, S.F. (1985) *The gender factory: The apportionment of work in American households*, New York, NY and London: Plenum Press.

Berlin, I. (1939) *Karl Marx: His life and environment*, Oxford: Oxford University Press.

Bernard, J. (1973) 'My four revolutions: an autobiographical history of the ASA', *American Journal of Sociology*, vol 78, pp 773-91.

Bernard, J. (1975) *Women, wives, mothers*, Chicago, IL: Aldine.

Bewley, S. and Bewley, T.H. (1992) 'Drug dependence with oestrogen replacement therapy', *The Lancet*, vol 339, pp 290-1.

Birdwell, B.G., Herbers, J.E. and Kroenke, K. (1993) 'Evaluating chest pain: the patient's presentation style alters the physician's diagnostic approach', *Archives of Internal Medicine*, vol 153, pp 1991-5.

Birke, L. (1986) *Women, feminism and biology*, Brighton, Sussex: Wheatsheaf Books.

Bittman, M. (1999) 'Parenthood without penalty: time use and public policy in Australia and Finland', *Feminist Economics*, vol 5, no 3, pp 27-42.

Blauner, R. (1964) *Alienation and freedom*, Chicago, IL: University of Chicago Press.

Blenkner, M., Bloom, M., Nielsen, M. and Weber, R. (1974) *Final report. Protective services for older people: Findings from the Benjamin Rose Institute Study*, Cleveland, OH: The Benjamin Rose Institute.

Blood, R.O. and Wolfe, D.M. (1960) *Husbands and wives*, New York, NY: Free Press.

Boath, E. and Henshaw, C. (2001) 'The treatment of postnatal depression: a comprehensive literature review', *Journal of Reproductive and Infant Psychology*, vol 19, no 3, pp 216-48.

Boaz, A., Ashby, D. and Young, K. (2002) *Systematic reviews: What have they got to offer evidence-based policy and practice?*, Working Paper 2, London: ESRC Centre for Evidence-based Policy and Practice.

Bonell, C. (1999) 'Evidence as a resource of control and resistance in advanced liberal health systems: the case of HIV prevention in the UK', PhD, University of London.

Bonney, N. and Reinach, E. (1993) 'Housework reconsidered: the Oakley thesis twenty years later', *Work, Employment and Society*, vol 7, no 4, pp 615-27.

Bose, C., Bereano, P. and Malloy, M. (1984) 'Household technology and the social construction of housework', *Technology and Culture*, vol 25, no 1, pp 53-82.

Boulton, M.G. (1983) *On being a mother*, London: Tavistock.

Boulton, M., Fitzpatrick, R. and Swinburn, C. (1996) 'Qualitative research in health care: a structured review and evaluation of studies', *Journal of Evaluation in Clinical Practice*, vol 2, pp 171-9.

Bourne, G. (1975) *Pregnancy*, London: Pan Books.

Bowen, E.S. (1956) *Return to laughter*, London: Gollancz.

Bowles, G. and Duelli Klein, R. (eds) (1983) *Theories of women's studies*, London: Routledge.

Bozoky, I. and Corwin, E.J. (2002) 'Fatigue as a predictor of postpartum depression', *Journal of Obstetric, Gynecologic and Neonatal Nursing*, vol 31, no 4, pp 436-43.

Bracken, M.B. (1984) 'Design and conduct of randomized clinical trials in perinatal research', in M.D. Bracken (ed) *Perinatal epidemiology*, New York, NY: Oxford University Press.

Brannen, J. (1992) 'Combining qualitative and quantitative approaches: an overview', in J. Brannen (ed) *Mixing methods: Qualitative and quantitative research*, Aldershot: Avebury.

Bricker, L. and Neilson, J.P. (2000) 'Routine ultrasound in late pregnancy (after 24 weeks gestation),' *The Cochrane Database of Systematic Reviews 2000*, Issue 1.

Brinig, M.F. (1999) 'Equality and sharing: views of household across the iron curtain', *European Journal of Law and Economics*, vol 7, no 1, pp 55-64.

Brodribb, S. (1992) *Nothing mat(t)ers: A feminist critique of postmodernism*, Melbourne, Australia: Spinifex Press.

Brody, H. (1977) *Placebos and the philosophy of medicine*, Chicago, IL: University of Chicago Press.

Broverman, I., Broverman, D., Clarkson, F., Rosenkrantz, P. and Vogel, S. (1970) 'Sex role stereotypes and clinical judgements of mental health', *Journal of Consulting and Clinical Psychology*, vol 34, pp 1-7.

Brown, G.W. and Davidson, S. (1978) 'Social class, psychiatric disorder of the mother and accidents to children', *The Lancet*, vol 1, pp 378-80.

Brown, R. (1991) 'Women as employees: some comments on research in industrial sociology', in D. Leonard and S. Allen (eds) *Sexual divisions revisited*, Houndsmill, Basingstoke: Macmillan.

Brown, S., Lumley, J., Small, R. and Astbury, J. (1994) *Missing voices: The experience of motherhood*, Melbourne: Oxford University Press.

Bryant, K., Kang, H., Zick, C.D. and Chan, A.Y. (2004) 'Measuring housework in time use surveys', *Review of Economics of the Household*, vol 2, no 1, pp 23-47.

Bryman, A. (1988) *Quantity and quality in social research*, London: Unwin Hyman.

Bryn Mawr (1945) 'Women during the war and after', cited in A. Myrdal and V. Klein (1956) *Women's two roles*, London: Routledge and Kegan Paul.

Bullough, V.L. (1974) *The subordinate sex: A history of attitudes towards women*, New York, NY: Penguin Books.

Bulmer, M. (1991) 'National contexts for the development of social-policy research: British and American research on poverty and welfare compared', in P. Wagner, C.H. Weiss, B. Wittrock and H. Woolman (eds) *Social sciences and modern states: National experiences and theoretical crossroads*, Cambridge: Cambridge University Press.

Butler, J. (1990) *Gender trouble*, London: Routledge.

Callender, C. (1988) *Gender and social policy: Women's redundancy and unemployment*, Cardiff: University of Wales, College of Cardiff.

Campbell, J.K. (1964) *Honour, family and patronage*, Oxford: Clarendon Press.

Caplow, T. (1954) *The sociology of work*, Minneapolis: University of Minnesota Press.

Carroli, G., Villar, J., Piaggio, G., Khan-Neelofur D., Gulmezoglu, Mugford, M., Lumbiganon, P., Farnot, U., Bergsjø, for the WHO Antenatal Care Trial Research Group (2001) 'WHO systematic review of randomised controlled trials of routine antenatal care', *The Lancet*, vol 357, pp 1565-70.

Cartwright, A. (1979) *The dignity of labour? A study of childbearing and induction*, London: Tavistock.

Cartwright, A. and Jefferys, M. (1958) 'Married women who work: their own and their children's health', *British Journal of Preventive Social Medicine*, vol 12, pp 159-71.

Chalmers, I. (1983) 'Scientific inquiry and authoritarianism in perinatal care and education', *Birth*, vol 10, no 3, pp 151-64.

Chalmers, I. (1986) 'Minimizing harm and maximizing benefit during innovation in health care: controlled or uncontrolled experimentation?', *Birth*, vol 13, pp 155-64.

Chalmers, I., Enkin, M. and Keirse, M.J.N.C. (eds) (1989) *Effective care in pregnancy and childbirth*, Oxford: Oxford University Press.

Chalmers, I. and Richards, M. (1977) 'Intervention and causal inference in obstetric practice', in T. Chard and M. Richards (eds) *Benefits and hazards of the new obstetrics*, London: Heinemann Medical Books.

Chapman, S. (1955) *The home and social status*, London: Routledge and Kegan Paul.

Chapman, S. (1979) 'Advertising and psychotropic drugs: the place of myth in ideological reproduction', *Social Science and Medicine*, vol 13A, pp 751-64.

Chase, C. (1998) 'Hermaphrodites with attitude: mapping the emergence of intersex political activism', *GLQ: Journal of Gay and Lesbian Studies*, vol 4, pp 189-211.

Charles, N. (1999) *Feminism, the state and social policy*, Basingstoke: Macmillan.

Chodorow, N. (1978) *The reproduction of mothering*, Berkeley, CA: University of California Press.

Cicourel, A.V. (1964) *Method and measurement in sociology*, New York, NY: Free Press.

Cobb, A.K. and Hagemaster, J.N. (1987) 'Ten criteria for evaluating qualitative research proposals', *Journal of Nursing Education*, vol 26, pp 138-43.

Cockburn, C. and Ormrod, S. (1993) *Gender and technology in the making*, London: Sage Publications.

Code, L. (1991) *What can she know? Feminist theory and the construction of knowledge*, Ithaca, NY: Cornell University Press.

Cohen, A. (1955) *Delinquent boys*, London: Routledge and Kegan Paul.

Cohen, I.B. (1994) *The natural sciences and the social sciences*, Dordrecht, the Netherlands: Kluwer Academic.

Cohen, P.N. (2004) 'The gender division of labor: "keeping house" and occupational segregation in the United States', *Gender and Society*, vol 18, no 2, pp 239-52.

Collins, R. (1972) 'A conflict theory of sexual stratification', in H.P. Dreitzel (ed) *Family, marriage and the struggle of the sexes, Recent Sociology*, no 4, New York, NY: Macmillan.

Coltrane, S. (2004) 'Elite careers and family commitment: it's (still) about gender', *Annals of the American Academy of Political and Social Science*, vol 596, pp 214-20.

Cook, J., Roberts, J. and Waylen, G. (eds) (2000) *Towards a gendered political economy*, Houndsmill, Basingstoke: Macmillan.

Cooke, W.R.I. (1945) 'The differential psychology of the American woman', *American Journal of Obstetrics and Gynecology*, vol 49, pp 457-72.

Corbin, M. (1971) 'Appendix 3', in J.M. Pahl and R.E. Pahl (eds) *Managers and their wives*, London: Allen Lane.

Cotten, S.S. (1897) 'A national training school for women', in *The work and words of the National Congress of Mothers*, New York, NY: D. Appleton.

Coulter, A. (1993) 'Assembling the evidence: outcomes research', in M. Dunning and G. Needham (eds) *But will it work, doctor? Report of a conference about involving users of health services in outcomes research*, London: Kings Fund Centre.

Cowan, R.S. (1974) 'A case study of technological and social change: the washing machine and the working wife', in M. Hartman and L.W. Banner (eds) *Clio's consciousness raised: New perspectives on the history of women*, New York, NY: Harper Colophon.

Cowan, R. (1983) *More work for mother: The ironies of household technology from the open hearth to the microwave*, New York, NY: Basic Books.

Coward, R. (1983) *Patriarchal precedents*, London: Routledge.

Cowles, M.L. and Dietz, R.P. (1956) 'Time spent in homemaking by a selected group of Wisconsin farm homemakers', *Journal of Home Economics*, January.

Crawford, M. and Gentry, M. (eds) (1989) *Gender and thought*, New York, NY: Springer Verlag.

Crawford, M. and Unger, R. (2003) *Women and gender: A feminist psychology*, Maidenhead: McGraw Hill Education.

Crook, J.H. (1970) 'Introduction – social behaviour and ethology', in J.H. Crook (ed) *Social behaviour in birds and mammals*, London: Academic Press.

Crouch, M. and Manderson, L. (1995) 'The social life of bonding theory', *Social Science and Medicine*, vol 41, no 6, pp 837-44.

Crouse, J.R. (1989) 'Gender, lipoproteins, diet and cardiovascular risk. Sauce for the goose may not be sauce for the gander', *The Lancet*, vol i, pp 318-20.

CSO (Central Statistical Office) (1973a) *Annual abstract of statistics*, London: HMSO.

CSO (1973b) *Advance census analysis 1971*, London: HMSO.

Culler, J. (1983) *Deconstruction: Theory and criticism after structuralism*, London: Routledge and Kegan Paul.

Curthoys, J. (1997) *Feminist amnesia: The wake of women's liberation*, London: Routledge.

Czaplinski, S.M. (1976) 'Sexism in award winning picture books', in Children's Rights Workshop, *Sexism in children's books: Facts, figures and guidelines*, London: Writers and Readers Publishing Co-operative.

Dalton, K. (1959) 'Menstruation and acute psychiatric illness', *British Medical Journal*, vol 1, pp 326-8.

Dalton, K. (1960) 'Menstruation and accidents', *British Medical Journal*, vol 2, pp 1752-3.

Dalton, K. (1961) 'Menstruation and crime', *British Medical Journal*, vol 2, pp 1425-6.

Dalton, K. (1966) 'The influence of the mother's menstruation on her child', *Proceedings of the Royal Society of Medicine*, vol 59, p 1014.

David, M.E. (2003) *Personal and political: Feminisms, sociology and family lives*, Stoke on Trent, Staffs: Trentham Books.

Davidoff, L. (1976) 'The rationalization of housework', in D.L.Barker and S. Allen (eds) *Sexual divisions and society*, London: Tavistock.

Davidson, C. (1982) *A woman's work is never done*, London: Chatto and Windus.

Davidson, N. (1988) *The failure of feminism*, New York, NY: Prometheus Books.

Davies, H.T.O., Nutley, S.M. and Smith, P.C. (eds) (2000) *What works? Evidence based policy and practice in public services*, Bristol: The Policy Press.

Davies, J. and Goodman, N. (1972) *Girl offenders aged 17 to 20 years*, Home Office Research Studies no 14, London: HMSO.

Davies, K. and Esseveld, J. (1986) 'Reflections on research practices in feminist research', Paper presented at the 4th Nordiska Symposiet for Kvinnoforskning, Uppsala, Sweden, 22-24 May.

Davis, D. (1966) *A history of shopping*, London: Routledge and Kegan Paul.

Davis, J.A. (1994) 'What's wrong with sociology', *Sociological Forum*, vol 9, no 2, pp 179-97.

De Beauvoir, S. (1960) *The second sex*, London: Four Square Books.

Delamont, S. (1980) *A sociology of women*, London: Allen and Unwin.

Delamont, S. (2003) *Feminist sociology*, London: Sage Publications.

Delphy, C. (1993) 'Rethinking sex and gender', *Women's Studies International Forum*, vol 16, no 1, pp 1-9.

Delphy, C. and Leonard, D. (1992) *Familiar exploitation: A new analysis of marriage in contemporary Western societies*, Cambridge: Polity Press.

Dench, S. Aston, J. Evans, C., Meager, N., Williams, M. and Willison, R. (2002) *Key indicators of women's position in Britain*, London: Women and Equality Unit, DTI.

Dennis, N. Henriques, F. and Slaughter, C. (1956) *Coal is our life*, London: Eyre and Spottiswoode.

Denzin, N. (ed) (1970) *Sociological methods: A source book*, London: Butterworth.

Denzin, N. (1987) *On understanding emotion*, San Francisco, CA: Jossey-Bass.

DH (Department of Health) (1993) *Changing childbirth: Part I: Report of the Expert Maternity Group*, London: HMSO.

DH (1995) *Variations in health: What can the Department of Health and the NHS do?*, London: HMSO.

Des Rivières-Pigeon, C., Saurel-Cubizolles, M.-J. and Romito, P. (2003) 'Psychological distress one year after childbirth', *European Journal of Public Health*, vol 13, pp 218-25.

Devine, F. (1994) 'Segregation and supply: preferences and plans among "self-made" women', *Gender, Work and Organisation*, vol 1, no 2, pp 94-109.

Dex, S. (1985) *The sexual division of work: Conceptual revolutions in the social sciences*, Brighton: Wheatsheaf.

Dexter, L.A. (1956) 'Role relationships and conceptions of neutrality in interviewing', *American Journal of Sociology*, LXI, no 4, p 153-7.

Diamond, M. (2002) 'Sex and gender are different: sexual identity and gender identity are different', *Clinical Child Psychology and Psychiatry*, vol 7, no 3, pp 320-34.

Di Stefano, C. (1990) 'Dilemmas of difference: feminism, modernity and postmodernism', in L. Nicholson (ed) *Feminism/postfeminism*, New York, NY: Routledge.

Donovan, J. (1990) 'Animal rights and feminist theory', *SIGNS: Journal of Women in Culture and Society*, vol 15, pp 350-75.

Doyal, L. (1998) *Women and health services*, Buckingham: Open University Press.

Douglas, M. (1970) *Purity and danger: An analysis of concepts of pollution and taboo*, Harmondsworth: Penguin.

Downes, D. (1966) *The delinquent solution*, London: Routledge and Kegan Paul.

Draper, H. (1971) 'Marx and Engels on women's liberation', in R. Salper (ed) *Female liberation*, New York, NY: Alfred A. Knopf.

Draper, P. (1975) '!Kung women: contrasts in sexual egalitarianism in foraging and sedentary contexts', in R.R. Reiter (ed) *Toward an anthropology of women*, New York, NY: Monthly Review Press.

Du Bois, C. (1944) *The people of Alor*, Minneapolis: University of Minnesota Press.

Duden, B. (1993) *Disembodying women*, Cambridge, MA: Harvard University Press.

Duffield, M. (2002) 'Trends in female employment 2002', *Labour Market Trends*, November, pp 605-16.

Eakins, B.W. and Eakins, R.G. (1978) *Sex differences in human communication*, Boston, MA: Houghton Mifflin.

Ebrahim, S. (2003) 'Pemberton, sex and gender' (editorial), *International Journal of Epidemiology*, vol 32, p 485.

Edmunds, L. (1975) 'Instead of paying housewives, why not make them happier?', *The Daily Telegraph*, 20 February.

Edwards, J.N. (ed) (1969) *The family and change*, New York, NY: Knopf.

Edwards, M. and Waldorf, M. (1984) *Reclaiming birth: History and heroines of American childbirth reform*, Trumansburg, NY: The Crossing Press.

Eisenstein, Z.R. (1981) *The radical future of liberal feminism*, New York, NY: Longman Press.

Ekins, R. and King, D. (1996) *Blending genders*, New York, NY: Routledge.

Elcock, H. (1976) *Political behaviour*, London: Methuen.

Elek, S.M., Hudson, D.B. and Fleck, M.O. (2002) 'Couples' experiences with fatigue during the transition to parenthood', *Journal of Family Nursing*, vol 8, no 3, pp 221-40.

Ellmann, M. (1968) *Thinking about women*, London: Macmillan.

Emerson, J. (1970) 'Behavior in private places: sustaining definitions of reality in gynecological examinations', in H.P. Dreitzel (ed) *Recent Sociology*, No 1, New York, NY: Macmillan.

England, P. (1999) 'The impact of feminist thought on sociology', *Contemporary Sociology*, vol 28, no 3, pp 263-8.

Erlich, C. (1971) 'The male sociologist's burden: the place of women in marriage and family texts', *Journal of Marriage and the Family*, vol 33, pp 421-30.

Fausto-Sterling, A. (1993) 'The five sexes: why female and male are not enough,' *The Sciences*, March–April, pp 20–5.

Feinberg, L. (1996) *Transgender warriors*, Boston, MA: Beacon Press.

Felson, D.T., Zhang, Y., Hannan, M.J., Kannel, W.B. and Kiel, D.P. (1995) 'Alcohol intake and bone mineral density in elderly men and women', *American Journal of Epidemiology*, vol 142, pp 485–92.

Ferber, M.A. and Nelson, J.A. (eds) (1993) *Beyond economic man: Feminist theory and economics*, Chicago, IL: University of Chicago Press.

Finch, J. (1984) '"It's great to have someone to talk to": the ethics and politics of interviewing women', in Bell and Roberts (eds).

Finch, J. and Groves, D. (1983) *A labour of love*, London: Routledge.

Firestone, S. (1972) *The dialectic of sex: The case for feminist revolution*, London: Paladin.

Firth, R. (1965) *Primitive Polynesian economy*, London: Routledge and Kegan Paul.

Fish, D.G. (1966) 'An obstetric unit in a London hospital: a study of relations between patients, doctors and nurses', PhD thesis, University of London.

Fisher, S, (1986) *In the patient's best interest: Women and the politics of medical decisions*, New Brunswick, NJ: Rutgers University Press.

Fishman, P. (1977) 'Interactional shitwork', *Heresies: A feminist publication on art and politics*, 2 May.

Fletcher, R. (1966) *The family and marriage in Britain*, Harmondsworth: Penguin.

Floro, M.S. and Miles, M. (2003) 'Time use, work and overlapping activities: evidence from Australia', *Cambridge Journal of Economics*, vol 27, pp 881–904.

Folbre, N. (2001) *The invisible heart: Economics and family values*, New York, NY: The New Press.

Fonow, M.M. and Cook, J.A. (eds) (1991) *Beyond methodology: Feminist scholarship as lived research*, Bloomington, IN: Indiana University Press.

Forbes, I. (2003) 'Perceptions of cutting edge research in UK social science', *Innovation: The European Journal of Social Sciences*, vol 3, pp 271–91.

Ford, C.S. and Beach, F.A. (1952) *Patterns of sexual behaviour*, London: Eyre and Spottiswoode.

Forde, C.D. (1957) *Habitat, economy and society*, London: Methuen.

Foster, P. (1995) *Women and the health care industry*, Buckingham: Open University Press.

Fox, B. and Worts, D. (1999) 'Revisiting the critique of medicalized childbirth: a contribution to the sociology of birth', *Gender and Society*, vol 13, pp 326–46.

Frank, R.T. (1931) 'The hormonal cause of premenstrual tension', *Archives of Neurology and Psychiatry*, vol 26, pp 1053–7.

Frankenberg, R. (1991) 'Sex and gender in British community studies', in D. Leonard and S. Allen (eds) *Sexual divisions revisited*, London: Macmillan.

Franklin, S. (1996) 'Introduction', in S. Franklin (ed) *The sociology of gender*, Cheltenham: Edward Elgar.

Fransella, F. and Frost, K. (1977) *How women see themselves*, London: Tavistock.

Fraser, N. (1995) 'Pragmatism, feminism and the linguistic turn', in S. Benhabib, J. Butler, D. Cornell and N. Fraser (eds) *Feminist contentions: A philosophical exchange*, New York, NY: Routledge.

Freidson, E. (1970) *Profession of medicine*, New York, NY: Dodd-Mead.

Freud, S. (1962, originally published 1905) *Three essays on the theory of sexuality*, translated by J. Strachey, London: Hogarth Press.

Freud, S. (1964, originally published 1933) 'Femininity', in *New introductory lectures on psychoanalysis*, translated by J. Strachey, New York, NY: Norton.

Friedan, B. (1963) *The feminine mystique*, London: Gollancz.

Frisco, M.L. and Williams, K. (2003) 'Perceived housework equity, marital happiness, and divorce in dual-earner households', *Journal of Family Issues*, vol 24, no 1, pp 51-73.

Galbraith, J.K. (1974) *Economics and the public purpose*, London: André Deutsch.

Galtung, J. (1967) *Theory and methods of social research*, London: Allen and Unwin.

Gamarnikow, E., Morgan, S., Purvis, J. and Taylorson, D. (eds) (1983) *The public and the private*, London: Heinemann.

Gans, H. (1967) *The Levittowners*, New York, NY: Pantheon.

Garcia, J. (1982) 'Women's views of antenatal care', in M. Enkin and I. Chalmers (eds) *Effectiveness and satisfaction in antenatal care*, London: William Heinemann Medical Books.

Gardiner, J. (1995) *New thinking on the domestic labour debate*, Research Working Paper no 11, Leeds: University of Leeds, Gender Analysis and Policy Unit.

Gardiner, J., Himmelweit, S. and Mackintosh, M. (1975) 'Women's domestic labour', *Bulletin of the Conference of Socialist Economists*, vol 4, no 11, pp 1-11.

Garforth, S. and Garcia, J. (1987) 'Admitting – a weakness or a strength? Routine admission of a woman in labour', *Midwifery*, vol 3, pp 10-24.

Garry, A. and Pearsall, M. (eds) (1989) *Women, knowledge and reality: Explorations in feminist philosophy*, London: Unwin Hyman.

Gatens, M. (1992) 'Power, bodies and difference', in M. Barrett and A. Phillips (eds) *Destabilizing theory: Contemporary feminist debates*, Cambridge: Polity Press.

Gauthier, A.H. and Furstenberg, F.F. (2002) 'The transition to adulthood: a time use perspective', *Annals of the American Academy of Political and Social Science*, vol 580, no 1, pp 153-71.

Gavron, H. (1966) *The captive wife*, Harmondsworth: Penguin.

General Register Office (1968) *Sample census 1966 England and Wales*, London: HMSO.

Gershuny, J. and Jones, S. (1987) 'The changing work/leisure balance in Britain 1961-84', *Sociological Review Monograph*, vol 33, pp 9-50.

Giddens, A. (1973) *The class structure of the advanced societies*, London: Heinemann.

Gijsbers van Wijk, C.M.T., van Vliet, K.P. and Kolk, A.M. (1996) 'Gender perspectives and quality of care: towards appropriate and adequate health care for women', *Social Science and Medicine*, vol 43, pp 707-20.

Gilligan, G. (1982) *In a different voice: Psychological theory and women's development*, Cambridge, MA: Harvard University Press.

Gilman, C.P. (1903) *The home: Its work and influence*, London and New York, NY: McClure, Phillips.

Giner, S. (1972) *Sociology*, London: Martin Robertson.

Girard, A. (1958) 'Le budget-temps de la femme mariée dans les agglomérations urbaines', *Population*, pp 591-618.

Girard, A. and Bastide, H. (1959) 'Une étude de budget-temps de la femme mariée dans la campagne', *Population*, pp 253-84.

Glazer-Malbin, N. (1976) 'Housework', *SIGNS: Journal of Women in Culture and Society*, vol 1, no 4, pp 905-22.

Gluckman, M. (1963) 'Gossip and scandal', *Current Anthropology*, vol 4, p 307-16.

Goetting, A. and Fenstermaker, S. (eds) (1995) *Individual voices, collective visions: Fifty years of women in sociology*, Philadelphia, PA: Temple University Press.

Goldberger, N., Tarule, J., Clinchy, B. and Belenky, M. (eds) (1996) *Knowledge, difference and power*, New York, NY: Basic Books.

Goldthorpe, J. (1983) 'Women and class analysis: a defence of the traditional view', *Sociology*, vol 17, pp 465-88.

Goldthorpe, J., Lockwood, D., Bechhofer, F. and Platt, J. (1968) *The affluent worker: Industrial attitudes and behaviour*, Cambridge: Cambridge University Press.

Goodale, J.C. (1971) *Tiwi wives*, Washington, DC: University Press.

Goode, W.J. and Hatt, P.K. (1952) *Methods in social research*, New York, NY: McGraw-Hill.

Gould, S.J. (1981) *The mismeasure of man*, Harmondsworth: Penguin.

Gouldner, A. (1971) *The coming crisis of western sociology*, London: Heinemann.

Gove, W.R. (1972) 'The relationship between sex roles, mental illness and marital status', *Social Forces*, vol 51, no 1, pp 34-44.

Gove, W.R. and Tudor, J.F. (1973) 'Adult sex roles and mental illness', *American Journal of Sociology*, vol 78, pp 812-35.

Graham, H. (1977) 'Images of pregnancy in antenatal literature', in R. Dingwall, C. Heath, M. Reid and M. Stacey (eds) *Health care and health knowledge*, London: Croom Helm.

Graham, H. (1983) 'Do her answers fit his questions? Women and the survey method', in Gamarnikow et al (eds).

Graham, H. (1984) *Women, health and the family*, Hemel Hempstead: Wheatsheaf.

Graham, H. and Oakley, A. (1981) 'Competing ideologies of reproduction: medical and maternal perspectives on pregnancy and birth' in H. Roberts (ed) *Women, health and reproduction*, London: Routledge.

Grant, J. (1993) *Fundamental feminism*, New York, NY: Routledge.

Gray, J.A. and Buffery, A.W.H. (1971) 'Sex differences in emotional and cognitive behaviour in mammals including man: adaptive and neural bases', *Acta Psychologica*, vol 35, pp 89-111.

Green, J., Coupland, V. and Kitzinger, J. (1990) 'Expectations, experiences, and psychological outcomes of childbirth: a prospective study of 825 women', *Birth*, vol 17, pp 15-23.

Gross, H. and Pattison, H. (2001) 'Pregnancy and working: a critical reading of advice and information on pregnancy and employment', *Feminism and Psychology*, vol 11, no 4, pp 511-25.

Guba, E.G. (ed) (1990) *The paradigm dialog*, Newbury Park, CA: Sage Publications.

Haavio-Mannila, E. (1969) 'Some consequences of women's emancipation', *Journal of Marriage and the Family*, vol 31, pp 123-34.

Hague, H. (2000) '2.3% and 9.8%...', *The Times Higher*, April 7, pp 18-19.

Haig, D. (2004) 'The inexorable rise of gender and the decline of sex: social change in academic titles, 1945-2001', *Archives of Sexual Behaviour*, vol 33, no 2, pp 87-96.

Haire, D. (1972) 'The cultural warping of childbirth', *Journal of Tropical Paediatrics and Environmental Child Health*, Special issue, vol 19, pp 171-91.

Hakim, C. (1996) 'The sexual division of labour and women's heterogeneity', *British Journal of Sociology*, vol 47, pp 178-88.

Hall, M., Macintyre, S. and Porter, M. (1985) *Antenatal care assessed*, Aberdeen: Aberdeen University Press.

Halsey, A.H. (2004) *A history of sociology in Britain*, Oxford: Oxford University Press.

Hammersley, M. (1989) *The dilemma of qualitative method: Herbert Blumer and the Chicago tradition*, London: Routledge.

Hamilton, R. (1978) *The liberation of women*, London: Allen and Unwin.

Hammond, D. and Jablow, A. (1976) *Women in cultures of the world*, Meno Park, CA: Cummings Publishing Co.

Hansson, R.E., Chernovetz, M.E. and Jones, H. (1977) 'Maternal employment and androgyny', *Psychology of Women Quarterly*, vol 2, pp 76-8.

Haraway, D. (1991) *Simians, cyborgs and women: The reinvention of nature*, New York, NY: Routledge.

Harden, A., Peesman, G., Oliver, A., Mauthner, M. and Oakley, A. (1999) 'A systematic review of the effectiveness of health promotion interventions in the workplace', *Occupational Medicine*, vol 49, no 8, pp 540-8.

Harding, S. (1986) *The science question in feminism*, Milton Keynes: Open University Press.

Harding, S. (ed) (1987) *Feminism and methodology*, Bloomington, IN: Indiana University Press.

Harding, S. (1991) *Whose science? Whose knowledge?*, Buckingham: Open University Press.

Harkness, R.A. (1974) 'Variations in testosterone excretion by man', in M. Ferin, F. Halberg, R.M. Richart and R.L. Vande Wiele (eds) *Biorhythms and human reproduction*, New York, NY: John Wiley.

Hartmann, H. (1979) 'Capitalism, patriarchy and job segregation by sex', in Z.R. Eisenstein (ed.) *Capitalist patriarchy*, New York, NY: Monthly Review Press.

Hartsock, N.C.M. (1987) 'The feminist standpoint: developing the ground for a specifically feminist historical materialism', in S. Harding (ed) *Feminism and methodology*, Bloomington, IN: Indiana University Press.

Hausman, B.L. (1995) *Changing sex: Transsexualism, technology and the idea of gender*, Durham and London: Duke University Press.

Hawkesworth, M. (1997) 'Confounding gender', *SIGNS: Journal of Women in Culture and Society*, vol 22, pp 649-85.

Hays, S. (1996) *The cultural contradictions of motherhood*, New Haven, CT: Yale University Press.

Heidensohn, F. (1968) 'The deviance of women', *British Journal of Sociology*, vol 19, pp 160-75.

Hemminki, E. (1995) 'The future of population strategies in drug prevention. Drugs for all?', *Scandinavian Journal of Social Medicine*, vol 23, pp 225-6.

Hemminki, E. (1996) 'Impact of Caesarean section on future pregnancy – a review of cohort studies', *Paediatric and Perinatal Epidemiology*, vol 10, pp 366-79.

Hemminki, E. and McPherson, K. (1997) 'Impact of postmenopausal hormone therapy on cardiovascular events and cancer: pooled data from clinical trials', *British Medical Journal*, vol 315, pp 149-53.

Henderson, A. (1964) *The family house in England*, Los Angeles, CA: Phoenix House.

Henry, J. (1964) *Jungle people*, New York, NY: Vintage Books.

Herdt, G. (1996) *Third sex, third gender: Beyond sexual dimorphism in culture and history*, New York, NY: Zone.

Herzberg, F., Mausner, B. and Snyderman, B.B. (1959) *The motivation to work*, New York, NY: John Wiley.

Hetherington, E.M. (1965) 'A developmental study of effects of sex of the dominant parent on sex-role preference, identification and imitation in children', *Journal of Personality and Social Psychology*, vol 2, pp 188-94.

Hetherington, E.M. and Frankie, G. (1967) 'Effects of parental dominance, warmth and conflict on imitation in children', *Journal of Personality and Social Psychology*, vol 6, pp 119-25.

Himmelweit, S. (1995) 'The discovery of "unpaid work": the social consequences of the expansion of "work"', *Feminist Economics*, vol 1, no 2, pp 1-19.

Hird, M.J. (2000) 'Gender's nature: intersexuality, transsexualism and the "sex"/ "gender" binary', *Feminist Theory*, vol 1, no 3, pp 347-64.

Hobson, D. (1975) 'Housewives: isolation as oppression', in Women's Studies Group, Centre for Contemporary Cultural Studies (eds), *Women take issue*, London: Hutchinson.

Hochschild, A.R. (1975) 'The sociology of feeling and emotion: selected possibilities', in M. Millman and R.M. Kanter (eds) *Another voice: Feminist perspectives on social life and social science*, New York, NY: Anchor Books.

Hochschild, A.R. (1989) *The second shift: Working parents and the revolution at home*, New York, NY: Viking.

Hoff, J. (1994) 'Gender as a postmodern category of paralysis', *Women's History Review*, vol 3, no 3, pp 149-68.

Hoffman, L.W. (1963) 'Parental power relations and the division of household tasks', in F.I. Nye and L.W. Hoffman (eds) *The employed mother in America*, Chicago, IL: Rand-McNally.

Hoffman, L.W. and Nye, F.I. (eds) (1974) *Working mothers: An evaluative review of the consequences for wife, husband and child*, San Francisco, CA: Jossey-Bass.

Hole, C. (1957) *A mirror of witchcraft*, London: Chatto and Windus.

Holte, A. (1991) 'Prevalence of climacteric complaints in a representative sample of middle aged women in Oslo, Norway', *Journal of Psychosomatic Obstetrics and Gynaecology*, vol 12, pp 303-17.

Holter, H. (1970) *Sex roles and social structure*, Oslo, Norway: Universitetsforlaget.

Homans, H. (ed) (1985) *The sexual politics of reproduction*, Aldershot: Gower.

Hood-Williams, J. (1996) 'Goodbye to sex and gender', *The Sociological Review*, vol 44, pp 1-16.

Hooks, B. (1981) *Ain't I a woman: Black women and feminism*, Boston, MA: South End Press.

Horney, K. (1974) 'The flight from womanhood', in J.B. Miller (ed) *Psychoanalysis and woman*, Harmondsworth: Penguin.

Howe, L.K. (1977) *Pink collar workers*, New York, NY: Avon Books.

Hoy, S. (1995) *Chasing dirt: The American pursuit of cleanliness*, New York, NY: Oxford University Press.

Huang, L. (1971) 'Sex role stereotypes and self concepts among American and Chinese students', *Journal of Comparative Family Studies*, vol 2, pp 215-34.

Hughes, E. (1958) *Men and their work*, Glencoe, IL: Free Press.

Hughes, H.E. (1973) *The status of women in sociology 1968-72*, American Sociological Association.

Humphreys, J. and Rubery, J. (eds) (1995) *The economics of equal opportunities*, Manchester: Equal Opportunities Commission.

Hunt, A. (1968) *A survey of women's employment*, London: HMSO.

Hunt, S. and Symonds, A. (1995) *The social meaning of midwifery*, London: Macmillan.

Hunter, M. (1990) 'Emotional well-being, sexual behaviour and hormone replacement therapy,' *Maturitas*, vol 12, pp 299-314.

Hurstfield, J. (1975) 'Extended review', *The Sociological Review*, August, pp 698-705.

Hyde, J.S. (1996) 'Meta-analysis and the psychology of gender differences', in B. Laslett, S.G, Kohlstedt, H. Longino and E. Hammonds (eds) *Gender and scientific authority*, Chicago, IL: University of Chicago Press.

Illsley, R. (1967) 'The sociological study of reproduction and its outcome', in S.A. Richardson and A.F. Guttmacher (eds) *Childbearing: Its social and psychological aspects*, Baltimore, MD: Williams and Wilkins.

Imber, J.B. (1999) 'Other-directed rebels', *Contemporary Sociology*, vol 28, no 3, pp 255-9.

Irigaray, L. (1985) *This sex which is not one*, Ithaca, NY: Cornell University Press.

Irvine, L., Crombie, I.K., Clark, R.A., Slane, P.W., Feyerabend, C., Goodman, K.E. and Cater, J.I. (1999) 'Advising parents of asthmatic children on passive smoking: randomised controlled trial', *British Medical Journal*, vol 318, pp 1456-9.

Jackson, S. (1975) 'Sinks of inequity', *Times Literary Supplement*, 28 February.

Janowsky, D.S., Gorney, R., Castelnuovo-Tedesco, P. and Stone, C.B. (1969) 'Premenstrual-menstrual increase in psychiatric hospital admission rates', *American Journal of Obstetrics and Gynecology*, vol 103, pp 189-91.

Jarrett-Macauley, D. (1996) *Reconstructing womanhood, reconstructing feminism: Writings on black women*, London: Routledge.

Jayaratne, T.E. and Stewart, A.J. (1991) 'Quantitative and qualitative methods in the social sciences: current feminist issues and practical strategies', in M.M. Fonow and J.A. Cook (eds) Bloomington, IN: Indiana University Press.

Jefferson, T. and King, J.E. (2001) '"Never intended to be a theory of everything": domestic labor in neoclassical and Marxian economics', *Feminist Economics*, vol 7, no 3, pp 71-101.

Jelliffe, D.B. and Jelliffe, E.F.P (1978) *Human milk in the modern world*, Oxford: Oxford University Press.

Jenkins, V. (1979) 'It's not what you are expecting', *Evening Chronicle*, 10 April.

Jephcott, P. (1962) *Married women working*, London: Allen and Unwin,

Johnson, A.G. (1997) *The gender knot: Unravelling our patriarchal legacy*, Philadelphia, PA: Temple University Press.

Johnstone, S.J., Boyce, P.M., Hickey, A.R., Morris-Yates, A.D. and Harris, M.G. (2001) 'Obstetric risk factors for postnatal depression in urban and rural community samples', *Australian and New Zealand Journal of Psychiatry*, vol 35, no 1, pp 69-74.

Jordanova, L. (1989) *Sexual visions: Images of gender in science and medicine between the eighteenth and twentieth centuries*, Hemel Hempstead: Harvester Wheatsheaf.

Kaberry, P. (1962) *Women of the grassfields*, London: HMSO.

Kahn, R.L. and Cannell, L.F. (1957) *The dynamics of interviewing*, New York, NY: John Wiley.

Kahn, R.P. (1995) *Bearing meaning: The language of birth*, Urbana and Chicago, IL: University of Chicago Press.

Kanter, R.M. (1977) *Men and women of the corporation*, New York, NY: Basic Books.

Katbamna, S. (2000) *'Race' and childbirth*, Buckingham: Open University Press.

Katz, E. and Lazarsfeld, P.F. (1964) *Personal influence*, Glencoe, IL: Free Press.

Kaufert, P.A., Gilbert, P. and Hassard, T. (1988) 'Researching symptoms of menopause: an exercise in methodology', *Maturitas*, vol 10, pp 117-31.

Kessler, S. (1998) *Lessons from the intersexed*, New Brunswick, NJ: Rutgers University Press.

King, J. (1986) 'Informed consent', *Bulletin of the Institute of Medical Ethics*, Supplement no 3, December.

Kitterød, R.H. (2002) 'Mothers' housework and childcare: growing similarities or stable inequalities?', *Acta Sociologica*, vol 45, no 2, pp 127-49.

Kitzinger, S. (1979) *The good birth guide*, London: Fontana.

Klein, V. (1965) *Women workers*, Paris: OECD.

Kohlberg, L. (1967) 'A cognitive-developmental; analysis of children's sex-role concepts and attitudes', in E.E. Maccoby (ed) *The development of sex differences,* London: Tavistock.

Kohlberg, L. and Ullian, D.Z. (1974) 'Stages in the development of psychosexual concepts and attitudes', in R.C. Friedman, R.M. Richart and R.L. Vande Wiele (eds) *Sex differences in behavior*, New York, NY: John Wiley.

Kornhauser, A. (1965) *Mental health of the industrial worker*, New York, NY: John Wiley.

Koutroulis, G. (1990) 'The orifice revisited: women in gynaecological texts', *Community Health Studies*, vol XIV, no 1, pp 73-84.

Krieger, N. (2003) 'Genders, sexes, and health: what are the connections – and why does it matter?', *International Journal of Epidemiology*, vol 32, pp 652-7.

Kristeva, J. (1981) 'Woman can never be defined', in E. Marks and I. de Courtivron (eds) *New French feminisms: An anthology*, New York, NY: Schocken Books.

Kroska, A. (2004) 'Divisions of domestic work: revising and expanding the theoretical explanations', *Journal of Family Issues*, vol 25, no 7, pp 900-32.

Kuhl, J.F.W, Lee, J.K., Halberg, F., Harris, E, Gunther, R. and Knapp, E. (1974) 'Circadian and lower frequency rhythms in male grip strength and baby weight', in M. Ferin, F. Halberg, R.M. Richart and R.L.Vande Wiele (eds) *Biorhythms and human reproduction*, New York, NY: John Wiley.

Kuhn, T.S. (1962) *The structure of scientific revolutions*, Chicago, IL: University of Chicago Press.

Kutner, N.G. and Brogen, G.M. (1990) 'Sex stereotypes and health care: the case of treatment for kidney failure', *Sex Roles*, vol 24, pp 257-63.

Laing, A.H., Berry, R.J., Newman, C.R, and Peto, J. (1975) 'Treatment of inoperable carcinoma of bronchus', *The Lancet*, 13 December, pp 1161-4.

Lake, A. (1975) 'Are we born into our sex roles or programmed into them?', *Women's Day*, January, pp 24-5.

Lakoff, R. (1975) *Language and woman's place*, New York, NY: Harper Colophon.

Laqueur, T. (1990) *Making sex: Body and gender from the Greeks to Freud*, Cambridge, MA: Harvard University Press.

LaRossa, R and LaRossa, M.M. (1981) *Transition to parenthood: How infants change families*, Beverly Hills, CA: Sage Publications.

Laslett, B. and Rapoport, R. (1975) 'Collaborative interviewing and interactive research', *Journal of Marriage and the Family*, November, pp 968-77.

Latour, B. (1993) *We have never been modern*, Hemel Hempstead: Harvester Wheatsheaf.

Laws, J. (1971) 'A feminist review of the marital adjustment literature: the rape of the Locke', *Journal of Marriage and the Family*, vol 33, pp 483-516.

Leavey, C. (1997) 'In conversation with Ann Oakley', *The Journal of Contemporary Health*, vol 5, pp 18-20.

Leifer, M. (1980) *Psychological effects of motherhood: A study of first pregnancy*, New York, NY: Praeger Publishers.

Leith-Ross, S. (1939) *African women*, London: Faber.

Lenski, G.E. (1966) *Power and privilege*, New York, NY: McGraw-Hill.

Lepenies, W. (1988) *Between literature and science: The rise of sociology*, Cambridge: Cambridge University Press.

Levi-Strauss, C. (1969) *The elementary structures of kinship*, Boston, MA: Beacon Press.

Levy, J. (1972) 'Lateral specialization of the human brain: behavioral manifestations and possible evolutionary basis', in J.A. Kiger (ed) *The biology of behavior*, Corvallis: Oregon State University Press.

Lewins, F. (1995) *Transsexualism in society*, Melbourne: Macmillan.

Lewontin, R. (2000) *It ain't necessarily so*, London: Granta Books.

Lie, M. (2002) 'Science as father? Sex and gender in the age of reproductive technologies', *The European Journal of Women's Studies*, vol 9, no 4, pp 381-99.

Lipset, S.M. (1963) *Political man*, London: Mercury Books.

Little, K. (1954) 'The Mende in Sierra Leone', in D. Forde (ed) *African worlds*, Oxford: Oxford University Press.

Lövdahl, U., Riska, A. and Riska, E. (1999) 'Gender display in Scandinavian and American advertising for antidepressants', *Scandinavian Journal of Public Health*, vol 27, pp 306-10.

Luce, G.H. (1970) *Biological rhythms in psychiatry and medicine*, USPHS Publication no 2088, Washington, DC: US Department of Health, Education and Welfare.

Luke, C. and Gore, J. (1992) 'Introduction', in C. Luke and J. Gore (eds) *Feminism and critical pedagogy*, London: Routledge.

Lukes, S. (1973) *Emile Durkheim: His life and work*, London: Allen Lane.

Lumley, J., Lester, A., Renon, P. and Wood, C. (1985) 'A failed RCT to determine the best method of delivery for very low birthweight infants', *Controlled Clinical Trials*, vol 6, pp 120-7.

Luxton, M. (1980) *More than a labour of love*, Toronto, Canada: The Women's Press.

Lyotard, J.-F. (1984, originally published 1979) *The postmodern condition: A report on knowledge*, translated by G. Bennington and B. Massumi, Manchester: Manchester University Press.

Macarthur, C., Lewis, M. and Knox, E.G. (1991) *Health after childbirth*, London: HMSO.

Maccoby, E.E. and Jacklin, C.N. (1974) *The psychology of sex differences*, Stanford, CA: Stanford University Press.

Macfarlane, A. (1977) *The psychology of childbirth*, London: Fontana.

Macfarlane, A., Mugford, M., Henderson, J., Furtado, A, Stevens, K. and Dunn, A. (2000) *Birth counts: Statistics of pregnancy and childbirth*, London: The Stationery Office.

Macintyre, S. (1977) 'The management of childbirth: a review of sociological research issues', *Social Science and Medicine*, vol 11, pp 477-84.

Mackinnon, C.A. (1990) 'Legal perspectives on sexual difference', in D. L. Rhode (ed) *Theoretical perspectives on sexual difference*, New Haven, CT: Yale University Press.

MacKinnon, P.C.B. and MacKinnon, I L. (1956) 'Hazards of the menstrual cycle', *British Medical Journal*, vol 1, p 555.

McBride, T. (1976) *The domestic revolution*, London: Croom Helm.

McCleary, G.F. (1933) *The early history of the infant welfare movement*, London: H.K. Lewis and Co.

McCord, J. (1981) 'Consideration of some effects of a counselling program', in S.E. Martin, L.B. Sechrest and R. Redner (eds) *New directions in the rehabilitation of criminal offenders*, Washington, DC: National Academy Press.

McCord, J. (1982) 'The Cambridge-Somerville Youth Study a sobering lesson on treatment, prevention and evaluation', in A.J. McSweeny, W.J. Freeman and R. Hawkins (eds) *Practical program evaluation in youth*, Springfield, IL: Charles C. Thomas.

McDonald, L. (1993) *The early origins of the social sciences*, Montreal, Canada: McGill-Queen's University Press.

McKee, L. and O'Brien, M. (1983) *The father figure*, London: Tavistock.

McKie, L. (1995) 'The art of surveillance or reasonable prevention? The case of cervical screening', *Sociology of Health and Illness*, vol 17, pp 441-57.

McLean, C., Carey, M. and White, C. (1996) *Men's ways of being*, Boulder, CO: Westview Press.

McMahon, A. (1999) *Taking care of men: Sexual politics in the public mind*, Cambridge: Cambridge University Press.

McNally, F. (1979) *Women for hire: A study of the female office worker*, London: Macmillan.

McPherson, K. (1995) 'Breast cancer and hormonal supplements in postmenopausal women', *British Medical Journal*, vol 311, pp 699-700.

McPherson, K. (2004) 'Where are we now with hormone replacement therapy?', Editorial, *British Medical Journal*, vol 328, pp 357-8

McQueen, A. and Mander, R. (2003) 'Tiredness and fatigue in the postnatal period', *Journal of Advanced Nursing*, vol 42, no 5, pp 463-9.

McRae, S. (1986) *Cross-class families*, Oxford: Clarendon Press.

Madge, N. and Marmot, M. (1987) 'Psychosocial factors and health', *The Quarterly Journal of Social Affairs*, vol 3, no 2, pp 81-134.

Madigan, F.C. (1957) 'Are sex mortality differentials biologically caused?', *The Milbank Memorial Fund Quarterly*, vol 35, no 2, pp 202-23.

Malinowski, B. (1963) *The family among the Australian Aborigines*, New York, NY: Shocken Books.

Malos, E. (1977) 'Housework and the politics of women's liberation', Reprinted from the January-February issue of *Socialist Review* by RSM Publications, 11 Waverly Road, Redland, Bristol BS6 6ES.

Mamak, A.F. (1978) 'Nationalism, race-class consciousness and social research on Bougainville Island, Papua New Guinea', in C. Bell and S. Encel (eds) *Inside the whale*, Oxford: Pergamon Press.

Mandell, A. and Mandell, M. (1967) 'Suicide and the menstrual cycle', *Journal of the American Medical Association*, vol 200, pp 792-3.

Manicas, P.T. (1987) *A history and philosophy of the social sciences*, Oxford: Basil Blackwell.

Manke, B., Seery, B.L., Crouter, A.C. and McHale, S.M. (1994) 'The three corners of domestic labor: mothers', fathers' and children's weekday and weekend housework', *Journal of Marriage and the Family*, vol 56, pp 657-68.

Maroney, H.J. (1986) 'Embracing motherhood: new feminist theory', in R. Hamilton and M. Barrett (eds) *The politics of diversity*, London: Verso.

Marshall, H. (1991) 'The social construction of motherhood: an analysis of childcare and parenting manuals', in A. Phoenix, A. Woollett and E. Lloyd (eds) *Motherhood: Meanings, practices and ideologies*, London: Sage Publications.

Martin, E. (1987) *The woman in the body: A cultural analysis of reproduction*, Boston, MA: Beacon Press.

Martin, M.K. and Voorhies, B. (1975) *Female of the species*, New York, NY: Columbia University Press.

Mass Observation Bulletin (1951) 'The housewife's day', no 42, May/June.

Mastroianni, A.C., Faden, R. and Federman, D. (eds) (1994) *Women and health research* (vol 1), Washington, DC: National Academy Press.

Maushart, S. (1999) *The mask of motherhood*, New York, NY: The New Press.

Mauthner, N. (1995) 'Postnatal depression: the significance of social contacts between mothers', *Women's Studies International Forum*, vol 18, no 3, pp 311-23.

Maynard, A. and Chalmers, I. (eds) (1997) *Non-random reflections on health services research*, London: BMJ Publishing.

Mays, N. and Pope, C. (1995) 'Rigour and qualitative research', *British Medical Journal*, vol 311, pp 109-12.

Mead, M. (1935) *Sex and temperament in three primitive societies*, New York, NY: William Morrow.

Mead, M. (1950) *Male and female*, London: Penguin.

Mead, M. (1962) *Male and female*, Harmondsworth: Penguin.

Medical Sociology Group (1996) 'Criteria for the evaluation of qualitative research papers', *Medical Sociology News*, vol 22, pp 69-71.

Meehl, P.E. (1986) 'What social scientists don't understand', in D.W. Fiske and R.A.Schweder (eds) *Metatheory in social science*, Chicago, IL: Chicago University Press.

Merchant, C. (1980) *The death of nature: Women, ecology and the scientific revolution*, New York, NY: Harper and Row.

Metherey, N.Y., Hunt, F.R., Patton, M.B. and Heye, H. (1962) 'The diets of preschool children', *Journal of Home Economics*, vol 54, pp 297-308.

Michael, R.P. and Glascock, R.F. (1963) 'The distribution of C^{14-} and H^{3-}labelled oestrogens in the brain', *Proceedings of the Fifth (1961) International Congress of Biochemistry*, vol 9, p 1137.

Michaels, G.Y. and Goldberg, W.A. (eds) (1988) *The transition to parenthood: Current theory and research*, Cambridge: Cambridge University Press.

Mies, M. (1983) 'Towards a methodology of feminist research', in G. Bowles and R. Duelli Klein (eds) *Theories of women's studies*, London: Routledge.

Miller, J.B. (1976) *Toward a new psychology of women*, Boston, MA: Beacon Press.

Millett, K. (1969) *Sexual politics*, London: Rupert Hart-Davis.

Millum, T. (1975) *Images of women: Advertising in women's magazines*, London: Chatto and Windus.

Mischel, W. (1967) 'A social-learning view of sex differences in behaviour', in E.E. Maccoby (ed) *The development of sex differences*, London: Tavistock.

Mischel, W. (1970) 'Sex-typing and socialization', in P.H. Mussen (ed) *Carmichael's manual of child psychology*, New York, NY: John Wiley.

Mitzman, A. (1970) *The iron cage: An historical interpretation of Max Weber*, New York, NY: Knopf.

Moir, A. and Jessel, D. (1989) *BrainSex: The real difference between men and women*, London: Mandarin Books.

Money, J. (ed) (1965) *Sex research: New developments*, New York, NY: Holt, Rinehart and Winston.

Money, J. (1994) 'The concept of gender identity disorder in childhood and adolescence after thirty nine years', *Journal of Sex and Marital Therapy*, vol 20, pp 163-77.

Money, J. and Ehrhardt, A.E. (1972) *Man and woman, boy and girl*, Baltimore, MD: Johns Hopkins Press.

Montagu, A. (1968) *The natural superiority of women*, London: Macmillan.

Morantz, S. and Mansfield, A. (1977) 'Maternal employment and the development of sex role stereotyping in five to eleven year olds', *Child Development*, vol 48, pp 668-73.

Morawski, J.G. (1994) *Practicing feminisms, reconstructing psychology: Notes on a liminal science*, Ann Arbor, MI: University of Michigan Press.

More, K. and Whittle, S. (1999) *Reclaiming genders*, London: Cassell.

Morgan, E. (1972) *The descent of woman*, London: Souvenir Press.

Morton, J.H., Additon, H., Addison, R.G., Hunt, L. and Sullivan, J.J. (1953) 'A clinical study of premenstrual tension', *American Journal of Obstetrics and Gynecology*, vol 65, pp 1182-91.

Moser, C.A. (1950) 'Social research: the diary method', *Social Service*, vol 24, pp 80-4.

Moser, C.A. (1958) *Survey methods in social investigation*, London: Heinemann.

Moss, H.A. (1967) 'Sex, age and state as determinants of mother-infant interaction', *Merrill-Palmer Quarterly*, vol 13, pp 19-36.

Myrdal, A. and Klein, V. (1956) *Women's two roles*, London: Routledge and Kegan Paul.

Natalier, J. (2003) '"I'm not his wife": doing gender and doing housework in the absence of women', *Journal of Sociology*, vol 39, no 3, pp 253-69.

Naughton, J. (1975) 'Life sentences', *New Statesman*, 10 January.

Neilson, J.P. (1998) 'Ultrasound for fetal assessment in early pregnancy', *The Cochrane Database of Systematic Reviews 1998*, Issue 4.

Newill, R. (1974) *Infertile marriage*, Harmondsworth: Penguin.

Nicholson, L.J. (ed) (1990) *Feminism/postmodernism*, London: Routledge.

Nicolson, P. (1998) *Postnatal depression: Psychology, science and the transition to motherhood*, London: Routledge.

Nomaguchi, K.M. and Milkie, M.A. (2003) 'Costs and rewards of children: the effects of becoming a parent on adults' lives', *Journal of Marriage and the Family*, vol 65, no 2, pp 356-74.

Nordenmark, M. and Nyman, C. (2003) 'Fair or unfair? Perceived fairness of household division of labour and gender equality among women and men: the Swedish case', *The European Journal of Women's Studies*, vol 10, no 2, pp 181-209.

Nowotny, H., Scott, P. and Gibbons, M. (2001) *Re-thinking science: Knowledge and the public in an age of uncertainty*, Cambridge: Polity Press.

Nye, F.I. and Hoffman, L.W. (eds) (1963) *The employed mother in America*, Chicago, IL: Rand-McNally.

Office of Health Economics (1978) *Perinatal mortality in Britain: A question of class*, OHE Briefing Pamphlet no 10, London.

Office of Technology Assessment, Congress of the United States (1995) *Effectiveness and costs of osteoporosis screening and hormone replacement therapy* (vols I and II), Washington, DC: Government Printing Office.

Ohmann, C. (1971) 'Emily Bronte in the hands of male critics', *College English*, vol 32, pp 906-13.

O'Laughlin, B. (1974) 'Mediation of contradiction: why Mbum women do not eat chicken', in M.Z. Rosaldo and L.K. Lamphere (eds) *Woman, culture and society*, Stanford, CA: Stanford University Press.

Oldenhave, A., Jaszmann, L.J.B., Haspels, A.A. and Everaerd, W.T.A.M. (1993) 'Impact of climacteric on well-being', *American Journal of Obstetrics and Gynecology*, vol 168, pp 772-80.

Ollenburger, J.C. and Moore, H.A. (1992) *A sociology of women: The intersection of patriarchy, capitalism, and colonization*, Englewood Cliffs, NJ: Prentice Hall.

Ortner, S. (1974) 'Is female to male as nature is to culture?', in M.Z. Rosaldo and L.K. Lamphere (eds) Stanford, CA: Stanford University Press.

Overstreet, E.W. (1963) 'The biological makeup of woman', in S.M. Farber and R.H.L. Wilson (eds) *The potential of woman*, New York, NY: McGraw Hill.

Oudshoorn, N. (1994) *Beyond the natural body: An archaeology of sex hormones*, London: Routledge.

Paglia, C. (1992) *Sex, art and American culture*, Harmondsworth: Penguin.

Pahl, J.M. and Pahl, R.E. (eds) (1971) *Managers and their wives*, London: Allen Lane.

Paige, K.E. (1971) 'Effects of oral contraceptives on affective fluctuations associated with the menstrual cycle', *Psychosomatic Medicine*, vol 33, no 6, pp 515-37.

Papaioannou, A. (1982) 'Informed consent after randomisation' (letter), *The Lancet*, 9 October, p 828.

Parker, R. (1995) *Torn in two: The experience of maternal ambivalence*, London: Virago.

Parker, S.R., Brown, R.K., Child, J. and Smith, M.A. (1967) *The sociology of industry*, London: Allen and Unwin.

Parkin, F. (1971) *Class inequality and political order*, London: MacGibbon and Kee.

Parlee, M.B. (1976) 'The premenstrual syndrome', in S. Cox (ed) *Female psychology: The emerging self*, Chicago, IL: Science Research Associates.

Parsons, T. and Bales, R.F. (1955) *Family, socialization and interaction process*, Glencoe, IL: Free Press.

Pascall, G. (1997) *Social policy: A new feminist analysis*, London: Routledge.

Patchen, M. (1970) *Participation, achievement and involvement on the job*, Englewood Cliffs, NJ: Prentice-Hall.

Patterson, G.R., Littman, R.A. and Bricker, W. (1967) 'Assertive behaviour in children: a step toward a theory of aggression', *Monographs of the Society for Research in Child Development*, vol 32, no 113.

Paul, B. (1954) 'Interview techniques and field relationships', in A.L. Kroeber (ed) *Anthropology today*, Chicago, IL: University of Chicago Press.

Paykel, E.S., Emms, E.M., Fletcher, J. and Rassaby, E.S. (1980) 'Life events and social support in puerperal depression', *British Journal of Psychiatry*, vol 136, pp 339-46.

Payne, G., Payne, J. and Chapman, T. (1983) 'Trends in female social mobility', in E. Gamarnikow, D.H.J. Morgan, J. Purvis and D.E. Taylorson (eds) *Gender, class and work*, London: Heinemann.

Pearson, K. (1892) *The grammar of science*, New York, NY: Meridian.

Peckham Rye Women's Liberation Group (1971). Paper on housework, in *A woman's work is never done*, London: Agitprop.

Phelan, S. (ed) (1997) *Playing with fire: Queer politics, queer theories*, New York, NY: Routledge.

Phillips, D.C. (1992) *The social scientist's bestiary*, Oxford: Pergamon Press.

Piaget, J. (1952) *The origins of intelligence in children*, New York, NY: International Universities Press.

Pierce, J. (1995) *Gender trials: Emotional lives in contemporary law firms*, Berkeley, CA: University of California Press.

Pittman, J.F., Teng, W., Kerpelman, J.L. and Solheim, C.A. (1999) 'Satisfaction with performance of housework: the roles of time spent, quality assessment and stress', *Journal of Family Issues*, vol 20, no 6, pp 746-70.

Plamenatz, J. (1970) *Ideology*, London: Macmillan.

Plant, M. (1952) *The domestic life of Scotland in the eighteenth century*, Edinburgh: Edinburgh University Press.

Plath, S. (1963) *The bell jar*, London: Faber and Faber.

Plath, S. (1977) *Letters home* (ed A.S. Plath), New York, NY: Bantam Books.

Platt, J. (1969) 'Some problems in measuring the jointness of conjugal role-relationships', *Sociology*, vol 3, pp 287-97.

Platt, J. (1985) 'Weber's *verstehen* and the history of qualitative research: the missing link', *British Journal of Sociology*, vol 36, pp 448-66.

Pollak, O. (1950) *The criminality of women*, University Park, PA: Pennsylvania University Press.

Pool, R. (1993) *The new sexual revolution*, London: Hodder and Stoughton.

Porter, M. (1983) *Home, work and class consciousness*, Manchester: Manchester University Press.

Powers, E. and Witmer, H. (1951) *An experiment in the prevention of juvenile delinquency: The Cambridge-Somerville Youth Study*, New York, NY: Columbia University Press.

Poynter, F.N.L. and Keele, K.D. (1961) *A short history of medicine*, London: Mills and Boon.

Poynter, F.N.L. and Keele, K.D. (1974) *The needs of children*, London: Hutchinson.

Pryzgoda, J. and Crisler, J.C. (2000) 'Definitions of gender and sex: the subtleties of meaning', *Sex Roles*, vol 43, no 7/8, pp 553-69.

Puner, H.W. (1947) *Freud: His life and mind*, New York, NY: Dell.

Purefoy, E. (1931) *Purefoy letters* (ed G. Eland), London: Sidgwick and Jackson.

Raffle, A.E. (1996) Presentation to National Cervical Screening Conference, Oxford. September.

Raffle, A.E., Alden, B. and Mackenzie, E.F.D. (1995) 'Detection rates of abnormal cervical smears: what are we screening for?', *The Lancet*, vol 345, pp 1469-73.

Reid, M. (1983) 'Review article: a feminist sociological imagination? Reading Ann Oakley', *Sociology of Health and Illness*, vol 5, pp 83-94.

Reiger, K.M. (1985) *The disenchantment of the home: Modernizing the Australian family 1880-1940*, Melbourne: Oxford University Press.

Reinharz, S. (1983) 'Experimental analysis: a contribution to feminist research', in G. Bowles and R. Duelli Klein (eds) London: Routledge.

Reinharz, S. (1992) *Feminist methods in social research*, New York, NY: Oxford University Press.

Renzetti, C. and Curran, J. (1992) *Women, men and society*, London: Allyn and Bacon.

Rheingold, H.L. and Cook, K.V. (1975) 'The content of boys' and girls' rooms as an index of parents' behaviour', *Child Development*, vol 46, no 2, pp 459-63.

Ribeiro, A.L. (1962) 'Menstruation and crime', *British Medical Journal*, vol 1, p 640.

Rich, A. (1977) *Of woman born*, London: Virago.

Richards, M.P.M. (1975) 'Innovation in medical practice: obstetricians and the induction of labour in Britain', *Social Science and Medicine*, vol 9, pp 595-602.

Richards, M.P.M., Bernal, J.F. and Brackbill, Y. (1976) 'Early behavioural differences: gender or circumcision?', *Developmental Psychobiology*, vol 9, no 1, pp 89-95.

Richards, M. and Oakley, A. (1990) 'Women's experiences of Caesarean delivery'. in J. Garcia, M. Richards and R. Kilpatrick (eds) *The politics of maternity care*, Oxford: Oxford University Press.

Richardson, D. (1993) *Women, motherhood and childrearing*, Basingstoke: Macmillan.

Richardson, S.A., Dohrenwend, B.S. and Klein, D. (1965) *Interviewing: Its forms and functions*, New York, NY: Basic Books.

Richter, C.P. (1968) 'Periodic phenomena in man and animals and their relation to neuroendocrinic mechanisms (in monthly or near monthly cycles)', in R.P. Michael (ed) *Endocrinology and human behaviour*, London: Oxford University Press.

Riley, D. (1983) *War in the nursery: Theories of the child and mother*, London: Virago.

Riley, D. (1988) *"Am I that name?" Feminism and the category of 'women' in history*, Basingstoke: Macmillan.

Roberts, H. (ed) (1981a) *Doing feminist research*, London: Routledge.

Roberts, H. (ed) (1981b) *Women, health and reproduction*, London: Routledge.

Roberts, H. (1985) *Patient patients: Women and their doctors*, London: Pandora.

Robinson, J.P. (1980) 'Housework technology and household work', in S.F. Berk (ed) *Women and household labor*, Beverly Hills, CA: Sage Publications.

Robinson, J.P. and Godbey, G. (1997) *Time for life: The surprising ways Americans use their time*, University Park, PA: Pennsylvania University Press.

Romalis, S. (ed) (1981) *Childbirth: Alternatives to medical control*, Austin, TX: Texas University Press.

Romito, P. (1989) 'Unhappiness after childbirth', in I. Chalmers, M. Enkin and M.J.N.C. Keirse (eds) Oxford: Oxford University Press.

Romito, P. (1993) 'The practice of protective legislation for pregnant workers in Italy', *Women's Studies International Forum*, vol 16, pp 581-90.

Romito, P. (1997) 'Studying work, motherhood and women's wellbeing: a few notes about the construction of knowledge', *Journal of Reproductive and Infant Psychology*, vol 15, pp 209-20.

Romito, P. and Hovelhaque, F. (1987) 'Changing approaches in women's health: new insights and new pitfalls in prenatal preventive care', *International Journal of Health Services*, vol 17, no 2, pp 241-58.

Romito, P., Saurel-Cubizolles, M-J. and Lelong, N. (1999) 'What makes new mothers unhappy: psychological distress one year after birth in Italy and France', *Social Science and Medicine*, vol 49, pp 1651-62.

Romney, M.L. (1980) 'Predelivery shaving: an unjustified assault?', *Journal of Obstetrics and Gynaecology*, vol 1, pp 33-5.

Romney, M.L and Gordon, H. (1981) 'Is your enema really necessary?', *British Medical Journal*, vol 282, pp 1269-71.

Rosaldo, M.Z. (1974) 'Woman, culture and society: a theoretical overview', in M.Z. Rosaldo and L.K. Lamphere (eds).

Rosaldo, M.Z. and Lamphere, L.K. (1974) *Woman, culture and society*, Stanford, CA: Stanford University Press.

Rose, A.M. (1945) 'A research note on experimentation in interviewing', *American Journal of Sociology*, vol 51, pp 143-4.

Rose, H. (1986) 'Women's work, women's knowledge', in J. Mitchell and A. Oakley (eds) *What is feminism?*, Oxford: Basil Blackwell.

Rose, H. (1994) *Love, power and knowledge*, Cambridge: Polity Press.

Rose, H. and Rose, S. (eds) (1976) *The political economy of science*, London: Macmillan.

Rose, R.M., Gordon, T.P. and Bernstein, I.S. (1972) 'Plasma testosterone levels in the male rhesus: influences of sexual and social stimuli', *Science*, vol 178, pp 643-5.

Rosenkrantz, P., Vogel, S. Bee, H., Broverman, I. and Broverman, D. (1968) 'Sex role stereotypes and self-concepts in college students', *Journal of Consulting and Clinical Psychology*, vol 32, pp 287-95.

Rossi, A. (1964) 'Equality between the sexes', in R.F. Lifton (ed) *The woman in America*, Boston, MA: Houghton Mifflin.

Rothblatt, M. (1995) *The apartheid of sex: A manifesto on the freedom of gender*, New York, NY: Crown.

Rothman, B.K. (1982) *In labor: Women and power in the birthplace*, New York, NY: W.W. Norton.

Rothman, B.K. (1988) *The tentative pregnancy: Prenatal diagnosis and the future of motherhood*, London: Pandora.

Rothman, B.K. (1989) *Recreating motherhood: Ideology and technology in a patriarchal society*, New York, NY: W.W. Norton.

Rowbotham, S. (1973) 'Women's liberation and the new politics', in M. Wandor (ed) *The body politic*, London: Stage I.

Rowbotham, S. (1990) *The past is before us*, Harmondsworth: Penguin.

Roxburgh, S. (2004) '"There just aren't enough hours in the day": the mental health consequences of time pressure', *Journal of Health and Social Behavior*, vol 45, no 2, pp 115-31.

Royal College of Obstetricians Clinical Effectiveness Support Unit (2001) *The national sentinel Caesarean section audit report*, London: RCOG.

Rubin, G. (1975) 'The traffic in women: notes on the "political economy" of sex', in R.R. Reiter (ed) *Toward an anthropology of women*, New York, NY: Monthly Review Press.

Rutter, M. (1972) *Maternal deprivation reassessed*, Harmondsworth: Penguin.

Rutter, M. and Brown, G.W, (1966) 'The reliability and validity of measures of family life and relationships in families containing a psychiatric patient', *Social Psychiatry*, vol 1, pp 38-53.

Ruzek, S.B. (1978) *The women's health movement*, New York, NY: Praeger.

Scheff, T.J. (1963) 'Decision rules, types of error and their consequences in medical diagnosis', *Behavioural Science*, vol 8, pp 97-105.

Scherer, R.A., Abeles, R.P. and Fischer, C.S. (1975) *Human aggression and conflict*, Englewood Cliffs, NJ: Prentice-Hall.

Schiebinger, L. (1989) *The mind has no sex?*, Cambridge, MA: Harvard University Press.

School of Public Health, University of Leeds/Centre for Health Economics, University of York/Research Unit, Royal College of Physicians in association with the Department of Health (1992) 'Screening for osteoporosis to prevent fractures', *Effective Care*, Bulletin 1, London.

Schutz, A. (1972, originally published in 1932) *The phenomenology of the social world*, London: Heinemann Educational.

Schwendinger, J. and Schwendinger, H. (1971) 'Sociology's founding fathers: sexists to a man', *Journal of Marriage and the Family*, vol 33, pp 784-99.

Scully, D. (1980) *Men who control women's health*, Boston, MA: Houghton Mifflin.

Scully, D. and Bart, P. (1973) '"A funny thing happened on the way to the orifice": women in gynecology textbooks', *American Journal of Sociology*, vol 78, no 4, pp 1045-50.

Segal, L. (1987) *Is the future female? Troubled thoughts on contemporary feminism*, London: Virago.

Selltiz, C., Jahoda, M., Deutsch, M. and Cook, S.W. (1965) *Research methods in social relations*, London: Methuen.

Sherwin, S. (1992) *No longer patient: Feminist ethics and health care*, Philadelphia, PA: Temple University Press.

Shipman, M.D. (1972) *The limitations of social research*, London: Longman.

Silva, E.B. (1995) *Household technologies and domestic labour*, Research Working Paper no 11, Leeds: University of Leeds, Gender Analysis and Policy Unit.

Silverman, C. (1968) *The epidemiology of depression*, Baltimore, MD: The Johns Hopkins Press.

Silverman, W. (1980) *Retrolental fibroplasia: A modern parable*, New York, NY: Grune and Stratton.

Silverman, W. (1985) *Human experimentation: A guided step into the unknown*, Oxford: Oxford University Press.

Sjoberg, G. and Nett, R. (1968) *A methodology for social research*, New York, NY: Harper and Row.

Skegg, D.C.G., Doll, R. and Perry, J. (1977) 'Use of medicines in general practice', *British Medical Journal*, 18 June, pp 1561-3.

Skolbekken, J.A. (1995) 'The risk epidemic in medical journals', *Social Science and Medicine*, vol 40, pp 291-305.

Smart, B. (1993) *Postmodernity,* London: Routledge.

Smart, C. (1979) 'The new female criminal: reality or myth?', *British Journal of Criminology*, vol 19, no 1, pp 50-9.

Smith, A. (1988) 'Cervical cytology screening', *British Medical Journal*, vol 296, p 1670.

Smith, D. (1987) *The everyday world as problematic: A feminist sociology*, Boston, MD: Northeastern University Press.

Smith, D. (1999) *Writing the social: Critique, theory and investigation*, Toronto: University of Toronto Press.

Smolensky, M.H., Reinberg, A., Elee, R. and McGovern, J.P. (1974) 'Secondary rhythms related to hormonal changes in the menstrual cycle: special reference to allergology', in M. Ferin, F. Halberg, R.M. Richart and R.L. Vande Wiele (eds) *Biorhythms and human reproduction*, New York, NY: John Wiley.

Solesbury, W. (2002) 'The ascendancy of evidence', *Planning Theory and Practice*, vol 3, no 1, pp 90-6.

Spallone, P. and Steinberg, D.L. (eds) (1987) *Made to order: The myth of reproductive and genetic progress*, Oxford: Pergamon Press.

Spencer, H.R. (1927) *The history of British midwifery from 1650 to 1800*, London: John Bale, Sons and Danielsson Ltd.

Spender, D. (1980) *Man made language*, London: Routledge.

Spender, D. (1985) 'Model knowledge-making: Ann Oakley's research', in D. Spender (ed) *For the record: The making and meaning of feminist knowledge*, London: The Women's Press.

Spender, S. (1966) 'Warnings from the grave', *New Republic*, 18 June.

Sperry, R.W. (1974) 'Lateral specialization in the surgically separated hemispheres', in F.O. Schmitt and R.T. Wardon (eds) *The neurosciences: Third study program*, Cambridge, MA: MIT Press.

Spruill, J.C. (1972) *Women's life and work in the southern colonies*, New York, NY: W.W. Norton.

Stacey, J. (1986) 'Are feminists afraid to leave home? The challenge of conservative pro-family feminism', in J. Mitchell and A. Oakley (eds) *What is feminism?*, Oxford: Blackwell.

Stacey, J. (1988) 'Can there be a feminist ethnography?', *Women's Studies International Forum*, vol 11, no 1, pp 21-7.

Stacey, M. (1969) *Methods of social research*, Oxford: Pergamon Press.

Stacey, M. (1988) *The sociology of health and healing*, London: Unwin Hyman.

Stanley, L. and Wise, S. (1983) *Breaking out: Feminist consciousness and feminist research*, London: Routledge.

Stanley, L. and Wise, S. (1993) *Breaking out again: Feminist ontology and epistemology*, London: Routledge.

Star, S.L. (1979) 'The politics of right and left: sex differences in hemispheric brain asymmetry', in R. Hubbard, M.S. Henifin and B. Fried (eds) *Women looking at biology looking at women*, Boston, MA: G.K. Hall and Co.

Stephenson, P.A., Bakoula, C., Hemminki, E., Knudsen, L., Levasseur, M., Schenker, J., Stembera, Z., Tiba, J., Verbrugge, H.P. Zupan, J., Wagner, M.G., Karagas, M., Pizacani, B., Pineault, R., Tuimala, R., Houd, S. and Lomas, J. (1993) 'Patterns of use of obstetrical interventions in 12 countries', *Paediatric and Perinatal Epidemiology*, vol 7, pp 45-54.

Stephenson, J., Strange, V., Forrest, S., Oakley, A., Copas, A., Allen, E., Babiker, A., Black, S., Ali, M., Monteiro, H., Johnson, A.M. and the RIPPLE study team (2004) 'Pupil-led sex education in England (RIPPLE study): cluster-randomised intervention trial', *The Lancet*, vol 364, pp 338-46.

Stewart, D. and Stewart, L. (eds) (1976) *Safe alternatives in childbirth*, Chapel Hill, North Carolina: Napsac Inc.

Stockman, N., Bonney, N. and Xuewen, S. (1995) *Women's work in East and West*, London: UCL Press.

Stoetzel, J. (1948) 'Une étude de budget-temps de la femme mariée dans les agglomérations urbaines', *Population*, pp 47-62.

Stoller, R.J. (1968) *Sex and gender*, New York, NY: Science House.

Strathern, M. (1976) 'An anthropological perspective', in B. Lloyd and J. Archer (eds) *Exploring sex differences*, London: Academic Press.

Strasser, S. (1982) *Never done*, New York, NY: Pantheon.

Strazdins, L. and Broom, D.H. (2004) 'Acts of love (and work): gender imbalance in emotional work and women's psychological distress', *Journal of Family Issues*, vol 23, no 3, pp 356-78.

Sullerot, E. (1971) *Woman, society and change*, London: Weidenfeld and Nicolson.

Swendsen, J. and Mazure, C. (2000) 'Life stress as a risk factor for postpartum depression: current research and methodological issues', *Clinical Psychology: Science and Practice*, vol 7, no 1, pp 17-31.

Swinscow, T.D.V. (1974) 'Personal view', *British Medical Journal*, 28 September.

Taylor-Gooby, P. (1994) 'Postmodernism and social policy: a great leap backwards', *Journal of Social Policy*, vol 23, no 3, pp 385-404.

Teare, L., Cookson, B. and Stone, S. (2001) 'Hand hygiene' (editorial), *British Medical Journal*, vol 323, pp 411-12.

Templeton, L., Velleman, R., Persaud, A. and Milner, P. (2003) 'The experiences of postnatal depression in women from black and minority ethnic communities in Wiltshire, UK', *Ethnicity and Health*, vol 8, no 3, pp 207-21.

Thomas, C. (1995) 'Domestic labour and health: bringing it all back home', *Sociology of Health and Illness*, vol 17, no 3, pp 328-52.

Thomas, J., Harden, A., Oakley, A., Oliver, S., Sutcliffe, K., Rees, R., Brunton, G. and Kavanagh, J. (2004) 'Integrating qualitative research with trials in systematic reviews', *British Medical Journal*, vol 328, pp 1010-12.

Thompson, C. (1974) 'Penis envy in women' (originally published in 1943), in J.B. Miller (ed) *Psychoanalysis and women*, Harmondsworth, Penguin.

Tiger, L. and Fox, R. (1971) *The imperial animal*, London: Secker and Warburg.

Tilly, L.A. and Scott, J.W. (1978) *Women, work and family*, New York, NY: Holt, Rinehart and Winston.

Tjio, D.H. and Levan, A. (1956) 'The chromosome number of man', *Hereditas*, vol 42, pp 1-6.

To, C.-Y. (2000) *The scientific merit of the social sciences: Implications for research and application*, Stoke-on-Trent: Trentham.

Tobin, J.N., Wassertheil Smoller, S., Wexler, J.P., Steingart, R.M., Budner, N., Lense, L. and Wachspress, J. (1987) 'Sex bias in considering coronary bypass surgery', *Annals of Internal Medicine*, vol 107, pp 19-25.

Toomey, D.M. (1971) 'Conjugal roles and social networks in an urban working class sample', *Human Relations*, vol 24, pp 417-31.

Topo, P. (1997) *Dissemination of climacteric and postmenopausal hormone therapy in Finland*, Helsinki, Finland: STAKES National Research and Development Centre for Welfare and Health, Research Reports 78.

Topo, P., Hemminki, E. and Uutela, A. (1993) 'Women's choice and physicians' advice on use of menopausal and postmenopausal hormone therapy', *International Journal of Health Services*, vol 4, no 3, pp 101-9.

Toroyan, T., Roberts, I., Oakley, A., Laing, G., Mugford, M. and Frost, C. (2003) 'Effectiveness of out-of-home day care for disadvantaged families: randomised controlled trial', *British Medical Journal*, vol 327, pp 906-9.

Tresemer, D. (1975) 'Assumptions made about gender roles', in M. Millman and R.M. Kanter (eds) *Another voice: Feminist perspectives on social life and social science*, New York, NY: Anchor Books.

Turnbull, C. (1965) *Wayward servants*, London: Eyre and Spottiswoode.

Turner, B. and Turner, C. (1974) 'Evaluations of women and men among black and white college students', *Sociological Quarterly*, vol 15, pp 442-56.

UNESCO (1962) 'Images of women in society', *International Social Science Journal*, vol XIV, no 1.

van Berkel, M. and de Graaf, N.D. (1999) 'By virtue of pleasantness? Housework and the effects of education revisited', *Sociology*, vol 33, no 4, pp 785-808.

van der Waals, F., Mohrs, J. and Foets, M. (1993) 'Sex differences among recipients of benzodiazepines in Dutch general practice', *British Medical Journal*, vol 307, pp 363-6.

Vanek, J. (1978) 'Household technology and social status: rising living standards and status residence differences in housework', *Technology and Culture*, vol 19, no 3, pp 361-78.

VanEvery, J. (1997) 'Understanding gendered inequality: reconceptualizing housework', *Women's Studies International Forum*, vol 20, no 3, pp 411-20.

Verbrugge, M.H. (1976) 'Women and medicine in nineteenth century America', *SIGNS: Journal of Women in Culture and Society*, vol 4, no 1, pp 957-72.

Vetter, N.J., Lewis, P.A. and Ford, D. (1992) 'Can health visitors prevent fractures in elderly people?', *British Medical Journal*, vol 304, pp 888-90.

Vroom, V. (1964) *Work and motivation*, New York, NY: John Wiley.

Wagner, M. (1994) *Pursuing the birth machine: The search for appropriate birth technology*, Camperdown, Australia: ACE Graphics.

Walby, S. (1988) 'Gender politics and social theory', *Sociology*, vol 22, no 2, pp 215-32.

Walby, S. (1990) *Theorizing patriarchy*, Oxford: Blackwell.

Walby, S. (1992) 'Post-post-modernism? Theorizing social complexity', in M. Barrett and A. Phillips (eds) *Destabilizing theory: Contemporary feminist debates*, Cambridge: Polity Press.

Walker, C.R. and Guest, R.H. (1952) *The man on the assembly line*, Cambridge, MA: Harvard University Press.

Wallerstein, I. (1999) 'The heritage of sociology, the promise of social science, Presidential address, XIVth World Congress of Sociology, Montreal, 26 July 1998', *Current Sociology*, vol 47, no 1, pp 1-37.

Walum, C.R. (1977) *The dynamics of sex and gender: A sociological perspective*, Chicago, IL: Rand McNally.

Wandor, M. (ed) (1973) *The body politic: Writings from the Women's Liberation Movement in Britain 1969-72*, London: Stage 1.

Ward, J.P. (1974) 'Adolescent girls: same or different?', Paper given at British Sociological Association Annual Conference at Aberdeen, Scotland, April 7-10.

Waring, M. (1988) *Counting for nothing: What men value and what women are worth*, London: Allen and Unwin with Port Nicholson Press.

Weber, M. (1947) *A theory of social and economic organization*, Glencoe, IL: Free Press.

Weideger, P. (1978) *Female cycles*, London: The Women's Press.

Weitz, S. (1977) *Sex roles: Biological, psychological and social foundations*, Oxford: Oxford University Press.

Weitzman, L.J., Eifler, D. Hokada, E, and Ross, C. (1976) 'Sex-role socialization in picture books for pre-school children', in Children's Rights Workshop, *Sexism in children's books: Facts, figures and guidelines*, London: Writers and Readers Publishing Co-operative.

Wells, C.K. and Feinstein, A.R. (1988) 'Detection bias in the diagnostic pursuit of lung cancer', *American Journal of Epidemiology*, vol 128, pp 1016-26.

Wharton, A.S. (2000) 'Feminism at work', *Annals of the American Academy of Political and Social Science*, vol 571, pp 167-82.

Whiffen, V.E. (1992) 'Is postnatal depression a distinct diagnosis?', *Clinical Psychology Review*, vol 12, pp 485-508.

Whitehead, R.E. (1934) 'Women pilots', *Journal of Aviation Medicine*, vol 5, pp 47-9.

Whiting, B.B. (ed) (1963) *Six cultures*, New York, NY: John Wiley.

WHO (World Health Organisation) (1994) *Assessment of fracture risk and its application to screening for postmenopausal osteoporosis*, Geneva: WHO Technical report Series 843.

Wickham, M. and Young, B. (1973) *Home management and family living*, London: National Council of Women.

Wiggins, M., Oakley, A., Roberts, I., Turner, H., Rajan, L., Austerberry, H., Mujica, R. and Mugford, M. (2004) 'The Social Support and Family Health Study: a randomised controlled trial and economic evaluation of two alternative forms of postnatal support for mothers living in disadvantaged inner-city areas', *Health Technology Assessment*, vol 8, no 32, pp 1-134.

Wight, D. and Obasi, A. (2003) 'Unpacking the "black box": the importance of process data to explain outcomes', in J.M Stephenson, J. Imrie and C. Bonell (eds) *Effective sexual health interventions: Issues in experimental evaluation*, Oxford: Oxford University Press.

Wild, R. and Hill, A.B. (1970) *Women in the factory: A study of job satisfaction and labour turnover*, London: Institute of Personnel Management.

Williams, D. (1975) 'Brides of Christ', in Ardener (ed).

Williams, R.J. (1962) *Biochemical individuality*, New York, NY: John Wiley.

Willmott, R. (1996) 'Resisting sex/gender conflation: a rejoinder to John Hood-Williams', *The Sociological Review*, pp 728-45.

Wilson, M. (1929) 'Use of time by Oregon farm homemakers', *Oregon Experiment Station Bulletin 256*, November.

Wise, J. (1996) 'HRT use in high risk women should be reviewed', *British Medical Journal*, vol 313, p 1102.

Witelson, S.F. (1976) 'Sex and the single hemisphere: specialization of the right hemisphere for spatial processing', *Science*, vol 193, pp 425-7.

Wittig, M. (1981) 'One is not born a woman', *Feminist Studies*, vol 1, no 2, pp 47-54.

Wittig, M. (1992) *The straight mind and other essays*, Boston, MA: Beacon Press/Hemel Hempstead: Harvester Wheatsheaf.

Wollstonecraft, M. (1929, originally published 1792) *Vindication of the rights of woman*, London: Everyman's Library.

Wood, A.D. (1974) '"The fashionable diseases"; women's complaints and their treatment in nineteenth century America', in M. Hartman and L.W. Banner (eds) *Clio's consciousness raised: New perspectives in the history of women*, New York, NY: Harper and Row.

Woodham-Smith, C. (1952) *Florence Nightingale 1820-1910*, London: The Reprint Society.

Wootton, B. (1959) *Social science and social pathology*, London: Allen and Unwin.

Wright, E.O. (1997) *Class counts: Comparative studies in class analysis*, Cambridge: Cambridge University Press.

Wright Mills, C. (1959) *The sociological imagination*, New York, NY: Oxford University Press.

Wright Mills, C. (1967) 'The professional ideology of social pathologists', in I.L. Horowitz (ed) *Power, politics and people*, New York, NY: Oxford University Press.

Young, I. (1974) *The private life of Islam*, London: Allen Lane.

Young, M. and Willmott, P. (1973) *The symmetrical family*, London: Routledge and Kegan Paul.

Zelditch, M. (1950) 'Role differentiation in the nuclear family: a comparative study', in T. Parsons and R.F. Bales (1955) *Family, socialization and interaction process*, Glencoe, IL: Free Press.

Zimmerman, D.H. and West, C. (1975) 'Sex roles, interruption and silences in conversation', in B. Thorne and N. Henley (eds) *Language and sex: Difference and dominance*, Rowley, MA: Newbury House publishers.

Zweig, F. (1949) *Labour, life and poverty*, London: Gollancz.

Bibliography of work by
Ann Oakley

This section provides details of work referred to in this volume.

1972

Sex, gender and society, London: Temple Smith [1981 Revised edition published by Gower Publishing, Aldershot].

1974

a) *Housewife*, London: Allen Lane.

b) *The sociology of housework*, London: Martin Robertson [revised edn 1985, published by Basil Blackwell, Oxford].

1976

'From wisewoman to medicine man: changes in the management of childbirth', in J. Mitchell and **A. Oakley** (eds) *The rights and wrongs of women*, Harmondsworth: Penguin.

1977

Oakley, A. and Mitchell, J. (eds) *Who's afraid of feminism?*, London: Hamish Hamilton; New York, NY: The New Press.

1979

Becoming a mother, Oxford: Martin Robertson [under the title *From here to maternity*, Harmondsworth: Penguin, 1981].

1980

Women confined: Towards a sociology of childbirth, Oxford: Martin Robertson.

1981

a) 'Interviewing women: a contradiction in terms?', in H. Roberts (ed) *Doing feminist research*, London: Routledge.

b) *Subject women*, Oxford: Martin Robertson.

1982

'Normal motherhood: an exercise in self control?', in B. Hutter and G. Williams (eds) *Controlling women*, London: Croom Helm.

1984

a) *Taking it like a woman*, London: Jonathan Cape [1985 paperback edn published by Fontana, London].

b) *The captured womb: A history of the medical care of pregnant women*, Oxford: Basil Blackwell.

c) 'The consumer's role: adversary or partner?', in L. Zander and G. Chamberlain (eds) *Pregnancy care for the 1980s*, London: Royal Society of Medicine/Macmillan Press.

1985

'Social support in pregnancy: the "soft" way to increase birthweight?', *Social Science and Medicine*, vol 21, no 11, pp 1259-68.

1988

'Is social support good for the heath of mothers and babies?', *Journal of Infant and Reproductive Psychology*, vol 6, pp 3-21.

1989

'Women's studies in British sociology: to end at our beginning?', *British Journal of Sociology*, vol 40, no 3, pp 442-70.

1990

Oakley, A. and Houd, S. *Helpers in childbirth: Midwifery today*, Washington, DC: Hemisphere Books, on behalf of the World Health Organization, Regional Office for Europe.

1992

Social support and motherhood: The natural history of a research project, Oxford: Basil Blackwell.

1994

'Who cares for women? Social relations, gender and the public health', *Journal of Epidemiology and Community Health*, vol 48, pp 427-34.

1995

Oakley, A, and Fullerton, D. *Young people and smoking*, London: Social Science Research Unit, Institute of Education.

a) **Oakley, A,** Fullerton, D. and Holland, J. 'Behavioural interventions for HIV/ AIDS prevention', *AIDS*, vol 9, pp 479-86.

b) **Oakley, A,** Fullerton, D., Holland, J., Arnold, S., France-Dawson, M., Kelley, P. and McGrellis, S. 'Sexual health interventions for young people: a methodological review', *British Medical Journal*, vol 310, pp 158-62.

1996

'Women's studies: theory or practice?', in C. Crouch and A. Heath (eds) *Social research and social reform*, Oxford: Oxford University Press.

Oakley, A, France-Dawson, M., Fullerton, D., Holland, J., Arnold, S., Cryer, C., Doyle, Y., Rice, J. and Russell Hodgson, C. 'Preventing falls and subsequent injury in older people', *Effective Health Care Bulletin*, vol 2, no 4, pp 1-16.

1997

'A brief history of gender', in **A. Oakley** and J. Mitchell (eds) *Who's afraid of feminism?*, London: Hamish Hamilton; New York, NY: The New Press.

1998

a) 'Experimentation and social interventions: a forgotten but important history', *British Medical Journal*, vol 317, pp 1239-42.

b) 'Gender, methodology and people's ways of knowing: some problems with feminism and the paradigm debate in social science', *Sociology*, vol 32 no 4, pp 707-31.

c) 'Living in two worlds', *British Medical Journal*, vol 316, pp 482-3.

d) 'Science, gender and women's liberation: an argument against postmodernism', *Women's Studies International Forum*, vol 21, pp 133-46.

2000

Experiments in knowing: Gender and method in the social sciences, Cambridge: Polity Press.

2002

Gender on planet earth, Cambridge: Polity Press.

2003

'Research evidence, knowledge management and educational practice: early lessons from a systematic approach', *London Review of Education*, vol 1, no 1, pp 21-33.

Oakley, A, Strange, V., Toroyan, T., Wiggins, M., Roberts, I. and Stephenson, J. 'Using random allocation to evaluate social interventions: three recent UK examples', *Annals of the American Academy of Political and Social Science*, vol 589, pp 170-89.

2004

'Qualitative research and scientific inquiry', *Australian and New Zealand Journal of Public Health*, vol 28, no 2, pp 102-4.

Oakley, A, Strange, V., Stephenson, J., Forrest, S., Monteiro, H. and the RIPPLE Study team 'Evaluating processes: a case study of a randomized controlled trial of sex education', *Evaluation*, vol 10, no 4, pp 440-62.

Please also refer to Ann Oakley's website: www.annoakley.co.uk

Ann Oakley: further reading

This section provides a selection of published work by Ann Oakley not referred to elsewhere in this volume. It includes some more recent work on social science methodology, much of which was undertaken collaboratively. A full bibliography can be found on the author's website (www.annoakley.co.uk).

Other academic and non-fiction books

1986
Telling the truth about Jerusalem: Selected essays, Oxford: Basil Blackwell.

1993
Essays on women, medicine and health, Edinburgh: Edinburgh University Press.

Edited and jointly authored books

1984
Oakley, A., McPherson, A., and Roberts, H. *Miscarriage*, London: Fontana [Revised edn, Penguin, 1990].

1994
Brannen, J., Dodd, K., **Oakley, A.** and Storey, P. *Young people, health and family life*, Buckingham: Open University Press.
Oakley, A. and Williams, A.S. (eds) *The politics of the Welfare State*, London: UCL Press.

1998
Williams, F., Popay, J. and **Oakley, A.** (eds) *Welfare research: A critical review*, London: UCL Press.

Chapters and articles

Gender, feminism and women's studies

1986
'Feminism, motherhood and medicine – Who cares?', in J. Mitchell and **A. Oakley** (eds) *What is feminism?*, Oxford: Basil Blackwell, pp 127-50.
'Feminism and motherhood', in M. Richards and P. Light (eds) *Children of social worlds*, Cambridge: Polity Press, pp 74-94.

1987

'Gender and generation: the life and times of Adam and Eve', in P. Allatt, T. Keil, A. Bryman and B. Bytheway (eds) *Women and the life cycle*, London: Macmillan, pp 13-32.

1992

'Women's studies: theory or practice?', in C. Crouch and A. Heath (eds) *Social research and social reform*, Oxford: Clarendon Press, pp 271-86.

1995

'Women and children first and last: parallels and differences between children's and women's studies', in B. Mayall (ed) *Children's childhoods*, Sussex: Falmer Press, pp 13-32.

1996

'Gender matters: man the hunter', in H. Roberts and D. Sachdev (eds) *Young people's social attitudes: Having their say – the views of 12-19 year olds*, Ilford: Barnardo's, pp 23-43.

1998

'Whatever's happening to women? Sex, gender and the politics of the backlash', in A. Despard (ed) *A woman's place: Women, domesticity and private life*, Kristiansand, Norway: Høgskolen i Agder, pp 1-20.

Childbirth and motherhood

1976

'Wisewoman and medicine man: changes in the management of childbirth', in J. Mitchell and **A. Oakley** (eds) *The rights and wrongs of women*, Harmondsworth: Penguin, pp 17-58.

1977

'Cross-cultural practice', in T. Chard and M. Richards (eds) *Benefits and hazards of the new obstetrics*, London: Heinemann Medical, pp 18-33.

1981

Oakley, A. and Chamberlain, G. (1981) 'Medical and social factors in postpartum depression', *Journal of Obstetrics and Gynaecology*, vol 1, pp 182-7.

1982

'Obstetric practice: cross-cultural comparisons', in P.M. Stratton (ed) *Psychobiology of the human newborn*, Chichester: John Wiley, pp 297-313.

1983

'Social consequences of obstetric technology: how to measure "soft" outcomes', *Birth*, vol 10, pp 99-108.

1985

'Doctors, maternity patients and social scientists', *Birth*, vol 12, no 3, pp 161-6.

1987

'From walking wombs to test-tube babies', in M. Stanworth (ed) *Reproductive technologies*, Cambridge: Polity Press, pp 36-56.

1989

'William Power Memorial Lecture. Who cares for women? Science versus love in midwifery today', *Midwives Chronicle*, pp 214-21.

1990

'A case of maternity: paradigms of women as maternity cases', in D. Pope, M. Wyer and J. O'Barr (eds) *Ties that bind: Essays on motherhood*, Chicago, IL: Chicago University Press, pp 61-85.

Oakley, A. and Rajan, L. 'Obstetric technology and maternal emotional wellbeing: a further research note', *Journal of Reproductive and Infant Psychology*, vol 8, pp 45-55.

Rajan, L. and **Oakley, A.** 'Low birthweight babies - the mother's point of view', *Midwifery*, vol 6, pp 73-85.

1992

'Setting the scene: the changing context of pregnancy care', in G. Chamberlain and L. Zander (eds) *Pregnancy care in the 1990s. Proceedings of a Symposium held at the Royal Society of Medicine*, Carnforth: Parthenon Publishing Group, pp 3-18.

1993

'The follow up survey', in G. Chamberlain, A.. Wraight and P. Steer (eds) *Pain and its relief in childbirth: The results of a national survey conducted by the National Birthday Trust*, Edinburgh: Churchill Livingstone, pp 101-13.

1996

'Becoming a grandmother - has childbirth really changed?', *British Medical Journal*, vol 312, p 1426.

1997

'The follow-up survey', in G. Chamberlain, A. Wraight, and P. Crowley (eds) *Home births: The report of the 1994 confidential enquiry by the National Birthday Trust Fund*, London: the Parthenon Publishing Group, pp 165-90.

Women's health

1983

'Women and health policy', in J. Lewis (ed) *Women's welfare, women's rights*, London: Croom Helm, pp 103-29.

1984

'Fertility control: a woman's issue? The 10th Jennifer Hallam Memorial Lecture', *Journal of Obstetrics and Gynaecology*, vol 4 (supplement 1), pp 1-10.

1989

'Smoking in pregnancy: smokescreen or risk factor? Towards a materialist analysis', *Sociology of Health and Illness*, vol 11, no 4, pp 311-35.

1991

'Tamoxifen: in whose best interest?', *New Scientist*, October, p 12.

1992

Oakley, A., Brannen, J. and Dodd, K. 'Young people, gender and smoking in the United Kingdom', *Health Promotion International*, vol 7, no 2, pp 75-88.

1993

Oakley, A., Rigby, A.S. and Hickey, D. 'Women and children last? Class, health and the role of the maternal and child health services', *European Journal of Public Health*, vol 3, pp 220-6.

'Women, health and knowledge: travels through and beyond foreign parts', *Health Care for Women International*, vol 14, pp 377-84.

1994

Oakley, A., Rigby, A.S., and Hickey, D. 'Life stress, support and class inequality', *European Journal of Public Health*, vol 4, pp 81-91.

Oakley, A., Rigby, A.S. and Hickey, D. 'Love or money? Social support, class inequality and the health of women and children', *European Journal of Public Health*, vol 4, pp 265-73.

1998

Oakley, A. and Rigby, A.S. 'Are men good for the welfare of women and children?' in J. Popay, J. Hearn and J. Edwards (eds) *Men, gender divisions and welfare*, London: Routledge, pp 101-27.

2003

Bonell, C.P., Strange, V.J., Stephenson, J.M., **Oakley, A.R.,** Copas, A.J., Forrest, S.P., Johnson, A.M. and Black, S. 'Effect of social exclusion on the risk of teenage pregnancy: development of hypotheses using baseline data from a randomised trial of sex education', *Journal of Epidemiology and Community Health*, vol 57, no 11, pp 871-6.

2005

Bonell, C., Allen, E., Strange, V., Copas, A., **Oakley, A.,** Stephenson, J. and Johnson, A. 'The effect of dislike of school on risk of teenage pregnancy: testing of hypotheses using longitudinal data from a randomised trial of sex education', *Journal of Epidemiology and Community Health*, vol 59, pp 223-30.

Social intervention evaluation

1990

Oakley, A., Rajan, L., and Grant, A. 'Social support and pregnancy outcome: report of a randomised controlled trial', *British Journal of Obstetrics and Gynaecology*, vol 97, pp 155-62.

1992

'Social support in pregnancy: methodology and findings of a one year follow-up study', *Journal of Reproductive and Infant Psychology*, vol 19, pp 219-31.

'Getting at the oyster: one of many lessons from the Social Support and Pregnancy Outcome Study', in H. Roberts (ed) *Women's health matters*, London: Routledge and Kegan Paul, pp 11-32.

1994

'Giving support in pregnancy: the role of research midwives in a randomised controlled trial', in S. Robinson and A.M. Thomson (eds) *Midwives, research and childbirth*, London: Chapman and Hall, pp 30-63.

1995

Oakley, A., Fullerton, D., Holland, J., Arnold, S., France-Dawson, M., Kelley, P. and McGrellis, S. 'Sexual health interventions for young people: a methodological review', *British Medical Journal*, vol 310, pp 158-62.

Oakley, A., Fullerton, D. and Holland, J. 'Behavioural interventions for HIV/AIDS prevention', *AIDS*, vol 9, pp 479-86.

1996

Oakley, A., Hickey, D., Rajan, L. and Rigby, A.S. 'Social support in pregnancy: does it have long-term effects?', *Journal of Reproductive and Infant Psychology*, vol 14, pp 7-22.

Oakley, A. and Fullerton, D. 'The lamppost of research: support or illumination?', in A. Oakley and H. Roberts (eds) *Evaluating social interventions: A report on two workshops*, Ilford: Barnardo's, pp 4-38.

1998

'Experimentation in social science: the case of health promotion', *Social Sciences in Health*, vol 4, pp 73-89.

'Public policy experimentation: lessons from America', *Policy Studies*, vol 19, no 2, pp 93-114.

Oakley, A., Rajan, L. and Turner, H. 'Evaluating parent support initiatives: lessons from two case studies', *Health and Social Care in the Community*, vol 6, no 5, pp 318-30.

Stephenson, J.M., **Oakley, A.**, Charleston, S., Brodala, A., Fenton, K., Petruckevitch, A. and Johnson, A. 'Behavioural intervention trials for HIV/STD prevention in schools: are they feasible?', *Sexually Transmitted Infections*, vol 74, pp 405-8.

Zoritch, B., Roberts, I. and **Oakley, A.** 'The health and welfare effects of day-care: a systematic review of randomised controlled trials', *Social Science and Medicine*, vol 47, no 3, pp 317-27.

1999

Harden, A., Peersman, G., Oliver, S., Mauthner, M. and **Oakley, A.** 'A systematic review of the effectiveness of health promotion interventions in the workplace', *Occupational Medicine*, vol 49, no 8, pp 540-8.

Peersman, G., Harden, A. and **Oakley, A.** 'Effectiveness reviews in health promotion: different methods, different recommendations', *Health Education Journal*, vol 58, pp 192-202.

Peersman, G., **Oakley, A.** and Oliver, S. 'Evidence-based health promotion? Some methodological challenges', *International Journal of Health Promotion and Education*, vol 37, no 2, pp 59-64.

2000

Toroyan, T., Roberts, I. and **Oakley, A.** 'Randomisation and resource allocation: a missed opportunity for evaluating health care and social interventions', *Journal of Medical Ethics*, vol 26, pp 319-22.

'A historical perspective on the use of randomised trials in social science settings', *Crime and Delinquency*, vol 46, no 3, pp 315-29.

2001

'Making evidence-based practice educational: a rejoinder to John Elliott', *British Educational Research Journal*, vol 27, no 5, pp 575-6.

Strange, V., Forrest, S. and **Oakley, A.** 'A listening trial: "qualitative" methods within experimental research', in S. Oliver and G. Peersman (eds) *Using research for effective health promotion*, Buckingham: Open University Press, pp 138-53.

'Evaluating health promotion: methodological diversity', in S. Oliver and G. Peersman (eds) *Using research for effective health promotion*, Buckingham: Open University Press, pp 16-31.

Harden, A., **Oakley, A.** and Oliver, S. 'Peer-delivered health promotion by young people: a systematic review of different study designs', *Health Education Journal*, vol 60, pp 362-70.

2002

'Social science and evidence-based everything: the case of education', *Educational Review*, vol 54, no 3, pp 277-86.

Sheldon, T. and **Oakley, A.** 'Why we need randomised controlled trials', in L. Duley and B. Farrell (eds) *Clinical trials*, London: BMJ Publishing, pp 13-24.

2003

Bonell, C., Bennett, R. and **Oakley, A.** 'Sexual health interventions should be subject to experimental evaluation', in J. Stephenson, J. Imrie and C. Bonell (eds) *Effective sexual health interventions: Issues in experimental evaluation*, Oxford: Oxford University Press, pp 3-16.

'Randomized controlled trial', in M. Lewis-Beck, A. Bryman and T. Futing Liao (eds) *The Sage encyclopaedia of social science research methods*, Thousand Oaks, CA: Sage Publications.

'Research evidence, knowledge management and educational practice: early lessons from a systematic approach', *London Review of Education*, vol 1, no 1, pp 21-33.

2004

Harden, A., Garcia, J., Oliver, S., Rees, R. Shepherd, J., Brunton, G. and **Oakley, A.** 'Applying systematic review methods to studies of people's views: an example from public health research', *Journal of Epidemiology and Community Health*, vol 58, no 9, pp 794-800.

Toroyan, T., **Oakley, A.**, Laing, G., Roberts, I., Mugford, M. and Turner, J. 'The impact of day care on socially disadvantaged families: an example of the use of process evaluation within a randomized controlled trial', *Child: Care, health and Development*, vol 30, no 6, pp 691-8.

2005

Wiggins, M., **Oakley, A.**, Roberts, I., Turner, H., Rajan, L., Austerberry, H., Mujica, R., Mugford, M. and Barker, M. 'Postnatal support for mothers living in disadvantaged inner city areas: a randomised controlled trial', *Journal of Epidemiology and Community Health*, vol 59, pp 288-95.

Oakley, A., Gough, D., Oliver, S. and Thomas, J. 'The politics of evidence and methodology: lessons from the EPPI-Centre', *Evidence and Policy*, vol 1, no 1, pp 5-32.

General social science methodology

1990

Oakley, A., Rajan, L. and Robertson, P. 'A comparison of different sources of information on pregnancy and childbirth', *Journal of Biosocial Science*, vol 22, pp 477-87.

Oakley, A. and Rajan, L. 'Social class and social support: the same or different?', *Sociology*, vol 25, no 1, pp 31-59.

1998

'People's ways of knowing', in B. Mayall, S. Hood, S. Oliver (eds) *Critical issues in social research: Power and prejudice*, Buckingham: Open University Press, pp 154-70.

Oakley, A., Peersman, G. and Oliver, S. 'Social characteristics of participants in health promotion research: trial and error?', *Education for Health*, vol 11, no 3, pp 305-17.

'Gender, methodology and people's ways of knowing some problems with feminism and the paradigm debate in social science', *Sociology*, vol 32, no 4, pp 707-31.

2003

Oakley, A,. Wiggins, M., Turner, H., Rajan, L. and Barker, M. 'Including culturally diverse samples in health research: a case study of an urban trial of social support', *Ethnicity and Health*, vol 8, no 1, pp 29-39.

2004

'Qualitative research and scientific inquiry' (Editorial), *Australian and New Zealand Journal of Public Health*, vol 28, no 2, pp 102-4.

'Response to "Quoting and counting: an autobiographical response to Oakley", *Sociology*, vol 38, no 1, pp 191-2.

Miscellaneous

1979

'Living in the present: a confrontation with cancer', *British Medical Journal*, vol 1, pp 861-2.

1983

'Millicent Garrett Fawcett', in D. Spender (ed) *Feminist theorists*, London: The Women's Press, pp 184-202.

1986

'Simone de Beauvoir: she came to stay', *Marxism Today*, June, pp 40-1.

1990

'Hannah Gavron: optimistic pioneer of modern feminism', *The Guardian*, 29 August, p 33.

1993

'Review article: telling stories: auto/biography and the sociology of health and illness', *Sociology of Health and Illness*, vol 15, no 3, pp 414-18.

2001

'Evidence, pain and the poor old NHS', *British Medical Journal*, vol 322, p 307.

Fiction

1988

The men's room, London: Virago [paperback edn published by HarperCollins, London and Atheneum, New York; both in 1989].

1990

[Under the name Rosamund Clay] *Only angels forget*, London: Virago.

1991

Matilda's mistake, London: Virago [HarperCollins paperback, 1991].

1992

The secret lives of Eleanor Jenkinson, London: HarperCollins.

1993

Scenes originating in the garden of Eden, London: HarperCollins.

1995

'Where the bee sucks', in R.G. Jones and A.S. Williams (eds) *The Penguin book of erotic stories by women*, London: Penguin Books, pp 384-97.

'Death in the egg', in A.S. Williams and R.G. Jones (eds) *The Penguin book of modern fantasy by women*, London: Penguin Books, pp 525-32.

1996

A proper holiday, London: HarperCollins.

1999

Overheads, London: HarperCollins.

Works relating to Richard Titmuss's literary estate

1991

'Eugenics, social medicine and the career of Richard Titmuss in Britain 1935-50', *British Journal of Sociology*, vol 42, no 2, pp 165-94.

1996

Man and wife: Richard and Kay Titmuss, my parents' early years, London: HarperCollins.

'Blood donation – altruism or profit? The gift relationship revisited', *British Medical Journal*, vol 312, p 1114.

1997

Oakley, A. and Ashton, J. (eds) *The gift relationship: From human blood to social policy. By Richard M. Titmuss*, London: LSE Books [New York: The New Press].

'Making medicine social: the case of two dogs with bent legs', in D. Porter (ed) *Social medicine and medical sociology in the twentieth century*, Amsterdam: Rodopi, Wellcome Institute Seminars on the History of Medicine, pp 81-96.

2001

Alcock, P., Glennerster, H., **Oakley, A.** and Sinfield, A. (eds) *Welfare and wellbeing: Richard Titmuss's contribution to social policy*, Bristol: The Policy Press.

2004

Oakley, A. and Barker, J. (eds) *Private complaints and public health: Richard Titmuss on the National Health Service*, Bristol: The Policy Press.

Works about Ann Oakley

1987

Mullan, B. Chapter on Ann Oakley, in B. Mullan (ed) *Sociologists on sociology*, London: Croom Helm.

1989

Forster, P., Sutton, I. 'Ann Oakley', in P. Forster (ed) *Daughters of de Beauvoir*, London: The Women's Press.

1990

Entry in Blair, V., Clements, P. and Grundy, I. *The feminist companion to literature in English: Women writers from the Middle Ages to the present*, London: Batsford.

1992

Griffiths, S. 'Women's work undone: profile of Ann Oakley', *Times Higher Education Supplement*, July 10, p 15.

1996/97

Benaiche, M. *Evolution de la pensée critique d'Ann Oakley, sociologue, dans le contexte de la théorie féministe en Grande-Bretagne*, DEA d'Etudes Anglophones, Université Michel de Montaigne Bordeaux.

1997

Leavey, C. 'In conversation with Ann Oakley', *The Journal of Contemporary Health*, vol 5.

1998

Baylis, D. 'Profile: Professor Ann Oakley', *Institute of Education Alumni Association Bulletin*.

2005

Crow, G. 'Ann Oakley: sociology as emancipation', Chapter 9 of *The art of sociological argument*, Basingstoke: Palgrave.

Index

Note: Page numbers in **bold** indicate extracts from a publication.

Gender regimes in transition in Central and Eastern Europe
Gillian Pascall and Anna Kwak

Understanding of welfare states has been much enriched by comparative work on welfare regimes and gender. This book uses these debates to illuminate the changing gender regimes in countries of Central and Eastern Europe. It has particular significance as countries in the region make the transition from communism and into a European Union that has issues of women's employment, work-life balance, and gender equality at the heart of its social policy.

HB £50.00 US$75.00 ISBN 1 86134 625 5
234 x 156mm 176 pages tbc October 2005

Gender inequality and social change
Segregation in the modern labour market
Jude Browne

This book presents a novel interpretation of the nature, causes and consequences of sex inequality in the modern labour market. Employing a sophisticated new theoretical framework, and drawing on original fieldwork, the book develops a subtle account of the phenomenon of sex segregation and offers a major challenge to existing approaches.

HB £50.00 US$74.50 ISBN 1 86134 599 2
234 x 156mm 224 pages tbc November 2005

Gender, pensions and the lifecourse
How pensions need to adapt to changing family forms
Jay Ginn

"When one of Europe's leading authorities on retirement pensions publishes a book of this quality one has to sit up and take notice. Jay Ginn has produced another tour de force." *Journal of Social Policy*

PB £17.99 US$28.95 ISBN 1 86134 337 X
HB £45.00 US$69.95 ISBN 1 86134 338 8
234 x 156mm 152 pages June 2003

The gender dimension of social change
The contribution of dynamic research to the study of women's life courses
Edited by Elisabetta Ruspini and Angela Dale

"... a testament to how a dynamic approach can aid researchers in unravelling the complex interactions between socio-economic factors and gendered outcomes across historical time and individual lives." *European Sociological Review*

HB £45.00 US$69.95 ISBN 1 86134 332 9

234 x 156mm 312 pages May 2002

To order further copies of this publication or any other Policy Press titles please contact:

In the UK and Europe:
Marston Book Services, PO Box 269, Abingdon, Oxon, OX14 4YN, UK
Tel: +44 (0)1235 465500
Fax: +44 (0)1235 465556
Email: direct.orders@marston.co.uk

In the USA and Canada:
ISBS, 920 NE 58th Street, Suite 300, Portland, OR 97213-3786, USA
Tel: +1 800 944 6190 (toll free)
Fax: +1 503 280 8832
Email: info@isbs.com

In Australia and New Zealand:
DA Information Services, 648 Whitehorse Road Mitcham, Victoria 3132, Australia
Tel: +61 (3) 9210 7777
Fax: +61 (3) 9210 7788
E-mail: service@dadirect.com.au

Further information about all of our titles can be found on our website:

www.policypress.org.uk